OBITUARIES
A GUIDE TO SOURCES

SECOND EDITION

Betty M. Jarboe

D1261530

G.K. HALL & CO.
BOSTON, MASSACHUSETTS
1989

CT
214
.Z99
J37
1989

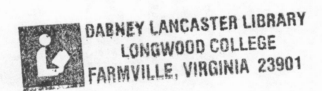 DABNEY LANCASTER LIBRARY
LONGWOOD COLLEGE
FARMVILLE, VIRGINIA 23901

Copyright 1989 by G. K. Hall & Co.
All rights reserved.

ISBN 0-8161-0483-2

This publication is printed on permanent/durable acid-free paper.
Manufactured in the United States of America.

CONTENTS

DABNEY LANCASTER LIBRARY
1000137415

CONTENTS

CONTENTS

PREFACE

This new edition contains all the entries found in the first edition with only a few exceptions. The same geographic arrangement has been maintained, and the same indexing policies and verification procedures have been used. The preface to the first edition explains the scope and methodology used in compiling the original bibliography and should be read if the user is unfamiliar with it.

The present work is much enlarged, with 3547 entries as compared to some 1600 in the first edition. Many of the new entries are for books published after 1982 which abstract or index obituaries from runs of newspapers, but in addition, another category of works has been included--tombstone inscriptions. Tombstone inscriptions often give valuable biographical information other than birth and death dates as many of the older tombstones give place of birth, military service, and sometimes family relationships. Recording tombstone inscriptions preserves information which often disappears over the course of time, as vandalism, weather, and urbanization take their toll. This category of publishing is often done by individuals or organizations with limited means and results in restricted availability. Nevertheless, these books often provide valuable information, and there needs to be bibliographic access to them. It has been necessary to limit the number of cemetery books, and this was done by including only those titles which appear on OCLC with two or more library locations.

To identify new titles for this edition, the Library of Congress, Indiana University Libraries, the Indiana State Library, the Library of the State Historical Society of Wisconsin, and the Public Library of Fort Wayne and Allen County have been visited. In addition, the online catalog of the Research Libraries Group (RLIN) has been searched, as well as the Library of Congress' information retrieval system named MUMS (Multiple Use Marc System) which provides access to bibliographic information about most of the books cataloged by the Library since 1968.

The first edition contained numerous references to articles in serials which indexed or abstracted obituaries. The second edition contains only a few additions of this type, as access to periodical articles has been well covered by the new publication Periodical Source Index (Allen County Public Library, 1987-). As in the first edition, the asterisk preceding an entry indicates the article is continued in subsequent issues of the periodical cited.

Obituaries can often be located by using online databases. Librarians who perform online searches through DIALOG and BRS might wish to refer to the list of databases in the Appendix. These databases cite a significant number of obituaries.

The Sheehy code and library symbols are still used, but they follow immediately after the entry rather than along the right-hand margin.

Finally, I want to express my appreciation to Indiana University for the research leave which enabled me to complete this second edition on schedule. I would also like to acknowledge the continued support of my colleagues in the Reference Department and our department head, Ann Bristow.

Betty M. Jarboe
Indiana University Library
Bloomington, Indiana
September 1988

PREFACE TO FIRST EDITION

It is an accepted fact that obituaries provide valuable biographical data since they are often the only printed source for obtaining information about an individual. This is particularly true for the ordinary citizen, but even for the famous, whose lives eventually are recorded in print, the obituary is important for its contemporary viewpoint.

This guide has been prepared to assist researchers in their pursuit of obituaries in newspapers or periodicals. Admittedly it is a rather curious collection of works of varying degrees of scholarship. Some of the works cited are very slight, in some instances only a few pages in a periodical, while other works are very comprehensive.

In addition to the books and articles which either index or abstract obituaries and death notices from newspapers and periodicals, this guide also includes references to annuals and yearbooks which contain necrology sections since these at least help establish a death date. Also, many indexes for the various disciplines have been included. It should be noted that for any serial entry, the editorial policy concerning necrology may vary over the years. If death information was found over an extended time period, it has been included; and when possible, the annotation will indicate what years contain death information. In some cases it has not been possible to examine complete runs of serials.

There are many additional sources of published death records: civil records, church and parish records, cemetery records, mortuary records, Bible records. These are too numerous to be included in this bibliography. Some ecclesiastical necrologies and obit books have been included for foreign countries. A few diaries and personal records of deaths have been included because researchers may be unaware of them and because these records may be particularly useful if they are for a community with no newspaper. Some manuscript material has been included and newspaper indexes are listed if they cite obituaries.

When searching for an obituary of a scholar or professional person, it should be remembered that the proceedings of professional organizations, particularly in the nineteenth and early twentieth century, often contained obituaries of their members. The proceedings of United States historical societies have been examined and many of them have been included since their members were inclined to write lengthy obituaries which often contained much family history. If the person for whom an obituary is sought had cultural ties with his community, the researcher should explore the possibility of society publications as a possible source.

The scholarly obituary often is concerned as much with the deceased's writings as with the details of his life, and in some cases these obituaries are cited in the body of the work without being entered in its index. An example of this is Bibliographie de la littérature française du Moyen Age à nos jours. It has a section entitled "Necrologies et Notices bio-bibliographiques," but the indexes do not list the deceased person's name. This situation exists in several of the indexes and bibliographies. In some indexes, obituaries are cited in the author index rather than the subject index; in some book catalogs they precede works by the deceased while in others they follow works by the deceased. There is little consistency and policy can change in the same title during its years of publication. Some of these peculiarities have been noted in the annotations. Most titles listed in this bibliography have been verified either in the National Union Catalog,[1] the Union List of Serials,[2] New Serial Titles,[3] or the OCLC data base.[4] These sources will indicate to users where the titles may be consulted.

Those titles which could not be found in any of these sources will have a library location symbol along the right hand margin indicating what library holds that title. In a few instances, the annotation will indicate where it can be consulted. If death information has been extracted from an American periodical which has been microfilmed by University Microfilms, Inc., reference is made to it in the citation, and the user should consult American Periodicals: 1741-1900.[5]

In order to identify items for this bibliography, the following collections were searched:

1. Library of Congress Catalog. Books: Subjects, 1950-81,[6] under the subject headings: Obituaries; Registers of Births, etc.; Newspapers--Indexes; and Necrologies.

2. New York. Public Library. Local History and Genealogy Division. Dictionary Catalog of the Local History and Genealogy Division. Boston: G. K. Hall, 1974. 20 vols

3. Library of Congress Shelflist on Microfiches, the F classification and parts of the Zs and CSs.

4. Genealogical Society of the Church of Jesus Christ of Latter-Day Saints. Microfilmed catalog. 1973 and updates.

5. Sheehy, Eugene P. Guide to Reference Books. Ninth edition. Chicago: American Library Association, 1976. Supplement, 1980.

6. Indexes and bibliographies of historical and genealogical material.

Letters were sent to libraries in most states requesting photocopies of their catalog cards which reflect their holdings of material which falls within the parameters of this bibliography. In most instances, these were the state libraries and the libraries of the major historical societies. The cooperation of these libraries has been remarkable and some items were provided which would otherwise have been missed. In most cases, if a library cataloged a book under the heading Obituaries, it was added to the bibliography without being examined by the compiler.

Many libraries were visited while compiling this bibliography, but the collections of the following libraries were especially useful: Library of Congress, New York Public Library, Indiana University Library, University of California Library, Berkeley, Stanford University Library, and the Indiana State Library. A visit was made to the Daughters of the American Revolution Library in Washington, D.C., and a few titles were taken from their card catalog. Unfortunately there is not always easy bibliographic access to the enormous amount of material that has been compiled by the many DAR chapters throughout the country.

Many libraries maintain card files of obituaries. Some of these have been microfilmed by the Genealogical Society of the Church of Jesus Christ of Latter-Day Saints and mention has been made of them in this bibliography. Milner's books, Newspaper Indexes[7] should also be consulted when the place of death is known; and if the newspaper needs to be consulted, Newspapers in Microform[8] should be used to identify libraries which hold microform copy that is available on interlibrary loan. At the end of the bibliography there is an Appendix which gives information on a few of the many card files located in libraries. Most of this information is the result of the letters of inquiry sent to libraries throughout the United States.

There is no claim that this bibliography includes everything published that falls within its scope. Persons familiar with the literature of specific fields will undoubtedly know of other sources not listed here. It is hoped, however, that enough items have been located to aid researchers. In addition, it is hoped that the sources mentioned may suggest similar types of material to be found in other libraries.

Searching for an obituary for some obscure figure can be interesting and challenging, but also it can be frustrating and disappointing. The searcher should use the sources mentioned here with caution and realize the chances of success are not great. Some of the titles may indicate coverage for a long span of years, but when examined, the user may be disappointed to find how few items were included. This may be due to the fact that complete runs of newspapers were not always available to the abstracter, and also, in early newspapers, the number of obituaries were very few.

The arrangement of the book is geographic. When searching for an obituary for a person associated with a given state, it is advisable not only to scan the works in the section for that state but also to consult the General Index, since titles that are regional have been put in the United States section but indexed under the various states represented in the collection. For titles in this bibliography which are annotated in Sheehy's Guide to Reference Books[9] that book's code designation is given along the right hand margin so that its annotations may be used in determining the scope of the work.

The General Index should be used to locate an obituary for a person who lived in a specific town or county by looking under the name of the town or county. If the title of a newspaper begins with the name of the town, there will be no entry in the index except for the title of the newspaper. If the title of the newspaper does not begin with the name of the town where it was published, there will be an entry in the index under the name of the town. With a few exceptions, the title entry in the index will indicate place of publication. For example, under Palmyra, N.Y. in the index, reference is made to 35.36, but that citation does not indicate that the Wayne Sentinel was published in Palmyra.

There is also access to obituaries for the various professions through the General Index. The terms Scholars and Scientists are used as well as the more specific titles, such as Botanists, Physicians, etc. There are several collections of obituaries dealing with soldiers of various wars, and the index should be used to locate them. Religious denominations and the term Clergy are also used in the index. The heading General is also used in the index to refer to works which should be used to locate obituaries of prominent persons in all fields. Such titles as the New York Times Obituary Index or the Annual Register of World Events are listed in the General Index under the heading General. In addition, some colleges and universities have published obituaries of their graduates. These can be located in the index under the name of the institution as well as under the heading Colleges and universities.

Finally, I wish to acknowledge the assistance of my colleagues in the Reference Department at Indiana University--Pauline Spulber, Pat Riesenman, and especially Tom Glastras who spent many evenings and weekends reading the manuscript. I also want to express my appreciation to Ann Bristow Beltran, our department head, for her encouragement and words of advice. In addition, the project could not have been completed without the sabbatical leave granted by Indiana University, and most especially without the assistance and encouragement of my husband.

LIBRARY SYMBOLS

A-Ar	Alabama Department of Archives and History, Montgomery
Ak	Alaska State Library, Juneau
BM	British Library, London
BN	Bibliothèque Nationale, Paris
C	California State Library, Sacramento
CHi	California Historical Society, San Francisco
CU-B	University of California, Berkeley. Bancroft Library
DNDAR	Daughters of the American Revolution, Washington, D.C.
GHi	Georgia Historical Society, Savannah
IHi	Illinois State Historical Library, Springfield
Ia	Iowa State Library, Des Moines
IaHi	State Historical Society of Iowa, Iowa City
In	Indiana State Library, Indianapolis
InFw	Public Library of Fort Wayne and Allen County, Fort Wayne
KHi	Kansas State Historical Society, Topeka
KyBgW	Western Kentucky State University, Bowling Green
KyLo	Louisville Free Public Library, Louisville
LN	New Orleans Public Library, New Orleans
MHi	Massachusestts Historical Society, Boston
MeHi	Maine Historical Society, Portland
MnHi	Minnesota Historical Society, Saint Paul
Nc	North Carolina State Library, Raleigh
NcC	Public Library of Charlotte and Mecklenburg County, Charlotte
NcU	University of North Carolina, Chapel Hill
NN	New York Public Library, New York City
O	Ohio State Library, Columbus
PHi	Historical Society of Pennsylvania
RHi	Rhode Island Historical Society, Providence
T	Tennessee State Library, Nashville
TxDa	Dallas Public Library
USIGS	Church of Jesus Christ of Latter-Day Saints, Genealogical Society, Salt Lake City[10]
WHi	State Historical Society of Wisconsin, Madison
Wa	Washington State Library, Olympia

1. INTERNATIONAL

1.1 <u>Almanach de Gotha, annuaire généalogique, diplomatique et statistique</u>, 1763-. Gotha: Perthes, 1763-1960. Annual. CJ224

1.2 <u>Alternative Press Index</u>, v. l, no. 1/2-, July/Dec. 1969-. College Park, Md.: Alternative Press Centre, 1970-. Quarterly. AE240

1.3 American Geographical Society of New York. <u>Current Geographical Publications: Additions to the Research Catalogue of the American Geographical Society</u>, v. 1-, 1938-. New York: The Society, 1938-. Monthly, except July and Aug. CL56

1.4 American Museum of Natural History, New York. Library. <u>Research Catalog of the Library of the American Museum of Natural History; Authors</u>. 13 vols. Boston: G. K. Hall, 1977. EC48

1.5 American Philosophical Society, Philadelphia. <u>Proceedings</u>, v. 1-, 1838/40-. Philadelphia: The Society, 1840-.

------. <u>General Index to the Proceedings</u>, v. 1-50, 1838-1911. Philadelphia: The Society, 1937.

------. <u>General Index to the Proceedings</u>, v. 51-75, 1912-35. Philadelphia: American Philosophical Society, 1937.

------. <u>Transactions</u>, v. 1-6, 1769-1809; n.s., v. 1, 1818-.

------. <u>Yearbook</u>, 1937-. The <u>Proceedings</u> and <u>Transactions</u> contain many obituaries of members. The <u>Yearbook</u> was started in 1937 and since that date has contained all obituaries.

------. Library. <u>Catalog of Books in the American Philosophical Society Library</u>. 28 vols. Westport, Conn.: Greenwood Press, 1970. EA200 Obituaries are entered under the deceased person's name. See also, vol. 1, p. 548, <u>Obituary notices of members of the American Philosophical Society</u>, 1844-1913, v. 1, A-L.

1.6 <u>Americana Annual: An Encyclopedia of Events</u>, 1923-. New York: Americana Corp., 1923-. AC13

1.7 <u>L'année philologique; bibliographie critique et analytique de l'antiquité greco-latine</u>, 1924/26-. Paris: Society d'Edition "Les Belles-Lettres," 1928-. Annual. BD1382

1.8 <u>L'année psychologique</u>, v. 1-, 1894-. Paris: Presses Universitaires de France, 1895-. Annual. CD66

1.9 <u>Annuaire du spectacle: théâtre, cinéma, musique, radio, télévision</u>, v. 1-, 1942/43-. Paris: Raoult, 1943-. Annual. BG262

1.10 <u>Annual Egyptological Bibliography. Bibliographie égyptologique annuelle</u>, 1947-. Leiden: Brill, 1948-. A publication of the International Association of Egyptologists. Annual. DD115

1. INTERNATIONAL

------. Indexes, 1947-56. Leiden: Brill, 1960.

1.11   Annual Library Index, 1905-10. 6 vols. New York: Publishers Weekly, 1906-11. AE242

1.12   Annual Literary Index, 1892-1904. 13 vols. New York: Publishers Weekly, 1893-1905. AE241

1.13   Annual Necrology for 1797-98 Including Also Various Articles of Neglected Biography. London, 1800.

1.14   Annual Obituary, 1st-, 1980-. New York: St. Martin's Press, 1981. Contains obituaries of persons from all walks of life who were nationally or internationally prominent.

1.15   Annual of Scientific Discovery: Or Year-book of Facts in Science and Art for 1850-71 . . . Obituaries of Eminent Scientific Men. . . . 21 vols. Boston: Gould and Lincoln, 1850-71.

1.16   Annual Register of World Events: A Review of the Year, v. 1-, 1758-. London, 1761-. Publisher varies. Recent volumes have very few obituary notices.

1.17   Appleton's Annual Cyclopaedia and Register of Important Events. . . . v. 1-15, 1861-75; v. 16-35 (n.s., v. 1-20), 1876-95; v. 36-42 (3d ser., v. 1-7), 1896-1902. 42 vols. New York: Appleton, 1862-1903. Indexes for 1861-87, 1876-95, 1896-1902. AC14

1.18   Applied Science and Technology Index, v. 1-, 1913-. New York: Wilson, 1913-. Monthly (except July), with quarterly and annual cumulations. No obituary citations could be found after 1973. EA66

1.19   Archäologische Bibliographie, 1913-: Beilage zum Jahrbuch des Deutschen Archaologischen Instituts. . . . Berlin: de Gruyter, 1914-. Annual. DA90

1.20   Arnim, Max. Internationale Personalbibliographie, 1800-1943. 2d ed. 2 vols. Leipzig: Hiersemann, 1944-52. AA26

------. v. 3, 1944-1959 und Nachträge. Stuttgart: Hiersemann, 1961-63.

------. v. 3-5, 1944-87. Stuttgart: Hiersemann. 1944-87. AA27

1.21   Art Index, v. 1-, 1929-. New York: Wilson, 1930-. Quarterly with annual cumulations. BE68

1.22   Arts and Humanities Citation Index, 1976-. Philadelphia: Institute for Scientific Information, 1978-. Three times a year with last issue being cumulative. AE220. The "Permuterm Index" will cite the author of the obituary under the deceased's name. Use the "Source Index" for full citation.

1. INTERNATIONAL

1.23 <u>Astronomischer Jahresbericht</u>, v. 1-68, 1899-1968. 68 vols. Berlin: de Gruyter, 1900-69. Annual. EB18 Continued by:

1.24 <u>Astronomy and Astrophysics Abstracts</u>, v. 1-, 1969-. Berlin: Springer-Verlag, 1969-. Semiannual. EB19

1.25 Barnhart, John Hendley. <u>Biographical Notes upon Botanists</u>. 3 vols. Boston: G. K. Hall, 1965.

1.26 Batty, Linda. <u>Retrospective Index to Film Periodicals, 1930-1971</u>. New York: Bowker, 1975. BG185

1.27 <u>Bibliographia zoologica</u>. . . . v. 1-43, 1896-1934. 43 vols. Zurich: Sumptibus Concilii Bibliographici, 1896-1934. EC179

1.28 <u>Bibliographie de la littérature française du Moyen Âge à nos jours</u>. Année 1953-. Paris: A. Colin, 1953-80. Annual. BD963. Index cannot be used to locate obituaries or necrology.

1.29 <u>Bibliographie der französischen Literaturwissenschaft</u>, v. 1-, 1956/58-. Frankfurt am Main: Klostermann, 1960-. Annual. BD964

1.30 <u>Bibliographie der fremdsprachigen Zeitschriftenliteratur; Répertoire bibliographique international des revues; International Index to Periodicals</u>, 1911-25, 1925/26-62/64. 1911-64. Reprint. New York: Kraus, 1961. AE221

1.31 <u>Bibliographie géographique internationale</u>, v. 1-, 1891-. Paris: Centre National de la Recherche Scientifique, 1894-. Annual. CL55

1.32 <u>Bibliographie linguistique des années</u>, v. 1-, 1939/47-. Utrecht: Spectrum, 1949-. Annual. BC29

1.33 <u>Bibliography and Index of Geology</u>, v. 33, no. 1-, Jan. 1969-. Boulder, Colo: Geological Society of America in Cooperation with the American Geological Institute, 1970-. Monthly with annual cumulation. EE31 Preceded by the following title:

1.34 <u>Bibliography and Index of Geology Exclusive of North America</u>, v. 1-32, 1933-1968. Boulder, Colo.: American Geological Institute, 1934-69. EE30

1.35 <u>Bibliotheca geographica: Jahresbibliographie der geographischen Literatur</u>. 1891/92-1911/12. 19 vols. Berlin: Kuhl, 1895-1917. CL11

1.36 <u>Bibliotheca zoologica I. Verzeichnis der Schriften über Zoologie welche in den periodischen Werken enthalten und vom Jahre 1846-1860 selbständig erschienen sind</u>. . . . 2 vols. Leipzig: Engelmann, 1861. EC170

------. <u>II. Verzeichnis der Schriften über Zoologie welche in den periodischen Werken enthalten und vom Jahre 1861-1880 selbständig erschienen sind</u>. . . . 8 vols. Leipzig: Engelmann, 1887-1923. EC171

1. INTERNATIONAL

1.37 <u>Biographisches Jahrbuch für Altertumskunde</u>, v. 1-63, 1878-1943. Berlin: Calvary, 1879-98; Leipzig: Reisland, 1899-1944. Annual. BD1399

1.38 <u>Biography Index: A Cumulative Index to Biographical Material in Books and Magazines</u>, v. 1-, 1946-. New York: Wilson, 1947-. Quarterly with annual and three-year cumulations. AJ10

1.39 <u>Biological & Agricultural Index: A Cumulative Subject Index to Periodicals in the Fields of Biology, Agriculture, and Related Sciences</u>, v. 19-, 1964-. New York: Wilson, 1964-. Monthly (except August) with annual cumulations. EC7. Continues the <u>Agricultural Index</u>. No obituaries after volume 27.

1.40 <u>Book News Monthly</u>, v. 1-36, Sept. 1882-Aug. 1918. 36 vols. Philadelphia: J. Wanamaker, 1883-1918. The section reporting literary deaths begins in volume 28.

1.41 <u>Britannica Book of the Year</u>, 1938-. Chicago: Encyclopaedia Britannica, 1938-. Annual. A necrology list can be found under "Obituaries." AC15

1.42 <u>British Archaeological Abstracts</u>, v. 1-, 1968-. London, Council For British Archaeology, 1970-. Use the index to locate obituaries in the section called History of Archaeology, Biographies, Obituaries.

1.43 <u>British Humanities Index</u>, 1962-. London: Library Association, 1963-. Quarterly with annual cumulations. AE238

1.44 <u>Brooklyn Daily Eagle Almanac . . . A Book of Information, General of the World and Special of New York City and Long Island</u>. . . . v. 1-. 1886-1929? Brooklyn: Brooklyn Daily Eagle, 1886-1929?

1.45 Cannons, Harry George Turner. <u>Bibliography of Library Economy: A Classified Index to the Professional Periodical Literature in the English Language Relating to Library Economy . . . from 1876 to 1920</u>. Chicago: American Library Association, 1927. AB2. Citations to obituaries for British and American librarians can be found on pp. 260-72.

1.46 <u>Catholic Almanac</u>. Huntington, Ind.: Our Sunday Visitor, 1969-. Annual. Change of title for the <u>National Catholic Almanac</u>, 1904-68, which also contained a necrology section. BB457

1.47 <u>Catholic Periodical Index: A Cumulative Author and Subject Index to a Selected List of Catholic Periodicals</u>, v. 1-13, 1930-66. New York: Catholic Library Association, 1939-67. Quarterly with biennial cumulations. Continued as <u>Catholic Periodical and Literature Index</u>, v. 14-, 1967/68-. Haverford, Pa.: Catholic Library Association, 1968-. Bimonthly with biennial cumulations. AE246-AE247

1.48 <u>Chamber's Encyclopaedia World Survey</u>. London: Newnes, 1952-65. Annual. Ceased publication. Superseded by <u>Chamber's Encyclopaedia Yearbook</u>.

1.49   Chemical Abstracts, v. 1-, 1907-. Columbus, Ohio: American Chemical
        Society, 1907-. Weekly. ED22

1.50   Chemisches Zentralblatt, v. 1-140, 1830-69. Berlin: Verlag Chemie,
        1830-1969. Weekly. Obituaries are listed under the heading Biographien
        und Nachrufe. ED25

1.51   Chicago. Art Institute. Ryerson Library. Index to Art Periodicals. 11 vols.
        Boston: G. K. Hall, 1962. Particularly helpful for locating obituaries of
        Chicago artists. BE69

1.52   Chicago Psychoanalytic Literature Index, 1920-1970. 3 vols. Chicago: CPL
        Publishers, 1971. CD12

1.53   Chicago Psychoanalytic Literature Index, 1971-1974. Chicago: CPL
        Publishing, 1979.

1.54   Chicago Psychoanalytic Literature Index, 1975-. Chicago: Institute for
        Psychoanalysis, 1975-. Quarterly, the 4th issue being an annual
        cumulation. CD12

1.55   Clairin, Pierre Eugene. Discours de Pierre Clairin. Paris: Firmin-Didot,
        1972. Obituaries of artists.

1.56   Columbia University. Libraries. Avery Architectural Library. Avery
        Obituary Index of Architects. 2d ed. Boston: G. K. Hall, 1980. BE293

1.57   ------. Law Library. Dictionary Catalog. 28 vols. Boston: G. K. Hall,
        1969. CK14

        ------. 1st Supplement. 7 vols. Boston: G. K. Hall, 1973.

1.58   Contemporary Authors; a Bio-bibliographical Guide to Current Authors and
        Their Works, v. 1-, 1962-. Detroit: Gale, 1962-. Annual. AJ48-AJ51

1.59   Cornell University. Faculty. Necrology of the Faculty of Cornell University.
        33 vols. Ithaca, N.Y., n.d. For the years 1938/39-1970/71.

1.60   Cotgreave, Alfred. A Contents-Subject Index to General and Periodical
        Literature. London: E. Stock, 1900.

1.61   Cumulated Magazine Subject Index, 1907-1949: A Cumulation of the F. W.
        Faxon Company's Annual Magazine Subject Index. 2 vols. Boston: G. K.
        Hall, 1964. AE244 Does not always cite obituaries from the many
        historical society publications which it indexes, but it is still useful for
        locating obituaries of prominent persons in many fields.

1.62   Current Biography, v. 1-, 1940-. New York: Wilson, 1940-. Monthly
        (except Aug.). Cumulated Index, 1940-85. AJ52

1.63   Current Index to Statistics, Applications, Methods and Theory, v. 1-, 1975-.
        Washington, D.C.: American Statistical Association, 1976-. Annual. EF16

1. INTERNATIONAL

1.64   <u>Current List of Medical Literature</u>, v. 19-36. Washington, D.C.: Army Medical Library, 1950-59. Monthly. EK51

1.65   <u>Current World Leaders: Almanac</u>, v. 1-12, 1957-78. Pasadena, Calif.: Almanac of Current World Leaders, 1957-78. Ceased.

1.66   <u>Dance World</u>, v. 1-14, 1966-79. New York: Crown, 1966-79. Annual. Ceased. BG137

1.67   <u>Dramatic Index for 1909-49, Covering Articles and Illustrations Concerning the Stage and Its Players in the Periodicals of America and England and Including the Dramatic Books of the Year</u>. 41 vols. Boston: Faxon, 1910-52. Cumulated and published by G. K. Hall, 1965. 2 vols. BD206-BD207

1.68   <u>Education Index: A Cumulative Subject Index to a Selected List of Educational Periodicals, Proceedings, and Yearbooks</u>, Jan. 1929-. New York: Wilson, 1932-. Monthly (except July and Aug.), cumulating throughout the year, with annual bound cumulation. CB131

1.69   <u>Encyclopaedia Judaica. Yearbook</u>, 1973-. Jerusalem: Encyclopaedia Judaica, 1973-. Frequently varies. BB582

1.70   <u>Excerpta botanica. Section A. Taxonomica et chorologica</u>, v. 1-, 1959-. Stuttgart: Gustav Fischer, 1959-. Monthly since Oct. 1962.

1.71   <u>Facts on File: A Weekly World News Digest with Cumulative Index</u>, v. 1-, Oct./Nov. 1940-. New York: Facts on File, 1940-. Loose-leaf. Weekly, with annual bound volumes available. DA193

         ------. <u>Five-year Index: The Index to World Events</u>. 1957-.

1.72   <u>Film Literature Index</u>, v. 1-, 1973-. Albany, N.Y.: Filmdex, 1974-. Quarterly with annual cumulations. BG186

1.73   France. Centre National de la Recherche Scientifique. <u>Bulletin signaletique</u>, v. 1-21, 1940-60. Paris: Centre de Documentation du Centre National de la Recherche Scientifique, 1940-60. Monthly. Title varies. AE277. Superseded by a number of separate series dealing with specific subject areas. Obituaries are cited in some of these separate series.

1.74   <u>Geographisches Jahrbuch</u>, v. 1-, 1866-. Gotha: Perthes, 1866-. Irregular. Index, 1866-1925, in vol. 40, pp. ix-xix. CL58

1.75   Gerlach, John C., and Lana Gerlach. <u>The Critical Index: A Bibliography of Articles on Film in English, 1946-1973, Arranged by Names and Topics</u>. New York: Teachers College Press, 1974. BG187

1.76   <u>Germanistik: internationales Referatenorgan mit bibliographischen Hinweisen</u>, v. 1-, 1960-. Tübingen: Max Niemeyer, 1960-. Quarterly. BD830

1. INTERNATIONAL

1.77 <u>Great Lives of the Century As Reported by the "New York Times."</u> Edited by Arleen Keylin. New York: Arno Press, 1977.

1.78 <u>Guide to Dance Periodicals</u>, v. 1-10, 1931/35-1961/62. 10 vols. Gainesville: University of Florida Press, 1948-63. BG134

1.79 <u>Guide to the Performing Arts</u>, 1957-68. New York: Scarecrow Press, 1960-72. Annual. BG45

1.80 Harvard University. Museum of Comparative Zoology. Library. <u>Catalogue</u>. 8 vols. Boston: G. K. Hall, 1968. EC172

1.81 ------. Peabody Museum of Archaeology and Ethnology. Library. <u>Catalogue: Authors</u>. 26 vols. Boston: G. K. Hall, 1963. CE12. Now called the Tozzer Library. Obituaries are cited following works by the deceased.

------. <u>Supplement</u>, 1st-4th. Boston: G. K. Hall, 1970-79.

1.82 Henrion, Mathieu Richard Auguste. <u>Annuaire biographique, ou Supplément annuel et continuation de toutes les biographies ou dictionnaires historiques, contenant la vie de tous les hommes célèbres</u>. . . . Années 1830-34. 2 vols. Paris: Méquignon, 1834. BN

1.83 <u>Historical Abstracts, 1775-1945: Bibliography of the World's Periodical Literature</u>. . . . v. 1, no. 1-, March 1955-. Santa Barbara, Calif.: Clio Press, 1955-. Quarterly. 1956/58-. Frankfurt am Main: Klostermann, 1960-. Annual. DA19

1.84 Houzeau, Jean Charles, and Albert Lancaster. <u>Bibliographie générale de l'astronomie jusqu'en 1880</u>. Rev. ed. 2 vols. in 3. London: Holland Press, 1964. EB9

1.85 Huyghebaert, Nicolas. <u>Les documents nécrologiques</u>. Turnhout: Brepols, 1972. (Typologie des sources du Moyen Age occidental, fascicule 4). Bibliography of necrologies on pages 9-12.

1.86 Hyamson, Albert M. "Jewish Obituaries in the <u>Gentleman's Magazine</u>." <u>Miscellanies of the Jewish Historical Society of England</u> 4 (1942): 33-60. An index of obituaries in the magazine from 1731 until 1868, when the publication of obituary notices ceased.

1.87 <u>Index Medicus</u>, v. 1-, 1960-. Washington: National Library of Medicine, 1961-. Monthly. Cumulates annually into the <u>Cumulated Index Medicus</u>. EK52. In the first four volumes, the subject heading "Obituaries" is used. From volume five on, obituaries are cited in the author section with the deceased's name in parentheses and preceding the other components of the entry.

1.88 <u>Index Medicus: A . . . Classified Index of the Current Medical Literature of the World</u>, v. 1-21, Jan. 1879-Apr. 1899; 2d ser. v. 1-18, 1903-20; 3d

1. INTERNATIONAL

ser. v. 1-6, 1921-June 1927. Washington: Carnegie Institution, 1879-1927. EK48

1.89   Index to Dental Literature, v. 1-, 1939-. Chicago: American Dental Association, 1943-. Quarterly with annual cumulations. EK190

1.90   Index to Dental Literature in the English Language; Including Periodicals from Australia, Canada, England, India, South Africa and the United States, 1839-1936/38. 15 vols. Chicago: American Dental Association, 1921-39. EK189

1.91   Index to Foreign Legal Periodicals, v. 1-, 1960-. London: Institute of Advanced Legal Studies, University of London, in cooperation with the American Association of Law Libraries, 1960-. Quarterly, cumulating annually and triennially. CK167. Obituaries are cited under "Biography: Individual."

1.92   Index to Jewish Periodicals, v. 1-, June 1963-. Cleveland, 1963-. Semiannual. BB577

1.93   Index to Legal Periodical Literature. 6 vols. Indianapolis: Bobbs-Merrill, 1888-1939. Imprint varies. CK169

1.94   Index to Legal Periodicals, 1908-. New York: Wilson, 1909-. Monthly with annual and three-year cumulations. CK170. Obituaries are cited under the heading "Biography: Individual."

1.95   Index to Periodical Articles by and about Negroes; Cumulated 1960-1970. Boston: G. K. Hall, 1971. Continued by annual volumes. Name changed in 1973 to Index to Periodical Articles by and about Blacks. AE252-AE253

1.96   Index to Selected Periodicals Received in the Hallie Q. Brown Library Decennial Cumulation, 1950-1959. Boston: G. K. Hall, 1961. AE251

1.97   International Bibliography of Economics. Bibliographie internationale de science economique, v. 1-, 1952-. London: Tavistock, 1955-. Annual. CH36

1.98   International Bibliography of Historical Sciences, v. 1-, 1926-. New York: Wilson, 1930-. Annual. DA22

1.99   International Bibliography of Social and Cultural Anthropology. Bibliographie internationale d'anthropologie sociale et culturelle, v. 1-, 1955-. London: Tavistock, 1958-. Annual. CE29

1.100   International Bibliography of Sociology. Bibliographie internationale de sociologie, v. 1-, 1951-. London: Tavistock, 1952-. Annual. CC15

1.101   International Catalogue of Scientific Literature, 1st-14th Annual Issues. 14 vols. London: Harrison, 1902-21. EA17. Obituaries are cited in the "History. Biography section." Covers the years 1901-14.

1. INTERNATIONAL

1.102   <u>International Index to Film Periodicals</u>, 1972-. New York: Bowker, 1973-. Annual. BG188

1.103   <u>International Who's Who</u>, 1935-. London: Europa, 1935-. Annual. Contains a list of deaths beginning with the 30th edition, 1966-67. AJ53

1.104   <u>Internationale Bibliographie der Kunstwissenschaft</u>, 1902-17/18. 15 vols. Berlin: Behr, 1903-20. Annual. BE35

1.105   <u>Internationale Bibliographie der Zeitschriftenliteratur aus allen Gebieten des Wissens</u>, v. 1-, 1963/64-. Osnabrück: Felix Dietrich, 1965-. Semiannual volumes. AE222

1.106   <u>Internationale Bibliographie des Buch- und Bibliothekswesens, mit besonderer Berücksichtigung der Bibliographie</u>, 1904-12, 1922-39. 13 vols. Leipzig: Harrassowitz, 1905-40. n.s. 1-14, 1926-39. AA25

1.107   <u>Internationale volkskundliche Bibliographie. International Folklore Bibliography</u>, 1939/41-. Bonn: Rudolf Habelt, 1949-. CF49. Supersedes <u>Volkskundliche Bibliographie</u>.

1.108   <u>Internationaler Nekrolog</u>, v. 1-, 1982-. Pullach: W. Gorzny, 1984-. Annual.

1.109   <u>ISIS Cumulative Bibliography: A Bibliography of the History of Science Formed from ISIS Critical Bibliographies</u> 1-90, 1913-65. 6 vols. London: Mansell, 1971-84. EA206

1.110   <u>ISIS Cumulative Bibliography, 1966-75; a Bibliography of the History of Science Formed from ISIS Critical Bibliographies 91-100d@. . . . 2 vols. London: Mansell, 1980-85. (In progress) EA207</u>

1.111   <u>Jahresbericht über die Erscheinungen auf dem Gebiete der germanischen Philologie</u>. . . . 1879-1936/39. 58 vols. Berlin: de Gruyter, 1880-1954. BC97

1.112   <u>Jewish Year Book: An Annual Record of Matters Jewish</u>, 5657-, (1896-). London: Jewish Chronicle, 1896-. BB602

1.113   <u>Keesing's Contemporary Archives: Weekly Diary of World Events with Index Continually Kept Up-to-Date</u>, v. 1-, July 1, 1931-. London: Keesing's, 1931-. Loose-leaf. Weekly. DA194-DA195

1.114   Levy, Felice D. <u>Obituaries on File</u>. 2 vols. New York: Facts on File, 1979. A compilation of all the obituaries from <u>Facts on File</u>, 1940-78. AJ36

1.115   <u>Library and Information Science Abstracts</u>, no. 1-, Jan./Feb. 1969-. London: Library Association, 1969-. Bimonthly. AB16

1.116   <u>Library Literature</u>, 1921/32-. New York: Wilson, 1934-. Bimonthly with annual cumulations. AB14

1.117 <u>Lives That Shaped Your Life</u>. Compiled by Bob Brecher. New York: Proteus, 1980. Contains obituaries or biographical articles of 365 persons who have influenced society significantly.

1.118 London. University. School of Oriental and African Studies. Library. <u>Index Islamicus, 1906-1955: A Catalogue of Articles on Islamic Subjects in Periodicals and Other Collective Publications</u>. 1958. Reprint. London: Mansell, 1972. BB518

------. Supplements, 1st-5th, 1956-80. London: Mansell, 1962-83. Imprint varies. Use author index for locating obituaries.

1.119 Lust, John. <u>Index Sinicus: A Catalogue of Articles Relating to China in Periodicals and Other Collective Publications, 1920-1955</u>. Cambridge, Eng.: W. Heffer, 1964. DE160

1.120 MacCann, Richard Dyer, and Edward S. Perry. <u>The New Film Index: A Bibliography of Magazine Articles in English, 1930-1970</u>. New York: Dutton, 1975. BG189

1.121 Mallett, Daniel Trowbridge. <u>Index of Artists: International-Biographical; Including Painters, Sculptors, Illustrators, Engravers and Etchers of the Past and the Present</u>. New York: Bowker, 1935. BE171

------. <u>Supplement to Index of Artists</u>. . . . New York: Bowker, 1940.

1.122 <u>Marquis Who's Who Publications: Index to All Books</u>, 1974-. Chicago: Marquis, 1975-. Biennial. Contains a section entitled "Supplementary Listing of Deceased Who's Who Biographies." AJ19

1.123 <u>Mathematical Reviews</u>, v. 1-, 1940-. Providence, R.I.: American Mathematical Society, 1940-. Monthly. EF19

1.124 <u>Music Index; the Key to Current Music Periodical Literature</u>, 1949-. Detroit, Mich.: Information Service, 1950-. Monthly with annual cumulations. BH105

1.125 <u>National Newspaper Index</u>, 1979-. Los Altos, Calif.: Information Access Corp., 1979-. Microfilm. Monthly. An index to the <u>Christian Science Monitor</u>, the <u>New York Times</u>, the <u>Wall Street Journal</u>. The <u>Los Angeles Times</u> and the <u>Washington Post</u> were added in 1982. AF75

1.126 <u>New International Year Book: A Compendium of the World's Progress</u>, 1907-65. New York: Funk and Wagnalls, 1908-66. Publisher varies. AC16

1.127 New York. Metropolitan Museum of Art. Library. <u>Library Catalog</u>. 2d ed. 48 vols. Boston: G. K. Hall, 1980. BE62

1.128 ------. Museum of Modern Art. Library. <u>Catalog of the Library</u>. 14 vols. Boston: G. K. Hall, 1976. BE63

1.129   ------. Public Library. Art and Architecture Division. <u>Dictionary Catalog</u>. 30 vols. Boston: G. K. Hall, 1975.   BE64

1.130   <u>New York Daily Tribune Index</u>, 1875-1906. 31 vols. New York: Tribune Association, 1876-1907. Deaths are listed under the heading <u>Obituaries</u> until 1898. Beginning in 1898, they are found by looking under the deceased's name.   AF76

1.131   <u>New York Times Biographical Edition: A Compilation of Current Biographical Information of General Interest</u>, v. 1-, 1970-. New York: New York Times, 1970-. Loose leaf. Monthly. Includes obituaries which have appeared in issues of the <u>New York Times</u>.

1.132   <u>New York Times Great Lives of the Twentieth Century</u>. Edited by A. M. Rosenthal and Arthur Gelb. New York: Times Books, 1988.

1.133   <u>New York Times Index</u>, v. 1-, 1913-. New York: New York Times, 1913-. Semimonthly with annual cumulations.   AF77

         ------. <u>Prior Series</u>. 15 vols. New York: Bowker, 1966-76. Covers 1851 to 1912.   AF78

1.134   <u>New York Times Obituaries Index, 1858-1968</u>. New York: New York Times, 1970.   AJ20-AJ21

         ------. <u>1969-1978</u>. New York: New York Times, 1980.

1.135   <u>Nineteenth Century Readers' Guide to Periodical Literature, 1890-1899, with Supplementary Indexing, 1900-1922</u>. 2 vols. New York: Wilson, 1944. AE230

1.136   <u>Numismatic Literature</u>, no. 1-, 1947-. New York: American Numismatic Society, 1947-. Semiannual.   BF151

1.137   <u>Obituaries from the "Times," 1951-1960, Including an Index to All Obituaries and Tributes Appearing in the "Times" During the Years 1951-1960</u>. Westport, Conn.: Meckler Books, 1979.   AJ39-AJ41

         ------. <u>1961-70</u>, <u>1971-75</u>. Westport, Conn.: Meckler Books, 1975-78.

1.138   <u>Palestine and Zionism: A Cumulative Author, Title and Subject Index to Books, Pamphlets and Periodicals</u>, v. 1-11, 1946-56. New York: Zionist Archives and Library of Palestine Foundation Fund, 1949-58.

1.139   Payne, William Morton. <u>Little Leaders</u>. Chicago: A. C. McClurg, 1902. Reprints of obituaries from the <u>Dial</u> which were written at the time of death of well known literary figures.

1.140   Perry, Jeb H. <u>"Variety" Obits: An Index to Obituaries in "Variety," 1905-1978</u>. Metuchen, N.J.: Scarecrow Press, 1980.   BG21

1. INTERNATIONAL

1.141   Physics Briefs, v. 1-, 1979-. Weinheim: Physik Verlag, 1979. Semimonthly. EG9. Supersedes the following title.

1.142   Physikalische Berichte, v. 1-57, 1920-78. Braunschweig: Vieweg, 1920-78. Monthly. Continued by Physics Briefs.

1.143   Poggendorf, Johann Christian. Biographisch-literarisches Handwörterbuch zur Geschichte der exakten Wissenschaften. 1863-1940. Reprint. 6 vols. in 11. Ann Arbor, Mich.: Edwards, 1945. EA231-EA232

------. Biographisch-literarisches Handwörterbuch der exakten Natur-wissenschaften, unter Mitwirkung der Akademien der Wissenschaften zu Berlin, Göttingen, Heidelberg, München und Wien. Berlin: Akademie-Verlag, 1955-85. V. 7a-7b. (In Progress)

1.144   Poole's Index to Periodical Literature, 1802-81. Rev. ed. 1891. Reprint. 2 vols. Gloucester, Mass.: Peter Smith, 1963. AE227

------. Supplements, Jan. 1882-Jan. 1, 1907. 5 vols. Boston: Houghton, 1887-1908.

1.145   Psychological Abstracts, v. 1-, 1927-. Lancaster, Pa.: American Psychological Association, 1927-. Monthly. CD69

------. Cumulated Subject Index to Psychological Abstracts, 1927/60-. Boston: G. K. Hall, 1966-.

1.146   Psychological Index, 1894-1935: An Annual Bibliography of the Literature of Psychology and Cognate Subjects. 42 vols. Princeton, N.J.: Psychological Review, 1895-1936. CD71

1.147   Quarterly Cumulative Index Medicus, 1927-56. 60 vols. Chicago: American Medical Association, 1927-56. Quarterly with semiannual cumulations. EK50

1.148   Quarterly Index Islamicus, v. 1-, Jan. 1977-. London: Mansell, 1977-. Quarterly, with five-year cumulations. BB519

1.149   Readers' Guide to Periodical Literature, v. 1-, 1900-. New York: Wilson, 1905-. AE231

1.150   Religion Index One: Periodicals, 1949-. Chicago: American Theological Library Association, 1953-. Semiannual, with biennial cumulation. Called Index to Religious Periodical Literature, 1949-75/76. BB41

1.151   Review of Reviews: Index to the Periodicals of 1890-1902, v. 1-13. 13, vols. London: Review of Reviews, 1891-1903. Annual. AE256

1.152   Richardson, Ernest Cushing. An Alphabetical Subject Index and Index Encyclopaedia to Periodical Articles on Religion, 1890-1899. 2 vols. New York: Scribner, 1907-11. BB44

1. INTERNATIONAL

1.153   Royal Society of London. <u>Catalogue of Scientific Papers</u>, 1800-1900.
1867-1925. Reprint. 19 vols. Metuchen, N.J.: Scarecrow Press, 1968.
EA23-EA24

------. <u>Subject Index</u>. 1908-14. Reprint. 3 vols. Metuchen, N.J.:
Scarecrow Press, 1968. v. 1. Pure Mathematics; v. 2. Mechanics; v. 3.
Physics: pt. 1. Generalities, Heat, Light, Sound; pt. 2. Electricity and
Magnetism. Obituaries in the indexes are found cited in the "History.
Biography" section. Obituaries for scientists in the fields for which no
indexes were issued can be found by going directly to the proper series
in the <u>Catalog of Scientific Papers</u> under deceased person's name.

------. <u>Obituary Notices of Fellows of the Royal Society</u>, v. 1-9,
1932/35-Nov. 1954. London: Royal Society of London, 1932-54. Annual.
Includes foreign members. EA233

1.154   <u>Science Citation Index</u>, 1961-. Philadelphia: Institute for Scientific Information, 1961-. Bimonthly with annual cumulations. EA72. The
"Permuterm Index" will cite the author of the obituary; the "Source Index"
will give full citation.

1.155   <u>Science Year: The World Book Science Annual</u>, 1965-. Chicago: Field
Enterprises, 1965-. Annual. EA34

1.156   <u>Screen World</u>, v. 1-, 1949-. New York: Greenberg, 1950-. Annual. BG268

1.157   <u>Social Sciences and Humanities Index: Formerly International Index</u>, v. 1-61,
1907/15-74. New York: Wilson, 1916-74. AE234. Since World War II,
foreign periodicals no longer indexed. The number of obituaries in recent
volumes is minimal and contains none after the index split into <u>Social
Sciences Index</u> and <u>Humanities Index</u>.

1.158   <u>Social Sciences Citation Index</u>, 1966-70, 71-. Philadelphia: Institute for
Scientific Information, 1973-. 3 times a year with annual cumulations.
CA36. The "Permuterm Index" will cite the author of the obituary; the
"Source Index" will give full citation.

1.159   Spencer, Leonard James. <u>Biographical Notices of Mineralogists Recently
Deceased; with an Index to Those Previously Published in This Magazine</u>.
London, 1921. Reprinted from the <u>Mineralogical Magazine</u>, December
1921, v. 19, no. 95. 2d series, v. 20, no. 107, 1924. 3d series, v. 21,
no. 117, 1927.

1.160   Stewart, William T. <u>International Film Necrology</u>. New York: Garland, 1980.
(Garland Reference Library of the Humanities, v. 215).

1.161   <u>Street's Pandex of the News and Cumulative Index to Current History</u>. New
York: Pandex of the Press, 1903-17. An index to the principal
newspapers of the United States. Serves primarily as a date book.

1.162   Stuckey, Frank. <u>Necrology of the Cinema: A Ready Reference for Librarians
and Laymen</u>. New York: Gordon Press, 1977.

1.163   Subject Index to Periodicals, 1915-61. London: Library Association, 1919-62. Annual (quarterly, 1954-61 with annual cumulations). AE237. Particularly useful for locating obituaries for British scientists, scholars and public figures.

1.164   Times, London. Index to the "Times," 1906-1972. London: Times, 1907-74. AF93

       ------. Palmer's Index to the "Times" Newspaper, 1790-June 1941. 1868-1943. Reprint. New York: Kraus, 1965. AF94. Obituaries are listed under the heading "Deaths."

1.165   "Times" Index, Jan./Mar. 1973-. Reading, England: Newspaper Archive Developments, 1973-. Monthly with annual cumulations beginning 1977. Supersedes Index to the "Times." AF95

1.166   Tod, Thomas Miller. A Necrology of Literary Celebrities, 1321-1943. Perth: Munro and Scott, 1948. Mainly British. Most of the information in this book can be found elsewhere. It does give place of burial in most instances.

1.167   Tribune Almanac and Political Register, 1838-1914. 76 vols. New York: G. Dearborn and Co., 1838-1914. Necrology section begins with volume for 1874, which has 1872-73 deaths.

1.168   U.S. Library of Congress. Geography and Map Division. Bibliography of Cartography. 5 vols. Boston: G. K. Hall, 1973. CL282

       ------. First Supplement. 2 vols. Boston: G. K. Hall, 1980.

1.169   U.S. National Library of Medicine. Index-Catalogue of the Library of the Surgeon General's Office, United States Army, Authors and Subjects, series 1-4. 58 vols. Washington: Government Printing Office, 1880-1955. EK31

1.170   Variety Obituaries, 1905-1986. 11 vols. New York: Garland Publishing, 1988. Over 90,000 obituaries reproduced in facsimile from Variety.

1.171   Volkskundliche Bibliographie, 1917-1937/38. 14 vols. Berlin: de Gruyter, 1919-57. CF49. Continued by International volkskundliche Bibliographie.

1.172   Whitman, Alden. Come to Judgment. New York: Viking Press, 1980. Contains 34 obituaries of twentieth century notables, originally appearing in the New York Times.

1.173   ------. The Obituary Book. New York: Stein and Day, 1971. Contains reprints of obituaries from the New York Times.

1.174   Who's Who in Art: Biographies of Leading Men and Women in the World of Art Today, 1st ed.-. London: Art Trade Press, 1927-. Biennial. BE179. British names predominate.

1. INTERNATIONAL

1.175   Who's Who in the Theatre: A Biographical Record of the Contemporary Stage, Ed. 1-17. London: Pitman, 1912-81. Irregular. BG105. Contains obituaries for personalities in the British and American theatre.

1.176   World Almanac and Book of Facts, 1868-. New York: World-Telegram, 1868-. Annual. AC87

1.177   Wylie, Alexander. Memorials of Protestant Missionaries to the Chinese: Giving a List of Their Publications, and Obituary Notices of the Deceased. Taipei: Ch'eng-wen Publishing Co., 1967.

1.178   Yearbook of Comparative and General Literature, v. 1-, 1952-. Bloomington, Ind.: Indiana University, 1952-. Annual. BD28. Beginning with v. 10, 1961, the section called "News and Notes" has obituaries for prominent scholars.

1.179   Year's Art, 1880-1947: A Concise Epitome of All Matters Relating to the Arts of Painting, Sculpture, Engraving and Architecture . . . Together with Information Respecting the Events of the Year. 64 vols. London: Macmillan, 1880-1947. Annual. BE133

1.180   Zappert, Georg. "Über sogenannte Verbrüderungsbücher und Nekrologien im Mittelalter." Sitzungsberichte der Kaiserlichen Akademie der Wissenschaften, Vienna. Philosophisch-historische Classe 10 (1853): 417-63.

1.181   Zeitschrift für romanische Philologie. Supplementheft: Bibliographie, v. 1-, 1875-. Tübingen: Max Niemeyer, 1878-. Biennial. BC120

1.182   Zentralblatt für Mathematik und ihre Grenzgebiete: Mathematics Abstracts, v. 1-, 1931-. Berlin: Springer, 1931-. EF21

1.183   Zionist Yearbook, 1951/52-. London: Zionist Federation of Great Britain and Ireland, 1951-. Annual. BB603

2. UNITED STATES

2.1   Abajian, James. <u>Blacks in Selected Newspapers, Censuses and Other Sources: An Index to Names and Subjects</u>. 3 vols. Boston: G. K. Hall, 1977. Nineteenth and twentieth century coverage, with emphasis on the American West.

    ------. First Supplement. 2 vols. Boston: G. K. Hall, 1985.

2.2   <u>Abstracts of Obituaries in the "Western Christian Advocate," 1834-1850</u>. Compiled by Margaret R. Waters, Dorothy Riker, and Doris Leistner. Indianapolis: Family History Section of the Indiana Historical Society, 1988.

2.3   <u>Air University Library Index to Military Periodicals</u>, v. 1-, Oct./Dec. 1949-. Maxwell Air Force Base, Ala.: Air University Library, 1949-. Quarterly with annual cumulative issues. CJ512

2.4   Alden, Timothy. <u>A Collection of American Epitaphs and Inscriptions, with Occasional Notes</u>. 5 vols. 1814. Reprint. New York: Arno Press, 1977.

2.5   <u>America: History and Life; A Guide to Periodical Literature</u>, v. 1, no. 1-, July 1964-. Santa Barbara, Calif.: Clio Press, 1964-. Quarterly. DB47

2.6   <u>American Almanac and Repository of Useful Knowledge</u>. . . . v. 1-32, 1830-61. 32 vols. Boston: Gray and Bowen, 1830-61. (American Periodicals: 1800-1850)

2.7   <u>American Annual Monitor . . . or, Obituary of the Members of the Society of Friends in America</u>. 6 vols. New York: Tract Association of Friends, 1858-63. Covers the years 1857-62.

2.8   American Antiquarian Society, Worcester, Massachusetts. <u>Index to Obituary Notices in the "Boston Transcript," 1875-1930</u>. . . . 5 vols. Worcester, Mass.: American Antiquarian Society, 1938-40. This index also includes notices in the <u>Boston Advertiser</u> from 1875 to 1885. The <u>Boston Transcript</u> in its obituaries is national in scope.

2.9   ------. <u>Index of Obituaries in "Massachusetts Centinel" and "Columbian Centinel," 1784-1840</u>. 5 vols. Boston: G. K. Hall, 1961. This newspaper printed notices of marriages and deaths from all of the United States. Indexes 102,000 obituaries from the South and West as well as from the East.

2.10   ------. <u>Proceedings of the American Antiquarian Society</u>, 1812-1849. Worcester, Mass.: American Antiquarian Society, 1912.

    ------. <u>Proceedings</u>. 31 May 1843-28 April 1880; n.s. v. 1-, 1880/81-.

    ------. <u>Index to the Proceedings of the American Antiquarian Society 1812-1916</u>. Compiled by Clifford Kenyon Shipton. Worcester, Mass.: American Antiquarian Society, 1978.

2. UNITED STATES

2.11 American Art Directory, v. 1-, 1898-. New York: Bowker, 1899-. Triennial, 1952-. BE134 Volume 30 is the last to contain an obituary section.

2.12 American Baptist Register for 1852. Edited by J. Lansing Burrows. Philadelphia: American Baptist Publication Society, 1853. Obituary notices for Baptist clergy, pp. 415-20.

2.13 American Baptist Year-Book, 1868-1940. Philadelphia: American Baptist Publication Society, 1868-1940. The volumes for 1874-1931 contain lists of deceased ministers.

2.14 American Bibliography of Russian and East European Studies, 1956-66. Bloomington, Ind.: Indiana University, 1957-67. Annual. DC39 Continued by the following:

2.15 American Bibliography of Slavic and East European Studies, 1967-. Columbus, Ohio: American Association for the Advancement of Slavic Studies, 1972-.

2.16 American Catholic Who's Who, 1934/35-80/81. Detroit: Walter Romig, 1934-80. Biennial. AJ89. Contains death information for prominent laymen as well as clergy.

2.17 American Jewish Year Book, v. 1-, 1899-. New York: Jewish Publishing Society of America, 1899-. Annual. BB601. Contains a necrology section for the United States and other countries through volume 48. The remaining volumes are for the United States only.

2.18 American Lutheran Church. Yearbook, 1961-. Minneapolis: Augsburg Publishing House, 1960-. Annual. BB377

2.19 American Men and Women of Science, Ed. 12-. New York: Bowker, 1971- . Represents a change of title for American Men of Science, 1st-11th ed., 1906-68. EA221

2.20 American Vital Records from "The Gentleman's Magazine," 1731-1868. Compiled by David Dobson. Baltimore: Genealogical Publishing Co., 1987. This volume has extracted the data for births, marriages, and deaths for persons with American connections.

2.21 American Year Book: A Record of Events and Progress, 1910-19, 1925-50. 36 vols. New York: Nelson, 1911-50. CG85

2.22 American Year-Book and National Register for 1869: Astronomical, Historical, Political, Financial, Commercial, Agricultural, Educational, and Religious. A General View of the United States, Including . . . Obituaries. Hartford: O. D. Case, 1869.

2.23 Baker, Russell P. Obituaries and Marriage Notices from the "Tennessee Baptist," 1844-1862. Easley, S.C.: Southern Historical Press, 1979. Includes obituaries for other Southern States in addition to Tennessee.

2.24   Beall, William R. _Index and Guide to "Harper's Weekly" and Frank "Leslie's Illustrated Newspaper" for the Year 1861_. [Washington, D.C.: Sourcebook Publications], 1962.

2.25   Benedictines. American Cassinese Congregation. _Necrologium Congregationis Americano-Cassinensis O.S.B. 1846-1946_. Collegeville, Minn.: Typis Abbatiae Sancti Ioannis Baptistae, 1948.

2.26   _Best Plays of 1894/99- and Year Book of the Drama in America_. New York: Dodd, 1926-. Annual. BD432

2.27   Biggerstaff, Inez Boswell. _Some Tombstone Inscriptions from Oklahoma, Arkansas, Louisiana, Mississippi, and Texas_. [Oklahoma City?], 1955.

2.28   Bowman, John Elliott. _Some Central Western States Veterans of the American Revolution: Items from Newspaper Files, 1790-1855_. N.p. 1928.

2.29   ------. _Some Southern States Veterans of the American Revolution: About 340 Newspaper Items Alphabetically Arranged, 1790-1857_. New Ipswich, N.H., 1928.

2.30   -----. _Some Southern States Veterans of the American Revolution: Items Alphabetically Arranged . . . 1790-1857_. Boston, 1930.

2.31   ------. _Some Veterans of the American Revolution in Various Parts of the United States: Items from Newspapers 1816-1850, About 1500 Items Alphabetically Arranged_. New Ipswich, N.H., 1923.

2.32   _Business Periodicals Index_, v. 1-, 1958-. New York: Wilson, 1958-. Monthly (except Aug.) with annual cumulations. CH203

2.33   Cameron, Kenneth W. _Research Keys to the American Renaissance_. . . . Hartford: Transcendental Books, 1967. Indexes the _Christian Examiner_, 1824-69, the _North American Review_, 1815-77, and the _New Jerusalem Magazine_, 1827-72. The first two are in the microfilm collection, American Periodicals: 1800-1850.

2.34   Cheek, John Carl. _Selected Tombstone Inscriptions from Alabama, South Carolina, and Other Southern States_. [N.p. 1970].

2.35   Christian Advocate (New Orleans). _Marriage and Death Notices, 1851-1915, except 1857, 1861-65, and 1903_. Jackson, Miss.: Mississippi Conference Historical Society, Millsaps College, [1966?]. Microfilm. WHi

2.36   _Clerical Directory of the Protestant Episcopal Church in the United States of America_. New York: Church Hymnal Corp., 1898-1968. BB400

2.37   Cowing, Elizabeth. "Some Vital Statistics of Revolutionary Worthies." _New York Genealogical and Biographical Record_ 50 (1919): 59-68.

2.38   Cropsey, Joyce Mackenzie. _Register of Revolutionary Soldiers and Patriots Buried in Litchfield County_. Canaan, N.H.: Phoenix Publishing, 1976.

2. UNITED STATES

2.39   Crosby, Nathan. <u>Annual Obituary Notices of Eminent Persons Who Have Died in the United States, for 1857-1858</u>. . . . 2 vols. Boston: Phillips, Sampson and Co., 1858-59.

2.40   <u>Current Law Index</u>, v. 1-, 1980-. Los Altos, Calif.: Information Access Corp., 1980-. 8 nos. per year with quarterly and annual cumulations. CK164

2.41   Curry, Emma. "Extracts from the <u>Columbian Magazine</u>, 1787." <u>National Genealogical Society Quarterly</u> 6 (1917): 43-44. (American Periodicals: 18th Century). This article includes a few death notices.

2.42   <u>Death and Marriage Notices from the "Rural Repository"</u> . . . <u>between June 4, 1831 and May 19, 1832</u>. Fairhope, Ala., 1936. (American Periodicals: 1800-1850) DNDAR

2.43   <u>Deaths of Revolutionary Soldiers Compiled from "American Almanac and Repository of Useful Knowledge"</u>. N.p., n.d. (American Periodicals: 1800-1850) DNDAR

2.44   Driscoll, Marion Lang. "Newspaper Clippings, New England. Deaths of Revolutionary Soldiers, Copied from the <u>New Hampshire Journal</u>." <u>National Genealogical Society Quarterly</u> 25 (1937): 84-86.

2.45   ------. "Vital Records from the <u>Christian Review</u>, Boston, Mass., March 1837." <u>National Genealogical Society Quarterly</u> 28 (1940): 84.

2.46   ------. "Vital Records from the <u>Columbian Star</u> and the <u>Christian Advocate</u> (Philadelphia, Pa.), 1829-30." <u>National Genealogical Society Quarterly</u> 28 (1940): 75-84. <u>Christian Review</u> and <u>Columbian Star</u> were Baptist publications and the <u>Christian Advocate</u> was Presbyterian. All are in the American Periodicals series.

2.47   <u>Dust to Dust: Obituaries of the Gunfighters</u>. Compiled by Jerry J. Gaddy. San Rafael, Calif.: Presidio Press, 1977.

2.48   *"Early Church Vital Records. Genealogical Items Gleaned from Early Publications of the Church and Original Sources, 1833-36." <u>Utah Genealogical and Historical Magazine</u> 27 (1936): 21-28.

2.49   <u>Episcopal Church Annual</u>, 1830-. New York: Morehouse-Gorham, 1830-. Annual. BB402

2.50   Fisher, Elizabeth J. "Abstracts of Obituaries in Publications of the Associate Presbyterian Church, 1831 to 1858." <u>National Genealogical Society Quarterly</u> 20 (1932): 98-110.

2.51   Ford, William H. "A List of Deceased Ministers, from a Manuscript of Rev. Ezra Stiles." <u>New England Historical and Genealogical Register</u> 62 (1908): 273-77. A list of New England ministers who died 1760-65.

2. UNITED STATES

2.52   Francis, Elizabeth Wheeler. Lost Links: New Recordings of Old Data from Many States. 1947. Reprint. Baltimore: Genealogical Publishing Co., 1975.

2.53   French, Esther Griswold. Revolutionary War Veterans Buried in Columbia County, New York. Hudson, N.Y.: Hendrick Hudson Chapter, National Society of the Daughters of the American Revolution, 1973.

2.54   Genealogical Data from Colonial New York Newspapers: A Consolidation of Articles from the "New York Genealogical and Biographical Record." Baltimore: Genealogical Publishing Co., 1977. Material extracted from the New-York Gazette, 1726-44; the New York Weekly Journal, 1733-51; the New York Mercury, 1752-68; and the New York Gazette and the Weekly Mercury, 1768-83. This data had been published in various volumes of the New York Genealogical and Biographical Record from October 1964 to October 1976.

2.55   Gray, Mr. and Mrs. R. D. Gray's Cemetery Records. Fort Worth, Tex.: American Reference Publishers, 1968. Includes records from Cherokee, Clay, Jack, Montague, Palo Pinto, Parker, Comanche, Eastland, Johnson, Knox, Callahan, and Wise counties, Texas; Huntsville, Auror, Ozark, Carolin and Witter, Arkansas; Montezuma and LaPlata Counties, Colorado; Washita and Comanche counties, Oklahoma; Tannytown, Missouri.

2.56   Haverford College. Library. Quaker Necrology. 2 vols. Boston: G. K. Hall, 1961. An index to approximately 59,000 entries from four Quaker periodicals. For the years 1828-1960 for the Middle Atlantic region.

2.57   Hayward, Elizabeth McCoy. American Vital Records from the "Baptist Register." 10 vols. Rochester, N.Y.: American Baptist Historical Society, 1956-65. For the years 1824-34.

2.58   ------. Deaths in Many Places, Reported in the "Boston Recorder and Telegraph." Ridgewood, N.J., 1948. For the years 1927-28.

2.59   ------. Soldiers and Patriots of the American Revolution Whose Deaths Were Reported in the "Boston Recorder and Telegraph" 1827 and 1828. Ridgewood, N.J., 1944.

2.60   ------. Vital Records from Scattered Issues of Nineteenth Century Periodicals. Ridgewood, N.J.: E. Hayward, 1954.

2.61   ------. Vital Records from the "Baptist Weekly Journal," 1832 and 1833 and the "Cross and Baptist Journal," 1834. Ridgewood, N.J., 1947.

2.62   Heiss, Jane Raoul. Obituary Notices in the "Christian Worker," a Quaker Periodical, 1871-1894. 2 vols. N.p. 1974.

2.63   *Hendrix, Mrs. Thomas D. "Marriage and Death Notices in the New Orleans Christian Advocate, 1851-1855." Journal of Mississippi History 25 (1963): 139-50. The New Orleans Christian Advocate was an official publication of the Methodist Church; however, it published marriage and death

2. UNITED STATES

notices of many people of other faiths. Coverage is from Texas to North Carolina and from Tennessee to Florida.

2.64 Holcomb, Brent. Marriage and Death Notices from the "Lutheran Observer," 1831-1861 and the "Southern Lutheran," 1861-1865. Easley, S.C.: Southern Historical Press, 1979.

2.65 ------. Marriage and Death Notices from the "Southern Christian Advocate". 2 vols. Easley, S.C.: Southern Historical Press, 1979-80. v. 1. 1837-60; v. 2. 1861-67.

2.66 Holloway, Lisabeth M. Medical Obituaries: American Physicians' Biographical Notices in Selected Medical Journals Before 1907. New York: Garland Publishing, 1981.

2.67 Hollywood Album 2: Lives and Deaths of Hollywood Stars from the Pages of of the "New York Times." New York: Arno Press, 1977.

2.68 Hollywood Alburm 2: Lives and Deaths of Hollywood Stars from the Pages of the "New York Times." New York: Arno Press, 1979.

2.69 Hough, Franklin B. American Biographical Notes . . . Gathered from Many Sources. 1875. Reprint. Harrison, N.Y.: Harbor Hill Books, 1974. Includes death notices from upstate New York newspapers.

2.70 Illinois. Veterans Commission. Honor Roll, State of Illinois. 102 vols. Springfield, 1956. Includes the names, burial places, and other related information concerning all members of the Armed Forces of the United States buried in the State of Illinois prior to 1 July 1955.

2.71 Index to Black Newspapers, 1977-. Wooster, Ohio: Bell and Howell Co., 1977-. Indexes ten newspapers published in major U. S. cities and cites obituaries which appear as news items in the Personal Names Index.

2.72 Ingmire, Frances Terry. Confederate P.O.W.'s: Soldiers and Sailors Who Died in Federal Prisons and Military Hospitals in the North. St. Louis: Ingmire Publications, 1984. Compiled from records in the National Archives.

2.73 Ivison, Hazle R. These Sacred Places. [Mobile? Ala.], 1965. Includes tombstone records from cemeteries in Alabama, Georgia, Louisiana, and Mississippi.

2.74 Johnson, Robert Foster. Wilderness Road Cemeteries in Kentucky, Tennessee, and Virginia. Owensboro, Ky.: McDowell Publications, 1981.

2.75 Koykka, Arthur S. Project Remember: A National Index of Gravesites of Notable Americans. Algonac, Mich.: Reference Publications, 1986.

2.76 Laney, Clara. Union County Cemeteries 1710-1914 and Roster of Confederate and Revolutionary Soldiers. Monroe, N.C.: C. Laney, 1958.

2. UNITED STATES

2.77   Lester, Memory Lee Alldredge. <u>Old Southern Cemetery Records</u>. Chapel Hill, N.C., 1960. Records copied from cemeteries in Alabama, Georgia, Mississippi, North Carolina, South Carolina, Tennessee, and Virginia.

2.78   Lewis, Eli Robert, and J. Seymour Currey. <u>The Roll of Honor, Containing the Names of Soldiers, Sailors, and Marines of All the Wars of Our Country Who Are Buried in the Cemeteries of Cook County, or the Garden of the Dead, Together with the Military Record and Place of Burial of Each of Them As Completely As They Can Be Ascertained</u>. [Chicago: Printing Products Corporation], 1922.

2.79   Lilley, David A. <u>Index: "Confederate Veterans"</u>. . . . Dayton, Ohio: Press of Morningside Bookshop, 1978. The <u>Confederate Veteran</u> was published monthly from 1893-1932 in Nashville. Obituaries were a regular feature from 1895, and this is a comprehensive index to these obituaries.

2.80   Lutheran Church. Missouri Synod. <u>Statistical Yearbook</u>, 1884-. St. Louis, Mo.: Concordia Publishing House, 1884-. Annual. BB379 Contains a necrology section which includes pastors and teachers, most from the Midwest. Published in German from 1884 to 1917.

2.81   Marble, Charles C. <u>Addresses of the Dead</u>. New York: G. W. Dillingham, 1887. Gives birth and death dates and place of burial for the famous.

2.82   Martin, George. <u>Marriage and Death Notices from the "National Intelligencer" (Washington, D.C.) 1800-1850</u>. Washington, D.C.: National Genealogical Society, 1976. Microfilm. (Special Publication of the National Genealogical Society, no. 41)

2.83   Moffett, Dorothy Ivison, and William R. Armistead. <u>Beneath Southern Sod</u>. [Mobile? Ala., 1964].

2.84   Murphy, Thelma. <u>Deaths and Marriages from "The Presbyterian," 1849-1855</u>. N.p. 1983.

2.85   ------. <u>Marriages and Obits, 1850-1856 from "The Presbyterian of the West."</u> N.p. 1982.

2.86   <u>Necrology of Rabbis</u>, n.s. 1-, 1952/53-. New York: Jewish Statistical Bureau, 1953. Annual. Includes Canadian rabbis until 1974.

2.87   <u>Negro Year Book</u>, 1912-52. 11 vols. Ceased. Tuskegee, Ala.: Tuskegee Institute, Department of Records and Research, 1912-52. CC425

2.88   <u>New England Historical and Genealogical Register</u>, v. 1-, Jan. 1847-. Boston: New England Historic Genealogical Society, 1847-.

      ------. <u>Subject Index</u>, vols. 1-50, 1847-96.

      ------. <u>Abridged Index</u>, vols. 51-112, 1897-1958. Obituaries for Society members as well as other prominent citizens of New England can be located by using the subject and abridged indexes. The Register ceased publishing obituaries with volume 113.

2.89   New England Library Association. Bibliography Committee. A Guide to Newspaper Indexes in New England. Holden, Mass.: The Association, 1978.

2.90   New York Clipper Annual Containing Theatrical and Sporting Chronologies . . . a List of Deaths in the Amusement Professions. . . . New York: F. Queen Publishing Co., 1853-1899?

2.91   Notable Names in the American Theatre. Rev. ed. Clifton, N.J.: James T. White & Co., 1976. This is a second edition of Walter Rigdon's Biographical Encyclopaedia and Who's Who of the American Theatre. Both have necrology. BG102

2.92   Obituary File of Prominent S.D.A. Workers, 1850-1959. N.p. 1981. This is a collection of obituaries for Seventh-Day Adventists.

2.93   Obituary Notices of the United States Taken from Vol. 17 of the "Christian Palladium" 1848-1849. DNDAR

2.94   Official Catholic Directory, 1886-. New York: Kennedy, 1886-. Annual. BB459

2.95   Overby, Mary Mckeown. Obituaries Published by the "Christian Index." 2 vols. Macon, Ga.: Georgia Baptist Historical Society, Mercer University, 1975-1982. v. 1. 1822-79; v. 2. 1880-99. (American Periodicals: 1800-1850)

2.96   Palmer, Pauline. An Index of Obituaries in the "Western Methodist" November 8, 1833 - October 17, 1834 and in the "Southwestern Christian Advocate" May 4, 1839 - October 25, 1844. Nashville: Daughters of the American Revolution, 1849. T Indexes over 1200 obituaries.

2.97   Piton, Mrs. Phillip. Register of Confederate Dead Interred in Camp Chase Confederate Cemetery, Columbus, Franklin County, Ohio, and in Johnson's Island Confederate Cemetery Near Sandusky, Ohio. Columbus, Ohio: Franklin County Chapter, Ohio Genealogical Society, 1980.

2.98   Popular Music Periodical Index, 1973-. Metuchen, N.J.: Scarecrow Press, 1973-. Annual.

2.99   Rankin, William. Memorials of Foreign Missionaries of the Presbyterian Church, U.S.A. Philadelphia: Presbyterian Board of Publication and Sabbath School Work, 1895. Necrological record of the Board of Foreign Missions.

2.100   *"Revolutionary Records: Obituary Notices of Revolutionary Soldiers." Daughters of the American Revolution Magazine 23 (1903): 439-40. This article is continued in subsequent volumes of the magazine. The DAR Magazine Index does not index these obituaries.

2. UNITED STATES

2.101   Rose Bibliography. Analytical Guide and Indexes to the "Colored American Magazine," 1900-1909. 2 vols. Westport, Conn.: Greenwood Press, 1974.

2.102   Rouse, Jordan K. Another Revolutionary War Hero Dies. Kannapolis, N.C.: Rouse, 1978.

2.103   St. Louis Genealogical Society. Cemetery Relocations by the U.S. Army Corps of Engineers in Illinois, Iowa, Missouri, Arkansas. St. Louis: St. Louis Genealogical Society, 1977. Provides known data about the deceased, along with the name of relocated cemetery and reinterment cemetery.

2.104   Sawyer, Ray Cowen. Deaths Published in the "Christian Intelligencer" of the Reformed Dutch Church from 1830 to 1871. . . . 7 vols. New York, 1933-34.

2.105   Scott, Kenneth. Abstracts from "American Weekly Mercury," 1719-1746. Baltimore: Genealogical Publishing Co., 1974.

2.106   ------. Abstracts from Ben Franklin's "Pennsylvanie Gazette," 1728-1748. Baltimore: Genealogical Publishing Co., 1975.

2.107   ------. Joseph Gavit's American Deaths and Marriages, 1784-1829: Index to Non-principals in Microfilm Copies of Abstracts in the New York State Library, Albany, New York. New Orleans: Polyanthos, 1976.

2.108   ------. "The New-York Magazine" Marriages and Deaths, 1790-1797. New Orleans: Polyanthos, 1975. (American Periodicals: 18th Century)

2.109   Some Black Hills Area Cemeteries, South Dakota. 3 vols. Rapid City, S.Dak.: Rapid City Society for Genealogical Research, 1973-81.

2.110   Spectator Insurance Year Book, 1874-1962. Philadelphia: Spectator Co., 1874-1962. Annual. CH636

2.111   Standard & Poor's Register of Corporations, Directors and Executives, United States and Canada, Ed. 1-. New York: Standard & Poor's Corp., 1928-. Annual. CH247

2.112   Starr, Edward Caryl. A Baptist Bibliography, Being a Register of Printed Material by and about Baptists, Including Works Written against the Baptists. 25 vols. Rochester, N.Y.: American Baptist Historical Society, 1947-76. BB349

2.113   Stevens, C. J. "Death Notices from the American Magazine, 1787-1788." National Genealogical Society Quarterly 63 (1975): 284-90. (American Periodicals: 18th Century) This periodical was published in New York City with coverage for New England.

2.114   Theatre World, v. 1-, 1944/45-. New York: Theatre World, 1945-. Annual. BG53

2.115   Tipton, Ennis Mayfield. <u>Marriage and Obituaries from the "New Orleans Christian Advocate," with Complete Index</u>. Bossier City, La.: Tipton Printing and Publishing Co., 1980-. v. 1. 1851-60.

2.116   United Church of Christ. <u>Yearbook</u>, 1962-. Philadelphia, 1962-. Annual. BB415

2.117   United Presbyterian Church in the U.S.A. General Assembly. <u>Minutes of the General Assembly</u>. Philadelphia, 1958-. Ser. 6, v. 1-. (Series 1-5, 1870-1957.) BB399

2.118   U.S. Army Medical Department. <u>Obituary Clippings of Medical Officers Who Died in World War I, 1917-19</u>. N.p., n.d.

2.119   U.S. Military Academy, West Point. Association of Graduates. <u>Annual Report</u>, 1st-72d; 1870-1940/41. Newburgh, N.Y.

2.120   United States Catholic Historical Society. <u>Historical Records and Studies</u>, v. 1-, 1899-. New York: United States Catholic Historical Society, 1900-. Index, 1-10, 1899-1917 in v. 11; 15-24 in v. 24. The indexes can be used to locate obituaries of prominent Catholics, both clergy and laymen.

2.121   Wall Street Journal. <u>Index</u>, 1958-. New York: Dow Jones, 1959-. Monthly with annual cumulations. AF82 Obituaries are listed under "Deaths" in the "General News" section.

2.122   <u>Who's Who in America: A Biographical Dictionary of Notable Living Men and Women</u>, v. 1-, 1899-. Chicago: Marquis, 1899-. Biennial. AJ84 The Marquis sectional <u>Who's Whos</u> do not have necrology. This title has necrology in v. 13-25, 39-, 1924/25-1948/49, 1976/77-.

2.123   <u>Who's Who in American Art</u>, v. 1-, 1936/37-. New York: Bowker, 1935-. Biennial (Irregular). BE186

2.124   <u>Who's Who in Colored America: A Biographical Dictionary of Notable Living Persons of Negro Descent in America</u>, v. 1-7, 1927-50. New York: Who's Who in Colored America Corp., [1927-50]. AJ93

2.125   Young, David Colby, and Robert L. Taylor. <u>Death Notices from Freewill Baptist Publications, 1811-1851</u>. Bowie, Md.: Heritage Books, 1985.

3. ALABAMA

3.1   Alabama. Department of Archives and History. <u>Revolutionary Soldiers in Alabama</u>. 1911. Reprint. Baltimore: Genealogical Publishing Co., 1975. Among the sources used for this list are obituaries. The citation is given to the newspaper from which the obituary is taken.

3.2   Barefield, Marilyn Davis. <u>Butler County, Alabama Obituaries, from "The Greenville Advocate," "Butler County News," "Spirit of the Times," "Weekly Echo," "Living Truth," "South Alabamian," " Southern Messenger," and "Alabama Christian Advocate."</u> Easley, S.C.: Southern Historical Press, 1985.

3.3   ------. <u>Cemeteries of Jefferson County, Alabama</u>. Birmingham, Ala.: Birmingham Public Library, 1982.

3.4   Biggerstaff, Inez Boswell. <u>Records of Walker County, Alabama, Including Inscriptions from Cullman, Fayette, Marion, Winston, Talladega and Tuscaloosa Counties</u>. Oklahoma City, 1959.

3.5   Birmingham Genealogical Society. <u>Bible and Cemetery Records</u>. 2 vols. Birmingham, Ala., 1962-66.

3.6   <u>Cemeteries of Clay County, Alabama</u>. LaGrange, Ga.: Family Tree, 1987.

3.7   <u>Cemeteries of East Lauderdale County, Alabama</u>. Rogersville, Ala.: Friends of the Rogersville Public Library, 1981.

3.8   <u>Cemetery Census of Shelby County, Alabama</u>. Montevallo, Ala.: Shelby County Historical Society, 1979.

3.9   <u>Cemetery Records of Tuscaloosa County, Alabama</u>. Compiled by Alton Lambert. 6 vols. Centre, Ala.: Stewart University Press, 1982.

3.10   Cochran, Mrs. Roy J. "1865-1866 Deaths from the <u>Christian Herald</u> As Reported in Obituaries, Tributes of Respect and Local News Items." <u>Valley Leaves</u> 9 (1974): 41-55. The <u>Christian Herald</u> was published in Moulton, Lawrence County.

3.11   <u>Coosa County Records: Cemeteries</u>. 2 vols. Rockford, Ala.: Coosa County Historical Society, 1980.

3.12   <u>Cullman County Churches and Cemeteries: A Countywide Project under the Auspices of the Cullman County Commission</u>. Compiled by the Cullman County Comprehensive Employment Training Act personnel and the Cullman County Public Library staff under the direction of Ann Cochrane Gregath. 2 vols. 198-.

3.13   "Death's Harvest, 1899-1900, from the <u>Leighton News</u>." <u>Valley Leaves</u> 9 (1974): 91-96.

3.14   Douthat, James L. <u>Guntersville Reservoir Cemeteries</u>. Signal Mountain, Tenn.: J. L. Douthat, 1986. Includes cemeteries in Jackson and Marshall counties.

3. ALABAMA

3.15   England, Flora D. <u>Cemetery Inscriptions from Perry County, Alabama</u>. Marion, Ala.: F. D. England, 1955?

3.16   ------. <u>Dallas County, Alabama Genealogical Records: Estate Settlements. Cemetery Records. Deed Book A</u>. Tuscaloosa, Ala.: Wills Publishing Co., 1963-.

3.17   Foley, Helen S. <u>Deaths: A Listing of Death Notices Appearing in Newspapers in Barbour, Henry and Pike Counties, Alabama, 1846-1890</u>. Fort Worth, Tex.: American References, 1969.

3.18   ------. <u>Events about People</u>. Eufaula, Ala.: Foley, n.d. vol. 2. From Barbour County, Alabama, newspapers 1890-1908. Contains death notices.

3.19   ------. <u>Marriage and Death Notices from Alabama Newspapers and Family Records, 1819-1890</u>. Easley, S.C.: Southern Historical Press, 1981.

3.20   ------. <u>Obituaries from Barbour County, Alabama, Newspapers, 1890-1905</u>. Eufaula, Ala.: Foley, 1976.

3.21   Garrett, Jill Knight, and Iris H. McClain. <u>Some Lauderdale County, Alabama Cemetery Records</u>. Columbia, Tenn.: J. K. Garrett, 1970?

3.22   Hahn, Marilyn Davis. <u>Butler County, Alabama Obituaries, from "Alabama Christian Advocate," "Greenville Advocate," "Spirit of the Times," "Butler News," "Weekly Echo."</u> N.p. 1977.

3.23   Hailes, Frances. "Dallas County, Alabama Obituaries, Compiled from the <u>Selma Free Press</u>, Selma, Alabama." (1835-1839) <u>Alabama Genealogical Register</u> 4 (1962): 136-37.

3.24   Haith, Dorothy May. <u>Triana, Alabama's Cemeteries and Deaths Recorded in Newspapers and Madison County Probate Records</u>. Fort Valley, Ga.: Information Exchange System for Minority Personnel, Inc., 1981.

3.25   Henshaw, Kittye Vandiver, Evelyn Smith Rochelle, and Addie Katherine Stovall Shaver. <u>Paint Rock Valley Pioneers</u>. N.p. 1986. Includes cemetery inscriptions.

3.26   Horn, Robert C. <u>Tap Roots: Epitaphs in East-Central Alabama Cemeteries</u>. 4 vols. Dadeville, Ala.: Genealogical Society of East Alabama, 1982-85. Includes cemeteries in Auburn, Camp Hill, Dadeville, Antioch, Fredonia, Milltown, and Rock Springs. Church records also included.

3.27   Johnson, Dorothy Scott. <u>Cemeteries of Madison County, Alabama</u>. Huntsville, Ala.: Johnson Historical Publications, 1971-78. v. 1. A record of tombstone inscriptions in all known white cemeteries in the west half of Madison County, Alabama, except Memory Garden; v. 2. A record of the tombstone inscriptions in all known white cemeteries in the northeast portion of Madison County, Alabama, except Valhalla Memory Garden and Mausoleum.

3. ALABAMA

3.28   Jones, Kathleen Paul. <u>Alabama Records</u>, v. 1-, 1932-. Compiled by
Kathleen Paul Jones, and Pauline Jones Gandrud. Tuscaloosa, Ala., 1932-.
The following volumes were found to contain some references to
newspaper death notices along with other material: v. 5. <u>Alabama
Newspaper Extracts</u>; v. 6. Includes abstracts from Huntsville and
Tuscaloosa newspapers, 18 Apr. 1828-22 Nov. 1836 (Huntsville) and 6 Apr.
1842 to 29 June 1842 (Tuscaloosa); v. 12. Includes extracts from the <u>Democrat</u>
published at Huntsville, 1833-40; v. 14. Includes newspaper items from the
<u>Greene County Gazette</u>, 1830; v. 15. Includes extracts from the <u>Democrat</u>
published at Huntsville, 1841-59; v. 16. Includes abstracts from newspapers of
Tuscaloosa, Greene, Franklin and Sumter counties, 1830s to 1860s; v. 34.
Includes newspaper extracts for 1823 from the <u>Halcyon</u> published at
Greensborough; v. 35. Includes extracts from Huntsville newspapers, 1819-30,
1846-47, 1880, 1884; v. 36. Includes extracts from Jackson County newspapers,
1872-76; v. 41. Includes newspaper extracts from Tuscaloosa newspapers,
1868-70; v. 42. Includes extracts from Huntsville newspapers, 1849, 1851, 1866,
1868, 1874-75, 1878-82; v. 43. Includes newspaper extracts from the <u>Florence
Gazette</u>, Lauderdale County, 1849-51. Continued in volumes 104, 199; v. 44.
Includes newspaper extracts for Sumter county, 1866-70; v. 47. Includes
newspaper extracts for Tuscaloosa county, 1831, 1870-72; v. 52. Includes
newspaper extracts for Sumter county, 1870-75; v. 54. Includes newspaper
extracts for Madison county, 1860-83; v. 56. Includes newspaper marriages
and obituaries for Colbert county, 1855-77; v. 57. Includes newspaper
extracts for Tuscaloosa county, 1824, 1873-75, 1879; v. 59. Includes
newspaper extracts for Madison county, 1869-73, Jan. 1877 to Apr. 21
1877, Feb. 4 1825 to Apr. 29 1825; v. 61. Includes newspaper extracts for
Limestone county, 1868-72, 1875, 1877; v. 63. Includes newspaper extracts
for Greene County, 1860s and 1870s; v. 66. Includes newspaper extracts
for Lawrence county, 1868-76; v. 67. Includes newspaper extracts for
Tuscaloosa county, 1869-77; v. 70. Includes newspaper extracts for Sumter
county, 1875-76; v. 74. Includes newspaper extracts for Morgan County,
1861-77. v. 77. Includes newspaper extracts for Dallas county, 1860-76;
v. 80. Includes newspaper extracts for Madison county, 1867, 1874, 1884;
v. 83. Includes newspaper extracts for Talladega county, 1860-77; v. 86.
Includes newspaper extracts from <u>Huntsville Democrat</u> 1823-28, Jan.
1878-Jan. 1879, <u>Southern Advocate</u>, Huntsville, 1846-51, <u>Northport
Spectator</u> 3 Nov. 1871-29 Feb. 1872, Jan. 1874-Oct. 1874, <u>Tuscaloosa Gazette</u>
6 Jan. 871-28 Dec. 1876, <u>Jacksonville Republican</u> 8 June 1852-19 Aug. 1857;
v. 87. Includes newspaper extracts for Greene county, May-Dec. 1859; v. 90.
Includes newspaper obituaries for Dallas county, 1835-41; v. 101. Includes
newspaper extracts from <u>Southern Advocate</u> (Huntsville) 11 May 1827-29, 31
Dec. 1851-7 Sept. 1853; v. 106. Includes paper extracts for Augauga county,
1839- 44; v. 108. Includes newspaper extracts for Greene county, 1867-76; v.
116. Includes newspaper abstracts from miscellaneous Alabama newspapers; v.
123. Includes extracts from Lauderdale county newspapers, 1860s and 1870s; v.
135. Includes Mont-gomery county newspaper items, 1867, 1872; v. 148.
Includes newspaper abstracts from the <u>Southern Advocate</u>, Huntsville, 1855-58;
v. 157. Includes newspaper abstracts from Huntsville newspapers, 1879, 1882,
1884-85, 1887, 1902; v. 161. Includes newspaper extracts for Madison county,
1876, 1881, 1883, 1886, 1890-91; v. 162. Includes newspaper extracts for
Jackson county, 1860s and 1870s; v. 165. Includes newspaper extracts for
Madison county, 1870, 1876-77, 1879-80; 1884, 1886-87; v. 173. Includes

newspaper extracts for Madison county, 1878, 1883, 1885, 1890-93; v. 176. Includes newspaper extracts for Sumter county, 28 Apr. 1852 to 29 Apr. 1854; v. 184. Includes newspaper extracts for Tuscaloosa county, 24 Aug. 1829 to 11 June 1830, 1875-76, 1878, 1880-81, 1886, 1870; v. 188. Includes newspaper extracts for Benton county (now called Calhoun) 1841-57; v. 203. Includes a few obituaries for Madison county, 1907-14; v. 209. Includes newspaper extracts for Limestone county, 1860s to 1910; v. 231. Includes newspaper extracts for Montgomery county, 2 Jan. 1851 to 29 Dec. 1851; v. 240. Includes newspaper extracts for Lowndes county, 6 Apr. 1860 to 20 Dec. 1860; v. 244. Includes newspaper extracts for Shelby county, 1871, 1873. Most volumes of this series were examined at the Library of Congress and the DAR Library in Washington.

3.29   Lancaster, Mary Holland, and Dallas M. Lancaster. <u>Parish Registers of Trinity Episcopal Church, Florence, Alabama with Marriages and Obituaries, 1836-1933</u>. Florence, Ala.: M. H. Lancaster, 1985.

3.30   <u>Limestone County Cemeteries</u>. Athens, Ala.: Limestone County Historical Society, 197-.

3.31   Luttrell, Carolyn Lane. <u>Early Tombstone Records of Talladega County, Alabama</u>. Weogufka, Ala.: Fixico Press, 1973.

3.32   McCord, Howard F. <u>Baptists of Bibb County: A Denominational Salute to the People Called Baptists, in Cahawba (Bibb) County, Alabama, 1817-1974</u>. N.p. 1979. Includes data from cemeteries: name of person interred, birth and death dates, and the name of cemetery.

3.33   McFarland, Reginald, Lennis Shelton, and Leslie Shelton. <u>Headstones and Heritages; Cemeteries of Escambia County, Alabama</u>. N.p. 1974.

3.34   McKnight, Helen Bowling. "<u>Lauderdale Times</u> 1871 Death Notices." <u>Valley Leaves</u> 12 (1977): 24-26.

3.35   *------. "Some Area Marriages and Deaths from <u>National Banner</u>, Nashville Newspaper." (1826-1831) <u>Valley Leaves</u> 9 (1974/75): 47-48.

3.36   ------. "Some Deaths from the <u>Florence (Ala.) Enquirer</u>, 1840-1847." <u>Valley Leaves</u> 9 (1974): 39-40.

3.37   ------. "Some 1828-29 Area Deaths from the <u>Democrat</u>, Huntsville, Alabama Newspaper." <u>Valley Leaves</u> 8 (1974): 143.

3.38   Mallon, Capt. and Mrs. John. <u>Bay and Bayou Burials</u>. 2 vols. Mobile, Ala., 1974. v. 1. South Mobile County, Alabama; v. 2. West Mobile County, Alabama.

3.39   Marine, Marilyn Sue Short, and Ivydene Simpson Walls. <u>Morgan County, Alabama Cemeteries</u>. Hartselle, Ala.: Marine/Walls Historical Publications, 1982.

3. ALABAMA

3.40 <u>Marriage, Death, and Legal Notices from Early Alabama Newspapers,</u>
<u>1819-1893</u>. Compiled by Pauline Jones Gandrud. Easley, S.C.: Southern
Historical Press, 1981.

3.41 Marshall, Mary Grantham. <u>Cemetery Records of Greene County, Alabama</u>
<u>and Related Areas: The Journal of Mrs. Mary Marshall</u>. Edited by
O'levia Neil Wilson Wiese. Waco, Tex.: Wiese, 1980.

3.42 ------. <u>Greene County, Alabama Records</u>. Edited by Elizabeth Wood
Thomas. Tuscaloosa, Ala.: Willo Publishing Co., 1960. Includes some
newspaper death notices for 1830-74, and cemetery inscriptions.

3.43 Milford, Margaret Parker, and Eleanor Davis Scott. <u>A Survey of Cemeteries</u>
<u>in Chambers County, Alabama</u>. Huguley, Ala.: Genealogical Roving Press,
1983. (Publication of the Chattahoochee Valley Historical Society, no. 14)

3.44 Mitchell, Lois Dumas, and Dorothy Ivison Moffett. <u>Burial Records, Mobile</u>
<u>County, Alabama</u>. Mobile, Ala.: Mobile Genealogical Society, 1963. v. 1,
1828-56.

3.45 Nall, Robert. <u>The Dead of the Synod of Alabama</u>. Mobile: Dade, Thompson, 1851. This synod was established in 1821.

3.46 Nelson, Col. and Mrs. Soren. <u>A History of Church Street Graveyard, Mobile,</u>
<u>Alabama</u>. Compiled under the auspices of the Historic Mobile
Preservation Society. Mobile, 1963. Includes epitaphs.

3.47 Newell, Mr. and Mrs. Herbert Moses. <u>Fayette County, Alabama, Cemetery</u>
<u>Records, 1958-1959</u>. Fayette, Ala., 1959.

3.48 *"Obituaries from the <u>Gurley Herald</u>." (1899-1910) <u>Valley Leaves</u> 9 (1975):
142.

3.49 <u>Obituary Clippings</u>. 13 vols. N.p. 1950-79. Microfilm. Death notices from
various Alabama newspapers, 1950-79. A-Ar

3.50 Owen, Thomas McAdory. <u>Owen's Obituary Clipping Scrap Book</u>. 2 vols.
Montgomery, Ala., n.d. A-Ar

3.51 <u>Pike County, Alabama Tomb Records</u>. Sponsored by the Pike County Historical
Society. Montgomery Ala.: Alabama State Department of Archives and History,
1973. (Alabama Historical Quartery, vol. 35)

3.52 Scott, Mrs. Marvin. <u>Henry County, Alabama Cemetery Records</u>. Tuscaloosa,
Ala.: Willo Publishing Co., 1964.

3.53 Spell, Catherine Pepper, and Nina Pepper. <u>Abstracts of Marriages and Death</u>
<u>Notices, Pickens County, Alabama</u>. Carrollton, Ala.: C. P. Spell, 1978.
Contains abstracts of deaths from Pickensville, Alabama papers, the
<u>Pickensville Register</u> and the <u>Pickensville Republican</u>, 1841-60.

3. ALABAMA

3.54 Stalcup, Dorothy Shores, and William Spann Stalcup. Cemetery Inscriptions of Marion County, Alabama. 3 vols. Winfield, Ala.: D. S. Stalcup, 1979-82.

3.55 Stewart, Mrs. Frank Ross. Cemetery Records of Cherokee County, Alabama, 1840-1960. Centre, Ala.: Stewart University Press, 1981.

3.56 Swanson, Florence Lambrecht. Reeves (Reaves) Chapel Methodist Church and Cemetery, Camden, Rt. 2, Wilcox County, Alabama, 1870-1978. N.p.: Swanson, 1979.

3.57 Taylor, Beverly M. "Items from Mobile Commercial Register." (1822-29) Deep South Genealogical Quarterly 6 (1968): 1-7.

3.58 Thomas, Sue Hardy. Chilton County, Alabama Cemetery Census. Birmingham, Ala.: S. H. Thomas, 1979.

3.59 Thompson, Helen A. Magnolia Cemetery: A Collection of Records from the Gravestones of One of the Oldest Cemeteries in Mobile, Alabama, Including the Confederate Rest, Dating from 1828 to 1971. New Orleans: Polyanthos, 1974.

3.60 Walker, James H. Tombstones along the Old Huntsville Road. Tuscaloosa, Ala.: Instant Heirloom Books, 1984.

3.61 Walker County Cemeteries. Compiled from the records of Bruce Myers for the Walker County Genealogical Group. Cullman, Ala.: Gregath Co., 1982.

3.62 Wellden, Eulalia Yancey. Death Notices from Limestone County, Alabama Newspapers, 1828-1891. N.p. 1986.

4. ALASKA

4.1   <u>Alaska's Kenai Peninsula Death Records and Cemetery Inscriptions</u>. Compiled by Kenai Totem Tracers. Kenai, Alaska: Kenai Totem Tracers, 1983.

4.2   <u>Anchorage Times Obituaries Index</u>. Edited by Tohsook P. Chang, and Alden M. Rollins. 2 vols. Anchorage, Alaska: University of Alaska, Anchorage Library, 1979-81. v. 1. 1915-65; v. 2. 1966-80. Also available in microfiche.

4.3   DeArmond, Robert N. <u>Subject Index to the "Alaskan," 1885-1907, a Sitka Newspaper</u>. Juneau, Alaska: Gastineau Channel Centennial Association, 1974. The <u>Alaskan</u> was the only newspaper published in Alaska during these years.

4.4   Hales, David A. <u>An Index to the Early History of Alaska As Reported in the 1903-1907 Fairbanks Newspapers</u>. Fairbanks, Alaska: Elmer E. Rasmuson Library, University of Alaska, 1980. All of the issues for this time period have not been preserved, but all issues available on microfilm have been indexed.

4.5   <u>Index of Births, Deaths, Marriages, and Divorces in Fairbanks, Alaska Newspapers, 1903-30</u>. Fairbanks, Alaska: Fairbanks Genealogical Society, 1986.

4.6   Tillotson, Marjorie. <u>A Guide to the "Pathfinder": A Monthly Journal of the Pioneers of Alaska 1919-1926</u>. Juneau, Alaska: Alaska Historical Library, 1977. The <u>Pathfinder</u> was the official organ of the Pioneers of Alaska and contains obituaries of early settlers.

5. ARIZONA

5.1   Arizona Daily Star. <u>Index to Arizona News in the "Arizona Daily Star,</u> 1953-. Compiled by Donald M. Powell, and Lutie L. Higley. Tucson, 1954-. Library of Congress holds 1953-65.

5.2   <u>Arizona Death Records: An Index Compiled from Mortuary, Cemetery, and Church Records: A Bicentennial Project of the Arizona State Genealogical Society.</u> 3 vols. Tucson, Ariz.: The Society, 1976-82.

5.3   <u>Arizona Historical Review</u>, v. 1-7, Apr. 1928-July 1936. Most issues contain obituaries of prominent Arizona Pioneers.

5.4   Arizona Pioneers' Historical Society. Records, 1884-1961. NUC MS 61-3546. Includes funeral notices of pioneer members held by the Arizona Pioneers' Historical Society, Tucson.

5.5   <u>Grave and Funeral Records of Mohave County, Arizona, 1882-1982</u>. Kingman, Ariz.: Mohave County Genealogical Society, 1982.

5.6   <u>Military Burials in Arizona</u>. Compiled by Elizabeth Jane Akey. Tucson, Ariz.: Arizona State Genealogical Society, 1987. Includes inscriptions from Ft. Huachuca Post Cemetery, Ft. Huachuca, Arizona, and veterans' graves in Evergreen Cemetery and Memorial Park, Tucson, Arizona.

5.7   Money, George David. <u>Index to the "Weekly Arizonian," v. 1, nos. 1-7; Indexed from the Standpoint of the History of the West</u>. Tucson, Ariz.: Money, 1974. The <u>Weekly Arizonian</u> was published in Tucson, 3 Mar. 1859 to 29 Apr. 1871.

5.8   Reader, Sally O'Donnal, and Leah Skousen O'Donnal. <u>Burial Records, 1872-1914, of the Following Cemeteries in Phoenix, Maricopa Co., Arizona: Independent Order of Odd Fellows, Knights of Pythias, City Cemetery, Rosedale, Porter and Masons</u>. N.p. 1970.

5.9   Shook, Sally. <u>Name Index to the "Arizona Champion."</u> Flagstaff, Ariz.: Northern Arizona University, 1974-. Vol. 8 has title <u>Name Index to the "Arizona Champion"-"Coconino Sun."</u> Vols. 9-11 have title <u>Name Index to the "Coconino Sun."</u> <u>Arizona Champion</u> was first published in 1882.

6. ARKANSAS

6.1   Allen, Chris Elmore. <u>Sebastian County, Arkansas Cemtery Records</u>. Fort Smith, Ark.: Century Enterprises of Ft. Smith, 1975.

6.2   <u>Arkansas Cemetery Inscriptions and Genealogical Records</u>. Compiled and edited by Counts Genealogical Research and Publications. North Little Rock, Ark.: Counts, 1966.

6.3   <u>Arkansas Newspaper Index 1819-1845: Index to Obituaries, Biographical Notes and Probate and Chancery Notices from Arkansas Newspapers 1819-1845</u>. Compiled by James Logan Morgan. Newport, Ark.: Morgan Books, 1981.

6.4   Bell, Kathleen S. <u>St. Francis County, Arkansas, Cemetery Records</u>. Forrest City, Ark.: Bell Books, 1981.

6.5   Bohannan, Larry C. <u>Tombstone Inscriptions of Madison County, Arkansas</u>. Huntsville, Ark.: Century Publishers, 1968.

6.6   <u>Cemeteries of Pope County, Arkansas</u>. 2d ed. Edited and compiled by J. B. Lemley. N.p. 1981. The first edition was compiled by the Pope County Genealogy and Family Group

6.7   <u>Cemeteries of Washington County, Arkansas</u>. 8 vols. Rogers, Ark.: Northwest Arkansas Genealogical Society, 1980-85.

6.8   <u>Cemetery Index, Van Buren County, Arkansas</u>. Edited by Maxine Jennings Kelley, and Eleanor Bowling Ryman. Conway, Ark.: River Road Press, 1980.

6.9   <u>Cemetery Records of Arkansas County, Arkansas</u>. DeWitt, Ark.: Arkansas County Extension Homemakers Council, 1984.

6.10   <u>Cemetery Records of Bradley County, Arkansas</u>. Warren, Ark.: Bradley County Extension Homemakers Council, 1983.

6.11   <u>Cemetery Records of Lawrence County, Arkansas</u>. Walnut Ridge, Ark.: Extension Homemakers Council of Lawrence County, 1982.

6.12   <u>Clark County Cemetery Record Book</u>. Gurdon, Ark.: Committee for Extension Homemakers Council, 1983.

6.13   <u>Cleveland County, Arkansas Cemetery Records</u>. 2 vols. N.p.: Cleveland County Extension Homemakers Council, 1981-86.

6.14   Cline, Inez E., and Bobbie Jones McLane. <u>Garland County, Arkansas, Tombstone Inscriptions</u>. 3 vols. Hot Springs National Park, Ark., 1969-86. v. 1. Eastern; v. 2. Western; v. 3. City of Hot Springs.

6.15   Counts, Gloria. <u>A Compendium of Arkansas Genealogy</u>. North Little Rock, Ark.: Counts, 1977. The largest part of this volume is devoted to the Oakland Cemetery in Little Rock.

6. ARKANSAS

6.16   Cross County, Arkansas, Cemetery Records. 2 vols. Wynne, Ark.: Cross County Genealogical Society and the Cross County Historical Society, 1983-84.

6.17   Dallas County, Arkansas, Cemetery Records. 2 vols. N.p.: Dallas County Extension Homemakers Council, 1981.

6.18   Daughters of the American Revolution. Arkansas. Prudence Hall Chapter, North Little Rock. Index to Sources for Arkansas Cemetery Inscriptions. North Little Rock, Ark.: The Chapter, 1976.

6.19   Desha County, Arkansas Cemetery Records. McGehee, Ark.: M. M. Stroud, 1983.

6.20   Drew County, Arkansas Cemetery Records. N.p.: Drew County Extension Homemakers Council, 1982.

6.21   Goodwin, Jane Allen. Cemetery Records of Jackson County, Arkansas: A Special Bicentennial Project. Newport, Ark.: Jackson County Historical Society, 1975-. v. 1. Swifton and vicinity.

6.22   Grant, Mollie Wisinger. Calhoun County Cemetery Records of Calhoun County, Arkansas. Hampton, Ark.: Grant, 1980.

6.23   Grant County, Arkansas, Cemetery Records. N.p.: Grant County Extension Homemakers Council, 1981.

6.24   Green, Chalman E., and Mae Chinn Green. Cemetery Records of Independence County, Arkansas. Newport, Ark.: Morgan Books, 1980.

6.25   Green, Mae Chinn, Chalman E. Green, and James Logan Morgan. Cemetery Records of the Newark-Magness Area of Big Bottom, Logan and Wycough Townships in Independence County, Arkansas. Newport, Ark.: James Logan Morgan, 1976.

6.26   Hancock, Juanita Butler. Cemetery and Bible Records of Union County, Arkansas. El Dorado, Ark.: Southern Printing and Stationery Co., 1971.

6.27   Headstone History, Cemetery Inscriptions: Hot Spring County, Arkansas. 4 vols. Malvern, Ark.: Hot Spring County Historical Society, 1979. v. 1. West of the Ouachita River; v. 2. City of Malvern; v. 3. East of the Ouachita River; v. 4. Borderline Cemeteries.

6.28   Henderson, Shannon J. "Arkansas Gazette" Index: An Arkansas Index. Russellville, Ark.: Arkansas Tech University Library, 1976-. Annual. Indexes being issued retrospectively. v. 1. 1819-29; v. 2. 1830-39; v. 3. 1840-49; v. 4. 1850-59; v. 5. 1860-69; v. 6. 1870-73; v. 7. 1874-79. The Arkansas Gazette was published in Little Rock.

6.29   Humphrey, Mary V., and Erma Lee Judkins Masters. Brearley Cemetery, Yell County, Arkansas. Russellville, Ark.: M. V. Humphrey, 1980.

6. ARKANSAS

6.30   Kannady, Nixby Daniel, and Loreda Hicks Daniel. Cemetery Inscriptions of Polk County, Arkansas. Cove, Ark.: N. D. Kannady, 1984.

6.31   Kittrell, Adelia C., and Curtis A. Houston. Cemetery Records of Woodruff County, Arkansas. Augusta, Ark.: Kittrell; McCrory, Ark.: Houston, 1978.

6.32   Lemley, J. B. Obituary and Death Notices of Pope County, Arkansas, 1875 through 1886. Russellville, Ark.: Lemley, 1977.

6.33   ------. Obituary and Death Notices of Pope County, Arkansas, 1894 through 1899. Russellville, Ark.: Lemley, 1978.

6.34   ------. Pope County, Arkansas Interviews and Obituaries, 1974. Russellville, Ark.: Lemley, 1977.

6.35   ------. Pope County, Arkansas Obituaries and Death Notices: February 2 1887-December 7 1893. Russellville, Ark.: Lemley, 1978. Volumes have been published also for the following years: Jan. 1900-Dec. 1903; Jan. 1904-Dec. 1906; 1907-1909; 6 Jan. 1910-1 Feb. 1912.

6.36   ------ Pope County, Arkansas Obituaries, February, 1973 thru December 1973. Russellville, Ark.: Lemley, 1974. Volumes for 1975-80 have also been published.

6.37   Lincoln County, Arkansas, Cemetery Records. Yorktown, Ark.: Lincoln County Extension Homemakers Council, 1984.

6.38   Little River County, Arkansas, Cemetery Census. Washington, Ark.: Southwest Arkansas Regional Archives, [1979?].

6.39   McConnell, Lloyd. Cemeteries in Washington County, Arkansas. Owensboro, Ky.: Cook-McDowell Publications, 1980.

6.40   Morgan, James Logan. Arkansas Newspaper Abstracts, 1819-1845. 4 vols. Newport, Ark.: Morgan, 1981.

6.41   ------. Genealogical Gleanings from Newspaper Files of Jonesboro, Arkansas, 1885-1887. Newport, Ark.: Northeast Arkansas Genealogical Association, 1979.

6.42   ------. Genealogical Records of Arkansas. Newport, Ark.: Arkansas Records Association, 1973. v. 1. 1804-30.

6.43   ------. Marriages, Deaths and Other Notices in the "Arkansas Advocate," 1830-1832. Newport, Ark.: Arkansas Records Association, 1971. The Arkansas Advocate was published in Little Rock.

6.44   ------. Marriages, Deaths and Other Notices in the "Arkansas Gazette," 1819-1822. Newport, Ark.: Northeast Arkansas Genealogical Association, 1971. The Arkansas Gazette was published in Little Rock.

6. ARKANSAS

6.45   Northwest Arkansas Genealogical Society. Cemeteries of Benton County, Arkansas. 4 vols. Rogers, Ark.: Northwest Arkansas Genealogical Society, n.d.

6.46   *"Obituaries." Backtracker 1, no. 2 (1972): 14. Obituaries are abstracted from the Springdale News from September 1971 to March 1972, for persons born before 1910.

6.47   Ouachita County, Arkansas, Cemetery Records. Camden, Ark.: Ouachita County Extension Homemakers Council, 1981.

6.48   Rowe, Imogene. Cemeteries, Van Buren County, Arkansas. Searcy, Ark.: Mrs. L. E. Presley, 1977.

6.49   St. Louis Genealogical Society. Cemetery Relocations by the U.S. Army Corps of Engineers in Illinois, Iowa, Missouri, Arkansas. St. Louis: St. Louis Genealogical Society, 1977.

6.50   Shaver, Jo, and Freda Roberts. Cemeteries of Randolph County, Arkansas. Flint, Mich.: J. Shaver, 1983?

6.51   Swinburn, Susan Stevenson, and Doris Stevenson West. History in Headstones: a Complete Listing of All Marked Graves in Known Cemeteries of Crawford County, Arkansas. Van Buren, Ark.: Press Argus, 1970.

6.52   Tiffee, Ellen. Sebastian County, Arkansas Cemeteries. Howe, Okla.: E. Tiffee, 1983.

6.53   Traxler, Doyle, and Mary V. Humphrey. 9 vols. Cemeteries of Yell County, Arkansas. Centerville, Ark., 1980-83.

6.54   Tweedle, Mrs. Earl. Monroe County, Arkansas, Cemetery Readings. Clarendon, Ark.: Monroe County Historical and Cemetery Association, 1982.

6.55   Vaughan, Mickey Weise. Madison County Arkansas Annotated Cemetery Enumerations. Rogers, Ark.: M. W. Vaughan, 1982.

6.56   Wade, Mrs. Jeff, Jr. Blytheville (Mississippi Co.) Arkansas Cemetery Inscriptions of Blytheville Cemetery, Dogwood Cemetery, Elmwood Cemetery, Maplegrove Cemetery, Memorial Park, North Chicksawaba Cemetery, Sandy Ridge Cemetery, Sawyer Cemetery. Bragg City, Mo., [1969].

6.57   Walls, Edwina, Rita Anderson, and Jeannette M. Shorey. Obituary Index from Arkansas Health Sciences Publications. Little Rock, Ark.: History of Medicine Division, Library/Archives, University of Arkansas for Medical Sciences, 1981.

6.58   Washington County Historical Society (Arkansas). Cemetery Records of Washington County, Ark. Fayetteville, Ark.: Washington County Historical Society, [1976?].

6. ARKANSAS

6.59   White, Rose Craig. <u>Records of Salem Baptist Church and Cypert Cemetery,</u>
<u>Eventide Cemetery, Smalley Cemetery, Gamble Cemetery, Area of Marvell,</u>
<u>Phillips County, Arkansas</u>. Marvell, Ark.: White, 1977.

6.60   <u>Yell County, Arkansas, Obituaries and Historical Items</u>. Compiled by Mary
Vinson Humphrey. Russellville, Ark., 1983. This is a compilation of
newspaper obituaries and other articles.

7. CALIFORNIA

7.1   Alsworth, Mary Dean. <u>Gleanings from Alta California: Marriages and Deaths Reported in the First Newspapers Published in California, 1846 through 1850</u>. Rancho Cordova, Calif.: Dean Publications, 1980.

7.2   ------. <u>More Gleanings from Alta California: Vital Records Published in California's First Newspaper, Year--1851</u>. Rancho Cordova, Calif.: Dean Publications, 1982.

7.3   <u>Amador County Cemeteries</u>. Auburn, Calif.: DuVall/Landrith, 1985.

7.4   <u>Anaheim Cemetery: 1400 E. Sycamore, Anaheim, California</u>. 2 vols. Orange, Calif.: Orange County California Genealogy Society, 1983. pt. 1. 1867-1902; pt. 2. 1903-1928.

7.5   Bayless, Dorothy Martin, and M. Georgeann Mello. <u>Rest in Peace: Early Records from Cemeteries in the City and County of Sacramento, California</u>. 7 vols. Sacramento, Calif.: D. M. Bayless, 1982-.

7.6   *"Births, Marriages and Deaths As Reported in the <u>Ferndale Enterprise</u>." (1878-85) <u>Redwood Researcher</u> 7, no. 3 (1974): 3-6.

7.7   Bower, Betty, and Elsa Anderson. <u>Denair Cemetery, Stanislaus County, CA., 1900-1981</u>. Modesto, Calif.: B. Bower, 1984.

7.8   *Buirch, Shirely [sic]. "<u>Lodi Sentinel</u> Vital Records; Vital Records Extracted from the <u>Lodi Sentinel</u> of Lodi, San Joaquin County, California." (July 1881-82) <u>Genealogical Research News</u> 6 (1968): 271-72.

7.9   <u>California Cemetery Records, Contra Costa County (Founded 1850)</u>. Compiled by Darlene Appell, et al. Concord, Calif.: Contra Costa County Genealogical Society, 1980. For the years 1854-1964.

7.10   <u>California Historical Society Quarterly</u>, v. 1-49, July 1922-70. San Francisco: California Historical Society, 1922-70. Name changed to <u>California Historical Quarterly</u>, 1971. There are indexes to volumes 1-40, 1922-61, and volumes 41-54, 1962-75. Contains many lengthy obituaries, particularly in the earlier years.

7.11   <u>California News Index</u>, v. 1-, July 1/15, 1970-. Claremont: Center for California Public Affairs, 1970-. Semimonthly with quarterly cumulations. Ceased? An index to California's leading newspapers and magazines.

7.12   Carpenter, Edwin H. <u>Early Cemeteries of the City of Los Angeles</u>. Los Angeles: Dawson's Book Shop, 1973.

7.13   Daughters of the American Revolution. California. <u>Pioneer Obituaries from the "San Francisco Chronicle," 1911-1928</u>. San Francisco, 1952. USIGS

7.14   ------. Genealogical Records Committee. <u>Vital Records from the "Daily Alta California," Including Records from the "Golden Era" and the "Wide West," 1854</u>. San Francisco, 1955. The <u>Daily Alta California</u> and the <u>Wide West</u> were published in San Francisco. CHi

7. CALIFORNIA

7.15   ------. <u>Vital Records from the "San Francisco Bulletin," October-December 1855, "Alta California" and "Wide West," 1855. Births, Marriages, and Deaths</u>. San Francisco, 1956.

7.16   ------. <u>Vital Records from the "San Francisco Daily Bulletin" (and Other San Francisco Newspapers) 1855-1906</u>. 20 vols. San Francisco, 1943, 1956-68. Filmed by Reproduction Systems for the Genealogical Society of Utah at the DAR Library, 1970. USIGS

7.17   ------. Collis P. Huntington Chapter. <u>Births, Marriages and Deaths from the "Los Angeles Daily Times," 1881-1886</u>. N.p. 1962. USIGS

7.18   ------. El Toyon Chapter. <u>Vital Records from Stockton, California Newspapers, 1850-1852</u>. Stockton, 1962. C

7.19   ------. Sequoia Chapter. <u>Annual Compilation of Births, Marriages, Deaths in the "Sacramento Union," 1859-1886</u>. 2 vols. San Francisco: Genealogical Records Committee, 1956.

7.20 "Deaths 'At Sea' in California, in San Francisco, As Listed in San Francisco Newspapers 1849-1850." <u>Quarterly of the Orange County (Calif.) Genealogical Society</u> 5 (1968): 31-32. Also contained in <u>San Francisco Historic Record and Genealogy Bulletin</u> 1, no. 11 (1964): 9-10, and continued in vols. 2 and 3.

7.21 <u>El Dorado County Cemeteries</u>. Auburn, Calif.: DuVall/ Landrith, 1985.

7.22 Eterovich, Adam S. <u>Jugoslav Cemetery Records of San Francisco, 1849-1930</u>. San Francisco, 1968. (His Jugoslav-American Immigrant History Series, 1492-1900, no. 3)

7.23 <u>Fresno County Cemetery Records: With Some Madera and Kings County Records</u>. Fresno, Calif.: Fresno Genealogical Society, 1985.

7.24 "<u>Fresno Weekly Expositor</u>, 1882-1883 Deaths." <u>Ash Tree Echo</u> 9 (1974): 82.

7.25 "Genealogical Notes from Early San Bernardino Newspapers, 1875-1880." <u>Valley Quarterly</u> 15 (1978): 34-35.

7.26 "Genealogical Notes from the <u>Argus</u>." (1876-77) <u>Valley Quarterly</u> 13 (1976): 18-19. The <u>Argus</u> was published in San Bernardino.

7.27 Genealogical Society of Riverside. <u>Newspaper Abstracts: Births, Marriages, Deaths, 1878-1879-1880-1881-1892, Riverside, California</u>. Riverside, Calif: Genealogical Society of Riverside, 1976.

7.28   ------. <u>Old Cemetery Records of Riverside, California</u>. Riverside, Calif.: Genealogical Society of Riverside, 1976. Includes inscriptions from Agua Mensa Cemetery, Temecula Cemetery, and Evergreen Memorial Park.

7.29 Hansen, Mary. "Deaths and Marriages, <u>Stockton Times</u>, Published in Stockton, California, 1850." <u>American Heritage Service</u> 2 (1969): 97-102.

7. CALIFORNIA

7.30   Harris, Billie. <u>Sacramento County Cemeteries</u>. Owensboro, Ky.: Cook and McDowell Publications, 1981.

7.31   Harter, Miriam Pruess. <u>Index to Oddfellows Cemetery and Mausoleum, Memorials, Crypts, and Gravestones, in San Luis Obispo, California</u>. Atascadero, Calif: California Central Coast Genealogical Society, 1978.

7.32   <u>Indexed Cemetery Records of Santa Cruz County, California</u>. Santa Cruz, Calif.: Genealogical Society of Santa Cruz County, 1980.

7.33   Lewis, Mary L. "Genealogical Notes from the <u>Guardian</u>, San Bernardino, 1867." <u>Valley Quarterly</u> 6 (1969): 31-32.

7.34   ------. "Genealogical Notes from the <u>Guardian</u>, San Bernardino, 1870." <u>Valley Quarterly</u> 5 (1966): 215-18.

7.35   *------. "Genealogical Notes from the <u>Guardian</u>, San Bernardino, 1873." <u>Valley Quarterly</u> 11 (1974): 6-8.

7.36   ------. "Genealogical Notes from the <u>Guardian</u>, San Bernardino, 1876." <u>Valley Quarterly</u> 13 (1976): 18.

7.37   Los Angeles (Archdiocese). <u>Necrologium</u>. . . . Compiled by Francis J. Weber. Los Angeles: Chancery Archives, 1966. Contains sacerdotal necrology for the Archdiocese of Los Angeles, 1840-1965.

7.38   Los Angeles Times. <u>Newspaper Index</u>. Wooster, Ohio: Bell and Howell Co., 1972-. Monthly with annual cumulations.

7.39   Morris, Joan M. <u>A Surname Guide to Heads of Families and Adult Children Residing in Nevada County, California in the Year 1880, and Births, Deaths and Marriages As Shown in the Incomplete Issues, 1874-1884 of the San Juan Times Weekly Newspaper, North San Juan, California</u>. Soquel, Calif.: Morris, 1980.

7.40   "North Coast Deaths, As Reported in the <u>San Francisco Daily Evening Bulletin, 1858-1874</u>." <u>Redwood Researcher</u> 7, no. 1 (1974): 3-8.

7.41   *"Obituaries As Published in the <u>Sun Telegram</u>, San Bernardino, California: Index for 1974." <u>Valley Quarterly</u> 11 (1974): 9-21.

7.42   Pomona Valley Genealogical Society. <u>Pomona Cemeteries</u>. Edited by Mary C. Swank. Pomona, Calif., 1973-.

7.43   Purdy, Tim I. <u>Enumeration of the Headstones of the Big Valley Cemeteries of Lassen and Modoc Counties, California</u>. Susanville, Calif.: Lahontan Images, 1986.

7.44   ------. <u>Enumeration of the Headstones of the Janesville Cemetery, Janesville, California</u>. Susanville, Calif.: Lahontan Images, 1986.

7. CALIFORNIA

7.45   ------. <u>Enumeration of the Headstones of the Summit and Vinton</u>
        <u>Cemeteries, Chilcoot and Vinton, California</u>. Susanville, Calif.: Lahonton
        Images, 1986.

7.46   ------. <u>Enumeration of the Headstones of the Susanville Cemetery,</u>
        <u>Susanville, California</u>. Susanville, Calif.: Lahontan Images, 1986.

7.47   ------. <u>Index to the Birth and Death Notices of the "Lassen Advocate"</u>
        <u>Newspaper of Susanville, California, 1868 to 1899</u>. Susanville, Calif.:
        Lahontan Images, 1986. Includes vital statistics for neighboring counties
        and former residents in addition to those for Lassen county.

7.48   Questing Heirs Genealogical Society. <u>Some Early Southern California Burials</u>.
        Long Beach, Calif.: The Society, 1974.

7.49   <u>Sacramento County Cemeteries</u>. Auburn, Calif.: DuVall/Landrith, 1985.

7.50   San Francisco Chronicle. <u>Newspaper Index</u>. Wooster, Ohio: Bell and Howell
        Co., 1976-. Monthly with annual cumulations.

7.51   San Joaquin Genealogical Society. <u>Gold Rush Days</u>. 5 vols. Stockton, Calif.:
        The Society, 1958-1984. v. 1. Vital statistics copied from early news-
        papers of Stockton, California, 1850-1855; v. 2. Deaths copied from early
        newspapers of Stockton, California, 1856-1862; v. 3. Miscellaneous
        records, 1856-1862, copied from early newspapers of Stockton, California;
        v. 4. Births and marriages copied from early newspapers of Stockton,
        California, 1856-1862; v. 5. Births, deaths, and marriages copied from
        early newspapers of Stockton, California, 1861-1866.

7.52   ------. <u>Old Cemeteries of San Joaquin County, California</u>. 3 vols.
        Stockton, Calif.: The Society, 1960-64.

7.53   "Santa Clara County Obituaries from the <u>San Jose Mercury News</u>." <u>Quarterly</u>
        <u>of the Santa Clara County Historical and Genealogical Society</u> 10 (1973):
        37.

7.54   <u>Santa Rose Rural Cemetery 1852-1980: A Listing of Burials in Fulkerson,</u>
        <u>Moke, Rural and Stanley Cemeteries</u>. Santa Rosa, Calif.: Sonoma County
        Genealogical Society, 1987.

7.55   <u>Scrapbook of Newspaper Clippings from the "Fresno Bee" and the "Hanford</u>
        <u>Sentinel," 1964-1966</u>. Salt Lake City, 1971. Contains obituaries and
        marriage information. USIGS

7.56   Setterquist, Ruth. <u>Solano County Cemeteries</u>. Fairfield, Calif.: Solano County
        Genealogical Society, 1986. v. 1. Rockville cemetery, Suisun Valley,
        Solano County, California, tombstone survey, 1852-1983.

7.57   Sonoma County Genealogical Society. <u>Sonoma County Cemetery Records,</u>
        <u>1846-1921</u>. Santa Rosa, Calif.: The Society, 197-.

7. CALIFORNIA

7.58   Stanley, Lucile. "Obituaries from the <u>Havilah Weekly Courier</u> Newspaper."
(1860-72)   <u>Kern-Gen</u> 3 (1966): 12-13.

7.59   ------. "Obituaries from the <u>Kern County Weekly Courier</u>."   (1870-75)
<u>Kern-Gen</u> 3 (1966): 26.

7.60   <u>Tombstone Inscriptions</u>. 4 vols. Orange, Calif.: Orange County California
Genealogical Society, 1969-. v. 1. Magnolia Memorial Park Cemetery,
Garden Grove, California, 1874-1967; v. 2. St. John's Lutheran Cemetery,
Section I and Section II, 1890-1968; v. 3. Holy Cross Cemetery, El Toro
Cemetery, San Juan Capistrano Mission Cemetery, Yorba Cemetery; v. 4.
The Broadway (Clark) Cemetery, Whittier, California.

7.61   Union Cemetery, Bakersfield, Calif.   <u>Union Cemetery Sexton Records,
Bakersfield, California</u>. Bakersfield, Calif.: Kern County Genealogical
Society, 1967. pt. 1. 1878-1882; pt. 2. 1883-October, 1904.

7.62   United States Work Projects Administration. California. <u>Descriptive Index to
Items Referring to the Mining Town of Columbia, California, 1851-1870,
in Tuolumne County Newspapers</u>. San Francisco, 1938. CU-B

7.63   Weight, Verl Frederick. <u>Cemeteries of El Dorado County, California</u>.
Carmichael, Calif.: Sacramento Branch Genealogical Library, 1967.

8. COLORADO

8.1   Denver. Public Library. Genealogy Division. <u>Obituary File of the Public Library, City and County of Denver, Colorado, Literature and History Department, Genealogy Division, 1944-1959</u>. Denver: Dakota Microfilm Service, 1963-65. Microfilm. Microfilm copies of the Division's obituary files, consisting of mounted clippings and typed notes from the <u>Rocky Mountain News</u>, Denver, and the <u>Denver Post</u>, and a few from other Colorado newspapers.

8.2   Denver Post. <u>Newpaper Index</u>. Wooster, Ohio: Bell and Howell Co., 1979-. Monthly with annual cumulations.

8.3   Drummond, Donna L. <u>Deaths and Burials of Garfield County, Colorado</u>. N.p.: Drummond, 1978-. v. 1. New Castle area.

8.4   Genealogical Society of the Church of Jesus Christ of L. D. S. Colorado Springs (Colorado Branch Genealogical Library). <u>Obituaries and Death Notices Taken from the "Free Press" and the "Gazette Telegraph," Colorado Springs, Colorado, January 1963 to December 1966</u>. Salt Lake City: Genealogical Society, 1967. Microfilm. USIGS

8.5   Houston, Grant E. <u>Cemeteries of Hinsdale County, Colorado: Comprising the Communities of Lake City, Capitol City, and Burrows Park Together with Cathedral, the Lake Fork Valley, Rio Grande and Debs, Representing the Years, 1874 to 1985</u>. Lake City, Colo.: Hinsdale County Historical Society, 1986.

8.6   <u>Littleton Cemetery, Littleton, Colorado</u>. Compiled by Mount Rosa Chapter, National Society, Daughters of the American Revolution. Littleton, Colo.: Mount Rosa Chapter, NSDAR, 1983.

8.7   <u>Logan County, Colorado, Cemetery Survey: A Centennial Project</u>. Sterling, Colo.: Logan County Genealogy Society, 1984.

8.8   Loudermilk-Edwards, Carol. <u>Teller County, Colorado, Church and Cemetery Records</u>. Westminster, Colo.: C. Loudermilk-Edwards, 1983.

8.9   <u>Obituaries, Non-Local</u>. Denver: Dakota, 1985. 7 microfilm reels. Microfilmed file of obituaries clipped from non-Denver Colorado Newspapers, 1934-1963, by staff of the Denver Public Library Genealogy Division.

8.10   <u>Ouray County Cemeteries: Including Information from Tombstone Inscriptions in Cedar Hill</u>. . . . N.p.: Ouray Genealogical Society, 1984.

8.11   Pease, Janet Kathleen. <u>Clear Creek County Cemetery Records: Idaho Springs, Colorado Cemetery Tombstone Inscriptions and Ledger Records</u>. Moline, Ill.: Pease, 1973.

8.12   ------. <u>Jefferson County, Colorado, Cemetery Records</u>. 2 vols. Moline, Ill., 1972.

8.13   Smith, Leah. <u>Archuleta County Cemeteries: One Hundred Years, 1878-1978</u>. Pagosa Springs, Colo.: L. Smith, 1985.

8. COLORADO

8.14 <u>Sons of Colorado: A Monthly Publication Devoted to the Interests of the Society and "for Colorado,"</u> v. 1-2, June 1906-May 1908. Denver. Superseded by <u>Trail: A Magazine for Colorado</u>, v. 1-20, June 1908-Mar. 1928. The library of the Colorado Historical Society, Denver, has an index to these two titles which can be used to locate obituaries of pioneers.

8.15 <u>Weld County, Colorado, Tombstone Inscriptions: Including Additional Records Taken from the Town Halls and Private Sources</u>. Greeley, Colo.: Genealogical Society of Weld County, Colorado, 1982.

9. CONNECTICUT

9.1   Abbott, Morris W., and Susan Woodruff Abbott. <u>Milford Tombstone Inscriptions</u>. Milford, Conn., 1967.

9.2   Andrews, Josiah Bishop. "Vital Records of Genealogical Interest Abstracted from the Diaries of Josiah Bishop Andrews of Connecticut, New York, and New Jersey." <u>New York Genealogical and Biographical Record</u> 57 (1926): 236-39.

9.3   Bowman, John Elliot. <u>Some Connecticut Veterans of the American Revolution; Items from Newspapers, 1816-1856; Including a Few Concerning Veterans of French and Indian Wars, of Whom No Service in Revolution Is Mentioned</u>. New Ipswich, N.H., 1927.

9.4   Caulkins, Frances Manwaring. <u>History of New London, Connecticut, from the First Survey of the Coast in 1612 to 1860</u>. New London: H. D. Utley, 1895. Contains obituaries. Index published in 1950.

9.5   Caulkins, Frances Manwaring, and Emily S. Gilman. <u>The Stone Records of Groton</u>. Norwich, Conn.: Free Academy Press, 1903. (Occasional Publication of the New London County Historical Society, v. 1)

9.6   Connecticut State Library, Hartford. <u>Charles R. Hale Collection of Newspaper Notices and Headstone Inscriptions</u>. Salt Lake City: Genealogical Society, 1949-50. Microfilm. For contents see: <u>A Reel Guide to the Charles R. Hale Collection of Connecticut Newspaper Notices and Headstone Inscriptions</u>. Compiled by the Local and Family History Section, The Newberry Library, Chicago, 1981. This collection consists of abstracts from Connecticut newspapers covering the period from 1755 to about 1870. USIGS

9.7   Daughters of the American Revolution. Connecticut. Abigail Wolcott Ellsworth Chapter. <u>Cemetery Inscriptions in Windsor, Connecticut; Appendix Containing Filley Records</u>. Windsor, Conn., 1929.

9.8   ------. Sarah Whitman Trumbull Chapter, Watertown. <u>The Old Burying Ground of Ancient Westbury and Present Watertown</u>. Watertown, Conn., 1938.

9.9   Dexter, Franklin B. "Inscriptions on Tombstones in New Haven, Erected Prior to 1800." <u>Papers of the New Haven Colony Historical Society</u> 3 (1882): 471-614. Includes copies of all the legible inscriptions prior to 1800 in the Grove Street Cemetery, in the crypt under the Center Church, and on the neighboring green.

9.10   Eardeley, William Applebie Daniel. <u>Connecticut Cemeteries, 1673-1911</u>. 9 vols. Brooklyn, N.Y., 1914-18. Microfilm. Gives headstone inscriptions, town of Stamford, Connecticut, copied in 1934, under the auspices of the F.E.R.A. and the W.P.A., sponsored by the Connecticut State Library and compiled under the supervision of Charles R. Hale.

9.11   Ellsberry, Elizabeth Prather. <u>Cemetery Records of New London County, Connecticut</u>. 2 vols. Chillicothe, Mo, 1968.

9. CONNECTICUT

9.12   ------. Cemetery Records of Windham County, Connecticut. Chillicothe,
        Mo, 1968.

9.13   First Congregational Church of Westbrook, Connecticut. First Congregational
        Church of Westbrook, Connecticut: Baptisms, Marriages, Deaths, Member-
        ships, 1725-1899, from the First Four Volumes of Records: Supplemented
        by Gravestone Inscriptions from Westbrook Cemeteries. Edited by Jean
        Rumsey. N.p. 1979.

9.14   Fowler, William Miles. "Inscriptions on Tombstones in Milford." Papers of
        the New Haven Colony Historical Society 5 (1894): 1-69. Copied from
        photographs taken by R. A. Lawrence.

9.15   Gilyard, Thomas. "Record Kept by Thomas Gilyard of Deaths Mainly in the
        Naugatuck Valley, Connecticut (1809-33); Transcribed by Donald Lines
        Jacobus." American Genealogist 32 (Oct. 1956): 245-49.

9.16   Gingras, Raymond. Quelques francos au Connecticut: notes, références et
        index des nécrologies parues dans des journaux de 1963 à 1975. Quebec,
        1976.

9.17   Hedden, James Spencer. Roster of Graves of, or Monuments to, Patriots of
        1775-1783, and of Soldiers of Colonial Wars, in and adjacent to New
        Haven County. 4 vols. New Haven, Conn., 1931-34.

9.18   Hempstead, Joshua. Diary of Joshua Hempstead of New London,
        Connecticut, Covering a Period of Forty-seven Years, from September,
        1711, to November, 1758. New London, Conn.: New London County
        Historical Society, 1901. Contains records of births, marriages and deaths.

9.19   Kinne, Manuel. "Record of Deaths Kept by Manuel Kinne of Plainfield,
        Connecticut, Communicated by Judge John Eben Prior, 1799-1818." New
        England Historical and Genealogical Register 71 (1917): 133-44. Of
        limited value. Gives only name, date of death, and occasionally the age
        at death.

9.20   Martin, Harold Secor. The Record of Inscriptions and Epitaphs Found on
        the Monuments and Headstones in East Norwalk Historical Cemetery, the
        Oldest Cemetery in Norwalk. East Norwalk, Conn., 1971.

9.21   Orcutt, Samuel. A History of the Old Town of Stratford and the City of
        Bridgeport, Connecticut. 2 vols. New Haven, Conn.: Press of Tuttle,
        Morehouse and Taylor, 1886. Epitaphs from the various cemeteries are
        included.

9.22   ------. History of the Towns of New Milford and Bridgewater, Connecticut,
        1703-1882. Hartford, Conn.: Press of the Case, Lockwood and Brainard
        Co., 1882. Includes a record of inscriptions in several cemeteries of New
        Milford and Bridgewater.

9. CONNECTICUT

9.23   Payne, Charles Thomas. <u>Litchfield and Morris Inscriptions; a Record of Inscriptions upon the Tombstones in the Towns of Litchfield and Morris, Ct</u>. Litchfield, Conn.: D. C. Kilbourn, 1905.

9.24   Perry, Kate E. <u>The Old Burying Ground of Fairfield, Conn.: A Memorial of Many of the Early Settlers in Fairfield, and an Exhaustive and Faithful Transcript of the Inscriptions and Epitaphs on the 583 Tombstones Found in the Oldest Burying Ground Now within the Limits of Fairfield</u>. Hartford, Conn.: American Publishing Co., 1882.

9.25   Pond, Nathan Gillet. <u>Inscriptions on Tombstones in Milford, Conn., Erected Prior to 1800, Together with a Few of Aged Persons Who Died after That Date</u>. New Haven, Conn.: New Haven Colony Historical Society, 1889.

9.26   Porter, George Shephard. <u>Inscriptions from Gravestones in the Old Burying Ground, Norwich Town, Connecticut</u>. Norwich, Conn.: Published for the Society of the Founders of Norwich, Connecticut by the Bulletin Press, 1933.

9.27   [Prentice, Edward]. <u>Ye Antient Buriall Place of New London, Conn</u>. New London, Conn.: Day Pub., 1899.

9.28   Prichard, Katherine Adelaid. <u>Ancient Burying-Grounds of the Town of Waterbury, Connecticut, Together with Other Records of Church and Town</u>. Waterbury, Conn.: Mattatuck Historical Society, 1917.

9.29   Salisbury, Connecticut. "Vital Records of Salisbury Town, Circa 1730-- Cemetery Records." <u>Historical Collections of the Salisbury Association</u> 1 (1913): 23-123.

9.30   Scott, Kenneth. <u>Genealogical Data from Colonial New Haven Newspapers</u>. Baltimore: Genealogical Publishing Co., 1979. Covers the years 1755-75.

9.31   <u>Scrapbook of Newspaper Clippings Containing Obituaries from Haddam, Conn. and Other Conn. Towns, Mostly in Middlesex and New London Counties, and a Few Marriages and Births</u>. 1890-1905.

9.32   Sisson, Mrs. Henry B. <u>Scrapbook of Newspaper Clippings Including Vital Records . . . Referring to Lyme, Haddam, East Haddam and Vicinity</u>. 1873-98.

9.33   "Some Connecticut Records." <u>National Genealogical Society Quarterly</u> 5 (1916): 41-42. Includes a few death notices for June 1805 and June 1806.

9.34   <u>Stonington Graveyards: A Guide</u>. Stonington, Conn.: Stonington Historical Society, 1980. This is an index for Stonington to the Hale Collection, a listing of all the graveyard inscriptions (names and dates only) in each of the 169 towns of Connecticut. The inscriptions were collected as a WPA project. The entire collection is on file cards and in bound volumes in the Genealogical Department of the Connecticut State Library. See also no. 9.6.

9.   CONNECTICUT

9.35   Tillotson, Edward Sweetser. Wethersfield Inscriptions; a Complete Record of the Inscriptions in the Five Burial Places in the Ancient Town of Wetherfield, Including the Towns of Rocky Hill, Newington, and Beckley Quarter (in Berlin), Also a Portion of the Inscriptions in the Oldest Cemetery in Glastonbury. Hartford, Conn.: W. F. J. Boardman, 1899.

9.36   Trinity College, Hartford. . . . Necrology: Trinity Men Who Died During the Years 1916-1918. Hartford, Conn., 1918.

9.37   Van Alystyne, L. Burying Grounds of Sharon, Connecticut, Amenia and North East, New York: Being an Abstract of Inscriptions from Thirty Places of Burial in the Above Named Towns. Interlake, N.Y.: Heart of the Lakes Publications, 1983.

9.38   Van Hoosear, David Herman. A Complete Copy of the Inscriptions Found on the Monuments, Headstones . . . in the Oldest Cemetery in Norwalk, Conn. September, 1892. Bridgeport, Conn.: Standard Association, Printers, 1895.

9.39   Watson, William. "Vital Records Kept by William Watson of Hartford, Connecticut, 1819-1834." New England Historical and Genealogical Register 79 (1925): 150-70. Most of the deceased were from Connecticut but there are others from nearby states.

9.40   Whittlesey, Marilyn, and Jack Scully. A Handbook of Cemeteries, Brookfield, Connecticut (Including Portions of New Milford and Newton), 1745-1985. N.p.: Old South Cemetery Association, 1986.

9.41   Yale University. Biographical Notices of Graduates of Yale College, Including Those Graduated in Classes Later Than 1815, Who Are Not Commemorated in the Annual Obituary Records. New Haven, Conn., 1913. Covers the years 1815-84.

------. Obituary Record of Graduates. . . . no. 1-110, 1859-1951. New Haven, 1860-1952.

10. DELAWARE

10.1   Dover. Delaware Public Archives Commission. Ridgely Family Papers, 1742-1899. NUC MS 61-1372. Includes obituary notices.

10.2   Wright, F. Edward. <u>Delaware Newspaper Abstracts</u>. Silver Spring, Md.: Family Line Publications, 1984. For the years 1786-95.

11. DISTRICT OF COLUMBIA

11.1 Columbia Historical Society. Records, v. 1-. Washington, D.C: Columbia Historical Society, 1895-. Analytical Index, v. 1-10, 1895-1907.

11.2 Howe, Henry. Historical Collections of Virginia. Charleston, S.C.: Babcock and Co., 1845. Pages 148-50 contain obituary notices taken from the American Almanac of public individuals and residents of Virginia and the District of Columbia for the years 1832-44. Reprinted in Tyler's Quarterly 10 (1928): 146-56.

11.3 Martin, George A., and Frank J. Metcalf. Marriage and Death Notices from the "National Intelligencer" (Washington, D.C.), 1800-1850. Washington, D.C.: National Genealogical Society, 1976. Microfilm. 3 reels. (Special Publication of the National Genealogical Society, no. 41)

11.4 Ridgely, Helen West. Historic Graves of Maryland and the District of Columbia, with the Inscriptions Appearing on the Tombstones in Most of the Counties of the State and in Washington and Georgetown. Edited under the auspices of the Maryland Society of the Colonial Dames of America. 1908. Reprint. Baltimore: Genealogical Publishing Co., 1967.

11.5 Sluby, Paul E. Civil War Cemeteries of the District of Columbia Metropolitan Area. Edited by Stanton L. Wormley. Washington, D.C.: Columbian Harmony Society, [1982].

11.6 ------. Holmead's Cemetery (Western Burial Ground), Washington, D.C. Edited by Stanton L. Wormley. Washington, D.C.: Columbian Harmony Society, 1985.

11.7 ------. Mt. Zion Cemetery: Washington, DC, Brief History and Interments. Edited by Stanton L. Wormley. Washington, D.C.: Columbian Harmony Society, 1984.

11.8 ------. Woodlawn Cemetery, Washington, DC: Brief History and Inscriptions. Edited by Stanton L. Wormley. Washington, D.C.: Columbian Harmony Society, 1984.

11.9 Washington Post. Newspaper Index. Wooster, Ohio: Bell and Howell Co., 1971-.

11.10 Wright, F. Edward. Abstracts of the Newspapers of Georgetown and the Federal City, 1798-1799: Advertisements, Insolvent Debtors, Notices of Escaped Servants and Slaves, Letters at the Post Offices (Georgetown and the Federal City), Marriages, Deaths, Stray Horses and Cows, Sales of Land in and around the District of Columbia: And Some Early Maps of the District of Columbia. Silver Spring, Md.: Family Line Publications, 1986.

12. FLORIDA

12.1   "Abstracted Deaths from the Palm Beach Post 1916." Ancestry 10 (1975): 35-36.

12.2   Brownell, Daphne M. Cemetery Inscriptions: West Volusia County, Florida. 4 vols. DeLand, Fla., 1972-78.

12.3   ------. Cemetery Records of East Volusia County, Florida. Melbourne, Fla.: Kellersberger Fund of the South Brevard Historical Society, 1981.

12.4   ------. Oakdale Cemetery Inscriptions, DeLand, Volusia Co., Florida, 21 June 1882-12 Aug. 1971. DeLand, Fla., 1972.

12.5   Bruington, Lola Lee Daniell, and James Clarke Bruington. Rural Cemeteries in Escambia County, Florida, 1826-1950. Pensacola, Fla.: L. L. D. Bruington, 1985.

12.6   ------. St. Michael's Cemetery, 1807 - ? Pensacola, Fla.: L. L. D. Bruington, 1986.

12.7   Cemetery Inscriptions of Okeechobee County, Florida: Basinger, Ft. Drum, Evergreen. Okeechobee, Fla.: Genealogical Society of Okeechobee, 1984.

12.8   Daughters of the American Revolution. Florida. Florida Cemetery Records. N.p.: Florida State Society, Daughters of the American Revolution, 1973.

12.9   Davis, Thomas Frederick. Digest of the Florida Material in "Niles' Register," 1811-1849. Jacksonville, Fla.: n.p., 1939. (American Periodicals: 1800-1850)

12.10   Edwards, Lucy Ames. Grave Markers of Duval County, 1808-1916. Jacksonville, Fla.: Edwards, 1976.

12.11   Hillsborough County, Florida, Cemeteries, 1840-1985. 3 vols. Tampa, Fla.: Florida Genealogical Society, 1986-87.

12.12   Langlais, Verna G. Cemetery Census of Brevard County, Florida: Including Sebastian (Indian River County). Titusville, Fla.: Yates Publishing Co., 1985.

12.13   Norman, Annie B., and Mr. and Mrs. David N. Brown. Cemeteries of Marion County, Florida. Prepared and presented through the Ocala Chapter of the Daughters of the American Revolution. 3 vols. N.p. 1977-79.

12.14   Paisley, Joy Smith. The Cemeteries of Leon County, Florida: Rural White Cemeteries: Tombstone Inscriptions and Epitaphs. Tallahassee, Fla.: Colonial Dames XVII Century, Dominie Everardus Bogardus Chapter, 1978.

12.15   Pamphilon, Doris E. Cemeteries of Jackson County, Florida. Cottondale, Fla.: D. E. Pamphilon, 1984.

12. FLORIDA

12.16   Smith, Leonard H. <u>The Records of the Key West Cemetery, Key West, Florida, 1888-1905</u>. Clearwater, Fla.: Owl Books, 1984.

12.17   Spencer, Elizabeth R. <u>They Are Here: Cemeteries of Clay County, Florida, and a Brief History of Clay County and Northeast Florida</u>. Orange Park, Fla., 1973.

12.18   Stirk, Kathryn London. <u>Tombstone Registry of Central Florida</u>. Orlando, Fla.: K. L. Stirk, 1984.

12.19   <u>A Survey of Graves in the Cemeteries of Northwest Pasco County, Florida</u>. New Port Richey, Fla.: West Pasco Genealogical Society, 1984.

12.20   <u>Tombstone Inscriptions in Cemeteries of Manatee County, Florida, 1850-1980</u>. 2d ed. Sarasota, Fla.: Manasota Genealogical Society, 1982.

12.21   Varick, Floreda Duke, and Phyllis Rose Smith. <u>Tallahassee and Leon County, Florida Cemeteries</u>. Tallahassee, Fla.: Varick, 1979.

13. GEORGIA

13.1   Abbott, Frank M. <u>History of the People of Jones County, Georgia</u>. 4 vols.
        Macon, Ga.: Lineage Unlimited, 1977. vol. 4 contains cemetery records.

13.2   <u>All Known Cemeteries of Clayton County, Georgia: A Record of Tombstone
        Inscriptions in Clayton County, Georgia</u>. Riverdale, Ga.: Ancestors
        Unlimited, 1979.

13.3   Andrus, Sara Margaret Stone. <u>Jefferson County, Georgia: Ebenezer Associate
        Reformed Presbyterian Church Cemetery, Stone Family Cemetery,
        Miscellaneous Bible Records of Families with Jefferson County, Georgia
        Ties</u>. Wrens, Ga.: John Franklin Wren Chapter, Daughters of the
        American Revolution, 1969.

13.4   Ayers, Ralph, and Jane Ayers. <u>Polk County, Georgia Cemeteries, in the
        Corners of Forever</u>. 2 vols. Cedartown, Ga.: R. and J. Ayers, 1986.

13.5   Baker, Pearl. <u>'Neath Georgia Sod: Cemetery Inscriptions</u>. Albany, Ga.:
        Georgia Pioneers Publications, 1970. Contains more than 2000 inscriptions
        from Warren, Columbia, Jefferson, McDuffie, Taliaferro, Richmond,
        Glascock and Wilkes counties.

13.6   *Bishop, William A. "Marriages and Deaths in Georgia Colony, 1763-1800."
        <u>Genealogical Quarterly Magazine</u> 4 (1903): 153-57.

13.7   Bulloch, Joseph Gaston Baillie. "Marriages and Deaths from the <u>Georgia
        Gazette</u> and the <u>Savannah Republican</u>." <u>National Genealogical Society
        Quarterly</u> 5 (1916): 29-32. Contains a small number of death notices
        1760s to 1810s.

13.8   <u>Carroll County Cemeteries</u>. Compiled and edited by the Carroll County
        Cemetery Committee. N.p. 1983.

13.9   Cashion, Mrs. Curran. "The <u>Sun</u>. Newspaper Published Weekly, Hartwell,
        Georgia." <u>Georgia Genealogical Magazine</u> 70 (1978): 273-82. Contains
        abstracts of death notices for 1881.

13.10   <u>Cemeteries of Spalding County, Georgia: Family Cemeteries, Oak Hill
        Cemetery, Stonewall Confederate Cemetery</u>. Griffin, Ga.: Griffin
        Historical and Preservation Society, 1986.

13.11   <u>Cemetery Records of Screven County, Georgia</u>. Compiled by Brier Creek
        Chapter, Daughters of the American Revolution. Sylvania, Ga.: Partridge
        Pond Press, 1981.

13.12   <u>The Cemetery Survey of Miller County, Georgia, 1824-1981</u>. [Colquitt, Ga.:
        Colquitt Garden Club, 1982.]

13.13   Cobb County Genealogical Society. <u>Cobb County, Georgia Cemeteries</u>.
        Edited by Ann Bishop Seymour. Marietta, Ga.: G. W. Publications, 1984.

13. GEORGIA

13.14   Coffee County, Georgia, Cemeteries, 1837-1978. Compiled by the Satilla
        Regional Library, Genealogy Department. Douglas, Ga.: The Department,
        1980.

13.15   "Confederate Necrology." Georgia Historical Quarterly, v. 1-. Savannah,
        Ga., 1917-. Volumes 12-37 contain obituaries taken from contemporary
        newspapers of the Civil War era. Name and date of the newspaper is
        given as well as the text of the obituary.

13.16   Cooper, Patricia Irvin, and Glen McAninch. Map and Historical Sketch of
        the Old Athens Cemetery, Jackson Street, Athens, Georgia. 2d ed.
        Athens, Ga.: Old Athens Cemetery Foundation, 1984.

13.17   Cornell, Nancy Jones. Campbell County, Georgia Cemeteries. Riverdale, Ga.:
        Inkwell Publications, [198-].

13.18   Daughters of the American Revolution. Georgia. Genealogical Records
        Committee. Obituaries (Abstracts) from the First Minutes of the
        Methodist Conference in the United States 1773-1813. N.p. 1945.
        DNDAR

13.19   ------. Archibald Bulloch Chapter. Cemeteries Located in Bulloch County,
        Georgia, Now or Previous to Creation of New Counties from Bulloch Co.,
        and the Identity of Many Persons Buried in Them. [N.p. 1980.]

13.20   ------. John Benson Chapter, Hartwell. Birth, Marriages and Death Notices
        of Hart County from Old Copies of the "Hartwell Sun" Published in
        Hartwell, Georgia 1881-1896. N.p. 1946. According to the Catalogue of
        the Georgia Society Library of the D.A.R., this is available in the
        Georgia Department of Archives and History.

13.21   ------. Mary Hammond Washington Chapter, Macon. Bibb County, Georgia:
        Early Wills and Cemetery Records. Compiled by Jean Saunders
        Willingham and Berthenia Crocker Smith. Macon, Ga., [1961?].

13.22   Death Notices, etc., Sept. 14, 1889 to Dec. 19, 1919, Copied from the
        "Quitman Free Press," of Quitman, Georgia. . . . Salt Lake City:
        Universal Microfilm Co., 1949. USIGS

13.23   "Death Notices from Old Georgia Newspaper Files: American Patriot,
        Louisville, Ga., April 18, 1816." Georgia Genealogical Magazine 12
        (1964): 730.

13.24   *"Death Notices from Old Georgia Newspaper Files: Augusta Chronicle and
        Gazette, 1790-1800." Georgia Genealogical Magazine 9 (1963): 505-6.

13.25   *"Death Notices from Old Georgia Newspaper Files: Columbian Museum and
        Savannah Advertiser, 1796-1818." Georgia Genealogical Magazine 3
        (1962): 119-20.

13. GEORGIA

13.26   *"Death Notices from Old Georgia Newspaper Files: <u>Columbian Museum and Savannah Daily Gazette</u>, 1817-1820." <u>Georgia Genealogical Magazine</u> 29 (1968): 2011-12.

13.27   "Death Notices from Old Georgia Newspaper Files: <u>Darien Gazette</u>, Darien, Ga., 1821-1825." <u>Georgia Genealogical Magazine</u> 21 (1966): 1399-1403.

13.28   *"Death Notices from Old Georgia Newspaper Files: <u>Georgia Gazette</u>, 1790-1802." <u>Georgia Genealogical Magazine</u> 1 (1961): 21-24. The <u>Georgia Gazette</u> was published in Savannah.

13.29   *"Death Notices from Old Georgia Newspaper Files: <u>Georgia Journal</u>, Milledgeville, 1809-1814." <u>Georgia Genealogical Magazine</u> 23 (1967): 1559-60.

13.30   *"Death Notices from Old Georgia Newspaper Files: <u>Georgia Messenger</u>, Macon, 1823-1835." <u>Georgia Genealogical Magazine</u> 24 (1967): 1587-88.

13.31   "Death Notices from Old Georgia Newspaper Files: <u>Georgia Republican and State Intelligencer</u>, Savannah, 1803-1805." <u>Georgia Genealogical Magazine</u> 14 (1964): 861-62.

13.32   "Death Notices from Old Georgia Newspaper Files: <u>Republican and Savannah Evening Ledger</u>, 1809-1810." <u>Georgia Genealogical Magazine</u> 14 (1964): 855-61.

13.33   *"Death Notices from Old Georgia Newspaper Files: <u>Southern Centinel and Universal Gazette</u>, Augusta, 1793-1799." <u>Georgia Genealogical Magazine</u> 8 (1963): 464.

13.34   "Death Notices from Old Georgia Newspaper Files: <u>Southern Patriot</u>, Savannah, 1804-1805." <u>Georgia Genealogical Magazine</u> 14 (1964): 853-54.

13.35   *"Death Notices from Old Georgia Newspaper Files: <u>Southern Recorder</u>, Milledgeville, 1823-1844." <u>Georgia Genealogical Magazine</u> 12 (1964): 730-34.

13.36   Dixon, Sara Anderson, and Mary Jane Dixon. <u>Newton County Georgia Cemeteries</u>. Starrsville, Ga., 1968.

13.37   Dorsey, James Edward, and John K. Derden. <u>Gone But Not Forgotten: A Tombstone Registry of Emanual County, Georgia</u>. Rev. ed. Swainsboro, Ga.: Magnolia Press, 1983.

13.38   Dumont, William H. "Burke County Georgia, Obituaries and Marriages, 1790-1812." <u>National Genealogical Society Quarterly</u> 54 (1966): 38-39. Lists only 30 obituaries in the twenty-two-year period. The name of the deceased with some information, date and name of newspaper given.

13.39   <u>Early Cemeteries and Gravestones: Elbert County, Georgia</u>. Elberton, Ga.: Elbert County Historical Society, 1984.

13. GEORGIA

13.40   Eller, Lynda S. Heard Co., Georgia Cemeteries. Lanett, Ala.: Eller, 1977.

13.41   Floyd County, Georgia Cemeteries. Edited by Shirley Kinney, Madge Tate, and Sandra Junkins. Rome, Ga.: Northwest Georgia Historical and Genealogical Society, 1985.

13.42   Futral, Jenny. Current Death Notices: Abstracted from Various Newspapers. 2 vols. Franklin, Ga.: J. Futral, 1980-83. v. 1. 1978-79; v. 2. 1980-81.

13.43   Garrason, Cecil Calder. Annotated Inscriptions of Long County, Georgia. Newark, N.J., 1968.

13.44   Genealogical Enterprises. The "Georgia Enterprise" and "Covington Star," 1865-1904. Morrow, Ga.: Genealogical Enterprises, 1969. Includes marriage and death notices appearing in these two newspapers.

13.45   General Index to Contents of Savannah, Georgia Newspapers, 1841-45. 9 vols. Savannah, Ga.: Public Library, 1975-.

13.46   [No entry].

13.47   Harvey, Mr. and Mrs. William David. Sumter County, Georgia Cemetery Records. Americus, Ga.: M. M. Harvey, [1972].

13.48   Hodge, Robert Allen. Some Georgia Reported Deaths, 1842-1848. Fredericksburg, Va.: Hodge, 1977. Deaths abstracted from three weekly newspapers: Southern Banner, Southern Reporter, and the Georgia Telegraph.

13.49   Howell, Addie Paramore. Cemeteries and Obituaries of Houston County, Georgia. Macon, Ga.: Omni Press, 1982.

13.50   Hubbard, Glenn. The History of Bascomb United Methodist Church and Cemetery Listing: Sesquicentennial 1830-1980, Cherokee County, Georgia. Woodstock, Ga.: Your Print Shoppe, 1980.

13.51   In Remembrance, Cemetery Readings of Walton County, Georgia. Monroe, Ga.: Historical Society of Walton County, 1981.

13.52   Jackson County Tombstones. Morrow, Ga.: Genealogical Enterprises, 1969.

13.53   Jefferson County, Georgia, Tombstone Inscriptions, a Beginning. Compiled by Wrens High School students. Wrens, Ga.: Wrens High School, 1980.

13.54   *Jones, Laura B. "Marriages and Deaths from the Southern Christian Advocate." Georgia Genealogical Magazine 6 (1962): 329-32. The Southern Christian Advocate was a Methodist publication published at Columbia, S.C. Most of the deaths are from the years 1837-1842, with a few later ones.

13.55   Jones, Wiley B. Rest in Peace: A Cemetery Census of Taliaferro County, Georgia. Washington, Ga.: Wilkes Publishing Co., 1984.

13. GEORGIA

13.56   Joyce, Wade H. Georgia Obituaries, June 1947-July 1948. 7 vols. N.p. 1954-55. Microfilm. Filmed by the Genealogical Society, Salt Lake City, 1972. USIGS

13.57   Kaufman, Marian Waxelbaum. The Burials of Congregation Beth Israel, Macon, Georgia in William Wolff Cemetery and in the Hebrew Burial Ground. [Macon, Ga., 1983?]

13.58   Lancaster, Jewel Moats. Jasper County, Georgia, Cemetery and Bible Records. Shady Dale, Ga., [1969].

13.59   LeMaster, Elizabeth Tidd. Abstracts of Georgia Death Notices from the "Southern Recorder," 1830-1855. Orange, Calif.: Orange County California Genealogical Society, 1971.

13.60   Levy, B. H. Savannah's Old Jewish Community Cemeteries. Macon, Ga.: Mercer University Press, 1983.

13.61   Lindsey, John Robert, and Barbara Moore Lindsey. A Tombstone Registry of Leila Cemetery, Colquitt County, Georgia. N.p. 1980.

13.62   Little, Mamie Burkhalter. "Miscellaneous from the Old Georgia State Gazette and Chronicle Published at Augusta, Georgia, 1769 to 1795." Daughters of the American Revolution Magazine 69 (1935): 370-73. Includes death notices.

13.63   McRay, Sybil Wood. Tombstone Inscriptions of Hall County, Georgia. Gainesville, Ga., 1971.

13.64   Maddox, Joseph T. Cemeteries, Wilkinson County, Georgia. [Irwinton, Ga., 1975.]

13.65   ------. Gravestone Inscriptions and Lineages, Wilkinson County, Georgia. Irwinton, Ga., 1980.

13.66   ------. Wilkinson County, Georgia Gravestones with Genealogical Information. Irwinton, Ga., 1971.

13.67   Marshall, Charlotte Thomas. Oconee Hill Cemetery; Tombstone Inscriptions for That Part of Cemetery West of Oconee River and Index to Record of Interments. Athens, Ga.: Athens Historical Society, 1971.

13.68   Martin, John H. Columbus, Georgia, from Its Selection As a "Trading Town" in 1827, to Its Partial Destruction by Wilson's Raid in 1865: History, Incident, Personality. 2 vols. Columbus, Ga.: Thomas Gilbert, 1874-75. Contains references to death notices and obituaries, giving dates, but does not identify the newspapers from which they were taken. No index.

13.69   Mathis, James A., and Betty Ann Waddell Mathis. Jackson County, Georgia Cemetery Records. Danielsville, Ga.: Heritage Papers, 1980.

13. GEORGIA

13.70   Medders, Mr. and Mrs. Jimmy. Marked Graves of Bacon County, Georgia As of December 1969: Excluding Rose Hill, Alma, Georgia. Alma, Ga.: Historical Society of Alma-Bacon County, Georgia, 1982.

13.71   Mize, Jessie Julia. The History of Banks County, Georgia, 1858-1976. Homer, Ga.: Banks County Chamber of Commerce, 1977. Cemetery inscriptions contained in appendix, pp. 276-409.

13.72   National Society Colonial Dames of America in the State of Georgia. Some Early Epitaphs in Georgia. Compiled by the Georgia Society of the Colonial Dames of America, with a foreword and sketches by Mrs. Peter W. Meldrim. . . . Durham, N.C.: Seeman Printery, Inc., 1924. Epitaphs from the Old Colonial cemetery, Frederica cemetery, Vernonburg (now White Bluff) and adjacent cemeteries, St. Paul's churchyard, Augusta, Midway cemetery, Sunbury cemetery, and the Old Jewish Cemetery.

13.73   Newsom, Elizabeth Pritchard. Washington County, Georgia, Tombstone Inscriptions. Sandersville, Ga., 1967.

13.74   Newsom, F. M., and Nell H. Newsome. Wilkes County Cemeteries and a Few from Adjoining Counties. Washington, Ga.: Wilkes Publishing Co., 1970.

13.75   Obituary Notices of Revolutionary Soldiers Buried in Georgia, from Milledgeville "Georgia Journal," 1819. DNDAR

13.76   Park, Orville Augustus. An Index to the Publications of the Various Bar Associations of America. Atlanta: Franklin Printing and Publishing Co., 1899. "Georgia necrology," p. 86.

13.77   Parker, Harold Travis. The Byrum Family Cemetery of Hart County, Georgia. [Lavonia, Ga.]: H. T. Parker, [1984].

13.78   Parrish, Donna, Bonnye T. Leary, and Garland C. Bagley. Cemeteries of Forsyth County, Georgia. Cumming, Ga., 1981.

13.79   Powell, Lillian Lewis, Dorothy Collins Odom, and Albert M. Hillhouse. Grave Markers in Burke County, Georgia, with Thirty-nine Cemeteries in Four Adjoining Counties. Waynesboro, Ga.: Chalker Publishing Co., 1974.

13.80   Powell, Nora. Historical and Genealogical Collections of Dooly County Georgia. Vienna, Ga., 1973-. Volume 1, pp. 64-70, gives obituaries from the Vienna Progress, 1893, 1895-96.

13.81   Rainer, Vessie Thrasher. Henry County, Georgia, Cemeteries: McDonough, Eastlawn, Stockbridge. McDonough, Ga.: R. A. Ranier, 1981.

13.82   ------. Henry County, Georgia, Churchyard Cemeteries. McDonough, Ga.: R. A. Ranier, 1980.

13.83   ------. Henry County, Georgia, Family Graveyards. McDonough, Ga.: R. A. Ranier, 1980.

13.84   "Revolutionary Obituaries - Georgia." National Genealogical Inquirer 2 (1978): 41-42.

13.85   Rocker, Willard L. Cemetery Records, Riverside Cemetery, Macon, Georgia. 2 vols. Macon, Ga.: Mary Hammond Washington Chapter, Daughters of the American Revolution, 1975.

13.86   ------. "The Georgia Journal (Milledgeville, Ga.) Oct. 6 1835 to Sept. 27 1836." Georgia Genealogical Magazine 67 (1978): 33-40.

13.87   ------. "The Georgia Messenger, Obituaries and Marriages, Published Weekly at Macon, Ga." Georgia Genealogical Magazine 68-69 (1978): 139-48. For the years 1836-38.

13.88   Savannah Morning News. Annals of Savannah, 1850-1937: A Digest and Index of the Newspaper Record of Events and Opinions, Abstracted from the Files of the "Savannah Morning News." Savannah, 1961-.

13.89   Simpkins, L. F. Marseilles Cemetery, West Point, Georgia. Shawmut, Ala.: Simpkins, 1979.

13.90   Stephens, J. Clayton. Marked Graves in Treutlen County, Georgia. Photography by Bill Ricks. [Soperton, Ga.], 1977.

13.91   ------. Supplement I to Marked Graves in Treutlen County, Georgia: Including Burials between August 1975 and December 31, 1980, As Well As Additions and Corrections to the First Edition. [Soperton, Ga.]: J. C. Stephens, [1982].

13.92   Temple, Sarah Blackwell. The First Hundred Years: A Short History of Cobb County, in Georgia. Atlanta: Walter W. Brown Publishing Co., 1935. pp. 590-860 contain cemetery records for Cobb county.

13.93   U.S. Work Projects Administration. Georgia. General Index to the Contents of Savannah, Georgia, Newspapers, 1763-1845. Savannah, 1937. Library of Congress holds 1763-1830. GHi

13.94   Varick, Floreda Duke. Grady County, Georgia, Tomb Index. 2d ed. Tallahassee, Fla., 1980.

13.95   Walker, Randall M. Marked Graves in Pierce County, Georgia. Jesup, Ga.: R. M. Walker, 1975.

13.96   Warren, Mary Bondurant. Chronicles of Wilkes County, Georgia, from Washington's Newspapers, 1889-1898. Danielsville, Ga.: Heritage Papers, 1978. Includes obituaries.

13.97   ------. Jackson Street Cemetery, Original City Cemetery of Athens, Georgia: Tombstone Inscriptions and Obituaries. Athens, Ga.: Heritage Paper, 1966. Includes 57 abstracted obituaries, 1827-1866, from the Southern Banner, Southern Watchman, the Athenian, and the Augusta Chronicle.

13. GEORGIA

13.98   ------. Marriages and Deaths Abstracted from Extant Georgia Newspapers.
2 vols. Danielsville, Ga.: Heritage Papers, 1968-. v. 1. 1763-1820; v. 2.
1820-30.

13.99   Washington County Deaths and Marriages. Morrow, Ga.: Genealogical
Enterprises, 1972. Contains abstracts of a few death notices. Arranged
alphabetically with name and date of newspaper, mostly for the 1820s and
1830s.

13.100   Wells, Catherine Fussell. The Complete Cemetery Records of Worth County,
Georgia. Tallahassee, Fla.: Rose Printing Co., 1984.

13.101   Wells, Joel Dixon, and Donald R. Schultz. All Known Cemeteries in Fayette
County, Georgia: A Genealogically Oriented Survey. [Hampton, Ga.]:
J. D. Wells, [1980].

13.102   Wilson, Caroline P. Annals of Georgia, Important Early Records of the State.
1928-33. Reprint. 3 vols. Easley, S.C.: Southern Historical Press, 1969.
Contains cemetery records.

13.103   Wilson, John Simpson. The Dead of the Synod of Georgia: Necrology, or
Memorials of Deceased Ministers Who Have Died During the First Twenty
Years After Its Organization. Atlanta: Franklin Printing House, 1869.

13.104   Wright, Buster W. Abstracts of Deaths Reported in the "Columbus (Georgia)
Enquirer," 1832-1852. Columbus, Ga.: Wright, 1980.

13.105   ------. Burials and Deaths Reported in the "Columbus (Georgia) Enquirer,"
1832-1872. [Columbus, Ga.?], 1984.

13.106   Youmans, W. M. Footprints . . . on the Sands of Time: Epitaphs of
Tombstones in Old Family Cemeteries in Screven County, Georgia.
Sylvania, Ga.: Partridge Pond Press, 1979.

14. HAWAII

14.1 Index to the "Honolulu Advertiser" and "Honolulu Star-bulletin," 1929/67-. Honolulu: Office of Library Services, 1968-. The first index issued included 1929-67. Annual supplements issued since 1968. The index includes obituaries.

15. IDAHO

15.1 <u>Forest Cemetery, Coeur d'Alene, Idaho</u>. Hayden Lake, Idaho: Kootenai County Genealogical Society, [1984].

15.2 Gammelle, William H. <u>Obituary Records Pocatello, Bannock County, Idaho, Copied from the "Idaho Journal" 1959</u>. Salt Lake City: Genealogical Society, 1961. USIGS

15.3 Groefsema, Olive De Ette. <u>Elmore County, Its Historical Gleanings: A Collection of Pioneer Narratives, Treasured Family Pictures, and Early Clippings</u>. . . . Mountain Home, Idaho, 1949. Contains reprints of newspaper obituaries of early pioneers of Elmore County who died during the period 1907-49.

15.4 Idaho Genealogical Society. <u>Idaho Vital Statistics</u>. Boise, Idaho, 1963. Includes cemetery records from Bingham, Bonneville, and Madison counties.

15.5 Idaho World News, Idaho City. <u>Births, Marriages, Divorces, Deaths (Boise Co., Idaho) 1863-1918</u>. 3 vols. in 2. N.p., n.d. vol. 3. Deaths. Microfilm. Filmed by the Genealogical Society, Salt Lake City, 1971. USIGS

15.6 Longeteig, Margaret Nell. <u>Cemetery Records, Lewis County, Idaho</u>. Lewiston, Idaho: Ilo Register, 1985.

15.7 Martin, Phyllis J. <u>Cemeteries in Bear Lake County, Idaho</u>. [Evanston, Wyo.]: P. J. Martin, [1984].

15.8 Shane, Alfred E. <u>Bonner County, Idaho Cemeteries</u>. Coeur d'Alene, Idaho: A. E. and B. J. Shane, [1986].

15.9 ------. <u>Kootenai County, Idaho Cemeteries</u>. 2 vols. Coeur d'Alene, Idaho: A. E. Shane, 1983.

15.10 ------. <u>Woodlawn Cemetery, St. Maries, Benewah County, Idaho</u>. Coeur d'Alene, Idaho: A. E. Shane, [1985].

15.11 Walker, Elaine. <u>Northwest Notes</u>. Post Falls, Idaho: Genealogical Reference Builders, 1975. Includes cemetery records.

16. ILLINOIS

16.1   Abstracts of the "Marshall Weekly Messenger": John Littlefield, Editor and Publisher: May 1868-April 1871. Abstracted by Louise Nelson. Marshall, Ill.: Clark County Genealogical Society, 1978.

16.2   Abstracts of the "Marshall Weekly Messenger": John Littlefield, Editor and Publisher: January 6, 1876-April 12, 1877. Abstracted by Louise Nelson. Marshall, Ill.: Clark County Genealogical Society, 1978.

16.3   Allaman, Durwood B. Obituaries, Knox County, Galesburg, Illinois, Newspapers. 6 vols. Galesburg, Ill.: Knox County Genealogical Society, 1985. v. 1. 1853-97; v. 2. 1898-1901; v. 3. 1902-4; v. 4. 1905-6; v. 5. 1907-8; v. 6. 1909-10.

16.4   ------. Obituaries of Founders and Patriots, Their Families and Friends in Hope Cemetery. Galesburg, Ill.: Knox County Genealogical Society, 1986.

16.5   Allers, Wanda, and Eileen Lynch Gochanour. Menard County, Illinois, Cemeteries. 3 vols. Springfield, Ill., 1984.

16.6   Anthony, Nelda Neer. Obituaries and Register of Deaths: Copied from "Greenville Advocate," 1858-1899. N.p.: N. N. Anthony, 1985.

16.7   Ball, J. Roger. Obituaries, 1861-1896. Springfield, Ill.: Sangamon County Genealogical Society of Illinois, 1982.

16.8   Bardolph Cemetery at Bardolph, Illinois. Macomb, Ill.: McDonough County Genealogical Society, 1981.

16.9   Black, Bessie Irene. Cemeteries of Lawrence County, Illinois. Bridgeport, Ill: Black, 1976.

16.10   Bland, Doris Ellen. Wayne County, Illinois, Cemetery Inscriptions. 9 vols. Fairfield, Ill.: Bland Books, 1971-83.

16.11   ------. Wayne County, Illinois, Newspaper Gleanings, 1855-1875. Fairfield, Ill.: Bland Books, 1974. (Daughters of the American Revolution. Illinois. Illinois Genealogical Records, 1974, v. 7)

16.12   Bockstruck, Lloyd D. "Vital Statistics from Bond County, Illinois Newspapers." (1846-1853) Quarterly of the Illinois State Genealogical Society 6 (1974): 127.

16.13   Bodman, Robert E., and Ruth E. Stotts. Bement, Illinois Cemetery Records. Monticello, Ill: Piatt County Historical and Genealogical Society, 1982. "Compiled from the Bement Cemetery trustees' records, the Cemetery sextons' records, Bement histories, and newspapers."--verso of title page.

16.14   Boedecker, Edward H. Inscriptions of Shelby County, Illinois Cemeteries. 10 vols. Shelbyville, Ill: Boedecker, 1971-85.

16. ILLINOIS

16.15   Bond County Historical Society. <u>Tombstone Inscriptions Found in the Cemeteries in Bond County, Illinois</u>. Greenville, Ill.: Bond County Historical Society, 1970.

16.16   Boyles, Harold. <u>Cemetery Records of Haines Township, Marion County, Illinois</u>. Salem, Ill.: Marion County Genealogical and Historical Society, 1980.

16.17   ------. <u>Cemetery Records of Romine Township, Marion County, Illinois</u>. Salem, Ill.: Marion County Genealogical and Historical Society, 1982.

16.18   Boyles, Harold, and Frank Brinkerhoff. <u>Cemetery Records of Raccoon Township, Marion County, Illinois</u>. Salem, Ill.: Marion County Genealogical and Historical Society, 1983.

16.19   Brieschke, Walter L. <u>Index of Obituaries Printed in the "Southern Illinois Herald" Newspaper, 1893-1922</u>. Murphysboro, Ill.: Jackson County Historical Society, 1985.

16.20   <u>Burials G.A.R. Cemetery, Homer, Champaign County, Illinois, 1886-1970</u>. Compiled by the Homer American Legion. Decatur, Ill.: Decatur Genealogical Society, 1971.

16.21   <u>Burlington Township Cemeteries, Kane County, Illinois</u>. Elgin, Ill: Elgin Genealogical Society, 1978.

16.22   <u>Bushnell Cemetery at Bushnell, Illinois</u>. Macomb, Ill.: McDonough County Genealogical Society, 1982.

16.23   Carlock, Mabel. <u>Obituaries: Attorneys and Physicians, Cook County, Illinois, January-September 1952, Copied from "Chicago Tribune."</u> Oak Park, Ill., 1952.

16.24   Carroll County Genealogical Society. <u>Tombstone Inscriptions, Carroll County, Illinois</u>. 14 vols. N.p.: Carroll County Genealogical Society, 1980.

16.25   Carter, Gertrude. "Old Newspaper Items." (1881-1889) <u>Illiana Genealogist</u> 3 (1967): 111-13. Includes some death notices from Vermilion County newspapers.

16.26   <u>Catholic Cemeteries of Knox County</u>. Galesburg, Ill.: Knox County Genealogical Society, [1982?]. Includes St. Augustine Cemetery, St. Mary's cemetery, and St.Joseph cemetery.

16.27   <u>Cemeteries of Calhoun County, Illinois, 1978</u>. Hardin, Ill: Calhoun County Historical Society, 1978.

16.28   <u>Cemeteries of [name of township]</u>. 8 vols. Springfield, Ill.: Sangamon County Genealogical Society, 1980-86. v. 1. Auburn Township; v. 2. Cotton Hill Township; v. 3. Loami Township; v. 4. Maxwell Township; v. 5. Mechanicsburg Township; v. 6. New Berlin Township; v. 7. Rochester

Township; v. 8. Williams Township. There are in addition volumes for Island Grove and Cooper townships.

16.29 <u>Cemeteries of Vermilion County, Illinois</u>. Compiled by the Illiana Genealogical and Historical Society. Utica, Ky.: McDowell Publications, 1982. For Blount and Newell townships.

16.30 <u>Cemeteries, Piatt County, IL</u>. Monticello, Ill: Piatt County Historical and Genealogical Society, 1985-86. v. 1. Blue Ridge Township; v. 2. Unity Township; v. 3. Monticello Township; v. 4. Goose Creek Township; v. 5. Cerro Gordo Township.

16.31 <u>Cemetery Inscriptions, Cave Township, Franklin County, Illinois</u>. West Frankfort, Ill: Frankfort Area Genealogy Society, 1980.

16.32 <u>Cemetery Inscriptions, Northern Township, Franklin County, Illinois</u>. West Frankfort, Ill.: Frankfort Area Genealogical Society, 1979.

16.33 <u>Cemetery Inscriptions, Stephenson County</u>. 3 vols. Freeport, Ill.: Stephenson County Historical Society, n.d.

16.34 <u>Cemetery Records of the Eastern Half of Whiteside Co., Illinois</u>. 6 vols. N.p.: Whiteside County Genealogists, 1984. vol. 1. Genesee Township; vol. 2. Tampico St. Mary's, Old Tampico, Old Hume; vol. 3. Hopkins Township; vol. 4. Jordan Township; vol. 5. Old Sterling Cemeteries (prior to 1886), Montmorency Township; vol. 6. Tampico Township.

16.35 Chicago, Illinois. Latter-Day Saints. Church. Northern States Mission. <u>Roselawn Memorial Cemetery Records and Obituary Notices, Springfield, Sangamon County, Illinois</u>. Salt Lake City: Genealogical Society, 1962. USIGS

16.36 Chicago Genealogical Society. Newspaper Research Committee. <u>Vital Records from Chicago Newspapers, 1833-1839</u>. Chicago: Chicago Genealogical Society, 1971.

16.37 ------. <u>Vital Records from Chicago Newspapers, 1840-1842</u>. Chicago: Chicago Genealogical Society, 1972.

16.38 ------. <u>Vital Records from Chicago Newspapers, 1843-1844</u>. Chicago: Chicago Genealogical Society, 1974.

16.39 ------. <u>Vital Records from Chicago Newspapers, 1845</u>. Chicago: Chicago Genealogical Society, 1975.

16.40 ------. <u>Vital Records from Chicago Newspapers 1846</u>. Chicago: Chicago Genealogical Society, 1976.

16.41 Chicago Sun-Times. <u>Newspaper Index</u>. Wooster, Ohio: Bell and Howell Co., 1979-. Monthly with annual cumulations.

16.42   Chicago Tribune. Newspaper Index. Wooster, Ohio: Bell and Howell Co., 1972-. Monthly with annual cumulations.

16.43   Clark County Genealogical Society. Clark County Cemetery Records. 6 vols. Marshall, Ill.: Clark County Genealogical Society, [197-].

16.44   Coltrin, Gerald Edward. Black Hawk War Veterans Buried in the State of Illinois. Peoria, Ill.: Coltrin, 1979.

16.45   Cook County Cemeteries. Compiled by Gertrude W. Lundberg. Homewood, Ill: Root and Tree Publication, for South Cook and North Will Counties Genealogical and Historical Society, 1971.

16.46   Craddock, Barbara J. Cemetery Inscriptions, Richland County, Illinois. Flora, Ill.: Martin Printing and Album Co., 1969.

16.47   Crumrin, Arthur, and Keith L. Strubbe. Old Cemeteries of Cass County, Illinois. N.p.: Cass County Historical Society, 1966.

16.48   Custer, Milo. Central Illinois Death Notices, 1848-1870. 1924. Reprint. Normal, Ill.: Bloomington-Normal Genealogical Society, [1985].

16.49   ------. Central Illinois Obituaries 1854-1870; Copied and Rearranged from Old Bloomington, Illinois Newspapers. Bloomington, Ill., 1911.

16.50   ------. Central Illinois Obituaries, 1871-1880, Compiled from Old Newspapers. 1912. Reprint. Normal, Ill.: Bloomington-Normal Genealogical Society, 1969.

16.51   ------. . . . Condensed Obituaries of Central Illinois for the Year 1908. Bloomington, Ill., 1911.

16.52   ------. Soldiers of the Revolution and the War of 1812 Buried in McLean County, Illinois. 1912. Reprint. Normal, Ill.: Bloomington-Normal Genealogical Society, 1969.

16.53   Daily Democratic Press, Chicago. The Chicago "Daily Democratic Press" Index for the Year 1855. 3 vols. Chicago: Work Projects Administration, 1940.

16.54   Daughters of the American Revolution. Illinois. Cook County Genealogical Records. 4 vols. N.p. 1972. vol. 1. Obituaries from Oak Leaves, Oak Park, Illinois, July-Nov. 1943; vol. 4. Marriages and obituary records from the Evanston Index 1873-75, 1880-87. In

16.55   ------. Alliance Chapter, Urbana-Champaign. Champaign County Obituaries, 1948; Wills 1866-1871. Urbana, Ill.: Daughters of the American Revolution, 1972. InFW

16.56   ------. Illinois Chapter. Seventeen Cemeteries--LaSalle County. 2 vols. Ottawa, Ill.: Daughters of the American Revolution, 1956. InFW

16. ILLINOIS

16.57 ------. Michael Hillegas Chapter, Harrisburg. Obituaries from Hardin County, Illinois (1900-1935). . . . Harrisburg, Ill.: Daughters of the American Revolution, 1965.

16.58 Davis, Chloe, and Ruby Henderson. Cemetery Inscriptions, Tyrone Township, Franklin County, Illinois. Utica, Ky: McDowell Publications, 1982.

16.59 "Death Notices and Obituaries from the Moline Workman 1854-1857." Quarterly of the Illinois State Genealogical Society 6 (1974): 195.

16.60 Deaths and Obituaries Extracted from Moffitt Book. Compiled by the Warren County, Illinois, Genealogical Society. 4 vols. N.p.: Warren County, Illinois, Genealogical Society, 1985. v. 1. July 1886-Dec. 1892; v. 2. January 1893-July 1897; v. 3. Feb. 1906-Jan. 1908; v. 4. June 1913-Jan. 1915. The Moffitt Books are scrapbooks which consist of articles written by Hugh R. Moffitt when he was editor of the newspapers in Monmouth, Illinois, in the late 1800s and early 1900s.

16.61 Decatur Genealogical Society. Christian County, Illinois, Cemetery Inscriptions. 4 vols. Decatur, Ill., 1969-70.

16.62 ------. DeWitt County, Illinois, Cemetery Inscriptions. 5 vols. Decatur, Ill., 1970-74.

16.63 ------. Logan County, Illinois Cemetery Inscriptions. 7 vols. Decatur, Ill., 1969-1982.

16.64 ------. Macon County, Illinois, Cemetery Inscriptions. 12 vols. Decatur, Ill., 1968-1979.

16.65 ------. Moultrie County, Illinois, Cemetery Inscriptions. 5 vols. Decatur, Ill., 1969-72.

16.66 ------. Sangamon County, Illinois, Cemetery Inscriptions. Decatur, Ill.: Decatur Genealogical Society, 1974.

16.67 ------. Shelby County, Illinois Cemetery Inscriptions. 3 vols. Decatur, Ill.: Decatur Genealogical Society, 1969-1972.

16.68 Dorris, Susan Doxsie. Cemetery Inscriptions of Denning Township in Franklin County, Illinois: Denning Cemetery, Bethel Cemetery, Rose Cemetery, Barber Cemetery, Hanes Cemetery, Follis Cemetery. West Frankfort, Ill., 1983.

16.69 Dugan, Dorothy, Harlin B. Taylor, and Linda S. Allison. Douglas County, Illinois, Cemetery Inscriptions. Decatur, Ill.: Vio-Lin Enterprises, 1972-.

16.70 Elmwood Cemetery, Section 32, City of Sycamore, Township of Sycamore, County of DeKalb, State of Illinois: Information Taken from Cemetery Tombstones and Other Cemetery Records Where Possible. Sycamore, Ill: Genealogical Society of DeKalb County, Illinois, 1982.

16. ILLINOIS

16.71   Epstein, Francis James. <u>Decet Meminisse Fratrum: A Necrology of the Diocesan Priests of the Chicago Archdiocese, 1844-1936</u>. Chicago: J. F. Higgins Printing Co., 1937.

16.72   Ettema, Ross. <u>From the Land of Windmills and Wooden Shoes in 1846: [Early Dutch Settlers of South Holland, Thornton, Lansing & Dolton, Illinois, Buried in the Old Holland Section of the Homewood Memorial Gardens, Homewood, Illinois]</u>. 2d ed. [South Holland, Ill.]: Ettema, 1976.

16.73   Fergus, Robert. "Obituary Compiled by Robert Fergus before 1900: Names, Places, Dates and Ages at Death of Some of Chicago's Old Settlers, Prior to 1843, and Other Well-known Citizens Who Arrived After 1843, Together with Others Prominently Connected with Illinois History." <u>Chicago Genealogist</u> 7 (1975): 96-101.

16.74   Frankfort Area Historical Society of Will County. <u>Pleasant Hill Cemetery Record, Frankfort, Will County, Illinois</u>. South Holland, Ill.: South Suburban Genealogical and Historical Society, [1975].

16.75   Fulton County Historical Society. Cemetery Records Committee. <u>Cemetery Inscriptions of Fulton County, Illinois</u>. 10 vols. Peoria, Ill.: Nationwide Speed Printing, 1971-85.

16.76   <u>Funeral Notices of Southern Illinois</u>. Owensboro, Ky.: Cook-McDowell; Boonville, Ind.: Published in cooperation with Capt. Jacob Warrick Chapter, NSDAR, 1980. Reproduces funeral notices for the period 1891 to 1931, primarily for the Grayville area.

16.77   <u>Galesburg Township, Knox County, Illinois Cemeteries</u>. Copied by Larry Thurman. 5 vols. Galesburg, Ill.: Knox County Genealogical Society, 1985-86.

16.78   Gerwick, Verda. <u>Burials in Lexington Cemetery, McLean County, Illinois</u>. Danville, Ill.: Heritage House, [1971].

16.79   Gilroy, Frank. <u>Obituary Records; Records from the Ministry; Family Histories</u>. Danville, Ill.: Illiana Genealogical and Historical Society, 1981. These are twentieth century obituaries for persons from Sidell.

16.80   Graven, Judy, and Phyllis Hapner. <u>Veterans Buried in Shelby County, Illinois</u>. Shelbyville, Ill.: Shelby County Historical and Genealogical Society, 1982. Includes veterans of all wars buried in Shelby County cemeteries.

16.81   Gray, Jeannette. <u>Obituaries of Hardin County, Illinois</u>. . . . Owensboro, Ky.: Cook-McDowell Publications, 1980.

16.82   Greenwood, Marie. <u>Cemetery Inscription, Ewing Township, Franklin County, Illinois</u>. Thomson, Ill.: Heritage House, 1974.

16.83   Grimes, Marilla R. "Items from Oneida County, New York Newspapers Having an Illinois Reference." (c1860) Quarterly of the Illinois State Genealogical Society 8 (1976): 57.

16.84   Grimm, E. Industry Cemetery, Industry, Illinois: Included are 1500 Burials, 1100 Obituary Abstracts. Macomb, Ill.: McDonough County Genealogical Society, 1984. Obituaries are from Macomb newspapers for persons interred in the twentieth century.

16.85   Groennert, Wanda Calloway. Obituaries Taken from the "Nashville Democrat" 1903-1908. Nashville, Ill.: Washington County Genealogical Society, 1978.

16.86   Hansen, Robert. Jo Daviess County, Illinois Newspaper Abstracts: Vital Statistics, 1840-1846. Galena, Ill.: R. Hansen, n.d.

16.87   ------. Jo Daviess County, Illinois, Newspaper Index. Galena, Ill.: Hansen, [1980?]. For the years 1828-40.

16.88   ------. Jo Daviess County, Illinois, Tombstone Index. 13 vols. Galena, Ill.: Hansen, 1979-85.

16.89   Harris, Marjorie Guy. Abstracts of "The Bardolph News," September 1893 to September 1912. [Macomb, Ill.: McDonough County Genealogical Society, 1981?].

16.90   ------. Burials in St. Paul's Catholic Cemetery, Macomb, Illinois: With Family Information for Genealogical Research, Including Burials in Old Macomb Catholic and Tennessee Catholic Cemeteries for Reference. Macomb, Ill.: McDonough County Genealogical Society, [1984?].

16.91   Heidlebaugh, James Ervin, and Louise Beckham Heidlebaugh. Coles County, IL Cemetery Inscriptions. 2 vols. Decatur, Ill: Decatur Genealogical Society, 1983. v. 1. Janesville Cemetery (New Gordon Cemetery), Pleasant Grove Township; v. 2. Shiloh (Old Gordon) Cemetery and Beals Cemetery in Pleasant Grove Township.

16.92   Helmuth, Orva. Amish and Mennonite Cemeteries of Moultrie and Douglas County [sic], Arthur, Illinois. Arthur, Ill.: Echo, [1985].

16.93   Herald. Elburn, Kane County, Illinois. Miscellaneous Obituaries, 1962-1965, Clipped from the "Herald." Elburn, Ill., 1965. Scrapbook. IHi

16.94   Hilton, Faye, and Dolores Hilton. Inscriptions, Records, and the Early History of Burritt Cemeteries and Area. . . . Pecatonica, Ill., 1983.

16.95   ------. Inscriptions, Records, and the Early History of Middle Creek and Winnebago Cemeteries and Area. Pecatonica, Ill., 1981.

16.96   ------. Inscriptions, Records, and the Early History of Pecatonica Township's Five Cemeteries, Pecatonica, Illinois: Rosehill, Thompson, St. Mary's, Hulse, Pecatonica. Pecatonica, Ill., 1981.

16. ILLINOIS

16.97   ------. Inscriptions, Records, and the Early History of the Twelve Mile Grove Cemetery and St. Thomas Cemetery of Seward, Illinois. Seward, Ill., 1980.

16.98   Hoffman, Esther Halford. Fayette County, Illinois, Cemetery Inscriptions. Decatur, Ill.: Decatur Genealogical Society, 1969.

16.99   *Hoffman, Muriel. "Obituaries Copied from the Colfax Press, a Weekly Newspaper, Colfax, Illinois." (1890-1905) Gleanings from the Heart of the Cornbelt 6 (1972): 96-99.

16.100   Hollowak, Thomas L., and William F. Hoffman. Index to the Obituaries and Death Notices Appearing in the "Dziennik Chicagnoski," 1890-1899. Chicago: Polish Genealogical Society, 1984.

16.101   ------. Index to the Obituaries and Death Notices Appearing in the Jedność-Polonia, 1926-1946. Chicago: Polish Genealogical Society, 1983.

16.102   Hutchinson, Ruth A. Abstracts of Marriage, Death, and Estate Notices from the "Oquawka Spectator," Henderson County, Ill, 1848-1852. Rowlett, Tex.: Hutchinson, n.d.

16.103   Hyde, Hazel M., and Taylor Decker. Winnebago County, Illinois Cemetery Inscriptions. Danville, Ill.: Heritage House, 1971.

16.104   Illinois. State Historical Library, Springfield. Index to the "Transactions" of the Illinois State Historical Society and Other Publications of the Illinois State Historical Library, Including "Publications" of the Illinois State Historical Library, I-III, "Transactions" of the Illinois State Historical Society, IV-XLIII. . . . 2 vols. Springfield, 1953. This index should be used to locate obituaries in the Publications.

16.105   Illinois State Historical Society. Journal, v. 1-, April 1908-. Springfield, Ill.: Illinois State Historical Society, 1908-. The early volumes contain many lengthy obituaries which are listed in the index for volumes 1-25.

16.106   Index to Prominent Decatur Persons, Obituaries and Features, Volumes 1-5, Pages 1-500, Scrapbook in "Decatur Herald and Review" Library. Decatur, Ill.: Decatur Herald and Review Library, 1968. Covers the years 1870 to 1968. IHi

16.107   Irgang, George L. Livingston County Cemeteries. Normal, Ill.: Bloomington-Normal Genealogical Society, 1971.

16.108   Jasper County Cemetery Survey Project. Some Jasper County, Illinois Cemeteries. Thomson, Ill.: Heritage House, 1972.

16.109   Jasper County, Illinois, Cemeteries, Crooked Creek and Fox Townships. Compiled by members of the Jasper County Cemetery Survey Project. Thomson, Ill.: Heritage House, 1973.

16. ILLINOIS

16.110   Knox County Genealogical Society. <u>Cemetery Records, Knox County Illinois</u>. 19 vols. Galesburg, Ill.: Knox County Genealogical Society, 197?-81.

16.111   Lake County (IL) Genealogical Society. Cemetery Committee. <u>Cemetery Inscriptions, Lake County, Illinois</u>. 6 vols. Libertyville, Ill.: Lake County Genealogical Society, 1980-86. For Grant, Lake Villa, Fremont, Wauconda, Libertyville and Avon townships.

16.112   <u>Leaf River Township Cemeteries, Ogle County, Illinois</u>. [Oregon, Ill.: Ogle County Historical Society, 1985?].

16.113   Lippincott, Mr. and Mrs. Lester. "Deaths from the <u>Lovington Reporter</u>, 1896." <u>Moultrie County Heritage</u> 2 (1974): 51.

16.114   Lynch, Phyllis. "DeWitt County (Ill.) Deaths, 1878." <u>DeWitt County Genealogical Quarterly</u> 3 (1977): 21-24.

16.115   McDonough County Genealogical Society, Illinois. <u>Mt. Auburn Cemetery, Colchester Twp., Colchester, Ill</u>. Compiled by Vera Cordell, Alice McMillan, and Genevieve Smalling. Macomb, Ill.: McDonough County Genealogical Society, 1983.

16.116   McKenzie, Mary, and Cynthia Leonard. <u>Obituary Index to 1897 "Staunton Times"</u>. Livingston, Ill.: M. McKenzie, 1986.

16.117   ------. <u>Obituary Index to the "Bunker Hill Gazette," 1898 and 1899</u>. Livingston, Ill.: M. McKenzie, 1986.

16.118   ------. <u>Obituary Index to the Carlinsville (IL) "Free Democrat," September 1856-December 1861</u>. Livingston, Ill.: M. McKenzie, 1987.

16.119   ------. <u>The "Staunton Times/Staunton Star" 1898, 1906-1907 Obituary Index</u>. Livingston, Ill.: M. McKenzie, 1986.

16.120   <u>McLean County Cemeteries</u>. 14 vols. Normal, Ill.: Bloomington-Normal Genealogical Society, 1976-1986.

16.121   McMakin, Dean. <u>Surname Guide to Kane County, Illinois Cemeteries</u>. Geneva, Ill.: Kane County Genealogical Society, 1986.

16.122   "Marriages and Deaths in Illinois, Copied from the <u>Quincy Weekly Herald</u>." <u>Bulletin of the Sons of the Revolution, California Society</u> 9, no. 4 (1932): 10-11. For 22 Dec. 1848; 5 Jan. 1849; 19 Jan. 1849; 23 Feb. 1849.

16.123   Marshall, Florence Houghton. <u>Fairview Cemetery Records, 1903-1982</u>. N.p. 1982.

16.124   ------. <u>Oakwood Cemetery, DeKalb, Illinois, 1865-1985</u>. [DeKalb, Ill.]: F. H. Marshall, 1985.

16.125   ------. <u>St. Mary's Cemetery, DeKalb, Ill., 1874-1984</u>. N.p.: F. H. Marshall, 1984.

16. ILLINOIS

16.126　Mason County, Illinois, Cemeteries. Havana, Ill.: Salt Creek Prairie Chapter, National Society of the Daughters of the American Revolution, and Havana, Illinois, Members of the Church of Jesus Christ of Latter-Day Saints, 1986. Originally published in individual township volumes in 1985 and 1986. Indexed, gathered, and bound as a single volume in 1986.

16.127　Matthews, James Alonzo. Early Marriages and Tombstone Inscriptions, Bond and Madison Counties, Illinois. Midland, Tex.: L. Pearce, 1980.

16.128　Memorial Park Cemetery, Staunton, Illinois. Staunton, Ill.: Staunton Area Genealogical Society, 1983.

16.129　Menard County Obituary Notices, 1875-1892. N.p., n.d. Mounted newspaper clippings. IHi

16.130　Meyer, Joyce. Cemeteries and Tombstone Inscriptions of Madison County, Illinois. 3 vols. Edwardsville, Ill.: Madison County Genealogical Society, 1984-86.

16.131　Middlesworth, Grace H. "Genealogical Excerpts from the Shelbyville Democrat (Shelby County, Illinois) June 16 1910-April 8 1915." Central Illinois Genealogical Quarterly 10 (1974): 99-103.

16.132　------. "Genealogical Gleanings from the Shelby Daily Union, Shelby Co., Illinois, Sept. 24, 1898 to Sept. 9, 1899." Central Illinois Genealogical Quarterly 10 (1974): 45-47.

16.133　------. "Genealogical Gleanings from the Vandalia Union, Vandalia, Fayette County, Illinois." (c1927) Central Illinois Genealogical Quarterly 10 (1974): 149.

16.134　"Milestones in the Central Transcript for the years 1858, 1859." DeWitt County Genealogical Quarterly 3 (1977): 82-86.

16.135　*"Milestones in the DeWitt Courier 1855." DeWitt County Genealogical Quarterly 1 (1975): 6-10. The DeWitt Courier was published in Clinton, Illinois.

16.136　Morgan, Mrs. Samuel. Union Co., Illinois Obituaries and Wedding Announcements. Murphysboro, Ill., 1974. Microfilm. Filmed by the Genealogical Society at Jackson County courthouse. USIGS

16.137　Morrison Chapter NSDAR Cemetery Records, Western Half of Whiteside County, Illinois. 5 vols. in 6. Sterling, Ill.: Whiteside County Genealogists, 1984.

16.138　Murphy, Bennie. Tazewell County, Illinois Cemeteries. 7 vols. Pekin, Ill.: Tazewell County Genealogical Society, 1979-84. v. 1. Dillon and Delavan Townships; v. 2. Boynton, Cincinnati, Deer Creek and Elm Grove Townships; v. 3. Fondulac and Hittle Townships; v. 4. Groveland and Hopedale Townships; v. 5. Little Mackinaw and Mackinaw Townships; v.

6. Malone, Sand Prairie, Spring Lake, and Tremont Townships; v. 7. Morton and Washington Townships.

16.139   Murphy, John V. <u>Cemeteries</u>. 8 vols. Carrier Mills, Ill.: Murphy, 1977-1983. Includes cemeteries in Saline and Williamson counties.

16.140   Newbill, Leona Hopper. <u>Early Settlers of Lagrange, Illinois and Vicinity</u>. 2 vols. LaGrange, Ill., 1941. Volume 2 is composed of obituaries of persons who were residents of LaGrange previous to 1900.

16.141   <u>Oak Ridge Cemetery: Section 27, Township of Somonauk-Sandwich, DeKalb County, State of Illinois: Information Taken from Cemetery Tombstones and Other Cemetery Records Where Possible</u>. Sycamore, Ill.: Genealogical Society of DeKalb County, Illinois, 1982.

16.142   <u>Obituaries from the "Virden Recorder," Virden, Illinois, 1985</u>. Springfield, Ill., 1985.

16.143   Parrick, Linda Kaufmann. <u>Deaths and Marriages from Early Quincy Papers, 1835-1850</u>. Quincy, Ill.: Great River Genealogical Society, 1979.

16.144   Patterson, Doris. "Central Illinois Obituaries, January-June, 1911." <u>Central Illinois Genealogical Quarterly</u> 10 (1974): 24-29. The obituaries are from the <u>Atlanta Argus</u>. Includes persons from Logan, DeWitt, McLean and Tazewell Counties. Many had moved to other states.

16.145   Pease, Janet K. "Deaths in Iowa Reported in the <u>Macomb Journal</u>, McDonough County, Illinois, 1880-1888." <u>Hawkeye Heritage</u> 11 (1976): 181-83.

16.146   ------. <u>Genealogical Abstracts from Rock Island County, Illinois Newspapers</u>. 2 vols. Moline, Ill., 1973-74. v. 1. The <u>Moline Review Dispatch</u>, 1878-82; v. 2. The <u>Rock Island Republican</u>, 1851-55. Includes births, marriages, deaths, estate notices, wedding anniversaries.

16.147   ------. <u>Genealogical Abstracts from the "Astoria Argus" (Fulton County, Illinois)</u>. Arvada, Colo., 1978. Includes material from Schuyler and McDonough counties, 1886-1892.

16.148   ------. <u>Genealogical Abstracts from the "Rock Island Republican," 1851-1855</u>. Rock Island, Ill.: Blackhawk Genealogical Society, 19--.

16.149   ------. "Newspaper Abstracts from McDonough County, Illinois (1880-1882) with Southern Connections." <u>Ridge Runners</u> 4 (1975): 204-13.

16.150   ------. "Obituaries from the <u>Astoria Argus</u>, 1886-1892." <u>Ridge Runners</u> 11 (1978): 217-24.

16.151   *------. "Obituaries from the <u>Macomb Journal</u> 1883-1894 with a Southern Nativity." <u>Ridge Runners</u> 4 (1976): 256-67.

16. ILLINOIS

16.152   ------. "Obituaries from the Port Byron Globe 1890-1893." Ridge Runners
          11 (1978): 224-25.

16.153   ------. "Oquawka, Henderson County, Illinois Burial Ground and Obituaries
          Included in Issue Thursday 5 May 1881 (Henderson County Spectator)."
          Quarterly of the Illinois State Genealogical Society 9 (1977): 158.

16.154   Peck, Sue, and Kay Jetton. St. Clair County's Cemeteries. Marissa, Ill.,
          1975.

16.155   Peoria County, Illinois, Cemeteries: Gravestone Inscriptions. Peoria, Ill.:
          Peoria Genealogical Society, 1980-85. There are volumes for Akron,
          Brimfield, Chillicothe, Elmwood, Hallock, Hollis, Kickapoo, Limestone,
          Logan, Medina, Millbrook, Princeville, Radnor, Rosefield, Timber, and
          Trivoli townships.

16.156   Peoria Journal Star Obituaries Jan. 1 1971-Dec. 31 1972. Springfield, Ill.:
          Illinois State Archives, 1973. Microfilm copy. IHi

16.157   Prairie City Cemetery, Prairie City, Illinois. Macomb, Ill.: McDonough
          County Genealogical Society, 1984.

16.158   The Prairie Sleeps. N.p.: Coles County, Illinois Genealogical Society, 1984.
          Includes cemeteries of Lafayette, Paradise and Pleasant Grove townships,
          Coles county, Illinois.

16.159   Reener, Lynn Boyd. Montgomery County, Illinois, Cemeteries. Litchfield,
          Ill.: L. B. Reener, 1985.

16.160   Richart, Fern J. Piatt County, Illinois, Marriage Records, 1841-1853, and
          Cemetery Records. Urbana, Ill., 1962. Includes epitaphs.

16.161   Richison, W. G. Cemeteries of Jackson County, Illinois. 6 vols.
          Murphysboro, Ill.: Jackson County Historical Society, 1978-86.

16.162   Ross, Virginia. Abstracts of the "Oquawka Spectator." Utica, Ky.: McDowell
          Publications, 1985.

16.163   Ross, Virginia., and Jane Evans. Henderson County, Illinois Cemeteries. 2
          vols. Gladstone, Ill.: Ross & Evans, 1979-81.

16.164   Round Prairie Cemetery of Schuyler County, Illinois. Augusta, Ill.:
          Tri-County Genealogical Society, [1981].

16.165   St. Boniface Cemetery, Quincy, Illinois. Quincy, Ill.: Great River
          Genealogical Society, [1984].

16.166   St. Peters Cemetery, Quincy, Illinois and Adams County Catholic Cemeteries.
          Quincy, Ill.: Great River Genealogical Society, [1985].

16.167   Schonert, Janet, and Wanda Shelby. Edwards County, Illinois, Cemetery
          Inscriptions. Decatur, Ill.: Decatur Genealogical Society, 1969.

16. ILLINOIS

16.168   Schuyler Brown Historical and Genealogical Society. Brown County Board.
          The Cemeteries of Brown County, Illinois, 1825-1972. Astoria, Ill.:
          Stevens, 1975.

16.169   Secrest, Edna McMahan. Cemeteries of Green[e] County, Illinois: Patterson
          Township. Jacksonville, Ill.: E. M. Secrest, 1983.

16.170   Secrest, Edna McMahan, and Carl L. Phillips. Cemeteries of Greene County,
          Illinois: White Hall Township. Sandy, Utah: E. M. Secrest, [1986].

16.171   Sherman, Nellie Cadle. Peoria County, Illinois Death Records 1837-1863.
          Peoria, Ill., 1945. Compiled from newspaper files in the Peoria Public
          Library.

16.172   Sweger, Jayne Kennedy. Deaths in Whiteside Co., Illinois, 1856-1881; 2000
          Obituarys [sic] Condensed from Early County Newspapers, the "Whiteside
          Sentinel" and the "Sterling Gazette," and others. N.p. 1972.

16.173   Tanner, John W. Cemetery Inscriptions of Clay County, Illinois. Olney, Ill.:
          Richland County Genealogical and Historical Society, n.d.

16.174   Taylor, Lola B. Gleanings from Old Newspapers, Clay and Richland
          Counties, Illinois. Olney, Ill.: Taylor Print Shop, 1975. Includes
          obituaries from the nineteenth and early twentieth century.

16.175   Terneus, Roy V. Deaths and Burials: Macon County Poor Farm, Decatur,
          Illinois. Decatur, Ill.: Decatur Genealogical Society, 1975. Includes
          obituaries.

16.176   Thomas, Mrs. Ross S. "Marriages and Deaths from Sangamo Journal March
          12, 1846." Quarterly of the Illinois State Genealogical Society 9 (1977):
          92. The Sangamo Journal was published in Springfield.

16.177   Thumbnail Sketches: Deaths and Obituaries, Warren Co., Il. Compiled by the
          Warren County, Illinois, Genealogical Society; extracted and typed by
          Donna Sheese. . . . N.p.: Warren County, Illinois, Genealogical Society, 1985.

16.178   Tombstone Revelations in Macoupin County, Illinois. Macoupin County, Ill.:
          Macoupin County Historical Society, [1983].

16.179   Vaccaro, Florence, Gertrude M. Pederson, and Hazel M. Hyde. Burritt Union
          Cemetery. . . . N.p.: Illinois Society, Daughters of the American Revolution,
          1968-69.

16.180   Vaught, Harriet. Hamilton County, Illinois, Cemetery Inscriptions. Indexed
          by Mrs. Harlin B. Taylor. Decatur, Ill.: Decatur Genealogical Society,
          1969-.

16.181   *"Vital Statistics, 1885." Gleanings from the Heart of the Cornbelt 2 (1968):
          70-71. Extracts from the Daily Pantagraph, McLean County.

16. ILLINOIS

16.182   Williams, Helen Maxwell. <u>3000 Obituaries from the "Belvidere Standard"</u>
<u>Newspaper, 1851-1899</u>. Belvidere, Ill.: H. M. Williams, 1986.

16.183   <u>Willow Branch Township Cemeteries</u>. Monticello, Ill.: Piatt County Historical
and Genealogical Society, 1985.

17. INDIANA

17.1 <u>Adams-Jefferson Township Cemeteries, Allen County, Indiana</u>. Fort Wayne, Ind.: Allen County Genealogical Society of Indiana, 1983.

17.2 Beeson, Cecil E. <u>Blackford County, Indiana Obituaries - 1983</u>. Hartford City, Ind.: C. E. Beeson, 1984.

17.3 ------. <u>Hartford City, Indiana "News-Times" Obituaries</u>. N.p., n.d. For 1966-74. InFw

17.4 ------. <u>Newspaper Items from the "Hartford City Telegram."</u> Fort Wayne, Ind.: Fort Wayne Public Library, 1972. Abstracts obituaries, giving date and page of the newspaper, for the years 1891-1900. In

17.5 ------ <u>Newspaper Items from the "Hartford City Telegram."</u> Fort Wayne, Ind.: Fort Wayne Public Library, 1974. Abstracts obituaries, giving date and page of the newspaper, for the years 1892-1939, but most of the obituaries are for the year 1901. In

17.6 ------. <u>Pennville, Indiana Scrapbook and Index</u>. N.p., n.d. Photocopy of newspaper clippings and pictures, chiefly obituaries and weddings for the late 1800s and early 1900s. Many are not dated. In

17.7 ------. <u>Scrapbook of Obituaries (1917-1955): Blackford County, Indiana</u>. Hartford City, Ind., n.d. Photocopy of Hartford City newspaper clippings. InFw

17.8 Binnie, Lester H. <u>Cemetery Records for Chester Township, Wabash County, Indiana</u>. North Manchester, Ind.: L. H. Binnie, 1983.

17.9 ------. <u>Cemetery Records for Jackson Township, Kosciusko County, Indiana</u>. Fort Wayne, Ind.: Fort Wayne Public Library, 1971.

17.10 ------. <u>Cemetery Records for Paw Paw and Pleasant Townships, Wabash County, Indiana</u>. Rev. ed. North Manchester, Ind.: L. H. Binnie, 1983.

17.11 ------. <u>Cemetery Records for the Gospel Hill Cemetery, Kosciusko County, Indiana</u>. Albion, Ind., 1974.

17.12 ------. <u>Kosciusko County, Indiana, Cemetery Records</u>. 8 vols. Albion, Ind.: Binnie, 1977-80. v. 1. Franklin and Seward Townships; v. 2. Lake and Clay Townships; v. 3. Jackson and Monroe Townships; v. 4. Tippecanoe and Washington Townships; v. 5. Harrison and Etna Townships; v. 6. Van Buren and Turkey Creek Townships; v. 7. Scott, Jefferson, Prairie and Plain Townships; v. 8. Wayne Township.

17.13 Bright, Velma. <u>Fulton County, Indiana Cemetery Inscriptions, Henry Township: Plus a 1933 Roll Call of the Akron American Legion Post</u>. Rochester, Ind.: Tombaugh, 1974.

17.14 <u>Brown Township Cemetery Records, Ripley County, Indiana</u>. Versaille, Ind.: Ripley County Historical Society, 1984.

17. INDIANA

17.15   Carvin, Mildred Hart. <u>Obituaries from the "Columbus Herald" and the "Republic," Columbus, Indiana</u>. 3 vols. Columbus, Ohio: M. H. Carvin, 1983. v. 1. 23 July 1982 to 16 May 1983; v. 2. 18 May 1983 to 31 Dec. 1983; v. 3. 3 Jan. 1984 to 11 Aug. 1984.

17.16   <u>Cemeteries in Pierce Township, Washington County, Indiana</u>. Salem, Ind.: Washington County Historical Society, 1985.

17.17   <u>Cemeteries of Eastern Greene County, Indiana</u>. Bloomfield, Ind.: Greene County Historical Society, [1982?].

17.18   <u>Cemeteries of Noble Township, Wabash County, Indiana: (Excludes Falls and Rodef Sholem)</u>. . . . Wabash, Ind.: Wabash Carnegie Public Library, 1979.

17.19   <u>Cemeteries of Washington Township, Washington County, Indiana</u>. Prepared by Washington County Historical Society. [N.p. 1981?].

17.20   <u>Cemetery Inscriptions, DeKalb County, Indiana</u>. Compiled by Kathleen Smith Vose. Utica, Ky.: McDowell Publications, 1987.

17.21   <u>Cemetery Records of LaPorte County, Indiana</u>. Fort Wayne, Ind.: Fort Wayne Public Library, 1974.

17.22   <u>Cemetery Records of LaPorte County, Indiana</u>. 4 vols. [LaPorte, Ind.: Miriam Benedict Chapter, Daughters of the American Revolution, 1949-78].

17.23   <u>Clark County Cemetery and Church Records</u>. New Albany, Ind.: Southern Indiana Genealogical Society, 1982.

17.24   <u>Clinton County Cemeteries</u>. Frankfort, Ind.: Gem City Genealogical Shoppe, 196-.

17.25   Correll, James L. <u>Obituaries from Hamilton County Newspapers.</u> 3 vols. N.p. [1987?].

17.26   Cowen, Carl C., and Janet C. Cowen. <u>Morgan County, Indiana Cemetery Records</u>. 1968.

17.27   Cox, Carroll O. <u>New Harmony, Indiana Newspaper Gleanings</u>. Owensboro, Ky.: Cook-McDowell Publications, 1980. Data taken from various newspapers published in the New Harmony area for the years 1825-1944.

17.28   ------. <u>Posey County Cemetery Records, 1814-1979</u>. Evansville, Ind.: Unigraphic, 1979. Includes index.

17.29   ------. <u>Poseyville, Indiana Newspaper Obituaries 1884-1960</u>. Poseyville, Ind.: C. and G. Enterprises, 1987.

17. INDIANA

17.30   Cox, Gloria M. Additional Posey County, Indiana, Cemetery Records (with Inscriptions from Scattered Cemeteries in Illinois, Kentucky, Warrick and Spencer Counties, Indiana). N.p. 1976. Photocopy of typescript.

17.31   ------. New Harmony, Indiana, Newspaper Gleanings. N.p., n.d. 3 vols. pt. 1. 1825-1899; pt. 2. 1900-1922; pt. 3. 1923-1943.

17.32   Crawford County Cemeteries. New Albany, Ind.: Southern Indiana Genealogical Society, 1982.

17.33   Current, Robert, and Leonore Current. Cemeteries of LaGrange County, Indiana. LaGrange, Ind.: LaGrange County Historical Society, 1984. Includes the years 1832-1982.

17.34   Daughters of the American Colonists. Indiana. Ensign Humphrey Madison Chapter, Pendleton. Cemetery and Obituary Records of Adams Township, Madison County, Indiana. Pendleton, Ind.: Daughters of the American Colonists, 1976.

17.35   ------. Muscatatuck Chapter, Seymour. Cemeteries, Jennings County, Indiana. 2 vols. 1970-71. Photocopy of typescript.

17.36   Daughters of the American Revolution. Indiana. Christopher Harrison Chapter, Salem. Washington County, Indiana, Condensed Obituaries; Copied from Clippings, from the Local Newspapers. 5 vols. Salem, Ind.: Daughters of the American Revolution, 1963-66. v. 1. 1960-63; v. 2. 1950-59; v. 3. 1849-1956; v. 4. 1950-60; v. 5. 1950-65. InFw

17.37   ------. Washington County, Indiana Records: Condensed Obituaries, Bible Records and Cemetery Records, 1968. Salem, Ind.: Daughters of the American Revolution, 1968. InFw

17.38   ------. Frances Dingman Chapter. Kendallville. Bible Records, Obituaries and Stories of Early Days, Noble County, Indiana. Kendallville, Ind.: Daughters of the American Revolution, 1952. InFw

17.39   ------. Church Histories, Obituaries, and Stories of Early Days, Noble County, Indiana. Kendallville, Ind.: Daughters of the American Revolution, 1952. InFw

17.40   ------. Obituaries and News Items of Early Settlers of Noble County, Indiana, As Published in the "Albion New Era" . . . Obituaries and News Items from Other Sources in Noble County. . . . Kendallville, Ind.: Daughters of the American Revolution, 1947. InFw

17.41   ------. General Francis Marion Chapter, Marion. Grant County, Indiana Records: Newspaper Items. Marion, Ind.: Daughters of the American Revolution, 1949. Data abstracted from county newspaper obituaries, 1867-1925. InFw

17. INDIANA

17.42 ------. John Paul Chapter. Madison. Newspaper Items from the "Madison Courier," Madison, Indiana. Madison, Ind.: Daughters of the American Revolution, n.d. (May 1874 to July 1879). In

17.43 ------. Julia Watkins Brass Chapter, Crown Point. Index to Cemeteries of Lake County, Indiana (Established Prior to 1880). Compiled by Frances Helmerick McBride. N.p. 1961. Photocopy of typescript

17.44 ------. Mary Penrose Wayne Chapter. A Collection of Cemetery Inscriptions of Allen Co., Indiana. [Fort Wayne, Ind.: Fort Wayne Public Library, 197-?]. Photocopy of typescript.

17.45 Davis, Lulie. Index of Obituaries from the "Christian Record," 1843-1884 (with Some Copies Omitted). Salem, Ind.: Davis, 1950.

17.46 Davis, Russell W. Alphabetical Index of Death Notices Appearing in the "Anderson Daily Bulletin" (1921-1925 Inclusive). N.p., 1974. Microfilm. In

17.47 ------. Madison County Obituaries, Jan. 1, 1968-Dec. 31, 1975, Collected from Anderson Newspapers. 8 vols. Anderson, Ind.: n.p., 1973-. Also on microfilm at the Indiana State Library, Indianapolis. InFw

17.48 "Deaths Reported in Indianapolis Locomotive, 1845-1860." Hoosier Genealogist 14 (1974): 40-44.

17.49 Dorrell, Dillon R. Ohio Counties Cemeteries. [Lawrenceburg, Ind.]: D. R. Dorrell, [1980?].

17.50 Eel River, Cedar Creek Township Cemeteries. Fort Wayne, Ind.: Allen County Genealogical Society of Indiana, 1986.

17.51 Eisen, David. "The Mishawaka Enterprise": Vital Statistics Index, 1858-1981. Evansville, Ind: Whipporwill Publications, 1987.

17.52 Evans, Nellie E. Hamilton County Cemeteries. Sheridan, Ind.: Evans, n.d.

17.53 Fairmount Cemetery, Huntingburg, Dubois County, Indiana, 1876-1982. N.p.: Dubois County Chapter, Daughters of the American Revolution, [1983?].

17.54 Floyd County Cemeteries. New Albany, Ind.: Southern Indiana Genealogical Society, 1982.

17.55 Fort Wayne and Allen County Public Library. Fort Wayne Obituaries from Newspapers, 1961-1965. Fort Wayne, Ind.: Fort Wayne and Allen County Public Library, 1966. Filmed by the Genealogical Society, 1971. USIGS

17.56 ------. Index to Obituaries in the "Fort Wayne Journal-Gazette," 1900-1918. Fort Wayne, Ind.: Fort Wayne and Allen County Public Library, 1973.

17.57 ------. Index to Obituaries in the "Fort Wayne Journal-Gazette," 1971-1975. Fort Wayne, Ind.: Fort Wayne and Allen County Public Library, 1976.

17.58   ------. <u>Index to Obituary Records As Found in the "Journal Gazette," Fort Wayne, Indiana, Mar. 1, 1938-Dec. 31, 1949; "Journal Gazette" on Strike July 8, 1945-Aug. 19, 1945; Obituaries Copied from the "News Sentinel" on These Dates</u>. Fort Wayne, Ind.: Fort Wayne and Allen County Public Library, 1976.

17.59   <u>Fourteen Cemeteries of Lagro Township, Wabash County, Indiana</u>. Wabash, Ind.: Wabash Carnegie Public Library, 1979.

17.60   <u>Fulton County, Indiana, Newspaper Excerpts</u>. Edited by Jean C. and Wendell C. Tombaugh. 7 vols. Rochester, Ind.: Tombaugh Publishing House, 1982-87. For the years 1858-77.

17.61   Garrett, Jill K. "Old News Items." (1863-1868) <u>Genealogical Reference Builders Newsletter</u> 11, no. 1 (1977): 45.

17.62   <u>Genealogical Sources</u>. Reprinted from the Genealogy Section, Indiana Magazine of History. Compiled by Dorothy L. Riker. Indianapolis: Family History and Genealogy Section, Indiana Historical Society, 1979. Includes cemetery and church records from Brown, Harrison, Hendricks, Henry, Jackson, Jefferson, Lawrence, Monroe, Sullivan, Switzerland, Vigo, and Washington counties.

17.63   Gradeless, Donald E. <u>Index and Surname Cross-reference to Nellie Riley Raber's Whitley County Obituaries, 1858-1910</u>. N.p.: Gradeless, 1979. Based on Mrs. Raber's abstracts which are available in the Columbia City and Fort Wayne libraries.

17.64   <u>Grant County, Indiana: Obituaries and Survivors</u>. 2 vols. Kokomo, Ind.: Selby Publishing and Printing, 1986. v. 1. 18 Sep. 1867-31 Dec. 1894; v. 2. 1 Jan. 1895-31 Dec. 1897.

17.65   Grove, Helen E., and Joan Cox Bohm. <u>Clinton County Cemeteries</u>. 3 vols. Owensboro, Ky.: McDowell Publications, 1980-82.

17.66   Hallett, Katherine, Harold E. McCormick, and Ruth G. McCormick. <u>Bonebroke Cemetery, Van Buren Township, Fountain County, Indiana</u>. N.p. 1977.

17.67   Hamm, Thomas D. <u>Blue River Township, Henry County, Indiana Cemetery Inscriptions</u>. New Castle, Ind.: Henry County Historical Society, 1982.

17.68   ------. <u>Cemetery Records, Dudley Township, Henry County, Indiana</u>. New Castle, Ind.: Henry County Historical Society, 1977.

17.69   ------. <u>Cemetery Records, Henry and Jefferson Townships, Henry County, Indiana</u>. New Castle, Ind.: Henry County Historical Society, 1976.

17.70   ------. <u>Cemetery Records, Stony Creek Township, Henry County, Indiana</u>. New Castle, Ind.: Henry County Historical Society, 1979.

17. INDIANA

17.71   Harrison County Cemeteries. New Albany, Ind.: Southern Indiana Genealogical Society, 1982.

17.72   Harrod, Mildred Dixon. "Hope Star," "Hope Star Journal" Obituaries, 1906-1933. [Flat Rock, Ind.: M. D. Harrod, 1983].

17.73   Harter, Stuart. Cemetery Readings of Eel River and Riverview Cemeteries, Allen County, Indiana. Churubusco, Ind.: S. Harter, 1980.

17.74   Henry, Marietta F. Master Index for Tipton Co., In. Cemetery Inscription Books: 24,960 Names. [Tipton, Ind.]: Henry, 1980.

17.75   Heuss, Lois Ione Hotchkiss. Driftwood Cemetery, Driftwood Township, Jackson County, Indiana. [Charlotte, N.C.]: Heuss, [1968].

17.76   Hinshaw, Don. Randolph County, Indiana Obituaries. 6 vols. Winchester, Ind.: D. Hinshaw, 1986. These obituaries begin with the year 1953.

17.77   Hodge, Robert Allen. An Index to the Marriage and Death Notices in the "Marion Chronicle," 1867-1882, a Newspaper of Marion, Grant County, Indiana. Fredericksburg, Va.: R. A. and L. L. Hodge, 1981.

17.78   Hofmann, Roberta. Cass County, Indiana, Some Pre-1880 Obituaries. Royal Center, Ind.: Hofmann, n.d.

17.79   ------. Cass County, Indiana: Some Pre-1900 Obituaries; Abstracted from "Democratic Pharos Weekly," June 2, 1858-May 25, 1859; Jan. 6, 1869-Dec. 27, 1871; July 31, 1872. Royal Center, Ind.: n.p., n.d. InFw

17.80   ------. Deaths in Logansport, Indiana Newspapers: "Democratic Pharos Weekly," 1858-1859, 1869-1871, July 31, 1872; "Logansport Weekly Journal," 1870-1876; "Logansport Daily Journal," 1876-1878. Kokomo, Ind.: Selby Publishing and Printing, 1983.

17.81   Howe, Zera Eleanor Hansell. Pioneer Churches and Cemeteries of Gillam Township, Jasper County, Indiana. [Medaryville, Ind.: Howe, 1979].

17.82   Hoyt, Arabelle Carter. Surname Index to Cemetery Records in Valparaiso-Porter County Public Library Genealogical Collection. N.p. 1978.

17.83   Index to Digest of Obituaries Published in Newspapers of Columbia City, Whitley County, Indiana, 1856-1910. Compiled by Nellie M. Raber. Fort Wayne, Ind.: Allen County Public Library, 1980.

17.84   Index to Obituary Records As Found in the "News-Sentinel" and the "Journal-Gazette," Fort Wayne, Indiana 1966-1970. Compiled by the Staff of the Public Library of Ft. Wayne and Allen County. Fort Wayne, Ind.: The Library, 1971.

17.85   Indiana Miscellaneous Records, Jackson and Jennings Counties Obituary and Cemetery Records. Compiled by the Muscatatuck Chapter, Daughters of the American Colonists.

17.86   Jenkins, Rosella Rasmussen, and Diana Marion Knowles. Sacred to the
         Memory: Inscriptions from Eastern Warren County, Indiana Cemeteries,
         1826-1974. 3 vols. N.p.: Jenkins, 1975-86.

17.87   Johnson Township Cemetery Records, Ripley County, Indiana. Versailles,
         Ind.: Ripley County Historical Society, 1984.

17.88   Kite, Marjorie J., and Mildred Schultz. Obituaries from "The Journal," the
         North Manchester, Ind. Newspaper, Dec. 1881 - Dec. 1893. N.p.: Dr.
         Manasseh Cutler Chapter, D.A.R., 1984.

17.89   Kraus, Loraine E. Cemeteries of Western Greene County, Indiana. 2 vols.
         N.p.: Greene County Historical Society, 1985.

17.90   Lake-Washington, Perry Township Cemeteries, Allen County, Indiana. Fort
         Wayne, Ind.: Allen County Genealogical Society of Indiana, 1984.

17.91   Lansaw, Simona. Woodlawn Cemetery, Terre Haute, Vigo County, Indiana:
         Index of Burials. 2 vols. Owensboro, Ky.: Cook-McDowell Publications,
         1980-83. v. 1. 1839 thru 1899; v. 2. 1900 thru March 1983.

17.92   Lantaff, Carol A, and Glenda K. Trapp. Cemetery Records of Vanderburgh
         County, Indiana. 2 vols. Owensboro, Ky.: Cook-McDowell Publications,
         1980-86.

17.93   Lewis, Audrée Seibel. Tombstone Inscriptions in Steuben County, Indiana:
         Carleton Cemetery, Jackson Prairie Cemetery, Memorial Grove Cemetery.
         Fort Wayne, Ind.: Fort Wayne Public Library, 1967.

17.94   McBride, Frances Helmerick. Obituaries from "Lake County Star," Crown
         Point, Indiana 3-6-1908--12-19-1913; Indexed. N.p., n.d.

17.95   McCarron, Helen. Surname Index to Obituaries, 1980, "Chesterton Tribune."
         N.p.: Valparaiso-Porter County Public Library, 1982.

17.96   ------. Surname Index to Obituaries, 1981, "Chesterton Tribune." N.p.:
         Valparaiso-Porter County Public Library, 1983.

17.97   McHenry, Chris. Dearborn County, Indiana Obituaries, 1820-1850,
         1851-1860. [Lawrenceburg, Ind.]: C. McHenry, [1983].

17.98   McPherson, Robert D. Mississinewa Memorial Cemetery, Wabash County,
         Indiana: Includes Bank Cemetery, Captain Dixon Cemetery, Chester E.
         Troyer Cemetery, Mt. Vernon Cemetery, Ogan Cemetery, Pleasant Grove
         Cemetery, William Ted Hosier Cemetery. Wabash, Ind.: Wabash Carnegie
         Public Library, 1977. Eleven Waltz and Liberty township cemeteries were
         moved to Mississinewa Memorial cemetery in the early 1960's to make
         way for the Mississinewa Reservoir.

17.99   McWhirter, David Ian. Index to the "Christian Record." Nashville, Tenn.:
         Disciples of Christ Historical Society, 1987. The Christian Record was

published in Bloomington and Bedford, 1843-1866, and contains many obituaries of Indiana Disciples.

17.100   <u>Madison-Monroe Township Cemeteries, Allen County, Indiana</u>. Fort Wayne, Ind.: Allen County Genealogical Society of Indiana, 1980.

17.101   <u>Marion, Pleasant, Lafayette, Aboite Township Cemeteries, Allen County, Indiana</u>. Fort Wayne, Ind.: Allen County Genealogical Society of Indiana, 1981.

17.102   Matson, Donald K. <u>Rose Hill Cemetery, 1821-1976</u>. Bloomington, Ind.: Monroe County Genealogical Society, 1976.

17.103   Mayer, Douglas L. <u>Index to Obituaries from the "Times-Union," Warsaw, Indiana, January 1960 thru December 1964</u>. Warsaw, Ind.: D. L. Mayer, 1985.

17.104   Mayhill, R. Thomas. <u>Cemetery Records of Greensboro Township and Harrison Township, Henry County, Indiana</u>. . . . Knightstown, Ind.: Eastern Indiana Publishing Co., 1968.

17.105   ------. <u>Early Cemetery Records of Wayne Township, Henry County, Indiana, Including the Town of Knightstown, the Village of Raysville, Grant City, Maple Valley, and the Former Villages of Elizabeth City and West Liberty</u>. Knightstown, Ind.: Eastern Indiana Publishing Co., 1968.

17.106   Mefford, Mrs. Robert R. <u>Genealogical Notes from the "Western Ranger" April 10, 1847-July 25, 1849, and the "Practical Observer," Porter County, Indiana, August 1, 1849-December 27, 1852</u>. Valparaiso, Ind.: Genealogy Department, Porter County Valparaiso Public Library System, [1982].

17.107   Miller, Mable Hale. <u>Keyhole to the Past</u>. Boonville, Ind.: Boonville Standard, 1968. Obituaries for 1871-1935 copied from <u>Boonville Enquirer</u> and <u>Boonville Standard</u>.

17.108   Minniear, Ingabee Brineman. <u>Wells County, Indiana Obituaries, 1969 to 1975</u>. Fort Wayne, Ind.: Fort Wayne and Allen County Public Library, 1978.

17.109   ------. <u>Wells County, Indiana, Obituaries, 1975-1979: Contained in This Volume Are Obituaries of Individuals Who Are Buried in Cemeteries Located in Wells County</u>. N.p. 1981.

17.110   Miskimens, Dorothea. <u>95 Cemeteries in Orange County, Indiana for Paoli Township, Orangeville Township, North West Township, Orleans Township, Northeast Township, Stampers Creek Township</u>. Sylmar, Calif.: D. Miskimens, 1986?

17.111   Morford, Wanda L. <u>Switzerland County, Indiana, Cemetery Inscriptions, 1817-1985</u>. Cincinnati, Ohio: W. L. Morford, [1986].

17.112   Murphy, Jane F. Obituaries and Miscellaneous Items Abstracted from Columbus, Indiana, Bartholomew County Newspapers, 1872-1884. Columbus, Ind.: Daughters of the American Revolution, 1979.

17.113   Murphy, Thelma M. Scrapbook of Vital Statistics, Indianapolis, Indiana from Newspapers. Indianapolis: n.p., 1950. 2 vols. v. 1 contains deaths Aug.-Dec. 1949. USIGS

17.114   Newhard, Malinda E. E. Allen County, Indiana Veterans Burial Records, 1906-1929. Harlan, Ind.: M. E. E. Newhard, 1981.

17.115   ------. Cemetery Inscriptions, Allen County, Indiana, Maumee, Milan, Scipio & Springfield Townships. N.p.: Newhard, 1978.

17.116   ------. Cemetery Inscriptions, De Kalb County, Indiana. Harlan? Ind., 1972.

17.117   19th Century Headstones of Tippecanoe Co. [Lafayette, Ind.: Tippecanoe County Historical Association, 1982].

17.118   Obituaries from the "Bunker Hill (Indiana) Press," 1904-1926. Collected by Clara McGee; collated and indexed by Charles Smith. Peru, Ind.: Peru Public Library, 1981.

17.119   Obituaries, Jennings County, Indiana, 1885-1890; and, Undertaker's Record, Jennings County, Indiana, 1901-1907. Seymour, Ind.: Indiana State Society, Daughters of the American Colonists, Muscatatuck Chapter, 1981.

17.120   Obituaries, Veterans, Madison County, Indiana. Anderson, Ind.: Indiana Room, Anderson Public Library, n.d. Began in 1985 with cumulation from 1982 newspapers. Contains obituaries which originally appeared in the Anderson Herald and Anderson Bulletin.

17.121   Obituary Records As Found in the "News-Sentinel" and the "Journal-Gazette," Fort Wayne, Indiana, 1841-1977. N.p., n.d. InFw

17.122   Palmer, Louise Martin. Index to Tri-state Obituaries (Indiana-Ohio-Michigan) from the "Fort Wayne Journal Gazette," 1977. Fort Wayne, Ind.: Fort Wayne and Allen County Public Library, 1978. Index for 1978 published in 1979.

17.123   Parkview Junior High School History Club. Henry County Cemetery Epitaphs and Inscriptions. Indianapolis: Indiana Junior Historical Society, 1973.

17.124   Pemberton, Dorothy Gilbert. Everyname Index to Wells County Indiana Cemetery Records. Compiled by Ingabee Brineman Minniear. Fort Wayne, Ind.: Fort Wayne Public Library, 1979.

17.125   ------. Everyname Index to Wells County, Indiana Obituaries, 1969-1975. Fort Wayne, Ind.: Fort Wayne and Allen County Public Library, 1979.

17. INDIANA

17.126   Phillips, J. Oscar, and Opal B. Phillips. <u>Spencer County, Indiana Cemeteries</u>. Owensboro, Ky.: Cook-McDowell Publications, 1980-. Published in cooperation with Capt. Jacob Warrick Chapter, National Society, Daughters of the American Revolution, Boonville, Ind. v. 1, Carter, Clay, Grass and Jackson Townships.

17.127   ------. <u>Warrick County, Indiana Cemeteries</u>. Owensboro, Ky.: Cook-McDowell Publications, 1980-. Published in cooperation with Capt. Jacob Warrick Chapter, National Society, Daughters of the American Revolution, Boonville, Indiana. v. 1. Greer and Campbell Townships.

17.128   <u>Pulaski County, Indiana, Cemetery Inscriptions: With Historical and Genealogical Notes</u>. Medaryville, Ind.: Pulaski County Historical Society, 1975.

17.129   Quinn, Frances. <u>Obituary Dates and Your Family Ties: Over 140 Years in Montgomery County, Indiana</u>. Cottage Grove, Oreg.: Cottage Grove Genealogical Society, 1987. Revision of a 1974 manuscript of the deaths recorded in Montgomery County, Indiana, compiled by Pauline Randel Walters.

17.130   Raber, Nellie Marie Riley. <u>Greenhill Cemetery, Columbia City, Indiana with Index</u>. N.p. 1974. Photocopy of typescript.

17.131   ------. <u>Digest of Obituaries Published in Newspapers of Columbia City, Whitley County, Indiana, 1856-1910</u>. N.p., n.d.

17.132   <u>Randolph County, Indiana Obituaries 1900-1935; the "Winchester Democrat."</u> 6 vols. Fort Wayne, Ind.: Fort Wayne and Allen County Public Library, 1973. Photocopy of clippings. v. 6 is an index with note on missing parts by W. C. Heiss. InFw

17.133   Ratcliff, Richard P. <u>Spiceland Township, Henry County, Indiana Cemetery Inscriptions, 1824-1981</u>. Rev. ed. New Castle, Ind.: Henry County Historical Society, 1981. Includes the following cemeteries: Old Friends Cemetery, Spiceland; Circle Grove Cemetery, Spiceland; Dunreith Cemetery, Dunreith.

17.134   Reeve, Helen H. <u>Brown County, Indiana Cemeteries</u>. Nashville, Ind.: Brown County Historical Society, 1977.

17.135   ------. <u>Brown County Indiana Obituaries 1914-1984</u>. 2 vols. Nashville, Ind.: Brown County Historical Society, 1986.

17.136   <u>Rest Haven: One Hundred Fifty Years</u>. Fort Wayne, Ind.: Fort Wayne Public Library, 1977. Includes approximately 40,000 names. Also includes information from mortuary records, from newspaper obituaries, Bible and family records.

17.137   <u>Scipio, Springfield, Maumee, Milan, St. Joseph Township Cemeteries, Allen County, Indiana</u>. Fort Wayne, Ind.: Allen County Genealogical Society of Indiana, 1985.

17. INDIANA

17.138   Sconce, Eva Mae. <u>Obituaries from Edinburg, Indiana Area Newspapers for the Year 1977</u>. Edinburg, Ind.: n.p., 1977. In

17.139   Scott County Historical Society (Indiana). <u>Cemetery Records</u>. Scottsburg, Ind.: Scott County Historical Society, 1978.

17.140   Smith, William Wright. <u>Newspaper Abstracts of Owensville and Gibson County, Indiana, 1872-1915</u>. Evansville, Ind.: Tri-state Genealogical Society, 1978. Reprint of the information contained in the several editions of <u>A True Record</u>, by W. W. Smith, published first in 1910 and 1916. Contains name and date of deaths that appeared in the <u>New Echo</u> published in Owensville, Indiana.

17.141   <u>Spencer County (Ind.) Cemetery Inscriptions</u>. 3 vols. Rockport, Ind.: Spencer County Historical Society, 1987. v. 1. Jackson, Grass, Hammond townships; v. 2. Ohio and Luce townships; v. 3. Huff, Clay, Harrison, Carter townships.

17.142   <u>Sullivan County, Indiana, Cemetery Records</u>. 5 vols. Sullivan, Ind.: Sullivan County Historical Society, 1983-85.

17.143   <u>Tipton County, Indiana, Cemetery Inscriptions and Histories</u>. Compiled and indexed by Indian Reserve Chapter, Daughters of the American Revolution and Tipton County Extension Homemakers Association. 7 vols. Rochester, Ind.: Tombaugh Publishing House, 1979-80. v. 1. Jefferson Township cemeteries, also Union (East Union) Cemetery, Hamilton county; v. 2. Madison Township cemeteries; v. 3. Prairie Township cemeteries, also Bacon Cemetery, Clinton county; v. 4. Liberty Township cemeteries; v. 5. Wildcat township cemeteries; v. 6. Rural Cicero township cemeteries; v. 7. City of Tipton cemeteries.

17.144   Tombaugh, Jean Cragun, and Wendell C. Tombaugh. <u>Fulton County, Ind., Cemetery Inscriptions (with Genealogical Notes)</u>. Rochester, Ind.: Tombaugh Publishing House, 1976. Includes Wayne, Liberty, and Henry townships.

17.145   ------. <u>Marshall County, Ind. Cemeteries</u>. 2 vols. Rochester, Ind.: Tombaugh Publishing House, 1985.

17.146   ------. <u>Miami County, Indiana Cemetery Inscriptions</u>. Rochester, Ind.: Tombaugh Pub. House, 1977.

17.147   Toph, Violet E. <u>Ripley County, Indiana Obituaries</u>. Versailles, Ind.: n.p., n.d. For the 1800s and 1900s. InFw

17.148   ------. <u>Ripley County, Indiana Records: Obituaries of Ripley County</u>. 2 vols. Versaille, Ind.: Toph, n.d. InFW

17.149   <u>Tri-State Obituaries (Indiana-Ohio-Michigan) 1964-1969</u>. 5 vols. Fort Wayne, Ind.: Fort Wayne and Allen County Public Library, 1975. Obituaries abstracted from the <u>Fort Wayne News Sentinel</u> and the <u>Fort Wayne Journal Gazette</u> and others.

17.150   ------.   <u>1970-1974</u>.   6 vols.   N.p.   1977.

17.151   Wagner, Beverly D. Hoot.   <u>Cemetery Inscriptions</u>.   2 vols.   Roanoke, Ind.: B. D. H. Wagner, 1982.   v. 1. Maxville/Woodlawn Cemetery of Randolph County; v. 2. Cemetery Inscriptions of Green Township, Monroe township, and Stony Creek Township.

17.152   Walters, Pauline Randel.   <u>Deaths in Montgomery County, Indiana, 1830's On</u>.   N.p.: Walters, 1973-.

17.153   Warren, Madge.   "Deaths from <u>Practical Observer</u> Newspapers 1850-52, Valparaiso, Indiana (Porter Co.)."   <u>Illiana Genealogist</u> 5 (1969): 105-6.

17.154   ------.   "Deaths from <u>Western Ranger</u> Newspapers 1847-1849, Valparaiso, Indiana (Porter Co.)."   <u>Illiana Genealogist</u> 4 (1968): 51-52.

17.155   <u>Washington County, Indiana, Madison Township, 1984: Copied from Death Records, Old Church Records, Grave Stones, Obituaries, Mortuary Records, Marriage Records, Newspaper Items</u>.   Copied by Virginia Miller.   N.p.: Washington County Historical Society, 1984. This is almost entirely made up of information from tombstone inscriptions.

17.156   <u>Wayne Township Cemeteries</u>.   Fort Wayne, Ind.: Allen County Genealogical Society of Indiana, 1982.

17.157   Wilhoit, Virginia.   <u>Some Wabash Valley Cemeteries in Parke, Sullivan, and Vigo Counties, Indiana</u>.   N.p. 1977.

17.158   Wilhoit, Virginia, and Nelson Eddy.   4 vols.   <u>Cemeteries, Vigo County, Indiana</u>.   Owensboro, Ky.: Cook & McDowell Publications, 1980-82.

17.159   Wilke, Katherine.   <u>Newspaper Gleanings, Union City, Randolph County</u>.   N.p. 1969.   v. 1. 1873-83.   Includes death notices.

17.160   Wilkens, Cleo Goff.   <u>Obituary Records As Found in Fort Wayne, Indiana Newspapers, 1841-1900</u>.   Fort Wayne, Ind.: n.p. 1962.

17.161   Woodard, Marian Cady.   <u>Names in Hamilton County Death Notices: An Index to the "Noblesville Ledger," September 11, 1874 to March 20, 1881</u>.   Noblesville, Ind.: Noblesville Public Library, 1978.

17.162   Woodhull, Joan.   <u>Pike County, Indiana, Cemetery Records</u>.   7 vols.   N.p.: Woodhull, 1976.

17.163   Woodward, Ronald L.   <u>Obituaries from the North Manchester, Indiana, Journal, May 1877--April, 1894</u>.   Wabash, Ind.: Wabash Carnegie Public Library, 1982.

17.164   ------.   <u>Obituaries from "Wabash Weekly Gazette," 1848-1856</u>.   Wabash, Ind.: Wabash Carnegie Public Library, n.d.

17. INDIANA

17.165   ------. <u>Obituaries, Wabash County, Indiana, 1873-1899</u>. Wabash, Ind.:
        Wabash Carnegie Public Library, 1984. Includes <u>Wabash Plain Dealer</u>,
        1873-1899; <u>Wabash Weekly Courier</u>, May 1876-Apr. 1886; <u>Wabash Times</u>,
        May 1884-1899; <u>Somerset Bugle</u>, June 1883-Dec. 1883; <u>Wabash Star</u>,
        Aug. 1896-1899; <u>North Manchester News-Journal</u>, Jan. 1892-June 1899.

17.166   Young, Christine, and Hazel M. Hyde. <u>Cemetery Inscriptions, Spencer
        County, State of Indiana</u>. Danville, Ill.: Heritage House, 1971.

        ------. <u>Cemetery Inscriptions, Spencer County, State of Indiana. Surname
        Index</u>. Danville, Ill.: Heritage House, 1975.

18. IOWA

18.1 "Abstracts from the <u>Dallas Weekly Gazette</u>." <u>Hawkeye Heritage</u> 2 (1967): 173 For Adel, Iowa, 1866-67.

18.2 Anderson, Richard L. <u>Deaths in Des Moines, Iowa, January-December, 1977, Compiled from the "Des Moines Evening Tribune" and the "Des Moines Sunday Register."</u> N.p., n.d. Ia

18.3 ------. <u>Deaths in Des Moines, Iowa, January-December, 1978 As Reported in the "Des Moines Sunday Register" and the "Des Moines Evening Tribune."</u> N.p., n.d. Ia

18.4 ------. <u>Deaths in Polk County, January-Dec. 1979, As Reported in the "Des Moines Evening Tribune" and the "Des Moines Sunday Register."</u> N.p., n.d. Ia

18.5 ------. <u>Polk County, Iowa Records: Deaths, July 1, 1976-December 31, 1976</u>. N.p., n.d. Taken from the <u>Des Moines Sunday Register</u>, <u>Des Moines Register</u> and the <u>Des Moines Tribune</u>. Ia

18.6 <u>Annals of Iowa</u>, 3d series, v. 1-, 1893-. Des Moines, Iowa.: Iowa State Department of History and Archives, 1893-. Volumes 1-36 of the 3d series contain a section called "Notable Deaths." The early volumes contain some long obituaries while in the later volumes the notices are brief.

18.7 Ashley, Freida. <u>Scrapbook, 1871-1888 Containing Newspaper Clippings of Vital Records, etc., Probably from Osceola Area</u>. Osceola, Iowa.: Genealogical Society, 1976. Microfilm. USIGS

18.8 Bartlen, Mrs. Vincent. <u>Jasper County, Iowa, Obituaries, 1880-1900, Taken from the Files of the "Prairie City News."</u> Prairie City, Iowa.: n.p., n.d. InFw

18.9 Beggs, G. H. <u>Van Buren County, Iowa, Obituaries, 1964-1967</u>. Keosauqua, Iowa.: n.p., 1976. InFw

18.10 Blevins, Scharlott Goettsch, and V. Lorraine Duncan. <u>Scott County, Iowa, Cemetery Records</u>. N.p. 1978.

18.11 Buchanan County Genealogical Society. <u>Buchanan County, Iowa, Cemeteries</u>. Independence, Iowa: The Society, 1980.

18.12 Caskey, Marjorie J. <u>Bedford City Cemetery, Bedford, Iowa; Annotated</u>. Bedford, Iowa: Caskey, 1977.

18.13 <u>Cemeteries, Clear Creek Township, Johnson County, Iowa</u>. Des Moines, Iowa: Iowa Genealogical Society, 1985.

18.14 <u>Cemeteries, Jefferson Township, Johnson County, Iowa</u>. Des Moines, Iowa: Iowa Genealogical Society, 1985.

18.15 <u>Cemeteries of Clay County, Iowa</u>. Spencer, Iowa: Speed Printers, 1983.

18.   IOWA

18.16   Cemeteries of Marion County, Iowa. Knoxville, Iowa: Marion County
         Genealogical Society, 1976.

18.17   Cemetery and Death Records of Warren County, Iowa. Marceline, Mo.:
         Walsworth Publishing Co., 1980.

18.18   Cemetery Records, Bremer County, Iowa. Waverly, Iowa: Bremer County
         Genealogical Society, 1983.

18.19   Cemetery Records, Montgomery County, Iowa: Townships of Douglas,
         Washington, East (Jackson). Des Moines, Iowa: Iowa Genealogical Society,
         1984.

18.20   Cerro Gordo County, Iowa Cemetery Records. Mason City, Iowa: North
         Central Genealogy Society, [1980?]. Includes Rockwell Cemetery, Sacred
         Heart Cemetery, Grant Center Cemetery, Pleasant Valley Cemetery,
         Richland Lutheran Cemetery, Owen's Grove Cemetery, Clear Lake
         Township Cemetery, Clear Lake Cemetery, I.O.O.F. Cemetery, and
         Memorial Park Cemetery.

18.21   Cronbaugh, Lois Emma Wilson. Abstracted Notes from Linn County
         Newspapers. 2 vols. N.p.: Lois W. Cronbaugh, 1970-71. v. 1. Notes
         from Mt. Vernon newspapers, Jan. 1916-25 Dec. 1919; v. 2. Mt. Vernon
         and Lisbon newspapers, Jan. 1922-July 1924.

18.22   ------. Cemetery Records and Additional Grave Stone Markers to
         Cemeteries Already Taken: Also, Abstracts of Obituaries of Burials in
         Linn County, Iowa, 1965-68. Cedar Rapids, Iowa: Ashley Chapter,
         Daughters of the American Revolution, 1968.

18.23   ------. Linn County, Iowa Cemetery Records, with a Few Pages of
         Miscellaneous Records. [Cedar Rapids, Iowa: Cronbaugh, 1962?].

18.24   ------. Obituaries from Cedar Rapids, Iowa "Daily Gazette," 1963 (Some in
         1961 and 1962) Mostly Linn County Residents. Cedar Rapids, Iowa.:
         Cronbaugh, 1964.

18.25   Daughters of the American Revolution. Iowa. Genealogical Collections.
         Washington, D.C.: Reproduction System for Genealogical Society, 1971.
         Microfilm. USIGS Contains records and obituaries from Cedar Rapids,
         Linn County; pioneer records taken from obituaries in the Grinnell
         Herald, 1871-1929, Poweshiek County; news items for early days in Spirit
         Lake which includes some obituary notices.

18.26   ------. Ashley Chapter, Cedar Rapids. Condensed Obituaries (Death
         Notices) 1965-1966-1967 of Linn County, Iowa Residents, from Cedar
         Rapids, Iowa, "Daily Gazette." Cedar Rapids, Iowa: Daughters of the
         American Revolution, 1968. IaHi

18.27   ------. Stars and Stripes Chapter, Burlington. Cemeteries of Des Moines
         County, Iowa. Burlington, Iowa: Daughters of the American Revolution,
         1968.

18. IOWA

18.28 Davis, Chester R. <u>Nodaway Township Cemeteries</u>. [Nodaway, Iowa: Davis, 1976].

18.29 Donnellson Review. <u>Obituaries, 1916-1922, 1926-1970</u>. 4 vols. N.p., n.d. Microfilm. Filmed by the Genealogical Society at the Public Library, Keokuk, Iowa, 1974. USIGS

18.30 Dyson, Geraldine. <u>Index of Marriage, Death, Probate and Divorce Notices Gleaned from "Vinton Eagle" Jan 10, 1855 through Mar 3, 1880</u>. Van Horne, Iowa.: Genealogical Society, 1976. Microfilm. USIGS

18.31 <u>Floyd County, Iowa Cemeteries</u>. Mason City, Iowa: North Central Iowa Genealogical Society, 1986.

18.32 Genealogical Society of the Church of Jesus Christ of Latter-Day Saints. <u>Vital Statistics from the "Frontier Guardian," Kanesville, Iowa, Feb. 1849-Jan. 1852</u>. Salt Lake City: n.p., n.d. USIGS

18.33 Gingerich, Mary A. <u>Cemetery Directory of Amish and Mennonites in Iowa, Johnson, and Washington Counties of Iowa</u>. Kalona, Iowa, 1972.

18.34 <u>Greene County, Iowa, Cemeteries</u>. Des Moines, Iowa: Iowa Genealogical Society, 1981. Includes cemeteries in Franklin and Willow townships.

18.35 Guess, Rosetta and Leo Guess. <u>Death Notices and Obituaries from the "New Virginian," New Virginia, Iowa, 1933-1937, Warren County</u>. . . . Des Moines, Iowa.: [Guess], 1974. IaHi

18.36 <u>Guthrie County Death Records, 29 April 1880-31 December 1915</u>. [Jamaica, Iowa]: Genealogical Society of Guthrie County, Iowa, [1982]. Includes cemetery records as well as civil records.

18.37 Guthrie County Genealogical Society. <u>Brethren Cemetery, Cass Township, Guthrie County</u>. Jamaica, Iowa: Guthrie County Genealogical Society, 1983.

18.38 Hansen, Charlene Mae. <u>Obituaries from the "Keystone Bulletin," 20 Jun 1912 - 30 Dec 1937</u>. Cedar Rapids, Iowa.: Hansen, n.d.

18.39 Higgins, Michael Robert. <u>Mitchell County, Iowa Obituaries from 1878-1978</u>. Iowa City, Iowa.: Higgins, 1978. Selected obituaries relating to the author's family.

18.40 <u>Highland Township Cemetery, Highland Township, Guthrie County, Iowa</u>. Jamaica, Iowa: Guthrie County Genealogical Society, 1983.

18.41 "Iowa Deaths Reported in the Macomb, Illinois <u>Journal</u>, 1880-1888." <u>Hawkeye Heritage</u> 11 (1976): 181-83.

18.42 "Iowa Related Deaths Reported in 1896 in the <u>Moline Daily Dispatch</u>." <u>Hawkeye Heritage</u> 13 (1978): 174.

18. IOWA

18.43 <u>Keokuk Obituaries, 1872-1946</u>. 12 vols. N.p., n.d. Filmed by the Genealogical Society at the Public Library, Keokuk, Iowa, 1974. USIGS

18.44 Lillie, Pauline. <u>Iowa County Cemetery Stones and History, 1844-1975</u>. N.p.: Iowa County Historical Society, 1976. For the years 1844-1976.

18.45 <u>Lucas County, Iowa Cemetery Records</u>. Compiled by the Lucas County Genealogical Society. Marceline, Mo.: Walsworth Publishing Co., 1981.

18.46 McKeeman, Opal. <u>Obituaries, 1972-1973, Iowa-born Kansans, Taken from "Hutchinson News" (Kansas) and "Dodge City Globe" (Kansas)</u>. N.p.: McKeeman, 1974.

18.47 ------. <u>Obituaries Taken from the "Oregonian," Portland, Oregon</u>. Portland, Oreg.: : McKeeman, 1974.

18.48 <u>Memorial Park Cemetery: Mason City, Iowa</u>. Mason City, Iowa: North Central Iowa Genealogical Society, 1982.

18.49 Meredith, Mrs. George W. <u>Excerpts from the Scrapbook Originally Compiled by Mrs. George W. Meredith and Abstracted by Mrs. Georgianna Meredith Wilson</u>. Keosauqua, Iowa.: Genealogical Society, 1974. Microfilm. Contains marriages and obituaries from 1876 to 1889. USIGS

18.50 <u>Montrose Obituaries, 1916-1929</u>. N.p., n.d. Filmed by the Genealogical Society at the Public Library, Keokuk, Iowa, 1974. USIGS

18.51 <u>Morrisburg Cemetery, Jackson Township, Guthrie County, Iowa</u>. Jamaica, Iowa: Guthrie County Genealogical Society, 1984.

18.52 <u>Newspaper Abstracts</u>. 4 vols. Jamaica, Iowa: Guthrie County Genealogical Society, 1984. v. 1 <u>Panora Weekly Umpire</u>, Panora, Iowa, 5 Jan. 1888-27 Dec. 1888; v. 2 <u>The Guthrian</u>, 1903-1904; v. 3 <u>Umpire-Vedette</u>, Panora, Iowa, Jan.-Dec. 1889; v. 4 <u>Vedette</u>, Panora, Iowa, Jan.-Dec. 1891.

18.53 <u>Obituaries Abstracted from the Daily Newspaper of Clinton, Iowa, the "Clinton Herald."</u> 4 vols. Clinton, Iowa.: Lockhart, n.d. v. 1. Jan.-June 1971; v. 2. Jan.-June 1972; v. 3. Jan.-June 1973; v. 4. July-Dec. 1973.

18.54 <u>Obituaries Abstracted from the Daily Newspaper of Davenport, Iowa, the "Times-Democrat," July 1, 1973 to September 30, 1973</u>. Compiled by Jane Lockhart. Clinton, Iowa: Lockhart, [197?].

18.55 <u>Obituaries from the "Clinton Herald" at Clinton, Iowa</u>. 2 vols. Clinton, Iowa.: Aitchison, n.d.

18.56 <u>Obituaries of Old Settlers Whose Deaths Occurred 1916-1918 As Given in Old Settlers Meeting Keosauqua Aug. 16, 1916 and August 21, 1918</u>. N.p., n.d. IaHi

18.57 O'Dell, Patricia Combs. <u>Obituaries and Death Notices from the "Bedford Free Press" in 1925, Taylor County, Ia</u>. Newmarket, Iowa.: n.p., n.d.

Also includes death notices from the <u>Iowa Southwest Democrat</u>, Bedford, and other papers, 1888-1920. InFw

18.58 ------. <u>Taylor County Index to Obituaries from Scrapbook of Patricia O'Dell, Taken from the "Bedford Times-Press" and "Clarinda Herald-Journal," Principally from 1971-72.</u> N.p., n.d.

18.59 O'Dell, Patricia Combs, Esther Stephens, and Helen Janson. <u>Tombstone Record of Taylor County, Iowa.</u> [New Market, Iowa: O'Dell], 1979.

18.60 Old Settlers' Association of Cedar County, Iowa. <u>Obituaries, April 1917-June 1934.</u> N.p. 1934. InFw

18.61 Pease, Janet. "Iowa Related Deaths Reported in Moline, Illinois Newspapers, 1893-1894." <u>Hawkeye Heritage</u> 10 (1975): 183-85.

18.62 ------. "Iowa Related Deaths Reported in Rock Island County, Illinois Newspapers 1851-1857." <u>Hawkeye Heritage</u> 10 (1975): 36.

18.63 ------. "Iowa Related Deaths Reported in the <u>Moline Review-Dispatch,</u> Rock Island County, Illinois, 1889." <u>Hawkeye Heritage</u> 10 (1975): 37.

18.64 Punelli, Janis. <u>Obituaries of Former Iowans, Taken from the "Oregonian," Portland, Oregon, 1963-1975.</u> N.p. 1975. IaHi

18.65 ------. <u>Obituaries Taken from the "Oregonian," Portland, Oregon, Listings from August 1964-October 1966, February 1967-March 1968.</u> N.p., n.d.

18.66 <u>Sac County-Wall Lake Township, Ferguson Cemetery.</u> Des Moines, Iowa: Iowa Genealogical Society, 1983.

18.67 Stephens, Esther, Patricial Combs O'Dell, and Helen Janson. <u>Supplement to Tombstone Record of Taylor County, Iowa.</u> N.p. 1979.

18.68 <u>Stones and Sites: Graves of Cedar County, Iowa.</u> [Cedar County, Iowa]: Cedar County Historical Society, 1986. For the years 1836-1986.

18.69 U.S. Work Projects Administration. Iowa. <u>Chickasaw County, Iowa Graves Registration.</u> Des Moines, Iowa: [W.P.A., 1938?].

18.70 Wayne County Genealogical Society. <u>Wayne County, Iowa, Cemeteries.</u> [Corydon, Iowa]: The Society, 1979.

19. KANSAS

19.1 Barton County Cemeteries. 3 vols. Great Bend, Kans.: Barton County Genealogical Society, 1983-84.

19.2 Branches and Twigs Genealogical Society. Cemetery Records of Kingman County, Kansas 1966-1969. [Kingman, Kans.: Branches and Twigs Genealogical Society, 1969].

19.3 Branigar, Thomas. Cemetery Survey. 2 vols. Abilene, Kans.: Dickinson County Historical Society, 1979-80. v. 1. Newbern Township, Newbern cemetery, Farmington cemetery. Buckeye Township, Union (Livingston) cemetery; v. 2. Grant Township, Abilene cemetery.

19.4 Casey, Lora Allen. Some Vital Records of Barton Co., Kansas. Claflin, Kans.: n.p., n.d. Contains deaths copied from the Claflin Clarion, 1899-1915. USIGS

19.5 Cemetery Inscriptions from Rural and Small Town Sites Found in the Northern Half of Montgomery County, Kansas: As Collected from the "Descender." Coffeyville, Kans.: Montgomery County Genealogical Society, 1983.

19.6 Cemetery Inscriptions from Rural and Small Town Sites Found in the Southern Half of Montgomery County, Kansas: As Collected from the "Descender." Coffeyville, Kans.: Montgomery County Genealogical Society, 1981.

19.7 Cemetery Records of Reno County, Kansas, 1865-1978. Hutchinson, Kans.: Reno County Genealogy Society, 1980.

19.8 Chanute Genealogical Society. Cemetery Inscriptions of Neosho County, Kansas. Marceline, Mo.: Walsworth, 1978.

19.9 City Cemetery, Altoona, Wilson County, Kansas, to March 25, 1977. Neodesha, Kans.: Heritage Genealogical Society, 1977.

19.10 Complete Tombstone Census of Douglas County, Kansas. Lawrence, Kans.: Douglas County, Kansas, Genealogical Society, 1987. Includes the Lawrence cemeteries of Oak Hill and Maple Grove.

19.11 Crozier, Micki. Mt. Hope Cemetery, Mt. Hope, Kansas. Sedgwick, Kans.: M. Crozier, 1981.

19.12 Deaths and Interments, Saline County, Kansas, 1859-1985: With Comprehensive Genealogical and Historical Data. Salina, Kans.: Smoky Valley Genealogical Society and Library, 1985.

19.13 Dupsky, Marguerite Watts. Goodland City Cemetery Inscriptions and Early Death Records, Including Bowers Funeral Home Records, Sherman County, Kansas. [Goodland, Kans.]: M. W. Dupsky, [1983].

19.14 Epitaphs and Inscriptions of Phillips County, Kansas. N.p.: Phillips County Genealogical Society, 1980.

19.15   Ford, Don L. Abandoned and Semi-Active Cemeteries of Kansas. 3 vols.
         N.p.: D. L. Ford, 1982-85?

19.16   ------. Cemetery Inscriptions, Atchison County, Kansas. Bowie, Md.:
         Heritage Books, 1987.

19.17   -----. Doniphan County, Kansas, Cemeteries and Burial Sites. Salem, Mass.:
         Higginson Books, 1986.

19.18   ------. Some Cemeteries of Brown County, Kansas. Salem, Mass.:
         Higginson Books, 1986.

19.19   Gardiner, Allen. Monumental Inscriptions from Jackson County, Kansas,
         Cemeteries. Topeka, Kans.: A. Gardiner, 1981.

19.20   Gilbert, Larry D. Nemaha County, Kansas, Cemeteries. N.p.: L. D. Gilbert,
         1982.

19.21   Gordon, Theresa. "News Items from the Cherokee Sentinel of Cherokee,
         Crawford County, Kansas." (2 June 1882-17 Nov. 1882) Lifeliner 13
         (1977/88): 70-75.

19.22   Hall, Mary L. Requiem: In Honor of and Dedicated to Our Pioneers That
         Their Names May Never Be Forgotten. N.p.: M. L. Hall, 1982.
         Inscriptions from cemeteries in Ness county.

19.23   ------. Requiem II: In Honor of and Dedicated to Our Pioneers That Their
         Names May Never Be Forgotten. N.p.: M. L. Hall, 1985.

19.24   Herrick, James L. Death Notices As Listed in "Neosho Valley/Hartford
         Times" and Burials in Hartford Cemetery, Lyon County, Kansas
         (Tombstone Inscriptions and Sexton's Records): Supplemented with
         Information from the "Hartford Call." Topeka, Kans.: Topeka
         Genealogical Society, 1978. The Neosho Valley and the Hartford Times
         were published 1874-1923. The Hartford Call, 1879-91?

19.25   Hodge, Robert A. An Index to the "Lawrence Daily World" (Lawrence,
         Kansas): 3 March, 1892-31 August, 1893. Fredericksburg, Va.: R. A.
         Hodge, 1985. Indexes obituaries as well as other events.

19.26   Index to Obituaries, "Neodesha Register," Wilson County, Kansas, 1883-1911.
         Neodesha, Kans.: Heritage Genealogical Society, [198-?]. Indexed by the
         W. A. Rankin Memorial Library, Neodesha, Kansas.

19.27   Jewell County Cemeteries: Records of Cemeteries Located in Jewell County,
         Kansas. 5 vols. Cawker City, Kans.: North Central Kansas Genealogical
         Society and Library, 1983. v. 1. Highland, Walnut, White Mound, Burr
         Oak townships; v. 2. Erving, Athens, Ionia, Odessa, Esbon, Limestone
         townships; v. 3. Harrison, Montana, Jackson, Holmwood, Richland,
         Sinclair townships; v. 4. Center, Washington, Grant townships; v. 5.
         Calvin, Buffalo, Vicksburg, Browns Creek Prairie, Allen townships.

19. KANSAS

19.28   Johnson County, Kansas, Cemetery Index. Shawnee Mission, Kans.: Johnson County Genealogical Society and Library, 1983.

19.29   Kansas, Mitchell County Cemeteries. 4 vols. Cawker City, Kans.: North Central Kansas Genealogical Society, 1981.

19.30   Kansas State Historical Society. The Annals of Kansas, 1886-1925. 2 vols. Topeka, Kans.: Kansas State Historical Society, 1954-56. Cites deaths of well known citizens giving place and date of death. Does not cite newspaper from which the information was taken. v. 1. 1886-1910; v. 2. 1911-1925.

19.31   ------. Library. Death Notices from "Proceedings" of Ancient Order of United Workmen (AOUW), Grand Lodge of Kansas, 1879-1908, and "Proceedings" of the Grand Lodge, Knights of Pythias (KP), 1877-1918. Topeka, Kans.: Kansas State Historical Society Library, 1973. KHi

19.32   ------. Death Notices from "Proceedings" of the Grand Lodge of Ancient, Free and Accepted Masons of Kansas, 1860-1935. 3 vols. Topeka, Kans.: Kansas State Historical Society Library, 1971. KHi

19.33   ------. Death Notices from "Proceedings" of the Grand Lodge of Independent Order of Odd Fellows of Kansas, 1873-1970. 3 vols. Topeka, Kans.: Kansas State Historical Society Library, 1972. KHi

19.34   ------. Death Notices from "Proceedings" of the Rebekah Assembly of Independent Order of Odd Fellows, 1891-1953. 2 vols. Topeka, Kans.: Kansas State Historical Society Library, 1974. KHi

19.35   ------. Index to Necrology Lists in G. A. R. Encampments 7, 11-62. 2 vols. Topeka, Kans.: Kansas State Historical Society Library, n.d. The Grand Army of the Republic was the largest organization of Union veterans of the Civil War. KHi

19.36   ------. Index to Obituaries from the "Kansas Medical Journal," 1889-1966. Topeka, Kans.: Kansas State Historical Society Library, 1967. KHi

19.37   Lowry, Mildred. The Lowell Kansas Cemetery and Other Records. [Pittsburg, Kans.]: Lowry, 1977.

19.38   McKeeman, Opal. Obituaries, 1972-1973, Iowa-Born Kansans, Taken from "Hutchinson News" (Kansas) and "Dodge City Globe" (Kansas). N.p.: McKeeman, 1974.

19.39   Miller, Marjorie, and Lucille O'Brien. Index to Cemetery Records of Ottawa County Kansas. N.p. [1980?].

19.40   "Morrill Journal." (1882) Topeka Genealogical Society Quarterly 6 (1976): 26. Includes a few death notices for Morrill, Kansas.

19.41   Mulanax, Katherine Schiller. Obituaries, Published in the "Manhattan Mercury," Manhattan, Kansas. 2 vols. [1985?]. v. 1. 1975; v. 2. 1976.

19. KANSAS

19.42   "Newspaper Excerpts from the North Topeka Mail, Topeka, Shawnee County, Kansas." (Feb-Apr 1884) Topeka Genealogical Society Quarterly 8 (1978): 96-98.

19.43   "Notes from the Conservative, Short-lived Leavenworth KS Newspaper." (Feb-June 1861) Topeka Genealogical Society Quarterly 8 (1978): 74.

19.44   "Notes from the Denison Star, Denison, Jackson County, Kansas." (1890) Topeka Genealogical Society Quarterly 4 (1974): 82.

19.45   "Notes from the Leavenworth (KS) Daily Conservative." Topeka Genealogical Society Quarterly 6 (1976): 73-75. For the period 3 Jan. 1867 to 2 July 1867.

19.46   "Notes from the Overbrook Herald, Overbrook, Osage County, Kansas." (1891-92) Topeka Genealogical Society Quarterly 7 (1977): 17-19.

19.47   "Notes from the Wyandotte Chieftain, Bonner Springs, Kansas." (1896) Topeka Genealogical Society Quarterly 4 (1974) 81-82.

19.48   Novotny, Velma McBride. "Obituaries from the Files of the Pratt Union, 1893-1915." Treesearcher 8 (1966): 29-32.

19.49   Obituaries from Chapman Newspapers, 1901-1930. N.p. [1930?].

19.50   Obituaries of the Marshall, Washington, and North Riley Counties, Kansas: Selected Obituaries. N.p., n.d. Photocopy of newspaper clippings, 1930?-73? InFw

19.51   *Paden, Pearl. "A Collection of Obituaries." Midwest Genealogical Register 1, no. 3 (1966): 19-20. From many Kansas cities, 1922-45.

19.52   Pantle, Alberta. "Death Notices from Kansas Territorial Newspapers, 1854-1861." Kansas Historical Quarterly 18 (1950): 302-23.

19.53   Pease, Janet K. "Kansas Deaths in Macomb Journal 1880-1881." Treesearcher 18 (1976): 147-53.

19.54   ------. "Kansas Deaths in Rock Island County, Illinois Newspapers." (1879-96) Treesearcher 19 (1977): 67-69.

19.55   Rice, Tina, and Wanda Houts. Tombstone Inscriptions, Labette County, Kansas. Parsons, Kans.: T. Rice and W. Houts, 1981.

19.56   Schmitt, Marilyn. Baxter Springs Cemetery (and Other Cemeteries in Spring Valley Township). [Columbus, Kans.]: Cherokee County Genealogical Society of Southeast Kansas, 1983.

19.57   Shimmick, Lillian, and Harwood G. Kolsky. Big Timber, 1873-1976, Altory Township, Decatur County, Kansas: A History of Big Timber Cemetery (Czech National Cemetery), the Final Resting Place of Pioneer Settlers from Czechoslovakia and Germany Who Helped Build This Nation. [Saratoga, Calif.]: Kolsky, [1976].

19.58   Smith, Stanley Clifford, and Patricia D. Smith. Cemetery Records of Cowley County, Kansas. Garden City, Kans.: Smith, 1978.

19.59   ------. 100 Years, Finney County, Kansas, Cemetery Inscriptions, 1879-1979. Garden City, Kans.: S. C. Smith, 1981.

19.60   Sterrett, Dorothy H. "The Holton Recorder, Holton, Kansas." (1875) Topeka Genealogical Society Quarterly 8 (1978): 56-57.

19.61   Streeter, Pauline. Obituaries from "Manhattan Republic," 1912-1914. N.p., n.d. InFw

19.62   Tombstone Inscriptions and Burials, Jefferson County, Kansas, 1854-1986. Oskaloosa, Kans.: Jefferson County Genealogical Society, 1986.

19.63   Tombstone Inscriptions, Cowley County, Kansas. Arkansas City, Kans.: Cowley County Genealogical Society, 1984.

19.64   Topeka Genealogical Society. Shawnee County Cemeteries. 2 vols. Topeka, Kans.: Topeka Genealogical Society, 1973-77.

19.65   Twentieth Century Club. Index to Six Cemeteries of Southeast Kansas. Kincaid, Kans., [1972?]. Includes cemeteries in Brown and Doniphan counties.

19.66   United Spanish War Veterans. Dept. of Kansas. Taps. 3 vols. N.p., n.d. Necrology lists arranged alphabetically. KHi

19.67   Walker, Vesta. "Deaths in 1911, from the Manhattan (Kansas) Weekly Republic, January 1912." Kansas Kin 16 (1978): 5.

19.68   Wasson, Beatrice Andrews. "Obituaries--Stafford (Kansas) Courier." Treesearcher 20 (1978): 55-62. For persons born before 1890 who died between the years 1931-56.

19.69   White Cloud, Kansas, Area Cemeteries and Other Information. St. Joseph, Mo.: Northwest Missouri Genealogy Society, [198-?].

19.70   "Wichita Eagle from April 12, 1873 to April 22, 1875. Deaths." Midwest Genealogical Register 1 (1966): 40.

19.71   "Wichita Vidette Newspaper from Aug. 1870 to March 1, 1871. Deaths." Midwest Genealogical Register 1 (1966): 39.

19.72   Winter, Lucile, and Frances Hill. Cemeteries of Allen County Kansas (except Highland and Mt. Hope). Iola, Kans. East Central Kansas Genealogical Society, 1979.

20. KENTUCKY

20.1   Ardery, Julia Hoge. <u>Kentucky Records . . . Tombstone Inscriptions. . . . Barren, Bath, Bourbon, Clark, Daviess, Fayette, Harrison, Jessamine, Lincoln, Madison, Mason, Montgomery, Nelson, Nicholas, Ohio, Scott, and Shelby Counties</u>. 2 vols. Baltimore: Genealogical Publishing Co., 1965-72.

20.2   Ashley, Linda Ramsey, and Elizabeth Tapp Wills. <u>Funeral Notices, Lexington, Ky., 1806-1887</u>. [Rochester, Mich.?], 1982. These funeral notices are in a collection at the Lexington Public Library. Before there were daily newspapers, the funeral notice or invitation was used to notify friends of funeral services to be held.

20.3   Barrickman, W. C. "Marriages and Deaths Published in the <u>Commentator</u>." <u>Register of the Kentucky Historical Society</u> 50 (1952): 134-51. For the period Apr. 8 1826-Mar. 29 1828. The <u>Commentator</u> was published in Frankfort.

20.4   Beam, Judith Ann. <u>Cemetery Records of Land Between the Lakes: (Betwixt the Rivers) 1814-1973</u>. N.p.: Winchester Printing Company, 1974.

20.5   Benningfield, Edward. <u>Larue County, Kentucky Cemeteries</u>. Owensboro, Ky.: McDowell Publications, 1982.

20.6   Biddle, Patty M. <u>Kentucky Straight Bourbon; Roots of Bourbon Co., Paris, Kentucky, and Surrounding Counties; "Western Citizen" Newspaper, 1808-1863</u>. N.p., n.d. Contains many obituaries recorded in full. Held by the DAR Library, Paris, Kentucky.

20.7   Blair, Juanita. <u>A Window to the Past: Cemetery Records: A Selection of Cemeteries from Rowan and Surrounding Counties</u>. Morehead, Ky.: J. Blair, 1981.

20.8   Bolin, Daniel Lynn. <u>Church Cemeteries of Mead, Breckinridge, and Hancock Counties, Kentucky</u>. N.p. 1974.

20.9   Bonham, Jeanne Snodgrass, and Patricia Heylmann Hiatt. <u>Inventory, Elmwood Cemetery, Mt. Vernon, Rockcastle County, Kentucky</u>. Greenwood, Ind.: High Grass Publications, 1983.

20.10   ------. <u>Rockcastle County, Kentucky, Cemetery Records</u>. Greenwood, Ind.: High Grass Publications, 1986.

20.11   Boone, Louis Raymond. "Kentucky Items from the <u>Platte County Reveille</u>, Missouri." (c1864) <u>Kentucky Genealogist</u> 16 (1974): 109-13.

20.12   ------. "Obituaries for Kentuckians in the <u>Bible Advocate</u> of Paris, Tennessee and Saint Louis, Missouri." <u>Kentucky Genealogist</u> 17 (1975): 66-70. <u>Bible Advocate</u> published 1842-50.

20.13   ------. "Obituaries for Kentuckians in the <u>Millennial Harbinger</u>." (1833, 1834, 1853, and 1856) <u>Kentucky Genealogist</u> 18 (1976): 20. <u>Millenial Harbinger</u> was published by the Christian Church, Bethany, Virginia.

20. KENTUCKY

20.14   Bridwell, Margaret M. A Record of Death Notices from Louisville, Ky. Papers from 1814 to 1842. Louisville, Ky., 1944. DNDAR

20.15   Burnette, Sonya, Billie Faye North, and Jakalyn Jackson. Cemeteries in Knox County, Kentucky. Barbourville, Ky.: Knox County Historical Society, 1980.

20.16   Butler County Cemeteries. N.p. 1975.

20.17   Cantrell, Timothy A. Stockton Valley Obituary Index. Bowling Green, Ky.: n.p., 1969. An index of the people from Clinton County whose obituaries have appeared in the minutes of the Stockton Valley Association. KyBgW

20.18   Cemetery Listings, Laurel County, Kentucky. London, Ky.: Published for the Laurel County Historical Society by Enterprise Publications, 1982.

20.19   Cemetery Records, Mercer County, Kentucky. 3 vols. Harrodsburg, Ky.: Harrodsburg Historical Society, 1969-70.

20.20   Chandler, Ora. Nine Hundred Twenty-Five Cemetery Records (Index) of Henderson County, Kentucky. Evansville, Ind.: O. Chandler, [1965].

20.21   ------. Two Thousand One Hundred (Index) Cemetery Records of Webster County, Kentucky. Evansville, Ind.: O. Chandler, [1966].

20.22   Church and Family Graveyards of Franklin County. Frankfort: Kentucky Genealogical Society, 1976.

20.23   Clift, Garrett Glenn. Kentucky Obituaries, 1787-1854; With an Index by Anita Comtois. Baltimore: Genealogical Publishing Co., 1977. Excerpted and reprinted from the Register of the Kentucky Historical Society, volumes 39-41, 1941-43, with index added.

20.24   *------. "Notes on Kentucky Veterans of the War of 1812." Register of the Kentucky Historical Society 50 (1952): 319-39. Newspaper obituaries were one of the sources used for this compilation. The name and date of the newspaper is given.

20.25   Coffey, Bennie, and Juanita Coffey. Cemeteries of Wayne County, Kentucky. [Monticello, Ky.?]: B. B. Coffey, Sr., 1982.

20.26   Coffey, Margie. Cemeteries of Adair County, Kentucky. Columbia, Ky.: Adair County Library, 1984.

20.27   Cornelius, Charley Maynard. Whitley County Cemeteries, Whitley County, Kentucky. 3 vols. 2d ed. Albuquerque, N.Mex.: C. M. Cornelius, [1982-83].

20.28   Craik, Susan Simmons. "Marriages and Deaths from the Western Monitor, Lexington, Kentucky." (1818) Kentucky Genealogist 4 (1962): 95-103.

20.29 <u>Crittenden County, Kentucky, Cemeteries</u>. 2 vols. Owensboro, Ky.: McDowell Publishing Co., 1981-82.

20.30 Darnell, Anita Whitefield, and Mary Lewis Roe Jones. <u>Cemetery Records of Fort Campbell, Kentucky</u>. Clarksville, Tenn., [1970].

20.31 Daughters of the American Revolution. Kentucky. <u>Genealogical Collections</u>. Washington, D.C.: Daughters of the American Revolution, n.d. Filmed by the Genealogical Society, 1971. Contains death notices from Louisville newspapers, 1814-42, and Warren County obituaries, 1938-39. USIGS

20.32 ------. Kentucky State Society. Kentucky Records Research Committee. <u>Kentucky Cemetery Records</u>. 5 vols. Lexington, Ky.: Daughters of the American Revolution, 1960-86.

20.33 ------. Samuel Davies Chapter, Bowling Green. <u>Obituaries: Kentucky, 1925-1941</u>. 2 vols. Bowling Green, Ky.: Daughters of the American Revolution, 1976. KyBgW

20.34 ------. <u>Obituaries: Kentucky, 1937-1942</u>. 3 vols. Bowling Green, Ky.: Daughters of the American Revolution, 1976. KyBgW

20.35 <u>Death Notices from Louisville Newspapers, 1814-1842, Most of Which Are in the Filson Club and the Louisville Free Public Library</u>. N.p., n.d. KyLo

20.36 *Dorman, John Frederick. "The <u>Licking Valley Register</u>, Covington, Kentucky Marriages and Obituaries, 1841-1845." <u>Kentucky Genealogist</u> 19 (1977): 123-28.

20.37 Dunn, Shirley. <u>Lincoln County, Kentucky, Marriages, 1780-1850 and Tombstone Inscriptions</u>. 2 vols. St. Louis: D. A. Griffith, 1977-80.

20.38 Ellsberry, Elizabeth Prather. <u>Cemetery Records, Mason County, Kentucky</u>. Chillicothe, Mo., 1970.

20.39 ------. <u>Cemetery Records of Boyle County, Kentucky</u>. Chillicothe, Mo., [1970?].

20.40 Fulton Genealogical Society. <u>Fulton County, Kentucky, Cemetery Readings</u>. 5 vols. Fulton, Ky.: Fulton Genealogical Society, 1976-85.

20.41 Givens, Mary Parks, and Weynette Parks Haun. <u>Butler County, Kentucky, Cemeteries</u>. Durham, N.C.: W. P. Haun, 1974. Includes some cemeteries in Logan, Muhlenberg, and Warren counties.

20.42 <u>Gone But Not Forgotten: Cemetery and Grave Plots in Henderson County, Kentucky</u>. N.p.: Henderson County Historical Society, 1982.

20.43 Gossum, Mary Louise, and Emily B. Walker. <u>Graves and Hickman County, Kentucky, Cemetery Records</u>. Owensboro, Ky.: Cook and McDowell Publications, 1981.

20.44   Graves County, Kentucky Cemeteries. 5 vols. Mayfield, Ky.: Graves County Genealogical Society, 1981-85.

20.45   Graves of the Lake Cumberland Basin. N.p.: Asher L. Young, 1974.

20.46   Hammers, Marian G. Muhlenberg County, Kentucky, Cemeteries. 4 vols. Madisonville, Ky.: Hammers, 1976-80.

20.47   Hardcastle, Mildred Tucker. Warren County, Kentucky, Obituaries, June 20, 1938-September 28, 1939; Extracts from Obituaries Published in the "Park City Daily News." Bowling Green, Ky.: n.p., n.d. USIGS

20.48   Hart County, Kentucky and Adjoining Counties Cemetery Records. N.p., n.d.

20.49   *Hartman, Mrs. Robert R., Jr. "Abstracts of Clippings." Kentucky Ancestors 3 (1967): 103-4. Abstracts of clippings from the scrapbook of Anna Newdigate, Mason County, Kentucky, 1890-1933.

20.50   Hasskarl, Eula Richardson. Milburn Cemetery Inscriptions, Milburn, Carlisle County, Kentucky. [Ada, Okla., 1968].

20.51   Headrick, Marcella Pickerel. Monroe County, Kentucky Obituaries, 1878-1984. Tompkinsville, Ky.: M. Headrick, 1985?

20.52   Hickman County Cemeteries. Clinton, Ky.: Hickman County Historical Society, 1984.

20.53   Hopkins County, Kentucky Cemeteries. 6 vols. [Madisonville, Ky.]: Hopkins County Genealogical Society; Utica, Ky.: McDowell Publications, 1970-82.

20.54   Houk, Martha T., and Judy Froggett. Cemeteries of Green County, Kentucky. 3 vols. [Green County, Ky.]: Green County Library, 1981-83.

20.55   Ingram, Barbara. Menifee Graveyards. N.p. 1981.

20.56   Jackson, Martha Werst, and Jimmie Harston Jones. Allen County, Kentucky Cemetery and Graveyards Revisited: With Genealogical Notes. Scottsville, Ky.: M. W. Jackson, 1983.

20.57   Jones, James Allison, and Mary Josephine Jones. Cemetery Inscriptions, Hardin County, Kentucky. 3 vols. Utica, Ky.: McDowell Publications, 1982.

20.58   Kenton County Cemeteries: Based on the Work of the Kenton County Historical Society's Cemetery Project Committee. Covington, Ky.: Kenton County Historical Society, 1981.

20.59   Kentucky Family Records. v. 1-, 1969/70-. Owensboro, Ky. Issued by the West-Central Kentucky Family Association. Contains cemetery records.

20.60   Knox County, Kentucky, Cemeteries. 5 vols. Louisville, Ky.: Knox County Genealogical Society, 1980-84.

20. KENTUCKY

20.61   Kyle, E. Arawana Thomas. Our Ancestral Plots. Dawson Springs, Ky.,
        [1967]. Includes a complete list of names and dates from 184 cemeteries
        of Caldwell county.

20.62   Leftwich, Holly M. Hancock County, Kentucky Cemeteries. Owensboro,
        Ky.: West-Central Kentucky Family Research Association, 1974.

20.63   Lewis, Elvira Breezeel. Marshall County, Kentucky, Cemeteries. Benton,
        Ky.: Lewis, 1979.

20.64   The Lexington, Kentucky Cemetery. Lexington, Ky.: Hisel's Headstones and
        Kentucky Tree-Search, 1986.

20.65   Livingston County, Kentucky, Cemeteries, 1738-1976. Smithland, Ky.:
        Livingston County, Kentucky, Homemaker Clubs, 1977.

20.66   Logan County, Kentucky Cemeteries. Russellville, Ky.: Logan County
        Genealogical Society, 1986.

20.67   McDowell, Samuel. Fort Knox Cemeteries in Bullitt, Hardin, and Meade
        Counties, Kentucky: With Historical and Genealogical Notations.
        Illustrated by Glenda Schultheis. Richland, Ind.: McDowell Publications,
        [1975].

20.68   McLean County, Kentucky Cemeteries. 2 vols. Owensboro, Ky.: West-
        Central Kentucky Family Research Association, 1977.

20.69   Maupin, Judith Ann. Cemeteries of Calloway County: "Heart of the Jackson
        Purchase." [Murray, Ky.: J. A. Maupin], 1981.

20.70   ------. The Kentucky Lake Cemetery Relocation Project. Winchester, Ky.:
        Winchester Printing Co., 1975.

20.71   ------. Trigg County Cemeteries, 1811-1979. Murray, Ky.: Maupin, 1980.

20.72   Meador, Anna Hunsaker. Cemetery Records, Northern Section of Christian
        County, Kentucky. Hopkinsville, Ky.: Meador, 1976.

20.73   Meador, Anna Hunsaker, and Timothy Reeves Meador. Cemetery Records of
        Southern Portion of Christian County, Kentucky. Hopkinsville, Ky.: A.
        H. Meador, 1980.

20.74   Meek, C. Price. Henry County, Kentucky Cemeteries. Eminence, Ky.:
        Henry County Historical Society, 1987.

20.75   Metcalfe County, Kentucky, Cemetery Records. Edmonton, Ky.: Metcalfe
        County Historical Society, 1983.

20.76   Nickell, Joe, J. Wendell Nickell, and Ella T. Nickell. Morgan County, Ky.,
        Cemetery Records. West Liberty, Ky., 1981.

20. KENTUCKY

20.77   Obituaries Abstracted from the "Sentinel-Echo," 1961-1971. Compiled by Wilma Parker Johnson. 2 vols. London, Ky.: Laurel County Historical Society, 1983-1984.

20.78   Ohio County, Kentucky, Cemeteries. 4 vols. Hartford, Ky.: Ohio County Historical Society, 1981-86.

20.79   Ohio County, Kentucky, Cemeteries. 2 vols. Owensboro, Ky.: West-Central Kentucky Family Research Association, 1975-77.

20.80   Owen, Kathryn, and Ann P. Couey. Early Winchester Cemetery Inscriptions, Winchester, Clark County, Kentucky. Utica, Ky.: McDowell Publications, 1983.

20.81   ------. Old Graveyards of Clark County, Kentucky. New Orleans: Polyanthos, 1975.

20.82   Patrick, Tracy R. More Cemeteries of Estill County, Kentucky. Irvine, Ky.: Powell Press, 1981.

20.83   Peden, Eva Coe. Barren County, Kentucky, Cemetery Records. Glasgow, Ky.: Peden, 1976.

20.84   ------. Monroe County, Kentucky, Cemetery Records. Glasgow, Ky.: Peden, 1974.

20.85   Potter, Clinton C. "Deaths." MS Western Kentucky University Library. A diary which contains deaths, 1870-73, for Warren County. Date and cause of death and occasionally family relationships are given.

20.86   Presbyterian Herald. Marriage and Death Abstracts 1850-1856. Indianapolis: n.p., 1948. The Presbyterian Herald was published weekly at Louisville. In

20.87   Pulaski County Historical Society. Pulaski County, Ky. Cemetery Records. Somerset, Ky.: The Society, 1976.

20.88   Rabold, Mary Moltenberry, and Elizabeth Moltenberry Price. Allen County, Kentucky, Cemetery Records. Bowling Green, Ky., 1971.

20.89   ------. Warren County, Kentucky, Cemetery Records. Bowling Green, Ky., 1971.

20.90   Rogers, Ellen Stanley, and Diane Rogers. Cemetery Records of Estill County, Kentucky, 1808-1976. Baltimore: Gateway Press, 1976.

20.91   Sanders, Faye Sea. Washington County, Kentucky, Cemeteries. 2 vols. Louisville: F. S. Sanders, n.d.

20.92   Savage, Jacob, and Bertha Savage. Greenup County, Kentucky Cemeteries. Utica, Ky.: McDowell Publications, 1985.

20.93   *Scott, Hattie Marshall. "Abstracts from Kentucky Newspapers, Franklin County, Kentucky." <u>Register of the Kentucky Historical Society</u> 44 (1946): 307-26. Includes death notices and obituaries for 1819 to Sept. 23 1829, from newspapers published at Frankfort and Lexington.

20.94   *-----. "Abstracts from Kentucky Newspapers, Mason County, Kentucky." <u>Register of the Kentucky Historical Society</u> 44 (1946): 187-93. The items are taken at random from old Maysville papers, a few from the <u>Tippecanoe Banner</u> of 1840, some from the <u>Western Star</u> for 1842, but most are from the <u>Maysville Eagle</u> of 1850 and 1860.

20.95   ------. <u>Scotts' Papers: Kentucky Court and Other Records</u>. Frankfort, Ky.: Kentucky Historical Society, 1953. Includes death notices and references to obituaries, 1831-70, pp. 159-92.

20.96   Shakers. South Union, Kentucky. <u>Necropolis: A List of the Names of the Brethren and Sisters Who Have Died, in the Society, Since the Year 1810</u>. N.p.: Shakers, 1906. An index of deaths cited in the Shaker records. KyBgW

20.97   Shelby County Historical Society. <u>Cemeteries in Shelby County, Kentucky</u>. Shelbyville, Ky.: The Society, 1979.

20.98   Sheridan, Richard C. "Some Deaths Reported in the <u>Princeton Banner</u> in 1873-1884." <u>Kentucky Genealogist</u> 17 (1975): 83-84.

20.99   Simmons, Don. <u>Graves County, Kentucky Newspaper Genealogical Abstracts</u>. Melber, Ky.: Simmons, 1978-. v. 1. <u>Mayfield Monitor</u>, 1876-85; v. 3. <u>Mayfield Monitor</u>, 1890-93.

20.100   ------. <u>Marshall County, Ky., Newspaper Genealogical Abstracts</u>. 2 vols. Melber, Ky.: Simmons, 1984.

20.101   ------. <u>Trigg County, Kentucky Newspaper Genealogical Abstracts</u>. Melber, Ky.: Simmons Historical Publications, 1986.

20.102   <u>Simpson County, Kentucky Cemeteries</u>. Franklin, Ky.: Simpson County Historical Society, 1983.

20.103   Smith, Randolph N. <u>Cumberland County, Kentucky Cemetery Records</u>. [Burkesville, Ky.]: Smith, [1979].

20.104   Talley, William M. "Old Newspaper Items." <u>Kentucky Genealogist</u> 18 (1976): 96. From the <u>Fleming Gazette</u>, Flemingsburg, Ky., 2 Oct. 1895, 9 Mar. 1904, and the <u>Ewing Inquirer</u>, Fleming County, 19 Apr. 1906. For 1871-89 in <u>Kentucky Genealogist</u> 19 (1977): 18-23.

20.105   ------. <u>Talley's Kentucky Papers</u>. Fort Worth, Tex.: Arrow Printing Co., 1966.

20.106   ------. <u>Talley's Northeastern Kentucky Papers</u>. Fort Worth, Tex.: American Reference Publishers, 1971. Chapter entitled "Old Newspaper Items,"

20. KENTUCKY

pp. 121-78, contains abstracts from several Ohio and Kentucky newspapers between the years 1816 and 1860.

20.107 Taylor County, Kentucky Cemeteries. N.p.: Kentucky Historical Society, 1986.

20.108 Thompson, Rita Adkisson. Meade County Cemeteries. Vine Grove, Ky.: Ancestral Trails Historical Society, 1973.

20.109 *Trabue, Alice E. "Kentucky Tombstone Inscriptions Contributed by the Colonial Dames in Kentucky [1700-1800]." Register of the Kentucky Historical Society 28 (1930): 47-60. These inscriptions are from the Old Jefferson Street cemetery in Louisville, and other small cemeteries in Nelson, Bourbon, Jefferson, Fayette, Woodford, and Mercer counties.

20.110 Visscher, Nina M. "Marriages and Obituaries from Kentucky Reporter, Lexington, 1827." Register of the Kentucky Historical Society 35 (1937): 360-63.

20.111 Webster County Cemeteries. Dixon, Ky.: Webster County Historical and Genealogical Society, 1981.

20.112 West-Central Kentucky Family Research Association. Daviess County, Kentucky Cemeteries. 3 vols. Owensboro, Ky.: West-Central Kentucky Family Research Association, 1977.

20.113 Whitley, Mrs. Wade Hampton. "Obituary Notices Taken from the Western Citizen, Published at Paris, Ky." Daughters of the American Revolution Magazine 47 (1915): 25-26. Contains selected obituaries from the Western Citizen for the years 1831-65.

20.114 Wood, Sue. Lewis County Cemeteries. [Tollesboro, Ky.]: S. Wood, [1983].

21. LOUISIANA

21.1   Ainsworth, Lucille Dickinson. <u>Cemeteries of Franklin Parish, Louisiana</u>
        <u>Public, Private and Abandoned</u>. Winnsboro, La.: L. D. Ainsworth, 1985.

21.2   Armstrong, Gladys Stovall. <u>Plaquemines Parish Obituary Notices, 1865-1898:</u>
        <u>Extracted from Newspapers Published in Plaquemines Parish</u>. [Buras, La.]:
        G. S. Armstrong, 1983.

21.3   Barnidge, Mary Alix Holt, and Janice Claire Oestriecher. <u>Rapides Cemetery,</u>
        <u>Pineville, Louisiana: Oldest Cemetery in Rapides Parish</u>. Alexandria, La.:
        Mar.-Jan., 1883.

21.4   Briley, Richard, Ida Martin Briley, and P. C. Lang. <u>Briley's Memorial</u>
        <u>History and Cemetery Directory of Winn Parish, Louisiana</u>. Montgomery,
        La.: Mid-south Publishers, [1966].

21.5   Broders, Mrs. E. A. "Death and Marriage Notices Appearing in the <u>Republic</u>
        Newspaper Published in Baton Rouge and New Orleans 1822-1823."
        <u>Genealogical Register</u> 14 (1967): 41-42.

21.6   Butler, Dolores Powe, and Doris Martin Holden. <u>Saint Tammany Parish,</u>
        <u>Louisiana, Cemetery Records</u>. N.p. 1977.

21.7   Catholic Church. Archdiocese of New Orleans. <u>The Necrology of the</u>
        <u>Archdiocese of New Orleans, 1702-1964</u>. Compiled by Henry C. Bezou.
        [New Orleans, 1964].

21.8   Chauvin, Phillip. <u>"Comet" Deaths 1982</u>. Houma, La.: [Terrebonne Genealogy
        Society, 1983].

21.9   ------. <u>"Comet" Deaths 1983</u>. [Houma, La.]: Terrebonne Genealogy Society,
        1983.

21.10   ------. <u>"Houma Courier" Deaths 1982</u>. [Houma, La.]: Terrebonne Genealogy
        Society, [1983].

21.11   ------. <u>"Houma Courier" Deaths 1983</u>. Houma, La.: Terrebonne Genealogy
        Society, [1984].

21.12   ------. <u>"Houma Courier" Microfilm Index Deaths</u>. 2 vols. [Houma, La.]:
        Terrebonne Genealogy Society, [1983]. v. 1. 1936-49; v. 2. 1950-59.

21.13   ------. <u>"Houma Courier" Selected Obituaries, 1981</u>. [Houma, La.]:
        Terrebonne Genealogy Society, [1984].

21.14   Conrad, Glenn R., and Carl A. Brasseaux. <u>"Gone But Not Forgotten":</u>
        <u>Records from South Louisiana Cemeteries</u>. Lafayette, La.: Center for
        Louisiana Studies, University of Southwestern Louisiana, 1983.

21.15   Daughters of the American Revolution. Louisiana Society. <u>Louisiana</u>
        <u>Tombstone Inscriptions</u>. 8 vols. Shreveport, La., 1957-. v. 1. Ouachita
        Parish, La., by Chief Tusquahoma Chapter; v. 2. Morehouse Parish, La.,
        by Abram Morehouse Chapter; v. 3. Bienville, Webster, Winn, and Lincoln

Parishes, by Long Leaf Pine, Chief Tusquahoma, Dugdemona, and Dorcheat Chapters; v. 4. Jackson Parish, by the Dugdemona Chapter; v. 5. Sabine, Vernon, and DeSota Parishes, by Long Leaf Pine and Bon Chasse Chapter; v. 6. East and West Carroll Parishes and some records from Ouachita; v. 7. West Feliciana, Arcadia, St. Mary, Lafayette, St. Martin, Evangeline, Calcisieu, St. Landry, Vermillion, Avoyelles; v. 8. Claiborne and Union Parish, by Chief Tusquahoma Chapter.

21.16   Frazier, John Purnell. Tombstone Inscriptions of Northwest Louisiana Cemeteries. [Pittsburg, Tex.]: J. P. Frazier, 1986.

21.17   Frazier, John Purnell, and Wanda Volentine Head. Cemetery Inscriptions of Claiborne Parish, Louisiana. Shreveport, La.: J&W Enterprises, 1985.

21.18   Hebert, Traise W. Cemeteries of Central Lafourche Parish, La. Thibodaux, La.: A. B. Westerman, 1984.

21.19   Johnson, Donald W. "The New Orleans Weekly Crescent, April 20, 1850." Genealogical Register 22 (1975): 97-99.

21.20   Knott, Clara Long. An Indexed Copy of the Cemetery Records of Sabine Parish, Louisiana. Center, Tex.: J. B. Sanders, [1966].

21.21   "Louisiana Newspaper Notices from the Franklin Planters' Banner." (1853) Genealogical Register 10 (1963): 4-5.

21.22   McManus, Jane Parker. L'est [sic] We Forget: Cemeteries of Vernon Parish, Louisiana. Seattle: McManus, 1978.

21.23   Magee, Zuma Fendlason, and Thelma S. Bateman. Cemetery Records, Louisiana. 5 vols. N.p. 1962-.

21.24   "Marriage and Death Notices from the Planters' Banner, Franklin, La., 1846-48." Genealogical Register 9 (1962): 6.

21.25   Mayers, Brenda LaGroue, and Gloria Lambert Kerns. Death Notices from Louisiana Newspapers. 4 vols. Baker, La.: Folk Finders, 1984-85. v. 1 1811-19 (3d rev. ed., c1984, 1985 printing); v. 2. 1822-1914 (rev. 2d ed., 1985); v. 3. Jan. 1833-Dec. 1917; v. 4. 1847-1893.

21.26   Mills, Elizabeth Shown. "Extracts of Births, Deaths, and Marriages from the Weekly Populist, Natchitoches, Louisiana." (1894-1899) Genealogical Register 22 (1975): 364-66.

21.27   ------. "Genealogical Notes from the Natchitoches Union October 1861-December 1862." Genealogical Register 22 (1975): 133-37.

21.28   ------. "Marriages and Deaths in Natchitoches Parish, 1825-1827." Genealogical Register 21 (1974): 167-69. Extracted from the Natchitoches Courier.

21. LOUISIANA

21.29 "Minutes of the Tangipahoa River Baptist Association." (September 22 1900) <u>Genealogical Register</u> 21 (1974): 66-74. Includes obituaries and death dates.

21.30 New Orleans Times-Picayune. <u>Newspaper Index</u>. Wooster, Ohio: Bell and Howell Co., 1972-. Monthly with annual cumulations.

21.31 <u>Obituaries: A Scrap Album (1885-1915?)</u>. New Orleans: New Orleans Public Library, 1972. LN

21.32 Pitcher, Mrs. Sargent P. "Newspaper Notices of Marriages and Deaths, Carroll Parish, La., 1868." <u>Genealogical Register</u> 16 (1969): 98. Contains only a few death notices.

21.33 Prud'homme, Lucile Keator, and Fern B. Christensen. <u>The Natchitoches Cemeteries: Transcriptions of Gravestones from the Eighteenth, Nineteenth, and Twentieth Centuries in Northwest Louisiana</u>. New Orleans: Polyanthos, 1977.

21.34 *Roberts, Mrs. Odile Lawler. "The <u>Daily Picayune</u>--New Orleans, Louisiana Deaths and Marriages, 1855-1856." <u>Genealogical Record</u> 18 (1976): 67-68.

21.35 Robertson, Billie Earp. <u>Sleeping by the Bayous: A History of the Cemeteries and Tombstone Inscriptions of the Houma, Louisiana, Area Including Gray, Schriever, Bayou Blue, and Little Bayou Black</u>. Thibodaux, La.: Library, Nicholls State University, [1982].

21.36 Scott, Thelmarie. <u>Catahoula Parish Cemeteries</u>. Baton Rouge, La.: VAAPR, 1984.

21.37 Sealy, Gwen Bradford. <u>Lest We Forget: A Record of Tombstone Inscriptions: Red River Parish, Louisiana, and Vicinity</u>. [Shreveport, La.: G. B. Sealy, 1983].

21.38 Slawson, J. A. H. <u>De Soto Parish History and Cemetery Records</u>. Center, Tex., [1967].

21.39 Westerman, Audrey B., and Lee Verret. <u>Death Notices, 1867-1954, Assumption Parish, Louisiana</u>. Thibodaux, La.: A. B. Westerman; L. Verret, 1983.

21.40 Williams, Ernest Russ. <u>Abstracts of Obituaries from the "Minutes" of the Magee's Creek Baptist Association (Mississippi and Louisiana) 1882-1924</u>. Monroe, La.: Williams, 1978.

21.41 Wingate, Ruby Brown, and Nelda Harrell Fleniken. <u>DeSoto Parish Cemetery Records</u>. Mansfield, La.: DeSoto Historical Society, 1980.

22. MAINE

22.1   Augusta, Maine. <u>Vital Records of Augusta, Maine, to the Year 1892</u>. Auburn, Maine: Press of Merrill and Webber Co., 1933. Newspapers were one of the sources used for this compilation.

22.2   Bowdoin College. <u>Obituary Record of the Graduates of Bowdoin College and the Medical School of Maine</u>. . . . Brunswick, Maine: Bowdoin College Library, 1911.

22.3   Bowman, John Elliot. <u>Some Maine Veterans of the American Revolution: Newspaper Items--Death Notices</u>. [1936?]. Photocopy of typescript presented to the Maine State Library by Clarence Brigham, Director, American Antiquarian Association, May 1936.

22.4   Brooks, Thelma Eye. <u>Inscriptions of Cemeteries in Hermon, Maine</u>. Waterville, Maine: T. E. Brooks, 1983.

22.5   Colby College, Waterville, Me. <u>An Obituary Record of Graduates of Colby University . . . from 1822 to 1870</u>. Lewiston, Maine.: Journal Press, 1870.

        ------. <u>Alumni of Colby University. Obituary Record from 1870 to 1873. Supplement no. 1</u>. . . . Waterville, Maine: n.p., 1873.

        ------. <u>Alumni of Colby University. Obituary Record from 1873 to 1877. Supplement no. 2</u>. . . . Waterville, Maine: n.p., 1877.

        ------. <u>Alumni of Colby University. Obituary Record from 1877 to 1884. Supplement no. 3</u>. . . . Cambridge, Mass.: J. Wilson and Son, 1884.

22.6   Daughters of the American Revolution. Maine. Colonel Dummer Sewall Chapter. <u>Bath Marriage and Death Records 1820-1853</u>. N.p., 1940. From the <u>Maine Gazette</u>, published in Bath. DNDAR

22.7   ------. <u>Marriages and Deaths Copied from the "Bath Daily Tribune" -May 1856 to January 1857, with Index</u>. Bath, Maine: n.p., 1946-47. DNDAR

22.8   Davis, Moses. "Extracts from the Diary of Moses Davis, J.P., of Edgecomb, Me., 1775-1823." <u>New England Historical and Genealogical Register</u> 82 (1928): 414-21.

22.9   "Deaths Copied from Newspapers, 1815-1830." <u>Maine Historical Magazine</u> 6 (1891): 156-60.

22.10   Demers, Mabel G. "Revolutionary Soldiers Appearing in the <u>Family Pioneer and Juvenile Key</u>, Published in Brunswick, Maine, 1833/4." <u>New England Historical and Genealogical Register</u> 104 (1950): 205-6.

22.11   Dodge, Christine H. <u>Vital Records of Old Bristol and Nobleboro in the County of Lincoln, Maine Including the Present Towns of Bremen, Damariscotta, South Bristol, and the Plantation of Monhegan</u>. 2 vols. N.p., 1947-51. v. 1. Births and Deaths; v. 2. Marriages.

22.12   Fisher, Carleton Edward. <u>Vital Records of Clinton, Maine, to the Year 1892:</u> <u>Births, Marriages and Deaths</u>. N.p., 1967.

22.13   Georgetown, Maine. <u>Vital Records of Georgetown, Maine, to the Year</u> <u>1892</u>. . . . Auburn, Maine: Press of Merrill and Webber Co., 1939. v. 3. Deaths. Contains references to death notices in the <u>Daily Bath</u> <u>Times</u> and the <u>Eastern Herald</u>, Portland.

22.14   Gorham, Maine. <u>Publishments, Marriages, Births and Deaths from the Earlier</u> <u>Records of Gorham, Maine</u>. Portland, Maine: Maine Genealogical Society, 1897. Newspapers were one of the sources used for this compilation.

22.15   Hallowell, Maine. <u>Vital Records of Hallowell, Maine, to the Year 1892</u>. . . . Auburn, Maine: n.p., 1924. Contains references to death notices in the <u>American Advocate</u> and <u>Hallowell Register</u>, 1797-1860.

22.16   Haskell, Jessica J. "Deaths of Revolutionary Soldiers, Copied from the <u>American Advocate</u>, Printed in Hallowell, Maine, 1810-1827, Also from Other Maine Papers." <u>Daughters of the American Revolution Magazine</u> 68 (1934): 695-99.

22.17   <u>Index of Selected Obituaries: "Kennebec Journal" 1825-1854, "Oxford</u> <u>Observer" 1826-1828, "Oxford Democrat" 1833-1855</u>. Farmington, Maine: University of Maine at Farmington, Mantor Library, 1977.

22.18   Jordan, William B. <u>Burial Records, 1717-1962, of the Eastern Cemetery,</u> <u>Portland, Maine</u>. Bowie, Md.: Heritage Books, 1987.

22.19   ------. <u>Burial Records 1811-1980 of the Western Cemetery in Portland,</u> <u>Maine</u>. Bowie, Md.: Heritage Books, 1987.

22.20   King, Luetta. <u>958 Obituaries of Revolutionary Soldiers Found in "Eastern</u> <u>Argus," a Portland, Maine Newspaper, Covering a Period Sept. 8,</u> <u>1803-Dec. 31, 1860</u>. Portland, Maine: [Elizabeth Wadsworth Chapter, Daughters of the American Revolution], 1933.

22.21   Labonté, Youville. <u>Necrologies of Franco-Americans Taken from Maine's</u> <u>Newspapers</u>. Auburn, Maine: n.p., 1977. v. 1. 1966-1976.

22.22   ------. <u>The Necrology of St. Peter and Paul's Cemetery, 1870-1976,</u> <u>Lewiston, Maine</u>. 2 vols. Auburn, Maine: Labonte, [1977?].

22.23   Leighton, Nellie Smith. <u>Addendum to North Yarmouth, Maine Vital Records</u> <u>to 1850</u>. Warwick, R.I.: Rhode Island Mayflower Descendants, 1986.

22.24   Maine Farmer. <u>Vital Statistics from the Paper "Maine Farmer" for the Period</u> <u>1833-1852</u>. N.P., 1945. (American Periodicals: 1800-1850). v. 1 and 2. marriages; v. 3. deaths. v. 3 lacks notices for the years 1849 and 1851. The notices from the <u>Maine Farmer</u> were for the whole state but were most numerous for the Kennebec Valley.

22.25   Maine Historical Society. Collections, v. 1-10. Portland, Me.: Maine Historical Society, 1831-87. v. 10 is an index. The Collections contain some obituaries.

22.26   Maine Old Cemetery Association Cemetery Inscription Project: Series One. Edited by Katherine W. Trickey. Augusta, Maine: Maine Old Cemetery Association, 1980. Microfilm. reel 1. Penobscot County cemeteries; reel 2. Franklin and Somerset County cemeteries; reel 3. Androscoggin and Kennebec counties.

22.27   Maine Old Cemetery Association Cemetery Inscription Project: Series Two. Edited by Katherine W. Trickey. Augusta, Maine: Maine Old Cemetery Association, 1982. Microfilm. reel 1. Lincoln, Oxford and York counties; reel 2. Knox, Penobscot, Sagadahoc, Somerset and Waldo counties; reel 3. Aroostock, Franklin, Hancock and Washington counties; reel 4. Androscoggin, Cumberland, Kennebec and Piscataquis counties.

22.28   Maine Old Cemetery Association Cemetery Inscription Project: Series Three. Edited by Katherine W. Trickey. Augusta, Maine: Maine Old Cemetery Association, 1987. Microfilm.

22.29   ------. Index to Cemeteries. Series Three. Edited by Katherine W. Trickey. Augusta, Maine: Maine Old Cemetery Association, 1987.

22.30   Marriages, Births and Deaths 1871-1903 from the "Portland Transcript" and the "Lewiston Weekly Journal." N.p. 1977.

22.31   Noyes, Benjamin Lake. Vital Records, Hancock County, Maine, 1899-1908, 1911, 1914-1915, 1917-1944, Published in Local Newspapers. Salt Lake City, Utah: Genealogical Society, 1950. USIGS

22.32   *"Obituaries Gathered from Different Sources." Maine Historical and Genealogical Recorder, v. 1-9, 1884-98. vols. 1,2,7 contain a few eighteenth and nineteenth century deaths.

22.33   Obituary Notices of Portland People, 1868 to Date. 11 vols. Most of the notices are for the years 1880-1930. All volumes are indexed in a separate card catalog. MeHi

22.34   Overlock, Leland. Warren Cemeteries 1735 to 1985. [Warren, Maine: Warren Historical Society, 1985].

22.35   Palmer, Lloyd E., Rundlette K. Palmer, et al. Whitefield Cemeteries in 1977 from the Readable Remaining Stones. N.p. 1977.

22.36   Phippsburg, Maine. Vital Records of Phippsburg, Maine, to the Year 1892. Auburn, Maine.: Press of Merrill and Webber Co., 1935. Some of the death records are taken from Brunswick newspapers and the Bath Daily Times.

22.37   Smith, Juliet Lesley. Cemetery Records of Hancock County, Maine. Chillicothe, Mo.: J. Smith, [197-].

22. MAINE

22.38 Spencer, Wilbur Daniel. Burial Inscriptions and Other Data of Burials in Berwick, York County, Maine, to the Year 1922. Sanford, Maine: Averill Press, 1922.

22.39 Topsham, Maine. Vital Records of Topsham, Maine, to the Year 1892. Concord, N.Y.: Rumford Press, 1929. 2 vols. The deaths, listed in vol. 2, pp. 295-402, are based on newspaper data.

22.40 Vital Records of North Yarmouth, Maine to the Year 1850. Edited by Ruth Wilder Sherman. Warwick, R.I.: Society of Mayflower Descendants in the State of Rhode Island, 1980. This is a revised version of the alphabetized vital records which were compiled by Carle D. Henry. Includes cemetery records.

22.41 Williamson, Joseph. History of the City of Belfast in the State of Maine. 2 vols. Portland, Maine: Loring, Short, and Harmon, 1877-1913. Contains obituaries.

22.42 Winslow, Maine. Vital Records of Winslow, Maine, to the Year 1892, Births, Marriages and Deaths. Auburn, Maine: Press of Merrill and Webber Co., 1937. Contains references to deaths in the Eastern Mail, the Watervillian, the Maine Farmer.

22.43 "York Necrology 1775-1807." Collections and Proceedings of the Maine Historical Society, 2d series. 10 (1899): 211-23. Copied from "A Book of Mortality," a manuscript record, and arranged alphabetically, by M. F. King. In most instances, only the name and date of death is given.

22.44 Young, David C. "Eastern Argus" Index, 1806-1820. Danville, Maine, 1983.

22.45 ------. "Eastern Argus" Index of Maine and NH Obituaries, 1821-1824. N.p. 1983?

22.46 ------. Index to Death Notices: Jenks's "Portland Gazette," 1798-1806. Danville, Maine: D. C. Young, 1983. Over 1400 death and obituary notices of York and Cumberland Counties in the District of Maine.

22.47 Young, David C., and Robert Taylor. "Morning Star" Index of Maine and New Hampshire Obituaries, 1826-1851. Lewiston, Maine, 1892. Microfilm. The Morning Star was a Freewill Baptist Church weekly newspaper.

23. MARYLAND

23.1   Baltimore Cemeteries. Compiled by the Baltimore County Historical Society. 2 vols. Silver Spring, Md.: Family Line Publications, 1985. v. 1. Northern Baltimore county; v. 2. Eastern Baltimore county and a few cemeteries in the northern area.

23.2   "Baltimore Young Men's Paper, vol. 1. June 7, 1834-November 24, 1835." Maryland Genealogical Bulletin 3 (1932): 2-4. Includes death notices.

23.3   Barnes, Robert William. Gleanings from Maryland Newspapers. 4 vols. Lutherville, Md.: Bettie Carothers, 1975. v. 1. 1727-75; v. 2. 1776-1785; v. 3. 1786-90; v. 4. 1791-95.

23.4   ------. Marriages and Deaths from Baltimore Newspapers, 1796-1816. Baltimore: Genealogical Publishing Co., 1978.

23.5   ------. Index to Marriages and Deaths in the "Baltimore County Advocate," 1850-1864. Silver Spring, Md.: Family Line Publications, 1985.

23.6   ------. Marriages and Deaths, 1802-1815, from the "Frederick-town Herald." Baltimore: n.p., 1970.

23.7   ------. Marriages and Deaths from the "Maryland Gazette," 1727-1839. Baltimore: Genealogical Publishing Co., 1973.

23.8   ------. "Obituaries of Revolutionary Soldiers." Bulletin of the Maryland Genealogical Society 6 (1965): 6-7. These obituaries were taken from Baltimore newspapers.

23.9   Beneath These Stones: Cemeteries of Caroline County, Maryland. Easton, Md.: Upper Shore Genealogical Society of Maryland, 1985.

23.10   Cemetery Inscriptions of Anne Arundel County, Maryland. Edited by John Thomas Gurney, III. Pasadena, Md.: Anne Arundel Genealogical Society, 1982.

23.11   Chance, Hilda Nancy Ersula Snowberger. Western Maryland Pioneers; Marriages, Early Settlers, Births and Deaths, with Location, Arranged and Alphabetized. 2 vols. Liberty, Pa: n.p., n.d. v. 1 contains extracts of obituaries for the Hagerstown area during the 19th century.

23.12   Daughters of the American Revolution. Maryland. Marlborough Towne Chapter. Genealogical Records Committee. Tombstone Inscriptions of Southern Anne Arundel County. Baltimore: Gateway Press, 1971.

23.13   "Emerald and Baltimore Literary Gazette, Vol. 1, no. 2, Saturday April 19, 1828-Saturday, October 18, 1828." Maryland Genealogical Bulletin 3 (1932): 4-5. (American Periodicals: 1800-1850). Contains death notices.

23.14   Gatewood, Gloria V. Marriages and Deaths from the Alleganian Newspaper of Cumberland, Maryland, May 16, 1864, through May 1, 1867. Huntingtown, Md.: G. V. Gatewood, [1984].

23.15   ------. Marriages and Deaths from the Cumberland Alleganian, Cumberland,
         Maryland, May 16, 1864-May 1, 1867. Silver Springs, Md.: Family Line
         Publications, 1986.

23.16   Henry, Effie. Extracts from the "Maryland Gazette" 1730-1790 . . . and
         Extracts from Newspapers Published at Rockville, Maryland 1825-1832.
         N.p., n.d. Contains obituary notices from several counties. The
         Maryland Gazette was published in Annapolis.

23.17   Historic Graves, Private Burial Grounds and Cemeteries of Kent County,
         Maryland: Gone But Not Forgotten. Silver Spring, Md.: Family Line
         Publications, 1972.

23.18   Holdcraft, Jacob Mehrling. More Names in Stone; Cemetery Inscriptions from
         the Peripheral Areas of Frederick County, Maryland. Ann Arbor, Mich.,
         1972.

23.19   ------. Names in Stone: 75,000 Cemetery Inscriptions from Frederick
         County, Maryland. 2 vols. 1966. Reprint. Baltimore: Genealogical
         Publishing Co., 1985.

23.20   Hollowak, Thomas L. Index to Marriages and Deaths in the "Baltimore Sun,"
         1837-1850. Baltimore: Genealogical Publishing Co., 1978.

23.21   Jacob, John E. Graveyards and Gravestones of Wicomico. [Salisbury, Md.:
         Salisbury Advertiser, 1971].

23.22   *Johnston, Christopher. "News from the Maryland Gazette." Maryland
         Historical Magazine 17 (1922): 364-79. Includes obituaries for 1728-1800.
         The Maryland Gazette was published in Annapolis.

23.23   "Marriages and Deaths from the Baltimore Sun, 1845." Maryland Genealogical
         Bulletin 19 (1948): 13-16.

23.24   Marshall, Nellie M. Additional Tombstone Records of Dorchester County,
         MD. St. Michaels, Md.: R. B. Clark, 1982.

23.25   ------. Tombstone Records of Dorchester County, Maryland, 1678-1964.
         Cambridge: Dorchester County Historical Society, 1965.

23.26   *Martin, George A. "Biographical Notes from the Maryland Gazette,
         1800-1821." Maryland Historical Magazine 42 (1947): 160-83. Includes
         obituaries. The Maryland Gazette was published in Annapolis.

23.27   Maryland's Garrett County Graves. Compiled by Youghiogheny Glades
         Chapter, National Society of the Daughters of the American Revolution,
         Oakland, Maryland. Parsons, W.Va.: McClain Printing Co., 1987.

23.28   Memoirs of the Dead, and Tomb's Remembrancer. Baltimore: Printed for the
         Editors, 1806. Contains epitaphs from Maryland cemeteries, mainly in
         Baltimore, and obituaries from the American, Federal Gazette, Evening
         Post, and Telegraphe. The introduction contains an account of the

funeral parade in honor of Washington, January 1, 1800. Claims to be the first publication in the United States to list tombstone inscriptions.

23.29   *Niccum, Norman. "Newspaper Clippings, Frederick Town, Frederick Co., Md." (1803-31) National Genealogical Society Quarterly 25 (1937): 56-59.

23.30   O'Brien, Jerry, and Merle L. Gibson. Calvert Co., Maryland, Old Graveyards. Sunderland, Md.: Calvert County Genealogical Newsletter, 1986.

23.31   O'Brien, Mildred Bowen. Calvert Co., Maryland, Family Records, 1670-1929: Church and Newspaper Records, Tombstone Inscriptions, Family Bible Records. . . . Baltimore: Gateway Press, 1978. Marriages and deaths, 1876-88.

23.32   *"Preliminary Index to Death and Marriage Notices in the Baltimore American, 1799-1801." Bulletin of the Maryland Genealogical Society 17 (1976): 122-26.

23.33   Republican Banner, Williamsport, Md. Marriages and Deaths, 1830-1837, Washington County, Maryland. . . . College Park, Md.: n.p., 1962.

23.34   St. John's College, Annapolis, Md. Memoirs of Deceased Alumni of St. John's College. Read, by Appointment of the Association, August 6th, 1856. . . . Annapolis: R. F. Bonsall, Printer, 1856.

------. Memoirs of Deceased Alumni of St. John's College, Annapolis, Read by Appointment of the Association. . . . Baltimore: W. K. Boyle, Printer, 1868.

------. Memoirs of Deceased Alumni of St. John's College, Annapolis, Read on Commencement Day, July 31st, 1872. . . . Annapolis: n.p., 1872.

23.35   "Some Marriage and Death Notices, 1848." Maryland Genealogical Bulletin 13 (1942): 19-20. These notices are from Baltimore newspapers.

23.36   "Some Notes from the Federal Gazette, Baltimore, Md." Maryland Genealogical Bulletin 16 (1944): 12-13. Contains a very few death notices for 1803-4.

23.37   Stones and Bones: Cemetery Records of Prince George's County, Maryland. Edited by Jean A. Sargent. Bowie, Md.: Prince George's County Genealogical Society, 1984.

23.38   Wright, F. Edward. Abstracts of Marriages and Deaths Recorded in Caroline County Newspapers, 1830-1874. Puerto Rico: Wright, 1975.

23.39   ------. Caroline County Marriages-Births-Deaths, 1850-1880: Abstracts of Newspapers, Federal Mortality Schedules, and Court Records. Silver Spring, Md.: Family Line, 1981.

23.40   ------. Maryland Eastern Shore Newspaper Abstracts. 8 vols. Silver Spring, Md.: Family Line, 1981. v. 1. 1790-1805; v. 2. 1806-12; v. 3.

1813-18; v. 4. 1819-24; v. 5. Northern counties, 1825-29; v. 6. Southern counties, 1825-29; v. 7. Northern counties, 1830-34; v. 8. Southern counties, 1830-34.

23.41   ------. <u>Newspaper Abstracts of Cecil and Harford Counties, 1822-1830</u>. Silver Spring, Md.: Family Line Publications, 1984.

23.42   ------. <u>Revised Index to Maryland Eastern Shore Newspaper Abstracts: Southern Counties, 1830-1834, Volume 8</u>. Silver Spring, Md., n.d.

23.43   ------. <u>Western Maryland Newspaper Abstracts: Compilation of Items Taken from the Available Newspapers of Hagerstown and Frederick, Maryland</u>. 2 vols. Silver Spring, Md.: Family Line Publications, 1985. v. 1. 1786-1798; v. 2. 1799-1805.

24. MASSACHUSETTS

24.1   Allen, Orrin Peer. Inscriptions from the Two Ancient Cemeteries of Palmer, Mass. [Palmer, Mass.]: Cemetery Commissioners, 1902. Covers the period 1729-1901.

24.2   "American Traveler (sic), October 31, 1834." Bulletin of the Sons of the Revolution, California Society 9, no. 4 (1932): 10. Contains a few death notices from the American Traveller, published in Boston.

24.3   "American Traveler (sic) of March 4, 1834, Boston, Mass." Bulletin of the Sons of the Revolution, California Society 9, no. 4 (1932): 6.

24.4   Amherst College, Amherst, Mass. Obituary Record of Graduates for the Academical Year Ending 1868, '70, '72, '74-1904, 1906-13. Amherst, Mass., 1868-.

24.5   Baker, Charlotte Alice, and Emma L. Coleman. Epitaphs in the Old Burying-Ground at Deerfield, Mass. Deerfield, Mass.: Pocumtuck Valley Memorial Association, 1924.

24.6   Baldwin, Thomas W. "The Drury Death Book." New England Historical and Genealogical Register 65 (1911): 356-66. Consists of a record of deaths in Natick, Framingham, Sudbury, Newton, Needham, and nearby Massachusetts towns from 1757 to 1803.

24.7   "Berkshire Star" Vital Records 1817-1849 and Index. Rollin H. Cooke Collection. Filmed by the Genealogical Society, Pittsfield, Massachusetts, 1961. USIGS The Berkshire Star was published in Pittsfield.

24.8   Blodgette, George Brainard. Inscriptions from the Old Cemetery in Rowley, Mass. Salem, Mass.: Salem Press, 1893.

24.9   Bowen, Nathan. "Extracts from Interleaved Almanacs of Nathan Bowen, Marblehead, 1742-1799." Historical Collections of the Essex Institute 91 (1955): 163-90. Entries relate to weather, births and deaths, marriages. After Nathan Bowen's death, the record was continued by his descen-dants.

24.10   Bowman, George Ernest. Gravestone Records in the Ancient Cemetery and the Woodside Cemetery, Yarmouth, Massachusetts: From Literal Copies of the Inscriptions Made at the Expense of Thomas W. Thatcher and Stanley W. Smith. Boston: Massachusetts Society of Mayflower Descendants at the Charge of the Cape Cod Town Record Fund, 1906.

24.11   Bridgman, Thomas. Epitaphs from Copp's Hill Burial Ground, Boston. Boston: J. Munroe and Co., 1851.

24.12   ------. Inscriptions on the Grave Stones in the Grave Yards of North-ampton, and of Other Towns in the Valley of the Connecticut, As Springfield, Amherst, Hadley, Hatfield, Deerfield. . . . Northampton, Mass.: Hopkins, Bridgman and Co., 1850.

24.13   ------. Memorials of the Dead in Boston; Containing Exact Transcripts of Inscriptions on the Sepulchral Monuments in the King's Chapel Burial Ground, in the City of Boston. . . . Boston: B. B. Mussey, 1853.

24.14   ------. The Pilgrims of Boston and Their Descendants: With an Introduction by Hon. Edward Everett, LL.D.; also, Inscriptions from the Monuments in the Granary Burial Ground Tremont Street. New York: Appleton; Boston: Phillips, Sampson and Co., 1856.

24.15   Brown, Francis Henry. Lexington Epitaphs. A Copy of Epitaphs in the Old Burying-Grounds of Lexington, Massachusetts. [Lexington, Mass.: Lexington Historical Society]; Boston: Spatula Press, 1905.

24.16   Buckland, Massachusetts. Vital Records of Buckland, Massachusetts, to the End of the Year 1849. Salem, Mass.: Essex Institute, 1934. Cites death notices in the Greenfield Gazette and Courier.

24.17   Catholic Church. The Solemn Obsequies, As Performed by the Reverend Clergy for a Brother Priest, with a Necrology of the Priests of Boston. Boston: Propagation of the Faith Press, 1943.

24.18   Clarke, George Kuhn. Epitaphs from Graveyards in Wellesley (Formerly West Needham), North Natick and Saint Mary's Churchyard in Newton Lower Falls, Massachusetts. Boston: T. R. Marvin, 1900.

24.19   Codman, Ogden. Gravestone Inscriptions and Records of Tomb Burials in the Central Burying Ground, Boston Common, and Inscriptions in the South Burying Ground, Boston. Salem, Mass.: Essex Institute, 1917.

24.20   ------. Gravestone Inscriptions and Records of Tomb Burials in the Granary Burying Ground, Boston, Mass. Salem, Mass.: Essex Institute, 1918.

24.21   ------. Index of Obituaries in Boston Newspapers, 1704-1800; Boston: G. K. Hall, 1968. 3 vols. Contains information from seven 18th century newspapers published in the Boston area. AJ12

24.22   Colrain, Mass. Vital Records of Colrain, Massachusetts, to the End of the Year 1849. Salem, Mass.: Essex Institute, 1934. Cites death notices in the Greenfield Gazette and Courier.

24.23   Cutter, William Richard, and Edward F. Johnson. Transcript of Epitaphs in Woburn First and Second Burial Grounds: Chronologically Arranged with Brief Illustrative Notes. [Woburn, Mass.], 1890.

24.24   Dall, Caroline Wells (Healy), 1822-1912. NUC MS 61-1782. A prolific writer of obituary tributes who lived in Boston and Washington, D.C. This manuscript collection is held by Radcliffe College Library, Women's Archives (A-72).

24.25   Damon, Jude. Deaths in Truro, Cape Cod, 1786-1826. Taken from the Diary of Rev. Jude Damon. [Salem, Mass.]: Salem Press, 1891.

24. MASSACHUSETTS

24.26 Daughters of the American Revolution. Massachusetts. Genealogical Collections. Washington, D.C.: Daughters of the American Revolution, Filmed by the Genealogical Society, 1971. USIGS This collection contains some newspaper vital statistics: Boston deaths reported in the Boston Recorder and Telegraph, 1827-28; Deaths published in the Quincy Patriot, 1837-62; Boston vital records from the Watchman and Reflector, 1865-66; Marlboro newspaper vital statistics from the Enterprise, 1889-1900; Vital records from the Melrose Journal, 1870-78, and the Melrose Record, 1875-76; Springfield deaths, marriages and ordinations from the Hampden Federalist, 1819-20.

24.27 Dodge, Reuben Rawson. Inscriptions in the Cemeteries of Sutton, Massachusetts. Worcester, Mass.: Press of Charles Hamilton, 1898.

24.28 Doten, Beryle C. The Old Cemetery. Hampden, Mass.: Historical Society of the Town of Hampden, 1978.

24.29 ------. Prospect Hill Cemetery, St. Mary's Cemetery. Hampden, Mass.: Historical Society of the Town of Hampden, 1984.

24.30 Drew, Benjamin. Burial Hill, Plymouth, Massachusetts: Its Monuments and Gravestones Numbered and Briefly Described, and the Inscriptions and Epitaphs Thereon Carefully Copied. Plymouth, Mass.: D. W. Andrews, [1894].

24.31 Drew, Thomas Bradford. Death Records from the Ancient Burial Ground at Kingston, Massachusetts. Boston: Massachusetts Society of Mayflower Descendants, 1905. Reprinted from vol. 7 of the Mayflower Descendant.

24.32 Durfee, Calvin. Williams Obituary Report, 1865-1875. North Adams, Mass.: J. T. Robinson, 1875.

24.33 Dyer, John Bensiah. Inscriptions from Gravestones in the Old North Cemetery, Truro, Mass. from 1713 to 1840. Provincetown, Mass.: Advocate Press, 1897.

24.34 Fiske, Arthur D. Cemetery Records of Leyden, Franklin County, Mass. to 1875: To Which is Appended a List of the Names of the Heads of Families Listed in the 1810 and 1820 Census Records. Seattle, Wash.: [Fiske], 1964.

24.35 ------. Cemetery Records of Wilbraham, Hampden County, Massachusetts to 1865. Seattle, Wash.: [Fiske], 1964.

24.36 ------. Cummings, Massachusetts [Cemetery Records]. [Seattle, Wash.: Seattle Genealogical Society, n.d.].

24.37 Flavell, Carol Willsey. "Death and Marriage Notices from the Christian Watchman." (Boston, 1819) National Genealogical Society Quarterly 65 (1977): 185-94.

24.38   Green, Samuel Abbott. <u>Epitaphs from the Old Burying Ground in Groton,</u> <u>Massachusetts</u>. Boston: Little, Brown, and Co., 1878.

24.39   ------. <u>Groton Historical Series: A Collection of Papers Relating to the</u> <u>History of the Town of Groton, Massachusetts</u>. 4 vols. Groton, Mass.: n.p., 1887-99. Volumes 2 and 4 contain obituary notices taken from the <u>New England Historical and Genealogical Register</u> for deceased members of the New England Historic Genealogical Society who had connections with the town of Groton. Volumes 2 and 3 contain death notices from newspapers for persons connected with Groton, and volume 2 also contains obituaries of Harvard, Amherst and Dartmouth graduates who had connections with Groton. Volume 4 contains obituaries taken from the annual necrology of alumni of Andover Theological Seminary of persons connected with Groton.

24.40   Greenwod, Charles Curtis. <u>Epitaphs from the Old Burying Ground,</u> <u>Needham, Massachusetts</u>. Dedham, Mass.: H. H. McQuillen, 1898. Reprinted from the <u>Dedham Historical Register</u>.

24.41   Hanover, Mass. First Congregational Church. <u>History and Records of the</u> <u>First Congregational Church, Hanover, Mass., 1727-1865, and Inscriptions</u> <u>from the Headstones and Tombs in the Cemetery at Centre Hanover,</u> <u>Mass., 1727-1894</u>. . . . Boston: W. Spooner, 1895.

24.42   Harris, William Thaddeus. <u>Epitaphs from the Old Burying Ground in</u> <u>Cambridge</u>. Cambridge, Mass.: J. Owen, 1845.

24.43   ------. <u>Epitaphs from the Old Burying Ground in Watertown</u>. Boston, 1869.

24.44   Harvard University. Harvard Alumni Association. <u>The Necrology of Harvard</u> <u>College, 1869-1872</u>. Cambridge, Mass.: J. Wilson and Son, 1872.

24.45   Hayward, Elizabeth. <u>Soldiers and Patriots of the American Revolution Whose</u> <u>Deaths Were Reported in "Boston Recorder and Telegraph," 1827 and</u> <u>1828</u>. N.p. 1944.

24.46   Historical Records Survey. Massachusetts. <u>Index to Local News in the</u> <u>"Hampshire Gazette," 1786-1937</u>. 3 vols. Boston: Historical Records Survey, 1939. v. 3. Personal Section, cites obituaries and death notices. The <u>Hampshire Gazette</u> was published in Northampton.

24.47   Hixon, Herbert N. <u>Epitaphs from the Old Burying Ground, West Medway</u>. Dedham, Mass., 1900. Reprinted from the <u>Dedham Historical Register</u>.

24.48   <u>Index to Lowell Newspapers, 1849-1940</u>. Waltham, Mass.: Graphic Microfilm, 197-. Microfilm. Microreproduction prepared by the Lowell Public Library. reel 2. Obituaries--War, 1914-18.

24.49   Johnson, Arthur Warren. <u>Memento Mori . . . Being an Accurate</u> <u>Transcription of the Tomb-stones, Monuments, Foot-stones, and Other</u> <u>Memorials in the Ancient Old Burial Yard in the Town of Ipswich,</u>

County of Essex, Massachusetts, from Its Beginnings in the Year Anno. Domi. 1634 to the Present Day. . . . Ipswich, Mass.: Ipswich Historical Society, 1935.

24.50   Kingman, Bradford. Epitaphs from Burial Hill, Plymouth, Massachusetts, from 1657 to 1892: With Biographical and Historical Notes. 1892. Reprint. Baltimore: Genealogical Publishing Co., 1977.

24.51   Lancaster, Mass. The Birth, Marriage, and Death Register, Church Records and Epitaphs of Lancaster, Massachusetts, 1643-1850. Edited by Henry S. Nourse. Lancaster, Mass.: W. J. Coulter, 1890.

24.52   Latham, Williams. Epitaphs in Old Bridgewater, Massachusetts: Illustrated with Plans and Views. Bridgewater, Mass.: Henry T. Pratt, Printer, 1882.

24.53   Lee, Harvey. "Abstractions from Waverly Magazine, 1863-64." Genealogical Reference Builders Newsletter 10, no. 3 (1976): 56-60. The Waverly Magazine was published in Boston.

24.54   McCoy, Norma E. "Newspaper Record; the Boston Recorder, Vital Records, Thursday, November 23, 1843." Searcher (Southern California Genealogical Society) 4 (1967): 130-31.

24.55   "Marriages and Deaths in Boston, February, 1862." Genealogist's Post 4 (1967): 11-12.

24.56   "Mary Endicott's Diary." Salem Press Historical and Genealogical Record 2 (1891-92): 111-22. Includes death information for many Essex county citizens for the years 1816-71.

24.57   Massachusetts Historical Society, Boston. Proceedings, v. 1-20, 1791/1835-1882/83. 2d series, v. 1-20, 1884/85-1906/7. 3d series, v. 41-, 1907/8-. Boston: Massachusetts Historical Society, 1859-. Obituaries are cited in its indexes.

24.58   Mayo, Charles Edwin. Mortuary Record from the Gravestones in the Old Burial Ground in Brewster, Massachusetts. . . . Yarmouth, Mass.: Register Publishing Co., 1898.

24.59   Methuen Historical Society. Ye Catalog of Epitaphs from Ye Old Burying Ground on Meeting-house Hill in Methuen, Massachusetts. Edited by Charles W. Mann. Methuen, Mass.: Press of the Methuen Transcript Co., 1897.

24.60   Milton Cemetery: A Catalogue of the Proprietors of Lots, Together with a Record of Ancient Inscriptions on All Tablets in the Cemetery Prior to and Including A.D. 1800: A.D. 1687-A.D. 1800. Boston: D. Clapp and Son, Printers, 1883.

24.61   Montague, Mass. Vital Records of Montague, Massachusetts to the End of the Year 1849. Salem, Mass.: Essex Institute, 1934. Cites deaths in the Greenfield Gazette and Courier.

24.62   Monumental Inscriptions in the Old Cemetery at Rutland, Worcester County, Mass.: "Laid Out" June 7, 1717. Edited by David Everett Phillips. Columbus, Ohio: "Old Northwest" Genealogical Society, 1902.

24.63   Moulton, John T. Inscriptions from the Old Burying Ground at Saugus Centre. N.p. 1888? Reprinted from the Historical Collections of the Essex Institute.

24.64   Nason, Elias. A History of the Town of Dunstable, Massachusetts, from Its Earliest Settlement to the Year of Our Lord 1873. Boston: A. Mudge, 1877. Contains inscriptions from the various cemeteries, pp. 228-68.

24.65   New Bedford, Masss. Vital Records of New Bedford, Massachusetts to the Year 1850. . . . Boston: New England Historic and Genealogical Society, 1932. Contains a few death notices from New Bedford newspapers.

24.66   New Salem, Mass. Vital Records of New Salem, Massachusetts to the Year 1849. Salem, Mass.: Essex Institute, 1927. Contains references to newspaper records of deaths in the Greenfield Gazette and Courier, Columbian Centinel, Boston Advertiser, Salem Gazette, and the Massachusetts Spy.

24.67   *"Newspaper Items Relating to Essex County." Historical Collections of the Essex Institute 42 (1906): 214-16.

24.68   Nourse, Henry Stedman. History of the Town of Harvard, Massachusetts. Harvard: W. Hapgood, 1894. Includes epitaphs in the Harvard burial grounds with dates prior to 1800.

24.69   The Old South Hadley Burial Ground, 1976. . . . South Hadley, Mass.: South Hadley Historical Society, 1976. An alphabetical index of names on markers.

24.70   Palmer, Joseph. Necrology of Alumni of Harvard College, 1851/52 to 1862/63. Boston: J. Wilson and Son, 1864.

24.71   Pemberton, Thomas Obituary Notices from the "Boston Gazette," 1723 to 1743. 2 vols. MSS. MHi

24.72   Pittsfield Sun, Pittsfield, Mass. Analytical Index to the "Pittsfield Sun" from 1800 to 1905. Pittsfield, Mass.: n.p., n.d.

24.73   Provincetown, Massachusetts, Cemetery Inscriptions. Compiled by Lurana Higgins Cook. Bowie, Md.: Heritage Books, 1980.

24.74   Pugh, Mary. Marriage Notices and Death Notices, 1852-1853, from Notices at Boston, Massachusetts. N.p.: Pugh, 1976. Does not give name of the newspapers from which the death notices are taken.

24.75   Pulsifer, David. Inscriptions from the Burying-grounds in Salem, Massachusetts. Boston: Press of James Loring, 1837.

24. MASSACHUSETTS

24.76   *"Record of Deaths in Boston and Vicinity, 1799-1815." New England Historical and Genealogical Register 77 (1923): 227-36.

24.77   Rice, Franklin Pierce. Marlborough, Massachusetts, Burial Ground Inscriptions: Old Common, Spring Hill, and Brigham Cemeteries. Worcester, Mass.: F. P. Rice, 1908.

24.78   ------. Paxton, Massachusetts, Burial Ground Inscriptions: to the End of the Year 1849. Worcester, Mass.: F. P. Rice, 1906.

24.79   Slafter, Carlos. Epitaphs in the Old Burial Place, Dedham, Mass. 1888. Reprint. Bowie, Md.: Heritage Books, 1986.

24.80   Springfield Republican, Springfield, Mass. Index to the "Springfield Daily and Sunday Republican." Springfield, Mass.: Republican Co., n.d. For the years 1899-1903.

24.81   Stevens, Cj. The "Massachusetts Magazine" Marriage and Death Notices, 1789-1796. New Orleans: Polyanthos, 1978. (American Periodicals: 18th Century)

24.82   Swansea, Mass. Swansea, Mass., Vital Records; Mounted Clippings from the "Boston Evening Transcript," June 1, 1938 to April 8, 1939. (Incomplete) Boston: n.p., 1938-39. Index to records of eighteenth century births, marriages and deaths published in installments, beginning 18 May 1938.

24.83   Townsend, Charles D., and Edna W. Townsend. Border Town Cemeteries of Massachusetts. West Hartford, Conn.: Chedwato Service, [1953].

24.84   "Vital Records from the Diary of Joseph Goodhue of Newbury, 1742-1763." Historical Collections of the Essex Institute 67 (1931): 401-7.

24.85   Vital Statistics of Berkshire County from the "Western Star" 1789-1806; the "Berkshire Star" 1815-1828 and the "Berkshire Star and County Republican" 1828. Filmed by the Genealogical Society, Pittsfield, Mass., 1961. USIGS

24.86   Waters, Wilson. History of Chelmsford, Massachusetts. Lowell, Mass.: Courier-Citizen, 1917. Contains a list of interments in Forefathers' burying ground, 721-53.

24.87   Whitmore, William Henry. The Graveyards of Boston; First Volume, Copp's Hill Epitaphs. Albany, N.Y.: Munsell, 1878.

24.88   Wilcox, Dorvil Miller. Gravestone Inscriptions, Lee, Mass.: Including All Extant of the Quarter Century, 1801-1825, Carefully Reproduced. Lee, Mass.: Press of the Valley Gleaner, 1901.

24.89   ------. Gravestone Inscriptions, Lee Mass., Including All Extant of the Quarter Century, 1826-1850, Carefully Reproduced. Lee, Mass.: Press of the Berkshire Gleaner, 1910.

24.90   Williams College. Alumni. <u>Obituary Record of Donors and Alumni of</u>
         <u>Williams College, 1882-3; Alumni Meeting, July 3, 1883</u> . . . .
         Williamstown, Mass.: n.p., n.d. The College also published obituaries of
         alumni in its <u>Bulletin</u>.

24.91   Williston, Josiah. "Extracts from the Diary of Josiah Williston of Boston,
         1808-1184." <u>New England Historical and Genealogical Register</u> 65 (1911):
         366-71.

24.92   Woburn, Masss. <u>Woburn Records of Births, Deaths, Marriages</u>. Woburn,
         Mass.: n.p., 1916. The Appendix lists deaths published in the <u>Woburn</u>
         <u>Journal</u> before 1891 and not found on the city records.

24.93   Wood, Alfred. <u>Records of Deaths, Middleboro, Massachusetts</u>. Boston:
         Genealogical Society of Mayflower Descendants, 1947. Some of the death
         records are taken from the <u>Namasket Gazette</u>, the <u>New Bedford Mercury</u>,
         <u>New Bedford Standard</u>, <u>Beverley Citizen</u>, <u>Boston Post</u>, <u>Boston Journal</u>, and
         <u>Boston Courier</u> for the 1850s and 1860s.

24.94   Woodbury, Louis Augustus. <u>Inscriptions from the Old Cemetery in Grove-</u>
         <u>land, Mass (Formerly East Bradford)</u>. Groveland, Mass., 1895.

24.95   Woodward, Harlow Elliott. <u>Epitaphs from the Old Burying Ground in</u>
         <u>Dorchester, Massachusetts</u>. Boston Highlands, Mass., 1869.

24.96   Worcester Historical Society, Worcester, Mass. <u>Inscriptions from the Old</u>
         <u>Burial Grounds in Worcester, Massachusetts, from 1727 to 1859: With</u>
         <u>Biographical and Historical Notes</u>. Worcester: Worcester Society of
         Antiquity, 1878-79. Microfiche. Louisville, Ky.: Lost Cause Press, 1969.
         The epitaphs in the old burial ground on the common were copied by W.
         S. Barton in 1846 and published in 1848. His copy as finally revised in
         1875 is given here. The epitaphs from the Mechanic street ground were
         copied by a committee of the Society consisting of E. B. Crane, A. A.
         Lovell, and F. P. Rice, who also supplied the notes.

25. MICHIGAN

25.1 Acheson, Donald R. "Death Records from the <u>Genesee Whig</u>, 1850-51." <u>Flint Genealogical Quarterly</u> 9 (1967): 25. The <u>Genesee Whig</u> was published in Flint.

25.2 ------. "Personal Items from the <u>Wolverine Citizen</u>, Flint, Michigan, 1862." <u>Flint Genealogical Quarterly</u> 11 (1969): 20-21.

25.3 Allegan County Pioneer Society. <u>Record of Members from 1876-1902</u>. . . . Lansing, Mich.: Michigan State Library, 1968. Includes obituaries of Allegan county.

25.4 *Barr, Ruth Feller. "Notes from Obituaries in the <u>Flushing Observer</u>." <u>Flint Genealogical Quarterly</u> 17 (1975): 82-83. For Genesee county, 1888-1932.

25.5 Beavis, Marjoria Estella. <u>Inscriptions in Bell Branch and Mount Hazel Cemeteries, Redford Township, Detroit, Wayne County, Michigan</u>. . . . Detroit, Mich., 1939.

25.6 <u>Bloomdale Cemetery, Trenton, Michigan</u>. Lincoln Park, Mich.: Downriver Genealogical Society, 1985.

25.7 Bowen, Harriet Cole. <u>Gravestone Records of Lenawee County, Michigan</u>. 5 vols. Adrian, Mich.: Daughters of the American Revolution of Adrian, 1935-43.

25.8 <u>Broken Ties, the Scrapbooks of Bessie Townsend: Obituaries of Central Michigan Pioneers</u>. Compiled by Fran Townsend Ewers. Owensboro, Ky.: McDowell Publication, 1981.

25.9 <u>Byron Cemetery, Burns Twp., Shiawassee Co., Byron, Michigan</u>. Compiled by Mrs. Frances Herber Hazelton, and Mrs. Katharine Goodnoe Adams. [Vernon? Mich.: F. H. Hazelton?, 1985].

25.10 <u>The Cemeteries of Overisel Township, Allegan County, Michigan: Old Overisel, Oakland, Diamond Springs, New Overisel, Bentheim</u>. Compiled by Amy Slotman Jansen. Holland, Mich.: Herrick Public Library, 1980.

25.11 <u>Cemetery Inscriptions and Records Branch County, Michigan</u>. 3 vols. Coldwater, Mich.: Branch County Genealogical Society, 1982-85. v. 1. Rural, 1837-1981; v. 2. Lakeview Cemetery, Quincy, 1837-1983; v. 3. Bronson Cemetery, Bronson, Michigan, 1839-1985.

25.12 <u>Cemetery Inscriptions of Saline Township, Washtenaw County, Michigan</u>. Ann Arbor, Mich.: Genealogical Society of Washtenaw County, Michigan, 1985.

25.13 <u>Cemetery Records of Galien Township in Berrien County, Michigan</u>. St. Joseph, Mich.: Genealogical Association of Southwestern Michigan, 1984.

25.14 <u>Cemetery Records of Muskegon Co., Mich</u>. 4 vols. Muskegon, Mich.: Muskegon County Genealogical Society, 1983.

25. MICHIGAN

25.15 Charboneau, Milton. Greenwood and Mount Olivet Cemeteries, Fowlerville, Michigan. Howell, Mich.: Livingston County Genealogical Society, 1985.

25.16 Cowles, Jane A., Melva Wilbur, and Paul Wilbur. Condensed Transcripts of Obituaries in the Region of Southeast Isabella County, Michigan, and Surrounding Areas. Owensboro, Ky.: McDowell Publications, 1980.

25.17 Daughters of the American Revolution. Michigan. Genealogical Collection. Washington, D.C.: Daughters of the American Revolution, n.d. Microfilm. Filmed for the Genealogical Society, 1971. USIGS Contains obituaries for Gratiot county, 1884-1924, Shiawassee county, 1887-1913, Clinton county.

25.18 Detroit Free Press. Vital Records from the "Detroit Free Press . . . 1931-1868. 17 vols. Lansing, Mich.: Michigan State Library, 1939. USIGS

25.19 Detroit News. Newspaper Index. Wooster, Ohio: Bell and Howell Co., 1976-. Monthly with annual cumulations.

25.20 Detroit Tribune. Scrapbook of Clippings from the Genealogical and Historical Department of the "Detroit Saturday Tribune," Sept. 3 - Dec. 10, 1904. Detroit, 1904. In addition to information about particular families it contains death notices from the Detroit Gazette, 1821-22.

25.21 Dexter, H. O. "Death Reports from the Weekly Observer of Fentonville, Michigan, 1853-1855." Flint Genealogical Quarterly 19 (1977): 130-32.

25.22 DeZeeuw, Donald J. Death and Marriage Items Abstracted from the "Lansing State Republican," 1861-1871. . . . Lansing, Mich.: Mid-Michigan Genealogical Society, 1978.

25.23 DeZeeuw, Donald J., and Fern Lawhead DeZeeuw. Cemetery Inscriptions and Records of Carmel Township, Eaton County, Michigan. Lansing, Mich.: Mid-Michigan Genealogical Society, 1976.

25.24 *Donelson, Emma E. "The Scrapbook of Emma E. Donelson." Detroit Society for Genealogical Research Magazine 16 (1952): 105-8. Contains obituaries for the area of Commerce, 1876-1917.

25.25 Druse, Joseph L. Death and Marriage Items Reported in the "Lansing State Republican," 1855-1860. Lansing, Mich.: Mid-Michigan Genealogical Society, 1968.

25.26 Eaton County Pioneer Society, Charlotte, Mich. Obituaries and Miscellaneous Records, 1874-1922. Microfilm. Filmed by the Genealogical Society at the University of Michigan Library, 1974. USIGS

25.27 Elliott, Sandra J. 1975 Kalkaska County, Michigan Obituary Gleanings from the "Kalkaskian and Leader" Newspaper, Published in Kalkaska, Michigan. N.p. 1975.

25. MICHIGAN

25.28 Ellis, J. Dee. "Genealogical Gleanings from Two Old Scrapbooks from Lapeer County, Michigan." Flint Genealogical Quarterly 11 (1969): 22-23. The scrapbooks were kept by Ina Abbott Rood for the period 1882-96, and contain obituaries.

25.29 Foster, Theodore F. Deaths and Marriages As Published in the "Signal of Liberty" of Ann Arbor, 1841-1847. N.p., 1931. Filmed by the Genealogical Society at the Michigan State Library, Lansing, Michigan, 1973. USIGS

25.30 ------. Deaths Mentioned in the "State Republican," April 28, 1855 to January 1, 1870. . . . Lansing, Mich.: n.p., 1932. Filmed by the Genealogical Society at the Michigan State Archives, 1973. USIGS

25.31 Fox, M. John. "Vital Records from the Family Favorite and Temperance Journal." Detroit Society for Genealogical Research Magazine 39 (1975): 21-22. (American Periodicals: 1800-1850). Family Favorite and Temperance Journal was published in Adrian, Michigan 1849-50.

25.32 Grand Rapids, Michigan. Public Library. Miscellaneous Soldiers Obituaries, 1890-1930. N.p., n.d. Filmed by the Genealogical Society, 1976. USIGS

25.33 Grimes, Marilla R. "Deaths and Marriages from an Oneida, N.Y. Newspaper Having Michigan References." Detroit Society for Genealogical Research Magazine 40 (1976): 163-66. These notices were taken from 15 Oneida County, New York newspapers, 1830s to 1870s.

25.34 Hazelton, Frances Herber. Greenwood Cemetery, Shiawassee Co., Vernon Twp., Vernon, Michigan. Vernon, Mich.: F. H. Hazelton, 1983.

25.35 ------. Oak Hill, Owosso Twp. and City of Owosso, Shiawassee Co., Michigan. Vernon, Mich.: F. L. Hazelton, 1986.

25.36 Hillcrest Memorial Gardens, Shiawassee Co., Owosso Twp., Michigan. Compiled by Mrs. Frances Herber Hazelton, and Mrs. Betty Clyde Critilos Blount. N.p. 1984.

25.37 Hilliard, Helen, James Hilliard, Joseph Wells, and Marjorie Wells. Cemetery Records of Coloma Township in Berrien County, Michigan. St. Joseph, Mich.: Genealogical Association of Southwestern Michigan, 1982.

25.38 Holland Genealogical Society. Committee on Cemetery Records and Research. Noordeloos Cemetery Recording. Edited by Adrian Trimpe. Holland, Mich.: Holland Genealogical Society, [1976].

25.39 ------. Pilgrim Home Cemetery Recording. Edited by Adrian Trimpe. Holland, Mich.: Holland Genealogical Society, 1977.

25.40 ------. Recordings of West Olive and Olive Township Cemeteries, Ottawa County, Michigan. [Holland, Mich.]: Holland Genealogical Society, 1982.

25. MICHIGAN

25.41   Index to Obituaries in the "Wolverine Citizen" and Other Old Flint Papers 1850-1876. Flint, Mich., n.d. Prepared at Flint by the Work Projects Administration.

25.42   Kent County, Michigan Vital Records and Obituaries, 1892-1913. . . . Lansing, Mich.: Michigan State Library, 1970.

25.43   *Kreage, Beulah Puffer. "Vital Records from the Detroit Gazette 1817-1830." Detroit Society for Genealogical Research Magazine 3 (1939): 14-15.

25.44   *Lambert, Marguerite N. "Washtenaw County, Michigan, Newspaper Death Notices, 1829-1867." Detroit Society for Genealogical Research Magazine 38 (1974): 23-28.

25.45   Liberty Township Historical Society. Jackson County, Michigan, Liberty Township Burials, 1838-1975. Edited by Paul R. Peck. [Clark Lake, Mich.: Liberty Town Press, 1976?].

25.46   Link, Muriel. Kent County, Michigan Vital Records and Obituaries, 1892-1913: Copied from Newspapers, Kent County, Michigan. [Lansing, Mich.: Michigan State Library], 1970.

25.47   ------. Obituaries Index 1933-1948. N.p., n.d. Filmed by the Genealogical Society at Grand Rapids, 1976. USIGS

25.48   Michigan Christian Herald. Michigan Vital Records from the "Michigan Christian Herald," 1850-1859. Microfilm. Filmed by the Genealogical Society at the Bentley Library, University of Michigan, 1974. USIGS The Michigan Christian Herald was a Baptist paper.

25.49   Michigan Historical Commission. Michigan Historical Collections, v. 1-40, 1874-1929. Lansing, Mich.: n.p., 1876-1929. Indexes. Contains obituaries for the members of the Michigan Pioneer and Historical Society.

25.50   [No entry].

25.51   Midland County, Michigan Cemetery Records: A Complete Listing of All Known Cemeteries, Including Sexton Records. Midland, Mich.: Midland Genealogical Society, 1981.

25.52   Mid-Michigan Genealogical Society. Cemetery Inscriptions and Records of Windsor Township, Eaton County, Michigan. Lansing, Mich.: Mid-Michigan Genealogical Society, 1976.

25.53   Milford Times. Items from "Milford Times" 1872-1875, Milford, Michigan. N.p., n.d. Microfilm. Filmed by the Genealogical Society at the State Library, Lansing, 1973. USIGS Includes deaths for 1873-1875.

25.54   Miller, Mrs. Lynn T. Death Records, Obituaries, 1884-1924, from the "Gratiot County Herald." Ithaca, Mich.: n.p., 1939.

25. MICHIGAN

25.55 Obituaries of the "Durand Express," 1985: Durand, Michigan, Shiwassee Co.
Compiled by Frances Herber Hazelton. Vernon, Mich.: H. Hazelton, 1986.

25.56 Obituaries Taken from the "Allegan Gazette," January 1, 1916 – April 1,
1922. Lansing, Mich.: Department of Education, Michigan State Library,
1968. Taken from the Collection of Mrs. Ruth Robbins Monteith; indexed
and typed by Emma A. Ervin.

25.57 Obituary Index for the "Birmingham Eccentric," Birmingham, Michigan,
Covering the Period, 1878-1977. Compiled by Merle Roninger, and Mrs.
R. George Ransford. Birmingham, Mich.: Baldwin Public Library, 1978.
Microform.

25.58 Obituary Index of the "Grand Haven Tribune," Ottawa County, Michigan,
1891-1905. Grand Haven, Mich.: C & S Enterprises, [1985?].

25.59 Perry, Merle. Genesee County, Michigan, Cemeteries. Flint, Mich.: Flint
Genealogical Society, 1983.

25.60 Recordings of Beaver Island Cemeteries: St. James Township, Holy Cross,
Also Beaver Island Death Records. Compiled by Irene Vander Meulen.
[Reidsma. Holland, Mich.: V. M. Reidsma], 1984.

25.61 Registers of Graves of Civil War Military Veterans Buried in Michigan.
[Lansing, Mich.: Michigan Civil War Centennial Observance Commission,
Graves Registration Committee, 1966?]. An alphabetical list of names
under each county, giving company/regiment, death date, cemetary and
location.

25.62 Reidsma, Irene Vander Meulen. New Groningen Cemetery Recording.
Holland, Mich.: Holland Genealogical Society, 1976.

25.63 ------. Recordings of East Saugatuck Cemetery (Fillmore Township, Allegan
County, Michigan), East Holland Cemetery (Fillmore Township, Allegan
County, Michigan), Gibson Cemetery (Laketown Township, Allegan
County, Michigan). Holland, Mich.: Holland Genealogical Society and the
Herrick Public Library, 1987.

25.64 ------. Recordings of the Cemeteries of Banks Twp., Antrim County, Mich.
and Bay View Cemetery, Central Lake Twp., Also Barnard Cemetery in
Marion Twp., Charlevoix County, Mich. [Holland, Mich.]: Reidsma, 1978.

25.65 Reidsma, Irene Vander Meulen, Vera Mulder Flight, Beulah Peck Plakke.
North Holland Local Cemetery Recording. Edited by Adrian Trimpe.
Holland, Mich.: Holland Genealogical Society, 1976.

25.66 ------. Recordings of Old Vriesland Cemetery and New Vriesland Cemetery,
Zeeland Township, Ottawa County, Michigan. Zeeland, Mich.: Zeeland
Historical Society, 1984.

25. MICHIGAN

25.67   Resig, Victor. <u>Cemetery Records of Baroda Township in Berrien County, Michigan</u>. St. Joseph, Mich.: Genealogical Association of Southwestern Michigan, 1983. Reprinted from <u>The Pastfinder</u>, 1973.

25.68   Savage, David. <u>Cemetery Records of Bertrand Township in Berrien County, Michigan</u>. St. Joseph, Mich.: Genealogical Association of Southwestern Michigan, 1978.

25.69   ------. <u>Cemetery Records of Chikaming Township in Berrien County, Michigan</u>. [St. Joseph, Mich.]: Genealogical Association of Southwestern Michigan, [1982].

25.70   ------. <u>Cemetery Records of Lake Township in Berrien County, Michigan</u>. St. Joseph, Mich.: Genealogical Association of Southwestern Michigan, 1983.

25.71   ------. <u>Cemetery Records of New Buffalo Township in Berrien County, Michigan</u>. St. Joseph, Mich.: Genealogical Association of Southwestern Michigan, 1978.

25.72   Schaldenbrand, Peter J. <u>"Farmington Enterprise" Obituaries, August 1, 1964 to April 30, 1967</u>. N.p., n.d. Microfilm. USIGS

25.73   Seelhoff, Mildred, Richard Welch, and Lucille Couzynse. <u>New Haven Township Cemeteries, Shiawassee County, Michigan: New Haven Cemetery, West Haven Cemetery, Easton Cemetery</u>. Owosso, Mich.: Shiawassee County Genealogical Society, 1985.

25.74   Skinner, Lulu Carpenter. <u>Vital Statistics of Washtenaw County Taken from the Ypsilanti Commercial Newspapers 1876-1883</u>. [Ypsilanti, Mich.: Ypsilanti Chapter, Daughters of the American Revolution]. Also Microfilmed by the Genealogical Society at the State Library, Lansing, 1973. USIGS

25.75   "Some Michigan Items from Old Chautauqua County, New York Newspapers." <u>Detroit Society for Genealogical Research Magazine</u> 7 (1943): 44. One page only of a few marriage and death notices for the years 1823-60.

25.76   Southern Michigan Genealogical Society. <u>Hillsdale County, Michigan, Burials: As Identified by Marker or Record</u>. . . . Fort Wayne, Ind.: Fort Wayne Library, 1978.

25.77   Tekonsha News, Tekonsha, Michigan. <u>Obituaries 1860-1951</u>. N.p., n.d. Microfilm. Filmed by the Genealogical Society at the Mid-Michigan Genealogical Society, Lansing, 1975. USIGS

25.78   <u>Tombstone Inscriptions in Kalamazoo County, Michigan: Bicentennial Project</u>. 2 vols. Kalamazoo, Mich.: Kalamazoo Valley Genealogical Society, 1980.

25.79   <u>Tombstone Inscriptions of Mendon and Nottawa Townships, St. Joseph County, Michigan</u>. Compiled by James H. Stahl. N.p. 1973.

25. MICHIGAN

25.80   Tombstone Recordings of the Cemeteries on Mackinac Island, Michigan.
         Compiled by Irene Vander Meulen Reidsma. Holland, Mich.: I. V. M.
         Reidsma, 1982.

25.81   University of Michigan. Death Notices; Supplementary to General Catalogue
         of Officers and Students, 1837-1921 (September 1926--September 1927).
         University of Michigan, 1927. (Bulletin of the University of Michigan,
         v. 29)

25.82   Wier, Mrs. Victor. Cemetery Records: Bainbridge Township in Berrien
         County, Michigan. St. Joseph, Mich.: Genealogical Association of
         Southwestern Michigan, 1983. Reprinted from The Pastfinder, 1973.

25.83   Winchester Cemetery, Kent County, Mich. [Grand Rapids, Mich.: Sandra J.
         Elliott, 198-].

25.84   Woodhull Township Cemetery, Graham, Kay Family, Oak Plain and Corcoran,
         Shiawassee County, Michigan. [Vernon, Mich.: F. H. Hazelton, 1985].

26. MINNESOTA

26.1   Anoka County Historical Society. The Silent Cities: A Survey of Anoka
        County Cemeteries, Public, Private, and Abandoned. [Anoka, Minn.]:
        Anoka County Historical Society, [1977].

26.2   Arends, Mrs. Charles. Anoka County Newspapers: From Anoka County
        Newspapers, Marriage Records, 1863-1870; From Anoka County
        Newspapers, Death Records, 1863-1870. [Anoka, Minn.: Anoka County
        Genealogical Society, 1975?].

26.3   Cemeteries of Clay County, Minnesota. 4 vols. [Fargo, N.Dak.?]: Red River
        Valley Genealogy Society, 1983-84. v. 1. City of Moorhead; v. 2. North
        half (north of Highway 10); v. 3. South half (south of Highway 10), and
        city of Barnesville.

26.4   Cemeteries of Norman County, Minnesota. 3 vols. West Fargo, N.Dak.: Red
        River Valley Genealogy Society, [1985?]. v. 1. Ada Cemetery; v. 2.
        Norman County, east half (all cemeteries east of Highway 9); v. 3.
        Norman county, west half (all cemeteries west of Highway 9).

26.5   ChiaraValle, Mrs. Alex. "Early Hibbing Newspaper Abstracts." Northland
        Newsletter 6 (1974): 65-66. For July to Dec. 1844.

26.6   Dahlquist, Alfred J., and Barbara L. Dahlquist. The Grave Markers of
        Hennepin County, MN. Brooklyn Park, Minn.: Park Genealogical Book
        Co., 1981.

26.7   Gibbons, Clare, Nora Willprecht, and Mel Trieglaff. Cemetery Records,
        Ottertail County, Minnesota. 5 vols. Frazee, Minn.: G.T.W., 1975-78. v.
        1. Perham township; v. 2. Norwegian Grove and Pelican townships; v. 3.
        Erhards Grove and Trondhjem townships; v. 4. Elizabeth, Friberg, Oscar,
        and Carlisle townships; v. 5. Maplewood, Maine, Star Lake, Amor, Everts,
        and Dead Lake townships.

26.8   Grimes, Marrilla. "Genealogical Items from Oneida County, New York
        Newspapers Having a Minnesota Reference." Minnesota Genealogist 6
        (1975): 5-7. For 1854-69.

26.9   A Guide to Graves in Kandiyohi County Cemeteries. [Willmar? Minn.]:
        Kandiyohi County Historical Society, 1981.

26.9a   Index to Gravestones of Stearns County, Minnesota As of 1974-1976; Index to
        Gravestones of Sherburne County, Minnesota As of 1978; Index to
        Gravestones of Benton County, Minnesota As of 1975-1977. St. Cloud,
        Minn.: St. Cloud Area Genealogists, 1982.

26.10   Leslie, Earl C., and Laura L. Leslie. Cemetery Records of Crow Wing
        County, Minnesota. [Brainerd, Minn., 1982].

26.11   Minneapolis Tribune and Minneapolis Star Index. Minneapolis: Minneapolis
        Public Library and Information Center, 1971-.

26. MINNESOTA

26.12   Minnesota Cemeteries. Compiled and edited by the Red River Valley
         Genealogy Society. 17 vols. West Fargo, N.Dak.: The Society, 1983-.

26.13   Minnesota Historical Society. Collections, v. 1-17. St. Paul, Minn.:
         Minnesota Historical Society, 1850-1920. Obituaries of deceased members,
         1889-98, 8: 495-533; for 1898-1902, 9: 637-80; for 1901-4, 10: 867-76;
         for 1905-8, 12: 767-804; for 1909-14, 15: 753-848. In addition there are
         long memorial addresses on other prominent citizens.

26.14   Scrapbook of Obituaries of Pipestone, Rock, and Lac Qui Parle County
         Pioneers. N.p., n.d. MnHi

26.15   Some Early Deaths and Marriages from Anoka County, Minnesota News-
         papers. Anoka, Minn.: Anoka County Genealogy Society, n.d. For the
         years from 17 Oct. 1863 to Jan. 1871. WHi

26.16   Tombstone Trails, v. 1-, 1978-. Austin, Minn.: Mower County Genealogical
         Society, 1978-.

26.17   Wittenberg, Marie C. Cemeteries in Eden Prairie and Chanhassen Catholic
         Cemetery. Eden Prairie, Minn.: M. C. Wittenberg, 1987.

27. MISSISSIPPI

27.1 Biggs, Rayma, and Irene Barnes. <u>Cemeteries of Tishomingo County, Mississippi</u>. Iuka, Miss.: Biggs, 1979.

27.2 Burton-Cruber, Betty Ann. <u>Cemetery Markings, Itawamba County, Mississippi</u>. Amory, Miss.: Amory Advertiser, 1978.

27.3 <u>Cemeteries of North Panola County, Mississippi</u>. [Batesville, Miss.]: Panola Historical and Genealogical Society, 1980.

27.4 <u>Cemeteries of Prentiss County, Mississippi</u>. Compiled by Maureen Crow, and Bill Gurney. [Booneville, Miss., 1981].

27.5 Chase, Rolfe B. <u>Lowndes County, Mississippi Cemetery Records</u>. Columbus, Miss.: Lowndes County Department of Archives and History, 1979.

27.6 Daniel, H. H. <u>History of Jones County, Miss., Church and Cemetery, 1830-1915, Index to Land Grants</u>. [Bay Springs, Miss.: H. H. Daniel, 1979].

27.7 ------. <u>History of Wayne County, Miss. Churches and Cemetery Records, 1800's-1915</u>. Bay Springs, Miss.: H. H. Daniel, [1979?].

27.8 Evans, William Augustus. <u>Monroe County, Mississippi, Cemetery Records</u>. Columbus, Miss.: Lowndes County Dept. of Archives and History, 1980.

27.9 Fly, Jean. "Marriage and Death Notices in Natchez Newspapers, 1805-1840." <u>Journal of Mississippi History</u> 8 (1946): 163-226.

27.10 <u>Forrest Co., Mississippi, Tombstone Inscriptions (Western Part of Old Perry Co., Miss.)</u> Petal, Miss.: South Mississippi Genealogical Society, 1986.

27.11 Gillis, Irene S. <u>Grave Registrations of Union Soldiers Buried in the Mississippi National Cemeteries of Corinth, Natchez, and Vicksburg</u>. [Shreveport, La.]: I. S. Gillis, 1983.

27.12 Gurney, Bill, Bobby Mitchell, and David Pryor. <u>Cemeteries of Marshall County, Mississippi</u>. Ripley, Miss.: Old Timer Press, 1983.

27.13 Harrell, Laura D. S. "Marriage, Death and Estate Notices in Holly Springs Newspapers, 1838-1847." <u>Journal of Mississippi History</u> 9 (1947): 135-51.

27.14 Hobgood, Cecilia Nabors, and Ann Jones Clayton. <u>Cemetery Records of Lauderdale County, Mississippi</u>. N.p. 1971.

27.15 Holman, Josie Worthy. <u>Tomb Records of Winston County, Mississippi</u>. [Louisville? Miss., 1968].

27.16 Hughes, Thomas Proctor. <u>Alcorn County, Mississippi, Cemetery Records</u>. Compiled by Thomas P. Hughes, Jr., and Jewel B. Standefer. Memphis, [1971].

27. MISSISSIPPI

27.17   "Items from the Star of Pascagoula, Pascagoula, Mississippi." (1875-77) Deep
         South Genealogical Quarterly 5 (1967): 76-78.

27.18   Martini, Don. Tippah County Death Notices. 3 vols. Ripley, Miss.: Tippah
         County Historical Society, 1976-1980. v. 1. 1837-1914; v. 2. 1915-36;
         v. 3. 1937-50.

27.19   Martini, Don, and Bill Gurney. Cemeteries of Benton County, Mississippi.
         Ripley, Miss.: Old Timer Press, 1985.

27.20   ------. Cemeteries of Tippah County, Mississippi. Ripley, Miss.: Old Timer
         Press, 1980.

27.21   Martini, Don, and Tommy Lockhart. Cemeteries of Tippah County,
         Mississippi. Ripley, Miss.: Tippah County Historical Society, 1975.

27.22   Mississippi Cemetery and Bible Records, v. 1-, 1954-. Jackson, Miss.:
         Mississippi Genealogical Society, 1954-.

27.23   Mississippi Genealogical Society. Newspaper Notices of Mississippians:
         1820-1860. N.p.: Mississippi Genealogical Society, 1960. An index of
         marriage, death, and estate notices appearing in the newspapers of Hinds,
         Madison, Noxubee, and Yazoo counties. This material appeared serially
         in the Journal of Mississippi History, volumes 18-21, January 1956-July
         1959.

27.24   Mogan, J. Paul, and Kathryn Cole Mogan. Franklin County, Mississippi
         Cemeteries. Osyka, Miss.: J. P. Mogan, 1982.

27.25   Mogan, J. Paul, Jr., Kathryn Cole Mogan, and Glen Huff. Amite County,
         Mississippi Cemeteries. Osyka, Miss.: J. P. Mogan, 1982.

27.26   Oktibbeha County Genealogical Society. Cemetery Records of Oktibbeha
         County, Mississippi. Starkville, Miss.: The Society, 1969.

27.27   Parish, Ray, and June Sartin Parish. Cemetery Inscriptions, Pike County,
         Mississippi, 1750-1978. [Pascagoula, Miss.?]: Parish, 1979.

27.28   Parker, James W. Friendship Cemetery, Columbus, Mississippi, Tombstone
         Inscriptions and Burial Records. 2 vols. Columbus, Miss.: Lowndes
         County Department of Archives and History, 1979.

27.29   Payne, Caledonia Jackson. Old Greenville Cemetery, Greenville, Mississippi,
         1880-1982. Leland, Miss.: C. J. Payne, 1983.

27.30   Pickering, Mrs. Archie, and Mrs. Mart Rogers. Cemetery Census: Covington
         County, Mississippi and Surrounding Counties. N.p. 1976.

27.31   Rankin County, Mississippi Cemetery Records, 1824-1980. Brandon, Miss.:
         Rankin County Historical Society, 1981.

27. MISSISSIPPI

27.32   Richards, E. Q. <u>Abstracts of Death Notices from the "Macon Beacon"</u> <u>(Macon, Mississippi), 1871-1912</u>. N.p.: E. Q. Richards, [1982].

27.33   Sanders, Delores Pickering. <u>Remember Me: Complete Directory of Cemeteries</u> <u>(White) in Scott County, Mississippi</u>. Cullman, Ala.: Gregath Co., 1986.

27.34   Skipwith Historical and Genealogical Society. <u>Lafayette County, Mississippi</u> <u>Cemetery Records</u>. 2 vols. [Oxford, Miss.]: The Society, 1978-79. Includes all pertinent information from the tombstones.

27.35   Slade, Leonard L. <u>Lamar County Heritage</u>. Baltimore: Gateway Press, 1978. Includes cemetery records.

27.36   <u>South Panola County, Mississippi, Cemeteries and Addenda for Other</u> <u>Cemeteries of Panola County</u>. [Panola, Miss.]: Panola Historical and Genealogical Society, 1981.

27.37   Southern Telegram, Rodney, Miss. <u>Newspaper Notices from "Southern</u> <u>Telegram" Rodney (Jefferson County) Mississippi, July 1834-July 1837</u>. N.p., 1967. TxDa The <u>Southern Telegram</u> was superseded by the <u>Rodney Telegraph</u>.

27.38   Strickland, Ben, and Jean Strickland. <u>George County, Mississippi Cemetery</u> <u>Records</u>. 2 vols. Moss Point, Miss.: B. & J. Strickland, 1984.

27.39   Strickland, Jean, and Patricia N. Edwards. <u>Records of Wayne County,</u> <u>Mississippi: Cemetery Records</u>. 2 vols. Moss Point, Miss.: J. Strickland, 1987.

27.40   <u>Tombstone Inscriptions of Noxubee County, Mississippi: A Bi-centennial Work</u> <u>of the Noxubee County Historical Society</u>. [Mason, Miss.]: The Society, 1975.

27.41   <u>Union County, Mississippi, Cemetery Records</u>. [New Albany, Miss.: Ish-te-ho-to-pah Chapter of the Daughters of the American Revolution, 1980].

27.42   Wiltshire, Betty Couch. <u>Marriages and Deaths from Mississippi Newspapers</u>. Bowie, Md.: Heritage Books, 1987. For the years 1837-1863.

27.43   <u>Yalobusha County, Mississippi: Cemetery Records</u>. 4 vols. Coffeeville, Miss.: Yalobusha County Historical Society, 1979-80. v. 1. Western Yalobusha county; v. 2. Eastern Yalobusha county; v. 3. Northern section, Water Valley, Mississippi; v. 4. Oak Hill Cemetery, Water Valley, Mississippi.

28. MISSOURI

28.1   Abbott, Nobel G., and Betty Beason Ammerman. <u>Tombstone Inscriptions in Western Polk County, Missouri: Madison, Union, and Jackson Townships: 33 Cemeteries</u>. Stockton, Mo: N. G. Abbott; Springfield, Mo: B. B. Ammerman, 1978.

28.2   <u>Accumulated Obituaries from Harrison County, Missouri and Dewey County, Oklahoma, Circa 1910</u>. N.p. 1979. InFw

28.3   "<u>Atchison County Journal</u>," <u>Rockport, Missouri, August 30, 1879 to December 31, 1882</u>. Compiled by John A. Ostertag. St. Joseph, Mo.: Missouri River Heritage Association, [1983]. This is a compilation of birth, death and marriage records for these years.

28.4   <u>Atchison Township Cemeteries, Nodaway County, Missouri</u>. [Maryville, Mo.: Nodaway County Genealogical Society, 1983].

28.5   Beckerman, Rob. <u>Ste. Genevieve County Tombstone Inscriptions</u>. 2 vols. Ste. Genevieve, Mo.: R. Beckerman, 1982-84].

28.6   Belk, Colleen. <u>Dade County, Missouri Tombstone Inscriptions and Historical Miscellany</u>. Huntsville, Ark.: Century Enterprises, 1972.

28.7   ------. <u>Tombstone Inscriptions of Jasper County, Missouri</u>. 8 vols. Huntsville, Ark.: Century Enterprises, 1968-82.

28.8   Belk, Colleen, and Mary M. Curry. <u>Newton County, Missouri Tombstone Inscriptions</u>. Duenweg, Mo.: Belk, 1974-.

28.9   Bernard, Charles L. <u>Cemetery Directory of Vernon County, Missouri</u>. Nevada, Mo.: Vernon County Historical Society, 1979.

28.10   Brinkman, Loyd R, and Lula M. Graff Brinkman. <u>Brewer Monument Company Sketches of Deceased and Cemetery Where Interred, Years 1916-1941</u>. Glendale, Mo.: L. M. Graff Brinkman, [1984].

28.11   Brown, Mary M. <u>1901-1913 New Madrid County, Missouri Newspaper Abstracts</u>. New Madrid, Mo.: Brown and Hedgepeth, 1977.

28.12   Browning, Ruth E. <u>Genealogical Notes from the "Fountain & Journal" (Mt. Vernon, Missouri) 1876-1880</u>. Mount Vernon, Mo.: Lawrence County Historical Society, 1981. These files are on microfilm at the State Historical Society of Missouri, Columbia, Missouri.

28.13   ------. <u>Obituaries, Death Notices, Memorials from "Spring River Fountain," 1867-71; "Lawrence County Journal," 1872, 1873; "Fountain and Journal," 1874, 1875, Lawrence County, Missouri</u>. Searcy, Ark: Browning, 1976 USIGS.

28.14   Brunetti, Marty Helm. <u>Jackson County, Missouri, Cemeteries</u>. 2 vols. Odessa, Mo.: M. H. Brunetti, 1984-86.

28.15   ------. Tombstone Inscriptions of Lafayette County, Missouri. 6 vols.
Odessa, Mo.: Brunetti, 1974–83.

28.16   Buckner, Marjorie Pearce, and Hazel Jennings Myers. Cemetery Records,
Pleasant Hill Township, Cass County, Missouri: The Pleasant Hill
Cemetery, the Thomas Cemetery, the Smith Cemetery. Kansas City, Mo.:
American Family Records Association, 1980.

28.17   Burial Sites and Cemeteries of Everett Township, Cass County, Missouri.
Harrisonville, Mo.: Cass County Historical Society, [197-].

28.18   Butler County, Mo. Cemeteries. 2 vols. N.p.: Genealogical Society of Butler
County, 1977–1980.

28.19   Carter, Genevieve L. Tombstone Inscriptions of Northeast Pettis County,
Missouri. [Sedalia, Mo.], n.d.

28.20   Catholic Cemetery Inscriptions of Jefferson County, Missouri. St. Louis: St.
Louis Genealogical Society, [1985].

28.21   Cemeteries in Cole County, Missouri As Recorded in the 1930s. Jefferson
City, Mo.: Capital City Family Research, 1986.

28.22   Cemeteries of Oregon County, Missouri. Alton, Mo.: Oregon County
Genealogical Society, 1982.

28.23   Cemetery Census of Clay County, Missouri. Liberty, Mo.: Cemetery
Committee, Clay County Historical Society, 1983.

28.24   Cemetery Directory of Polk County, Missouri. Bolivar, Mo.: Historical
Society of Polk County, Missouri, 1979. Lists burial sites and birth and
death data for persons buried in Polk County, prior to 1974.

28.25   Cemetery Inscriptions of Salt Fork, Old Lamine, McMahan, Campbell and
Hoke Family Cemeteries. Gilliam, Mo.: Saline Sentiments, [198-].

28.26   Cemetery Inscriptions of Sullivan County, Missouri. Compiled by the
Daughters of the American Revolution, General John Sullivan Chapter,
Milan, Mo. 5 vols. Milan, Mo.: Daughters of the American Revolution,
1951–54.

28.27   Cemetery Records of Daviess County, Missouri. Copied by Gallatin Chapter
of the Daughters of the American Revolution, Gallatin, Missouri. 2 vols.
Chillicothe, Mo.: Elizabeth Prather Ellsberry, 196-.

28.28   Cemetery Records of Platte County, Missouri. Compiled by the Platte
County Historical Society. 2 vols. [Platte City, Mo., 1961–68].

28.29   Christiansen, E. J. Bates County, Missouri, Cemeteries, 1980. 2 vols.
Clinton, Mo.: The Printery, 1980.

28.30   Coppage, Maxim. "From Salisbury Press, Chariton County, Missouri, Deaths."
Kansas City Genealogist 8 (1967): 10. Includes death notices for 1877-78.

28.31   ------. "Kentucky Natives Who Died in Missouri." Kentucky Ancestors 3
(1967): 32-33. Contains a few abstracts from Columbia, Missouri
newspapers between the years 1879-97.

28.32   Couch, Robert, and May Barter Couch. Chariton County, Missouri
Cemeteries. 9 vols. [Marceline, Mo.]: R. Couch, 1985.

28.33   Cunningham, Mary Bean. Webster County, Missouri Cemetery Inscriptions.
Springfield, Mo.: M. B. Cunningham, 1980.

28.34   Dade County Historical Society (Mo.). Cemetery Records of Dade County,
Missouri. 17 vols. Greenfield, Mo.: The Society, 1972-79. v. 1.
Arcola-Hickory Grove Cemetery; v. 2. Weir Cemetery; v. 3. Stockton
Family Cemetery; v. 4 Ray Spring Cemetery; v. 5. Daughtrey Cemetery;
v. 6. Pennsboro Cemetery; v. 7. Rice Cemetery; v. 8. Wetzel Cemetery; v.
9. King's Point Cemetery; v. 10. Collins Cemetery; v. 11. Pleasant Grove
Cemetery, "Old Baptist"; v. 12. Pemberton Cemetery; v. 13. Hays
Cemetery; v. 14. Stockton Lake Cemetery; v. 15. Ruth Chapel Cemetery;
v. 16. Buchanan Cemetery; v. 17. Cedarville Cemetery.

28.35   Dallas County Historical Society. A Reading of Dallas County, Missouri
Cemeteries, 1834-1977. 3 vols. Buffalo, Mo.: The Society, 1979.

28.36   Daughters of the American Revolution. Missouri. Genealogical Collection.
Washington, D.C.: Reproduction System for the Genealogical Society, 1971.
Microfilm. USIGS Data from obituaries in the Memphis Reveille,
1890-92 is included.

28.37   ------. Kansas City Chapter. Vital Historical Records of Jackson County,
Missouri, 1826-1876. Kansas City, Mo., 1933-34. Includes family
burying grounds and early cemeteries of Jackson county.

28.38   ------. Nancy Hunter Chapter, Cape Girardeau. A Historic Record of
Lorimer Cemetery, Cape Girardeau, Missouri, 1820-1944. Chillicothe,
Mo.: E. P. Ellsberry, 1962.

28.39   ------. Rachel Donelson Chapter, Springfield. Cemeteries of Texas County,
Missouri. Springfield, Mo.: Daughters of the American Revolution, 1976.

28.40   DeKalb County Historical Society (Missouri). Cemetery Census, DeKalb
County. Maysville, Mo., [1972].

28.41   Dodge, Eugene. Cemetery Inscriptions of Scotland County, Missouri. 3 vols.
St. Louis: W. Dunlap, [1971].

28.42   Dunlap, Wilma Walker. Cemetery Inscriptions of Clark County, Missouri.
4 vols. St. Louis, 1973.

28.43   Edwards, Ruth, and Flo Malaney. <u>Laclede County, Missouri: Lebanon City Cemetery, 1857-1979, Calvary (Catholic) Cemetery</u>. [Lebanon, Mo.]: Laclede County Historical Society, 1983.

28.44   Ellis, Sharon. <u>Shannon Co., Mo. Cemeteries</u>. Imperial, Mo.: D. Hopper, 1983.

28.45   Ellsberry, Elizabeth Prather. <u>Cemetery Records for Barton County, Missouri</u>. Chillicothe, Mo.: Ellsberry, n.d. Includes Howe Cemetery, Milford; Iantha Cemetery, Iantha; and Oakton Cemetery, Oakton.

28.46   ------. <u>Cemetery Records of Bates County, Missouri</u>. 4 vols. Chillicothe, Mo.: Ellsberry, n.d.

28.47   ------. <u>Cemetery Records of Boone County, Missouri</u>. 7 vols. Chillicothe, Mo.: Ellsberry, [1963].

28.48   ------. <u>Cemetery Records of Caldwell County, Missouri</u>. Chillicothe, Mo.: Ellsberry, n.d.

28.49   ------. <u>Cemetery Records of Callaway County, Missouri</u>. 6 vols. Chillicothe, Mo., 1970.

28.50   ------. <u>Cemetery Records of Camden County, Missouri</u>. Chillicothe, Mo.: Ellsberry, n.d.

28.51   ------. <u>Cemetery Records of Cape Girardeau and Adjoining Counties in Missouri</u>. Chillicothe, Mo.: Ellsberry, 1962.

28.52   ------. <u>Cemetery Records of Carroll County, Missouri</u>. 4 vols. Chillicothe, Mo.: Ellsberry, 1962.

28.53   ------. <u>Cemetery Records of Cedar County Missouri</u>. Chillicothe, Mo.: Ellsberry, 1965.

28.54   ------. <u>Cemetery Records of Chariton County, Missouri</u>. Chillicothe, Mo., n.d.

28.55   ------. <u>Cemetery Records of Grundy County, Missouri</u>. 6 vols. Chillicothe, Mo.: Ellsberry, 1963.

28.56   ------. <u>Cemetery Records of Holt County, Missouri</u>. Chillicothe, Mo.: Ellsberry, 1968? The records are from Maple Grove, Oregon, Missouri.

28.57   ------. <u>Cemetery Records of Howard County, Missouri</u>. 5 vols. Chillicothe, Mo.: Ellsberry, 1963.

28.58   ------. <u>Cemetery Records of Linn County, Missouri</u>. 8 vols. Chillicothe, Mo., 1957-. v. 1. Northwestern Linn County; v. 2. Central Linn County; v. 3. Laclede, Meadville; v. 4. Rose Hill and St. Michael of Brookfield, Missouri: pt. 1. St. Michael, pt. 2. Rose Hill; v. 5. Marceline; v. 6-7. Southern Linn County; v. 8. North Salem and vicinity.

28.59   ------. Cemetery Records of Livingston County, Missouri. Chillicothe, Mo.: Ellsberry, 1962.

28.60   ------. Cemetery Records of Macon County, Missouri. 11 vols. Chillicothe, Mo.: Ellsberry, 1963.

28.61   ------. Cemetery Records of Marion County, Missouri. Chillicothe, Mo.: Ellsberry, [1961?].

28.62   ------. Cemetery Records of Miller County, Missouri. Chillicothe, Mo.: Ellsberry, n.d.

28.63   ------. Cemetery Records of Monroe County, Missouri. Chillicothe, Mo.: Ellsberry, n.d.

28.64   ------. Cemetery Records of Montgomery County, Missouri. Chillicothe, Mo., n.d.

28.65   ------. Cemetery Records of Northern Carroll County, Missouri. 2 vols. Chillicothe, Mo.: Ellsberry, 1962.

28.66   ------. Cemetery Records of Northern Livingston County, Missouri. Chillicothe, Mo., n.d.

28.67   ------. Cemetery Records of Pettis County, Missouri. Chillicothe, Mo., n.d.

28.68   ------. Cemetery Records of Randolph County, Missouri. Chillicothe, Mo., n.d. Includes biographical sketches of persons buried in Randolph county cemeteries.

28.69   ------. Cemetery Records of Shelby County, Missouri. Chillicothe, Mo: E. Prather, n.d.

28.70   ------. Clay County, Missouri Cemetery Records. 2 vols. Chillicothe, Mo.: Ellsberry, 1962.

28.71   ------. Death Records of Livingston County, Missouri, 1883-1890; and Agency Roll of Pensioners of Missouri. Chillicothe, Mo.: Ellsberry, n.d. Includes death notices from newspapers. InFw

28.72   ------. Livingston County, Missouri, Cemetery Records. 5 vols. Chillicothe, Mo.: Ellsberry, 1961-62. vol. 1 and 2 have title: Edgewood Cemetery, Chillicothe, Missouri.

28.73   ------. Wright County, Missouri; South Central Cemetery Records. 3 vols. Chillicothe, Mo., 1961.

28.74   Ellsberry, Elizabeth Prather, Juliette L. Smith, and Mrs. Carlton Richardson. Cemetery Records of Ray County, Missouri. 6 vols. Chillicothe, Mo.: E. P. Ellsberry, 1971.

28.75   Evans, Rella, and Mrs. J. Frank Thompson. <u>Tombstone Records of Boone County, Missouri</u>. Columbia, Mo., [1934]. Includes the tombstones of adults in Boone county when the birth date was prior to 1860.

28.76   Feezor, Joan Tinsley. "<u>Charleston-Enterprise</u>" Obituaries, Mississippi County, <u>Missouri, 1879-1888</u>. Charleston, Mo.: Feezor, 1982.

28.77   ------. <u>Death Notices from Mississippi County, Missouri Newspapers 1858-1899</u>. N.p. 1981.

28.78   Gammon, Sharon. <u>Survey of Private Cemeteries at Ft. Leonard Wood, Missouri</u>. Sherman, Tex.: S. Gammon, 1981.

28.79   <u>Gasconade County Cemetery Survey</u>. [Hermann, Mo.]: Gasconade County Historical Society, 1985.

28.80   Geary, Mrs. Ross R. <u>Cemetery Record of Woodland Cemetery and (Old) City Cemetery, 1000-1022 East McCarty Street, Jefferson City, Cole County, Missouri</u>. Jefferson City, Mo.: Jane Randolph Jefferson Chapter, National Society of the Daughters of the American Revolution, 1976.

28.81   <u>Greene County, Missouri Cemeteries</u>. 3 vols. Springfield, Mo.: Ozarks Genealogical Society, 1986-87.

28.82   Hall, William Kearney. <u>Index to Items of Genealogical Interest (Deaths, Estates, Marriages, etc.) in the Springfield, Greene County, Missouri Newspapers</u>. 2 vols. St. Louis: W. K. Hall, [1983?]. v. 1. 8 June 1865 to 30 June 1896; v. 2. 1 July 1896 to 30 Dec. 1900.

28.83   <u>Harrison County Cemetery Records, to 1984</u>. Compiled by Maxine Taraba, et al, for the Harrison County Genealogical Society. Decorah, Iowa: Anundsen Publishing Co., n.d.

28.84   Haynes, Shirley, and Avlyn Conley. <u>Missouri Obituaries Index</u>. 4 vols. Gilliam, Mo.: Saline Sentiments, n.d. For Saline county.

28.85   ------. <u>Obituaries and Newsworthy Items, with Some Saline County, Missouri, Marriages: Index Volume IV</u>. Gilliam, Mo.: Saline Sentiments, n.d.

28.86   ------. <u>Saline County, Missouri Birth and Death Records 1882, 1884, 1885</u>. Gilliam, Mo.: Saline Sentiments, 1977.

28.87   <u>Hickory County, Missouri, Tombstone Inscriptions</u>. Warrensburg, Mo.: J. H. Williams and B. H. Williams, 1968.

28.88   Hodges, Nadine. <u>Genealogical Notes from the "Liberty Tribune," 1846-58, Published at Liberty, Clay County, Missouri</u>. Independence, Mo., 1975.

28.89   ------. <u>Genealogical Notes from the "Liberty Tribune," 1868-74, Published at Liberty, Clay County, Missouri</u>. Independence, Mo., 1976. InFw

28.90   ------. <u>Missouri Obituaries: Abstracts of Obituaries Published Weekly . . .</u> in the "St. Louis Christian Advocate." Kansas City, Mo.: n.p., 1966-. v. 1. 1880-82. The <u>St. Louis Christian Advocate</u> was a periodical of the Methodist Episcopal Church.

28.91   ------. <u>Missouri Obituaries, 1880, 1881 and 1882: Abstracts of Obituaries Published in the "St. Louis Christian Advocate," Publication of the Methodist Episcopal Church, South.</u> Independence, Mo., 1975.

28.92   ------. <u>Missouri Pioneers: County and Genealogical Records.</u> 30 vols. Independence, Mo.: Hodges and Woodruff, 1970-76. v. 5. 1851-54; v. 10. 1855; v. 13. 1856; v. 18. 1857; v. 26. 1858; v. 30. 1860.

28.93   ------. "Obituaries and Death Notices Published in the <u>Savannah Sentinel</u>." <u>Kansas City Genealogist</u> 9 (1969): 10-11. For the period 1 Nov. 1851 through 23 Oct. 1852. The <u>Savannah Sentinel</u> was published in Andrew County, Missouri.

28.94 Hopper, Rosalea. <u>Jefferson County Cemetery Records.</u> 2 vols. DeSoto, Mo.: Hopper, [197-?].

28.95   ------. <u>Small Cemeteries of St. Francois County, Missouri.</u> . . . Desoto, Mo.: R. Hopper, [197-?].

28.96 Howard, Gail, and Mozelle Hutchison. <u>A Personal History: The Cemeteries and Gravestones of Maries County, Missouri: A Complete Transcription of Tombstones and Their Epitaphs, Including Old County Newspaper References, Maps, and Photographs, Together with a History and Description of 122 Burying Grounds.</u> Vienna, Mo.: G. Howard, 1986.

28.97 <u>Index to Burial Sites and Cemeteries of Coldwater Township, Cass County, Missouri.</u> Harrisonville, Mo.: Cass County Historical Society, [197-?].

28.98 <u>Index to Obituaries or Newsworthy Items of Saline County, Missouri.</u> Gilliam, Mo.: Saline Sentiments, 198-?

28.99 <u>Index to Saint Louis Magazines and Obituaries.</u> St. Louis, Mo.: St. Louis Public Library, Jan./Mar. 1980-. Quarterly with the last issue being cumulative for the year.

28.100 <u>Index to St. Louis Newspapers.</u> St. Louis, Mo.: St. Louis Public Library, 1975-. Beginning with the Jan. 1977 issue, there is a separate obituary section.

28.101 James, Larry A. <u>Pioneers of the Six Bulls: The McDonald County, Missouri, Saga.</u> Neosho, Mo.: Newton County Historical Publications, 1981-. vol. 1. Cemeteries and pioneer families.

28.102   ------. <u>Pioneers of the Six Bulls: The Newton County, Missouri Saga.</u> Neosho, Mo.: Newton County Historical Society, 1978-. v. 1, pt. 1 is an extraction of obituaries from the <u>Neosho Times</u>, 1901-44, alphabetically listing about 3,036 persons.

28. MISSOURI

28.103   Kliethermes, Sharon, and Rita Kliethermes. The Cemeteries of Osage
          County, Mo. Jefferson City, Mo.: S. Kliethermes, 1984.

28.104   Kunkel, Joan. Barry County Missouri Cemeteries. 4 vols. Carthage, Mo.:
          Kunkel, 1982. Compiled by members of the Southwest Missouri
          Genealogical Society.

28.105   ------. McDonald County, Mo. Cemeteries. 3 vols. Carthage, Mo.: Kunkel,
          1983. Compiled by members of the Southwest Missouri Genealogical
          Society.

28.106   Kunkel, Joan, and Marie Miller. Lawrence Co. Missouri Cemeteries.
          Carthage, Mo.: Kunkel, 1984.

28.107   Kunkel, Joan, Marie Troxel, Frances Fleming, and Beulah Courter. Barton
          Co. Missouri Cemeteries. 3 vols. Carthage, Mo.: J. Kunkel, 1984.

28.108   Laclede County, Missouri Rural Cemeteries. 3 vols. Lebanon, Mo.: Laclede
          County Historical Society, 1983-. v. 1. Townships of Phillipsburg,
          Washington, Union, Franklin; v. 2. Townships of Auglaize, Hooker,
          Lebanon-West, Eldridge, Lebanon-East, Springhollow; v. 3. Townships of
          Gasconade, Mayfield, Osage, Smith.

28.109   Lasater, Mildred Vaughan. Cemetery Records, Scott County, Missouri.
          2 vols. Sikeston, Mo.: King's Highway Chapter, National Society of the
          Daughters of the American Revolution, 1982.

28.110   Lawrence County Missouri Tombstone Inscriptions. Mt. Vernon, Mo.:
          Lawrence County Historical Society, 1983.

28.111   Lesh, Delsa, and Roger Lesh. Ellington City Cemetery. [Ellington, Mo.:
          D. and R. Lesh, 1976?].

28.112   Lincoln Township Cemeteries, Nodaway County, Missouri. Maryville, Mo.:
          Nodaway County Genealogical Society, 1983.

28.113   McClure, Jeanette Henson. Listings of Iron County, Missouri, Cemeteries.
          Wyatt, Mo.: J. H. McClure, 1982.

28.114   McElhiney, Mary Johnson. Genealogical Records: Inscriptions Personally
          Transcribed from the Tombstones in Old Family Burying Grounds and in
          the Public Cemeteries in St. Charles, Montgomery, Warren, Lincoln and
          St. Louis Counties, Missouri. Edited by Emma R. Porter and Gertrude P.
          Johnson. N.p.: Edna McElhiney Olson, 1970.

28.115   McManus, Thelma S. Grandin (Carter) Missouri Records, 1888-1912.
          Doniphan, Mo.: T. S. McManus, 1984. Indexes The Grandin Herald,
          19 Oct. 1905 to 11 Nov. 1909; also includes cemetery and other records.

28.116   ------. Ripley County Records. 4 vols. [Doniphan, Mo.]: McManus,
          [1972-81]. v. 3. Obituaries, 1874-1910; v. 4. Cemeteries.

28. MISSOURI

28.117   McManus, Thelma S., and Grace E. Burlison. Macedonia Cemetery Inscriptions, Ripley County, Missouri. [Doniphan, Mo.], 1970.

28.118   Mears, Phyllis E. Macon County, Missouri Obituaries, 1889-1903. Decorah, Iowa: Anundsen Publishing Co., 1987.

28.119   Merrill, J. Wayne, Shirley Haynes, and Avlyn Conley. Ridge Park Cemetery: Marshall, Saline County, Missouri. Gilliam, Mo.: Saline Sentiments, [1977?].

28.120   Missouri Cemetery Records: Reprinted from Twenty Years of the "Kansas City Genealogist." Kansas City, Mo.: Heart of America Genealogical Society and Library, 1981-. "A unique asset of this volume is the data from the Missouri Survey Department pertaining to the removal of cemeteries for the formation of two large Missouri lakes and the reinterrment in other cemeteries. For some, this volume may be the only source available for finding this data."--Foreword.

28.121   Missouri Historical Review, v. 1-, 1906-. Columbia, Mo.: State Historical Society of Missouri, 1906-. Indexes; v. 1-25, 1906-31; v. 26-45, 1931-51. Contains obituaries of prominent Missouri citizens.

28.122   "Missouri Obituaries, from Alexander Campbell's Millenial Harbinger, 1841-1860." Missouri Pioneers 6 (1969): 51-58. The Millenial Harbinger was a monthly bulletin of the Christian Church published by Alexander Campbell at Bethany, Virginia. Only deaths of Missourians are included here.

28.123   Murdick, Mrs. William G. Cemetery Records: St. Francois County, Missouri. [Farmington, Mo.?]: Missouri Society, Daughters of the American Revolution, [1985?].

28.124   Nodaway Township Cemeteries, Nodaway County, Missouri. Maryville, Mo.: Nodaway County Genealogical Society, 1983.

28.125   Obituaries, 1908-1917: The "Browning Leader Record," Browning, Linn County, Missouri. Copied by Willo Haney Harwood. Brookfield, Mo.: Hannah Hull Chapter, Daughters of the American Revolution, 1983.

28.126   Old Cemeteries, St. Louis County, Mo. St. Louis: St. Louis Genealogical Society, 1982.

28.127   One Hundred Twenty One Cemeteries of Reynolds County, Missouri: Dedicated to Those Buried in Reynolds County in Lost and Unmarked Graves. Compiled by Delsa Lesh, and Glenda Stockton. St. Louis: Genealogical R. and P., [1982].

28.128   Painter, Dixie. Index of Deaths Taken from the "St. Joseph Daily Gazette," January 1, 1876 to December 31, 1880. [St. Joseph, Mo.: D. Painter, 198-?].

28. MISSOURI

28.129   ------. Index of Deaths Taken from the "St. Joseph Daily Gazette," July 1, 1868 to Dec. 31, 1875. St. Joseph, Mo.: D. Painter, [198-?].

28.130   Pease, Janet K. "Genealogical Abstracts from Early Missouri Newspapers." Ridge Runners 5 (1976): 77-81.

28.131   ------. "Vital Records from the Missouri Daily Democrat April-June 1854." Genealogical Reference Builders Newsletter 10 (1976): 48-51. This newspaper was published in St. Louis.

28.132   Pemiscot County Historical Society. Pemiscot County, Missouri Cemetery Inscriptions. Caruthersville, Mo., 1972.

28.133   Penning, Erma E., and Mary Lee Patten. Burials in Fee Fee Cemetery, Bridgeton, Missouri, 1722 [i.e. 1822]-1961. N.p. 1961.

28.134   Porter, Emma Ruckman. Genealogy Gleanings, St. Charles County, Missouri. St. Charles, Mo.: Porter, 1979. From St. Louis, St. Charles, O'Fallon, Wentzville and Warrenton newspapers.

28.135   Richardson, Bobbie Hatton. Dunklin County, Missouri, Cemetery Inscriptions. 6 vols. Bragg City, Mo., 1972-81.

28.136   St. John, Lucretia L. Book of Obituaries: Missouri. Lawson, Mo.: St. John, 1978. Obituaries, 1914-77, of people connected with Ray, Clay and surrounding counties.

28.137   St. Louis. Archdiocese. The Necrology of the Archdiocese of Saint Louis, 1705-1967. 3d ed. St. Louis: n.p., 1968.

28.138   St. Louis Post Dispatch. Newspaper Index. Wooster, Ohio: Bell and Howell Co., 1980-. Monthly with annual cumulations.

28.139   Saint Peters Cemetery: 1200 West Main Street, Jefferson City, Missouri. Jefferson City, Mo.: Mid-Missouri Genealogy Society, 1981.

28.140   Saline County, Missouri, Cemeteries. 6 vols. Gilliam, Mo: Saline Sentiments, 1981.

28.141   Selleck, Bessie Janet Woods. Early Settlers of Douglas County, Missouri. N.p., 1952. Includes abstracts of obituaries in the Douglas County Herald, published in Ava, for the 1940s and early 1950s.

28.142   Sinking Creek Cemetery: Rock Prairie Township, Section 16, Township 30N, Range 25W. Compiled by John and Mary Ellen Gifford. Greenfield, Mo.: Dade County Missouri Historical Society, 1983.

28.143   Sisson, Sarah, and Janice Mercer. Newspaper Articles, Volume 1 Giving Information Mainly on These Missouri Counties--Ray, Caldwell, Livingston, and a Few Others. Lawson, Mo.: Sisson, 1977. Includes some death information for the early 1800s through the 1940s.

28.144   Spence, Dorothy, and Elizabeth Prather Ellsberry. Edgewood Cemetery, Chillicothe, Missouri. Chillicothe, Mo.: Elizabeth Prather Ellsberry, [1961?].

28.145   Stanley, Lois, and Maryhelen Wilson. "Death and Estate Notices from the Missouri Gazette, 1808-1816." National Genealogical Society Quarterly 65 (1977): 226-33.

28.146   Stanley, Lois, George F. Wilson, and Maryhelen Wilson. Death Records from Missouri Newspapers. 3 vols. St. Louis: L. Stanley, 1982-84. v. 1. Jan. 1854-Dec. 1860; v. 2. The Civil War Years, Jan. 1861-Dec. 1865; v. 3. Jan. 1866-Dec. 1870.

28.147   ------. Death Records of Pioneer Missouri Women, 1808-1849. Decorah, Iowa: Anudsen Publishing Co, 1980.

28.148   ------. Death Records of Pioneer Missouri Women 1808-1853. Rev. ed. N.p. 1984.

28.149   ------. More Death Records from Missouri Newspapers, 1810-1857. [St. Louis]: L. Stanley, [1985].

28.150   Strader, Floyd H. Tombstone Transcriptions of Boone County, Missouri. Columbia, Mo.: F. W. Strader, 1981.

28.151   Texas County Cemeteries. 5 vols. Houston, Mo.: Texas County, Missouri Genealogical Society, 1983. v. 1. Boone, Sherrill, Lynch townships; v. 2. Roubidoux, Upton, Morris townships; v. 3. Clinton, Burdine, Sargent, Pierce and Date townships; v. 4. Jackson, Current, Ozark and Carroll townships; v. 5. Piney and Cass townships.

28.152   31 Benton County, Missouri Cemeteries, 1969. Clinton, Mo.: The Printery, [1969?].

28.153   Thompson, Martha McDaniel. Cemetery Records, Buchanan County, Missouri. 4 vols. Redding, Calif.: Thompson, 1973-79.

28.154   Tombstone Inscriptions, Miller County, Missouri. Compiled by Carl G. Kelsay. 7 vols. [Rocky Mount, Mo.: C. G. Kelsay, 1972?]. v. 1. Equality Township; v. 2. Franklin Township; v. 3. Jim Henry Township; v. 4. Osage Township; v. 5. Richwoods Township; v. 6. Saline Township; v. 7. Glaize Township.

28.155   Tombstone Inscriptions, Mississippi County, Missouri. Compiled by the Mississippi County Genealogical Society. Charleston, Mo.: The Society, 1985.

28.156   Tombstone Inscriptions throughout Pulaski County, Missouri. 2 vols. Waynesville, Mo.: Pulaski County Historical Society and Museum, 1984-85.

28.157   Union Township Cemeteries, Nodaway County, Missouri. Maryville, Mo.: Nodaway County Genealogical Society, 1985.

28.158 Usry, John M. <u>Phelps County, Missouri Cemetery Records</u>. 3 vols. Gilliam, Mo.: Saline Sentiments, [197-].

28.159 Vann, Jane, and Vera Ashley. <u>New Madrid County Cemetery Inscriptions</u>. N.p. 1985.

28.160 <u>Wayne County, Missouri Cemeteries</u>. St. Louis: St. Louis Genealogical Society, [1981?].

28.161 Williams, Betty Harvey. <u>Tombstone Inscriptions, Henry County, Missouri</u>. 2 vols. Warrensburg, Mo., 1966.

28.162 ------. <u>Tombstone Inscriptions, Johnson County, Missouri</u>. 6 vols. Warrensburg, Mo., 1966-68.

28.163 ------. <u>Tombstone Inscriptions, Taney County, Missouri</u>. 3 vols. Warrensburg, Mo., 1966.

28.164 Williams, Jacqueline Hogan, and Betty Harvey Williams. <u>Camden County, Missouri, Tombstone Inscriptions</u>. 3 vols. Warrensburg, Mo. 1968.

28.165 ------. <u>Dallas County, Missouri Tombstone Inscriptions</u>. Warrensburg, Mo., n.d.

28.166 ------. <u>Early Tombstone Inscriptions of Lafayette County, Missouri</u>. Warrensburg, Mo.: Williams, 197-.

28.167 ------. <u>Laclede County, Missouri Tombstone Inscriptions</u>. Warrensburg, Mo.: Williams, 1968.

28.168 ------. <u>Records of St. Clair County, Missouri</u>. Warrensburg, Mo.: Williams and Williams, 1968.

28.169 ------. <u>Tombstone Inscriptions of Christian Co., Mo</u>. [Warrensburg, Mo., 1969].

28.170 Wills, Ralph, and Lena Wills. <u>Christian County, Missouri, Cemeteries</u>. 4 vols. [Springfield, Mo.: Wills, 1978].

28.171 Wilson, George F. <u>Death Records of Missouri Men from Newspapers 1808-1854</u>. St. Louis: L. Stanley, 1981. These records are from many different Missouri newspapers.

28.172 Wilson, George F., Maryhelen Wilson, and Lois Stanley. <u>Death Records of Missouri Women from Newspapers, January 1850-December, 1853</u>. 1981.

28.173 Winger, Beulah. <u>Censuses of Six Cemeteries near Stewartsville, Mo.: In Clinton County, Stewartsville South Cemetery, Old School Presbyterian Cemetery, Lebanon Cemetery, Keller Cemetery, Independence Cumberland Cemetery: In Buchanan County, Kerns-Freeman Cemetery</u>. Stewartsville, Mo.: B. Winger, [1982?].

28. MISSOURI

28.174   Woodruff, Audrey Lee. <u>Missouri Miscellany: State-Wide Missouri Genealogical Records</u>. Independence, Mo.: Woodruff, 1976-. v. 1. Camden County, Missouri Early Pioneer Obituaries, p. 103; v. 2. Selected Obituaries from Northwest Missouri, 1885-1895. Published in the Liberty, Missouri <u>Tribune</u>, p. 55; v. 4. Some Obituaries for the Years 1865-1866. Taken from the <u>St. Louis Christian Advocate</u>, p. 1; v. 7. Some Obituaries for the Year 1867 from the <u>St. Louis Christian Advocate</u>, p. 1; v. 10. Some Obituaries from the <u>St. Louis Christian Advocate</u> for the Year 1868, p. 65.

28.175   ------. <u>Missouri Obituaries: Abstracts of Obituaries Published Weekly in the "St. Louis Christian Advocate."</u> 5 vols. Independence, Mo.: Woodruff, 1985. v. 1. Jan. 1870-June 1872; v. 2. July 1872-Dec. 1874; v. 3. Jan. 1875-June 1877; v. 4. July 1877-Dec. 1879; v. 5. 1880-82.

28.176   Yarnell, Ilene Sims. "Confederate War Dead, As Reported in the <u>Leader</u>, a Newspaper Published at Versailles, Missouri, February 21, 1895." <u>Kansas City Genealogist</u> 15 (1974): 37.

28.177   Yates, William A. <u>Christian County, Missouri Cemetery Inscriptions, Volume VI</u>. Sparta, Mo.: Yates, 1972.

29. MONTANA

29.1   Miller, Vicki M. Cemetery Inscriptions, Jefferson County, Montana. [Butte, Mont.]: V. M. Miller, 1980.

29.2   Montana. Historical Society. Contributions to the Historical Society of Montana, v. 1-9, 1876-1923; v. 10, 1940. Helena: The Society, 1876-1923, 1940.

29.3   Moog, Una. Cemetery Inscriptions and Church Records from Hingham, Rudyard, Inverness, Whitlash, Lothair, Joplin, and Chester, Montana. Chester, Mont.: Broken Mountains Genealogical Society, [1986].

29.4   Yellowstone County, Montana Cemeteries. 2 vols. [Billings, Mont.: Yellowstone Genealogy Forum of Billings, Montana, 1984-85].

30. NEBRASKA

30.1   Baumann, Louise Bloom. Nebraska, Douglas County Cemeteries: A Recording of All Rural Douglas County, Nebraska, Cemeteries. Omaha, Nebr.: Greater Omaha Genealogical Society, 1981.

30.2   Buffalo Co. Cemetery Inscriptions. 4 vols. Kearney, Nebr.: Fort Kearny Genealogical Society, [1981]. v. 1. Cemetery Inscriptions of Central Buffalo County, Nebraska; v. 2. Cemetery Inscriptions of Eastern Buffalo County, Nebraska; v. 3. Western Buffalo County, Nebraska, Cemetery Inscriptions; v. 4. Cemetery Inscriptions, City of Kearney, Collins Township, Buffalo County, Nebraska.

30.3   Cemeteries of Lancaster County, Nebraska. 6 vols. Lincoln, Nebr.: Lincoln-Lancaster County Genealogical Society, 1977-81. v. 1. Southeast quarter; v. 2. Southwest quarter; v. 3. Northwest quarter; v. 4. Northeast quarter; v. 5. Alphabetical index of Wyuka Cemetery, Lincoln, Nebraska; v. 6. City of Lincoln, Fairview and Grasshopper Hill.

30.4   [No entry].

30.5   Czech Cemeteries in Nebraska = Ceské hřbitovy v Nebrasce. Edited by Vladimír Kučera, and Alfréd Nováček. N.p. 1972.

30.6   Dakota County, Nebraska Tombstone Inscriptions As of Summer of 1979. Compiled by Jody K. Boyd, and Jane A. Byerly. N.p. [1979?].

30.7   *Dale, Raymond E. "Early Nebraska Vital Records, February 21, 1857 - November 1, 1862." Nebraska and Midwest Genealogical Record 11 (1933): 8-11. Includes death records from the Nebraska City News.

30.8   ------. Nebraska Newspaper Index: "The Beatrice Express," April, 1871-April, 1877. 6 vols. N.p. 1938.

30.9   ------. Nebraska Newspaper Index: "Nebraska Advertiser," Brownville, June, 1856-June 1865. 4 vols. [Lincoln, Nebr.: Dale], 1941.

30.10   Hall County, Nebraska Cemetery Index. 2 vols. Grand Island, Nebr.: Prairie Pioneer Genealogical Society, 1981-85.

30.11   Heil, Lelia R. Genealogical Abstracts from the "Tecumseh Chieftan," Johnson County, Nebraska, Official Newspapers, 1873 to 1900. N.p. 1970.

30.12   Hicks, Ruth Anna. Cemeteries of Pawnee County, Nebraska. Lincoln, Nebr.: R. A. Hicks, 1978.

30.13   Hollingsworth, Ruby. Historical Record of Evergreen Cemetery, Lexington, Nebraska. [Lexington, Nebr.]: Hollingsworth, [1975].

30.14   Laughlin, Mabel G. Sheffer Pioneer Cemetery: Lives of Those Interred. Revised and expanded by Ethel M. Buck. Ashland, Nebr.: [Ashland Gazette], 1967.

30.15   Martin, Phyllis J. <u>Fairview Cemetery, Scottsbluff, Nebraska</u>. [Evanston, Wyo.: P. J. Martin, 1983].

30.16   ------. <u>Mitchell City, Mitchell Valley Cemeteries, Scottsbluff County, Nebraska</u>. [Evanston, Wyo.]: P. J. Martin, [1984].

30.17   ------. <u>Seven Valleys Cemeteries, Custer County, Nebraska</u>. [Evanston, Wyo.]: P. J. Martin, [1983].

30.18   ------. <u>Sunset Memorial Garden, Scottsbluff County, Nebraska</u>. [Evanston, Wyo.]: P. J. Martin, [1986?].

30.19   ------. <u>West Lawn, Creighton Cemeteries, Gering, Nebraska</u>. [Evanston, Wyo.]: P. J. Martin, [1986?].

30.20   Nebraska State Historical Society. <u>Index-Guide to the Contents of the Publications, 1885-1956, and the Magazine, 1918-1958, of the Nebraska State Historical Society</u>. Lincoln, Nebr.: Nebraska State Historical Society, 1958. (Its Publications, v. 24). This index can be used to locate obituaries in the Society's magazine, <u>Nebraska History</u>.

30.21   <u>Obituary Index, 1978-1982</u>. 2 vols. Scottsbluff, Nebr.: Rebecca Winters Genealogical Society, 1984. Contains abstracts of obituaries that appeared in the Scottsbluff <u>Star-Herald</u> and the Gering <u>Courier</u> newspapers.

30.22   Plattsmouth Weekly Herald. <u>Index to the "Nebraska Herald," Plattsmouth, Nebraska, April 1865-February 1872</u>. 4 vols. Lincoln, Nebr.: Nebraska State Historical Society, 1957.

30.23   Rice, Marlys. <u>Stones of Time: Dixon County, Nebraska Cemeteries</u>. [Concord, Nebr.]: M. Rice, 1981.

30.24   Sobotka, Margie. <u>"Nova Doba" (New Era): Deaths and Obits: Abstractions & Translations</u>. [Omaha, Nebr.?]: M. Sobotka, [1984].

30.25   Switzer, Mrs. Harold. <u>Loup and Blaine County Cemetery Headstone Inscriptions, 1800-1970</u>. [Almeria? Nebr., 1970].

30.26   <u>York County Cemetery, York, Nebraska</u>. York, Nebr.: Greater York Area Genealogical Society, 1984.

31. NEVADA

31.1   <u>Draft and Enlistment Lists, Lyon County, 1917-1918, Together with Notices of Marriages, Divorces, Births and Deaths</u>. Copied by Nona Parkin. Reno, n.d.

31.2   Parkin, Nona. <u>Births, Marriages and Deaths, 1871-1879 (with Missing Dates) Published in the "Nevada State Journal."</u> N.p. 1964. USIGS

31.3   ------. <u>Death Records, March 1909-March 1919, from the "Yerington Times" and Births, Marriages, Divorces and Deaths from "Yerington Times" and "Lyon County Wasp" Published Yerington, Nevada</u>. Reno: n.p., 1964. USIGS

31.4   Round Mountain Nugget, Round Mountain, Nevada. <u>Births, Deaths and Miscellaneous Information Gleaned from "Round Mountain Nugget," 1908-1909</u>. Reno: n.p., 1964. USIGS

31.5   Taylor, Richard B. <u>The Nevada Tombstone Record Book</u>. Las Vegas, Nev.: Nevada Families Project, 1986.

31.6   White Pine News, Ely, Nevada. <u>Extracts of Vital Statistics Taken from "White Pine News," 1890, Ely, Nevada</u>. N.p. 1964. USIGS

32. NEW HAMPSHIRE

32.1   Bowman, John Elliot. Some New Hampshire Veterans of the American Revolution: Four Hundred Items Alphabetically Arranged from Newspaper Files, 1790-1855 Relating to Deaths of Veterans in or from New Hampshire. Boston: J. E. Bowman, 1929.

32.2   Burnham, Helen S. Vital Records Taken from Various Newspapers. N.p., n.d. Microfilm. Filmed by the Genealogical Society at the New Hampshire Historical Society, Concord, 1951. USIGS Contains death notices for 1809-1829.

32.3   Coddington, John Insley. "Deaths at Concord, New Hampshire 1792-1836." New England Historical and Genealogical Register 92 (1938): 268-86.

32.4   Dartmouth College. Necrology, 1876-1900. Hanover, N.H., 1877-1900.

        ------. Class of 1846. Catalogue of the Class of 1846, in Dartmouth College: Including a Record of the Meetings of the Class since Graduation; Sketches of Living Members; Obituary Notices, etc., to 1863. Concord, N.H.: McFarland and Jenks, 1863.

32.5   Dodge, Nancy L. Northern New Hampshire Graveyards and Cemeteries: Transcriptions and Indexes of Burial Sites in the Towns of Clarksville, Colebrook, Columbia, Dixville, Pittsburg, Stewartstown, and Stratford. Salem, Mass.: Higginson Books, 1985.

32.6   Dover, New Hampshire, War Record, 1861-1865. Newspaper Clippings and Pamphlets, Collected and Bound Together by Dr. John R. Ham. N.p., n.d. Contains a necrology of Dover soldiers published in the Dover Enquirer, 9 Jan. 1868.

32.7   Driscoll, Marion Lang. "Deaths Copied from New Hampshire Newspapers 1801-1846." National Genealogical Society Quarterly 24 (1936): 106-7.

32.8   Evans, Helen F. Index of References to American Women in Colonial Newspapers through 1800. Bedford, N.H.: The Bibliographer, 1979-. v. 1. New Hampshire, 1756-1770.

32.9   From Journey's End to Hardscrabble: A Guided Tour of the Cemeteries and Burying-grounds of Chesterfield, New Hampshire. Chesterfield, N.H: Chesterfield Historical Society, 1980.

32.10   Gill, Maryan R. Keene, New Hampshire Cemetery Headstone Inscriptions. N.p. 197-.

32.11   Goss, Winifred Lane. Colonial Gravestone Inscriptions in the State of New Hampshire. 1942. Reprint. Baltimore: Genealogical Publishing Co., 1974.

32.12   Granite Monthly; a New Hampshire Magazine Devoted to History, Biography, Literature, and State Progress, v. 1-63, Apr. 1877-Dec. 1930. Concord, N.H.: N. H. Metcalf, 1877-1930. Index, v. 1-34. Contains many obituaries of prominent New Hampshire citizens.

32. NEW HAMPSHIRE

32.13   <u>Graveyards of Barrington, New Hampshire</u>. Barrington, N.H.: Barrington New Hampshire Historical Society, 1976.

32.14   Hammond, Otis G. <u>Notices from the "New Hampshire Gazette," 1765-1800</u>. Lambertville, N.J.: Hunterdon House, 1970. Also published serially in the <u>Genealogical Magazine</u>, 1905.

32.15   Hills, Thomas. <u>Three Ancient Cemeteries in New Hampshire, Near Junction Boundary Lines of Lebanon, Plainfield and Grantham</u>. Boston: Press of D. Clapp and Son, 1910.

32.16   Hoyt, Olive F. "Record Kept by Mrs. Olive F. Hoyt of Newington, N.H." <u>New England Historical and Genealogical Register</u> 73 (1919): 188-206. For the years 1824-65.

32.17   Kingsbury, Frank B. <u>Epitaphs and Known Unmarked Graves in the Cemetery Known As the "New" Cemetery</u>. [Acworth, N.H.]: Acworth Historical Society, 1956.

32.18   Locke, Arthur Horton. <u>Portsmouth and Newcastle, New Hampshire Cemetery Inscriptions: Abstracts from Some Two Thousand of the Oldest Tombstones</u>. Portsmouth, N.H., 1907.

32.19   National Society of the Colonial Dames of America. New Hampshire. <u>Gravestone Inscriptions Gathered by the Old Burial Grounds Committee</u>. Compiled by Mrs. Josiah Carpenter. Cambridge, Mass.: Riverside Press, 1913.

32.20   Nichols, Ann Louise. <u>Lyndeborough, Hillsborough County, N.H. Tombstone Inscriptions, 1764-1980</u>. Washington, D.C.: A. L. Nichols, 1984.

32.21   Pike, John. "Journal of Rev. John Pike." <u>New Hampshire Genealogical Record</u> 3 (1905-6): 77-85. Contains considerable death information for the Dover area, 1678-1709.

32.22   <u>Portsmouth Newspaper Records</u>. N.p., n.d. Microfilm. Filmed by the Genealogical Society at the New Hampshire Historical Society, Concord, 1951. USIGS Records of marriages and deaths for 1761-1870.

32.23   Putnam, Berenice Webb. <u>Marriages and Deaths Copied from Portsmouth, New Hampshire "Oracle and Advertiser."</u> N.p., n.d. Microfilm. Filmed by the Genealogical Society at the New Hampshire Historical Society, Concord, 1951. USIGS Contains marriages and deaths for 1801-5.

32.24   Rice, Franklin P. <u>New Hampshire, Lake Region Inscriptions: Whiteface Intervale, Sandwich, Perkins Ground, New Durham, Further Memorials of Meredith</u>. Worcester, Mass.: F. P. Rice, 1900.

32.25   Ripley, William. "Record of Deaths Kept by William Ripley of Cornish, N.H. 1811-1815." <u>New England Historical and Genealogical Register</u> 71 (1917): 338-42. Gives only the name, date of death, and age at death.

32.26   Spofford, Charles B. <u>Grave Stone Records: From the Ancient Cemeteries in the Town of Claremont, New Hampshire, with Historical and Biographical Notes</u>. Claremont, N.H.: G. I. Putnam, 1896.

32.27   ------. <u>Inscriptions from the Ancient Gravestones of Acworth, N.H.: A Transcript of the Records in the Old Cemetery of That Town, Settled in 1769</u>. . . . Claremont, N.H.: E. L. Elliott, 1908.

32.28   Young, David Colby, and Robert L. Taylor. <u>Death Notices from Freewill Baptist Publications, 1811-1851</u> Bowie, Md.: Heritage Books, 1985.

33. NEW JERSEY

33.1   Andrews, Frank D. <u>Tombstone Inscriptions in the Old Presbyterian Burying Ground at Greenwich, New Jersey: With a Historical Sketch</u>. Vineland, N.J., 1915.

33.2   Bowman, John Elliot. "Some Jersey Veterans of the American Revolution." <u>Proceedings of the New Jersey Historical Society</u>, n.s. 13 (1928): 325. Contains abridged death notices of American Revolution veterans from New England newspapers prior to 1857.

33.3   Canfield, Frederick A. <u>Death Notices Copied from Newspapers Published in Morristown, N.J. 1798-1849, Morris County</u>. N.p. 1932. DNDAR Also available in microform.

33.4   Cape May Ocean Wave. <u>Marriages and Deaths from the "Cape May Ocean Wave," from June 5, 1856 to May 21, 1863</u>. Philadelphia, n.d. Microfilm. Filmed by the Genealogical Society at the Historical Society of Pennsylvania, 1965. USIGS

33.5   Crayon, J. Percy. <u>Rockaway Records of Morris County, N.J., Families, Cemetery Records, Church History, Military Records, Local History</u>. Rockaway, N.J.: Rockaway Publishing Co., 1902.

33.6   Daughters of the American Revolution. New Jersey. <u>Genealogical Collection</u>. Washington, D.C.: Daughters of the American Revolution Library, n.d. Microfilm. Filmed for the Genealogical Society at the DAR Library, 1971. USIGS Contains Morris County death notices copied from Morristown newspapers 1798-1848; New Jersey death notices as published in the <u>Christian Intelligencer</u> of the Reformed Dutch Church from 1830-71.

33.7   ------. Jersey Blue Chapter. <u>Marriage and Death Notices from Old New Jersey Newspapers, 1792-1816, Together with Bible and Other Records</u>. N.p. 1931. DNDAR

33.8   <u>Documents Relating to the Colonial History of the State of New Jersey, 1631-1809</u>, v. 1-42, 1880-1949. Newark, N.J.: New Jersey Historical Society, 1880-1949. Index, v. 1-10. (Archives of New Jersey, 1st series). Some of the volumes contain extracts of newspaper death notices.

33.9   Eppler, Mary Elinor. <u>Behold and See, As You Pass By: Epitaphs in the Old Cemetery of the First Presbyterian Church of Sparta, 1787-1924</u>. Sparta, N.J.: Eppler, 1976.

33.10   <u>Extracts from American Newspapers</u>. 5 vols. 1901-17. Reprint. New York: AMS Press, 1977. v. 1. 1776-77; v. 2. 1778; v. 3. 1779; v. 4. Nov. 1 1779-Sept. 30 1780; v. 5. Oct. 1780-July 1782. Includes obituaries and death notices, mostly from the <u>New Jersey Gazette</u>, but also from Pennsylvania and New York newspapers. The <u>New-Jersey Gazette</u> was published in Burlington 5 Dec. 1777-25 Feb. 1778, in Trenton Mar. 4 1778-Nov. 27 1786.

33. NEW·JERSEY

33.11   George, Shirley J., and Sandra E. Glenn. <u>Index to Tombstone Inscriptions in Vincentown, New Jersey</u>. Columbus, N.J.: G & G Genealogical Book Co., 1982.

33.12   Hollingsworth, Josephine Marsh. <u>Cemetery Inscriptions: Old Part of the Baptist Church Cemetery, Scotch Plains, New Jersey</u>. Edited by Virginia W. Barden Ripley. 1972. Microfilm. University Microfilms International.

33.13   Hutchinson, Elmer T. <u>Collection: Abstracts of Death and Marriage Notices from New Brunswick, N.J. Newspapers, 1792-1865</u>. New Brunswick, n.d. Microfilm. Filmed by the Genealogical Society at Rutgers University Library, 1971. USIGS

33.14   Lupp, Robert E. <u>New Jersey Obituaries Index, 1974-1983</u>. Trenton, N.J.: Division of State Library, New Jersey State Department of Education, 1983.

33.15   New Jersey. Bureau of Archives and History. <u>Vital Statistics Index from Trenton Newspapers, 1800-1900</u>. Trenton, N.J.: Bureau of Archives and History, 1969. Microfilm. USIGS

33.16   New Jersey Historical Society. <u>Proceedings</u>, v. 1-, 1845-. Newark, N.J.: New Jersey Historical Society, 1845-. Index, v. 1-36, 1845-1919 in <u>Proceedings</u>, 1920; 1920-31 in v. 61, 1943.

33.17   *"New Jersey Obituaries from the <u>Philadelphia Mirror</u> 1836." <u>Genealogical Magazine of New Jersey</u> 38 (1963): 7.

33.18   <u>New Jersey Vital Records from "Monmouth Democrat" 1937-1942: Obituaries, Marriages, etc</u>. Compiled by F. S. Deskam and B. C. Waldenmair. Freehold, N.J., n.d. InFw

33.19   "Obituary Notices from the <u>Centinel of Freedom</u>, Newark, N.J., 1796-1810." <u>Proceedings of the New Jersey Historical Society</u>, 3d series 1 (1896): 17-31. Gives only the name, date, and occasionally age at death.

33.20   Perinchief, Elizabeth Marren. <u>Index to Cemetery Transcriptions, Baptismal, Burial, Church, and Marriage Records in the "Genealogical Magazine of New Jersey" through 1980</u>. Mount Holly, N.J.: Burlington County Library, [1978].

33.21   Sawyer, Ray C. <u>New Jersey Death Notices As Published in the "Christian Intelligencer": Of the Reformed Dutch Church from 1830 to 1871</u>. 1933. Microfiche. University Microfilms International.

33.22   Scott, William W. <u>Inscriptions from Tombstones in the Old-Reformed Church Burying-ground Covering a Period of 160 Years, 1737-1897</u>. 1919. Microfilm. University Microfilms International.

33. NEW JERSEY

33.23   Siegel, Alan A. <u>Clinton Cemetery Irvington, New Jersey, 1842-1971; History, Register of Lots, Inscriptions</u>. Irvington, N.J.: Irvington Environmental Conservation and Improvement Commission, 1971.

33.24   *Stratford, Dorothy M. "Obituaries from the <u>Mount Holly Mirror</u>." <u>Genealogical Magazine of New Jersey</u> 38 (1963): 2. For the years 1818-50.

33.25   Thomas, George W. <u>Inscriptions from the Cemetery of the Presbyterian Church at Westfield in New Jersey from the Year 1740 to the Year 1899: Copied from the Old Tombstones in the Year 1899</u>. San Francisco, Calif.: Pioneer Press, 1923.

33.26   <u>Tombstone Inscriptions from Hunterdon County Cemeteries</u>. N.p., n.d. Inscriptions copied by Hiram E. Deats and others.

33.27   Wheeler, William Ogden. <u>Inscriptions on Tombstones and Monuments in the Burying Grounds of the First Presbyterian Church and St. Johns Church at Elizabeth, New Jersey, 1664-1892</u>. [New Haven, Conn.: Press of Tuttle, Morehouse and Taylor, 1892].

33.28   Wheeler, William Ogden, and Edmund D. Halsey. <u>Inscriptions on the Tomb Stones and Monuments in the Grave Yards at Whippany and Hanover, Morris County, N.J</u>. 1894. Reprint. Lambertville, N.J.: Hunterdon House, 1984.

34. NEW MEXICO

34.1 Brewer, Mary. New Mexico Cemeteries. 2 vols. Albuquerque, N.Mex.: New Mexico Genealogical Society, 1979-80. v. 1 Bernalillo County, Mount Calvary; v. 2 Some Valencia County cemeteries.

34.2 Colfax County Roots: Cemetery, and Probate Records. Edited by Nancy Robertson. Raton, N.Mex.: Friends of Raton Anthropology, [1980].

34.3 Lanning, Virginia Curnutt. Cemeteries, Lea County, New Mexico; Births and Deaths Recorded As of 1919. 1972. Reprint. Hobbs, N.Mex.: Lanning, 1984.

34.4 New Mexico Historical Review, v. 1-, 1926-. Santa Fe: New Mexico Historical Society, 1926-. The first 23 volumes contain a necrology section with obituaries of early pioneers and prominent citizens. There are indexes for these volumes: v. 1-15, 1926-40, and v. 16-30, 1941-55, as well as indexes for later volumes.

34.5 Steward, Ouida Davis. Cemeteries of San Juan County, New Mexico. 2 vols. Farmington, N.Mex.: San Juan County Museum Association and the Totah Tracers Genealogical Society, 1984.

35. NEW YORK

35.1   "Abstracts from the <u>Trumansburg Advertiser</u> 1832." <u>Tree Talks</u> 3 (1963): 100. For the period 5 July 1832-5 Dec. 1832.

35.2   Adams, James Truslow. <u>Memorials of Old Bridgehampton</u>. Port Washington, N.Y.: I. J. Friedman, 1962. (Empire State Historical Publication, v. 13).

35.3   American Antiquarian Society, Worcester, Massachusetts. <u>Index of Marriages and Deaths in "New York Weekly Museum," 1788-1817</u>. Worcester, Mass., 1952. (American Periodicals: 1800-1850)

35.4   [Ancestry, George]. <u>Katonah, Westchester Co., N.Y.</u> [Brooklyn, N.Y., 1907]. This is a compilation of gravestone records from cemeteries in Katonah, and neighboring villages in Westchester county, New York, and Fairfield county, Connecticut.

35.5   Andrews, Frank D. <u>Burials in the Old Stone Fort Cemetery at Schoharie, New York</u>. . . . Vineland, N.J., 1917.

35.6   Barber, Gertrude A. <u>Death Notices Copied from the "Cooperstown Federalist" from 1808-1809. Death Notices Copied from "Watch Tower" from 1828-1831</u>. New York, 1933.

35.7   ------. <u>Deaths Taken from the "Brooklyn Eagle."</u> 27 vols. New York, 1963-66. For the years 1841-80.

35.8   ------. <u>Deaths Taken from the "New York Evening Post."</u> 54 vols. New York, 1933-47. For the years 1801-90.

35.9   ------. <u>Deaths Taken from the "Otsego Herald and Western Advertiser" and "Freeman's Journal."</u> 3 vols. Cooperstown, N.Y., 1942-. v. 1. 1795-1840; v. 2. 1841-62; v. 3. 1862-75.

35.10   ------. <u>Deaths Taken from the "Republican Watchman," a Newspaper Published Every Saturday Morning at Greenport, Suffolk County, N.Y. Covering Death Records for the Entire County</u>. N.p. 1949-. For the years 1859-61, 1867-68, 1870-75.

35.11   ------. <u>Gravestone Inscriptions of Cadiz Cemetery, Town of Franklinville, Sugartown Cemetery, Town of Franklinville, Delevan Cemetery, Town of Yorkshire, Cattaraugus County, N.Y</u>. 1930. Microform. University Microfilms International.

35.12   ------. <u>Gravestone Inscriptions . . . Sullivan County, N.Y</u>. . . . 10 vols. [New York?] 1929-34.

35.13   ------. <u>Graveyard Inscriptions of the Bloomingburgh Cemetery, Bloomingburgh, Sullivan County, N.Y</u>. [New York], 1930.

35.14   ------. <u>Marriages and Deaths from the "Cayuga Patriot" . . . Published at Auburn, Cayuga County, New York from 1825 to 1834</u>. New York, 1947. NN

35. NEW YORK

35.15   ------. Marriages and Deaths Taken from the "Delaware Gazette" at Delhi, Delaware County, N.Y. 4 vols. Delhi, N.Y., 1933. v. 1. Nov. 1819-31 July 1844; v. 2. 7 Aug. 1844-17 June 1868; v. 3. 17 June 1868-3 Dec. 1880; v. 4. 1880-95.

35.16   ------. Marriages and Deaths Taken from the "Orange County, New York Patriot," a Newspaper Published at Goshen, N.Y. from May 1828 to Dec. 1831. New York, 1939.

35.17   Becker, Howard I. Town of Clifton Park Cemeteries. [Rexford, N.Y.]: Becker, [1954].

35.18   Births, Deaths and Marriage Records of Madison and Northern Chenango County, N.Y., Compiled from Newspapers Published in Hamilton, Madison Co., New York, 1818-1886 Inclusive. Sherburne, N.Y., 1956. (Daughters of the American Revolution. New York. Cemetery, Church and Town Records of New York State, v. 219). NN

35.19   Bowman, John Elliot. Some New York Veterans of the American Revolution; Items Alphabetically Assembled, from Newspaper Files, etc. 1790-1855. Boston, Mass., 1928.

35.20   Broderick, Frances Dotter. The Burial Grounds of Lansingburgh, Rensselaer County, New York. Lansingburgh, N.Y.: Broderick, [1965].

35.21   ------. "Obituary Notices Appearing in Lansingburgh, New York Newspapers 1787-1897." Tree Talks 8 (1968): 222.

35.22   Brooklyn Eagle. Index, July 1 1891-Dec. 31 1902. Brooklyn, n.d. Published by the newspaper under its earlier name, Brooklyn Daily Eagle.

35.23   Buys, Barbara Smith. Old Gravestones of Putnam County, New York, Together with Information from Ten Adjacent Dutchess County Burying Grounds: Eleven Thousand Eight Hundred Inscriptions of Persons Born up to and including 1850. Baltimore: Gateway Press, 1975.

35.24   Cemeteries of Chester, New York. Monroe, N.Y.: Library Research Associates, 1977.

35.25   Cemeteries of Town of Hamptonburgh. Goshen, N.Y.: Orange County Genealogical Society; Campbell Hall, N.Y.: Hamptonburgh Presbyterian Church Historical Society, 1980.

35.26   Cemetery Inscriptions in the Davenport Historical Area. Edited by Davenport Historical Society. Interlaken, N.Y.: Heart of the Lakes Publishers, 1978.

35.27   Cherry Valley, New York. Gazette. Marriages and Deaths Copied from the "Cherry Valley Gazette," Cherry Valley, Otsego County, New York, 1783-1908. N.p., n.d. Microfilm. Filmed at the New York Genealogical and Biographical Society, New York City, 1941. USIGS

35. NEW YORK

35.28   Cooley, La Verne C. <u>Tombstone Inscriptions from the Abandoned Cemeteries and Farm Burials of Genesee County</u>. Batavia, N.Y., 1952.

35.29   Cowen, Minnie. <u>"Delhi Gazette," Published at Delhi, Delaware County, New York: Deaths</u>. 3 vols. New York, 1933-34. v. 1. Nov. 1819-31 July 1844; v. 2. 7 Aug. 1844-17 June 1868; v. 3. 17 June 1868-31 Dec. 1870.

35.30   ------. <u>Gravestone Inscriptions of Chautauqua Cemetery, Chautauqua, N.Y: Hunt Family Private Cemetery, Chautauqua, N.Y., Magnolia Cemetery, Magnolia Springs, N.Y., Bemus Point, N.Y.</u> 1932. Microform. University Microfilms International.

35.31   *Dann, Mrs. Cecile M. "Deaths Compiled from the <u>Broome County Courier</u>, Binghamton, N.Y." <u>Tree Talks</u> 9 (1969): 22. For the years 1834-37.

35.32   Daughters of the American Revolution. New York. Captain John Harris Chapter. Norwich. <u>Newspaper Items 1847-1856</u>. Norwich, N.Y.: Filmed by Brigham Young University at Guernsey Memorial Library, 1970. Microfilm. USIGS

35.33   ------. New Rochelle Chapter. <u>New Rochelle Tombstone Inscriptions, a Record of All Inscriptions in the Old Cemeteries</u>. . . . New Rochelle, N.Y., 1941.

35.34   Davis, William Thompson, Charles W. Leng, and Royden W. Vosburgh. <u>The Church of St. Andrew, Richmond, Staten Island; Its History, Vital Records, and Gravestone Inscriptions</u>. Staten Island, N.Y.: Staten Island Historical Society by W. T. Davis, 1925.

35.35   ------. <u>Gravestone Inscriptions in the Asbury Methodist Cemetery; First Transcribed in 1922</u>. [New Springville? N.Y.] 1971.

35.36   <u>Death and Marriage Dates from the "Black River Gazette" of 1831-32 and the "Northern Journal" of 1838-45, 1847-53, 1855-59, Published at Lowville, Lewis Co., N.Y</u>. Filmed at the New York State Library, Albany, N.Y., 1941. Microfilm. USIGS

35.37   <u>Death and Marriage Records Copied from the "Saratoga Sentinel," Saratoga Springs, Saratoga County, New York</u>. Filmed at the New York Genealogical and Biographical Society, New York City, 1941. Microfilm. USIGS. Death notices for 1819-37, with index.

35.38   "Death Notices in <u>East Norwich Enterprise</u>, East Norwich, Queens County, N.Y., Saturday Jan. 21, 1882." <u>Ancestral Notes from Chedwato</u> 12 (1965): 10-11.

35.39   "Death Notices in the <u>East Norwich Enterprise</u>, East Norwich, January 28, 1882." <u>Ancestral Notes from Chedwato</u> 11 (1964): 120.

35.40   Death Notices, 1755-1787, Oct. 1812-June 1813, Copied from the <u>Gaines Mercury and Commercial Advertiser</u>. Uncataloged material. NN. The

Gaines Mercury and Commercial Advertiser was published in New York City.

35.41   "Deaths from Auburn, N.Y. Newspapers." Tree Talk 18 (1978): 25-26.

35.42   "Deaths from the New York Evening Post, 1851-1852." Ancestral Notes from Chedwato 11 (1964): 78-79.

35.43   *"Deaths 1816-1824 from Auburn Gazette and Cayuga Republican." Tree Talk 4 (1964): 182.

35.44   "Deaths Recorded in the New York Evening Post 1802-1816." Ancestral Notes from Chedwato 14 (1967): 86.

35.45   "Deaths Taken from the Rome Telegraph." Tree Talk 7 (1967): 149. For 1836-37.

35.46   Divine, Gerda E. Old Tombstones and Unusual Cemeteries in Columbia County, New York; a Collection of Inscriptions from Old Tombstones. Hillsdale, N.Y., 1973.

35.47   Dutchess County Historical Society. Poughkeepsie, New York. Card Index of Deaths, Marriages, and Some Births Collected from Local Newspapers 1778-1871. Poughkeepsie, N.Y. Filmed by the Genealogical Society at Adriance Memorial Library, 1973. Microfilm. USIGS

35.48   Early Newspapers: Records, Marriages and Deaths, Chautauqua County, New York, 1826-1880. Compiled by Edna Ingham. Jamestown, 1978-79. (Daughters of the American Revolution. New York. Cemetery, Church, and Town Records of New York State, v. 490) NN

35.49   Early Settlers of New York State, Their Ancestors and Descendants. 9 vols. Akron, N.Y.: T. J. Foley, 1934-42. These volumes contain extracts of obiturary records of former residents of Erie County. They are taken from Buffalo newspapers from 1810 to the 1860s.

35.50   *Eckert, Mrs. William H. "Deaths in 1840 from the Roman Citizen, Rome, New York." Tree Talks 3 (1963): 125-26.

35.51   Ellsberry, Elizabeth Prather. Cemetery Records of Saratoga County, New York. Chillicothe, Mo.: Ellsberry, [197-].

35.52   [Emery, Rufus]. A Record of the Inscriptions in the Old Town Burying Ground of Newburgh, N. Y. . . . Newburgh, N.Y.: Historical Society of Newburgh Bay and the Highlands, 1898. (Historical Papers of the Historical Society of Newburgh Bay and the Highlands, no. 5).

35.53   "Excerpts from the Brooklyn Eagle and King's County Democrat Wednesday January 19, 1842." Ancestral Notes from Chedwato 9 (1962): 99.

35.54   "Extracts from the Brooklyn Daily Union November 1, 1867." Ancestral Notes from Chedwato 11 (1964): 46.

35.55   "Extracts from the Journal and Diary of Richard I. Woolsey of Milton, New York." New York Genealogical and Biographical Record 54 (1923): 265-66. For the years 1822-52.

35.56   Extracts from the "Wayne Sentinel" and Other Wayne Co. Papers. Compiled by S. D. Van Alstine. N.p. 1913. Microfilm. Filmed at the New York State Library, Albany, N.Y., 1941. USIGS. Includes deaths for 1823-54.

35.57   Federal Writers' Project. New York (State). Private Burial Grounds in Schenectady County, N. Y. Albany, 1938.

35.58   Fegley, Chrystal W. Marriages and Deaths from Miscellaneous Newspapers for Waterloo, Seneca Falls, Ovid, Trumansburg and Geneva, 1807-1908. Waterloo, N.Y., 1969. Microfilm. Filmed by Brigham Young University Library at Waterloo Library and Historical Society, Waterloo, New York, 1970. USIGS

35.59   Finch, Jessie Everts Howell. Some Cemeteries of the Between the Lakes Country (Portions of Seneca, Schuyler, and Tompkins Counties, N.Y.). Edited by Carl W. Fischer, and Harriet Jackson Swick. 3 vols. Trumansburg, N.Y.: Chief Taufhannock Chapter, Daughters of the American Revolution, 1974.

35.60   ------. Vital Records from the "Ovid Bee": Published at Ovid Village, Seneca Co., N.Y., 1822-1869. N.p. 1971. Microfiche. Ann Arbor, Mich: University Microfilms International, 1988.

35.61   Fisher, Floyd. They All Rest Together; Burial Sites of Early Settlers-- Southern Dutchess and Putnam Counties. [Holmes? N.Y., 1972].

35.62   Freer, Elmirah. Death Notices of People of Ulster County, N.Y. from the Scrapbook of Elmirah Freer from Newspapers of Kingston, New Paltz and Poughkeepsie . . . 1865-1890. Compiled and edited by Kenneth E. Hasbrouck. New Paltz, N.Y., 1965.

35.63   Furman, Consuelo. Marriage and Death Notices from the "New York Weekly Museum," 1789-1796. New York, 1950.

35.64   Furman, Robert. Marriage and Death Notices from the "New York Weekly Museum," 1790-1793. New York, 1936.

35.65   Garden, Alice Payne. Death Notices and Obituaries from New York State Newspapers, 1804-1869 and 1891-1895. N.p. 1939-40. (New York Cemetery Records, vol. 133) DNDAR

35.66   Gardner, George. Death Notices, 1851-1865. Middletown, N.Y.: Hartwell Associates, 1978. Compiled from notices appearing in the Whig Press, 1851-65, published in Middletown, N.Y.

35.67   "Gleanings from Steuben Republican, 1893: A People on the Move." Ancestry 10 (1975): 20-25.

35. NEW YORK

35.68   Goerlich, Shirley Boyce. <u>At Rest in Unadilla, Otsego County, New York</u>. Sidney, N.Y.: RSG Publishing, 1987.

35.69   Gould, Jay. <u>History of Delaware County</u>. 1856. Reprint. New Orleans: Polyanthos, 1977. Pp. 357-77 contain a few obituaries from various county newspapers, for the years 1824-55. Names of the newspapers from which the obituaries are taken not given.

35.70   Haacker, Frederick C. <u>New Rochelle, New York, Deaths 1853-1881: Copied from the "New Rochelle Press Almanacs," 1879-1882, and Records of Deaths in New Rochelle from Account Books of Cornelius Seacord, Coffin Maker</u>. N.p.: Haacker, 1955.

35.71   Hall, Mary F. <u>Cemetery Inscriptions, Town of Spencer, New York, 1795-1906</u>. 1906. Microfiche. Ann Arbor, Mich.: University Microfilms International, 1986.

35.72   Hamilton College, Clinton, N.Y. <u>Fifty Years After: The Golden Anniversary of the Class of '87 of Hamilton College with Biographies and Necrology</u>. Boston, Mass., 1937

       ------. <u>Necrology, Commencement Announcements, 1918-24</u>. 7 vols. Clinton, N.Y., 1918-24. (Hamilton College Bulletin, v. 1-7)

       ------. <u>Obituary Record of the Deceased Alumni</u>. Clinton, N.Y., n.d.

35.73   Harris, Edward Doubleday. <u>Ancient Long Island Epitaphs, from the Towns of Southold, Shelter Island and Easthampton, New York</u>. Boston: Press of David Clapp, 1903.

35.74   Hasbrouck, Kenneth E. <u>Births, Deaths, Marriages from Ulster County Newspapers, 1842-1890; Collection of Huguenot Historical Society, New Paltz, New York</u>. 2 vols. New Paltz, N.Y., n.d.

35.75   Hobart College, Geneva, N.Y. <u>Necrology</u>. Geneva, N.Y. (Hobart College Bulletin, v. 1-, 1902-)

35.76   <u>"Ithaca Journal" Obituary Index</u>. Compiled by Joan E. Smith, and Julian C. Smith. Ithaca, N.Y., n.d.

35.77   Jewitt, Joyce S. <u>Some Deaths in Erie County, N.Y., 1863</u>. [Hamburg, N.Y.]: J. S. Jewitt, [1984].

35.78   Jordan, Mable L. <u>Tombstone Records of Eighteen Cemeteries in Pound Ridge, Westchester County, New York; with an Appendix, Burials in and around Pound Ridge, N.Y., 1860 to 1871</u>. 1941 and 1947. Reprint. Harrison, N.Y.: Harbor Hill Books, 1983.

35.79   Keefer, Donald A. "Deaths from Nineteenth Century Schenectady Newspapers." <u>Tree Talks</u> 16 (1976): 195.

35.80   ------. "Obituaries from the Schoharie Patriot." Tree Talks 5 (1965): 90.
         For the period Feb. 1838 to Sept. 1839.

35.81   Keefer, Donald A., and Catherine L. Keefer. Cemetery Records of the
         Town of Charlton, Saratoga County, N.Y. Glenville, N.Y., 1971.

35.82   Kelly, Arthur C. City of Hudson Burying Grounds: Interments, 1829-1873:
         Hudson, Columbia County, New York. Rhinebeck, N.Y.: A.C.M. Kelly,
         1986.

35.83   ------. Deaths, Marriages and Miscellaneous from Hudson, New York
         Newspapers: the "Balance and Columbian Repository," 1802-1811, the
         "Rural Repository; or Bower of Literature," 1824-1851. Rhinebeck, N.Y.:
         Kelly, 1979. v. 1. Deaths. (American Periodicals: 1800-1850)

35.84   ------. Deaths, Marriages, and Much Miscellaneous from Rhinebeck, New
         York Newspapers, 1846-1899. Rhinebeck, N.Y.: Kelly, 1978. v. 1.
         Deaths.

35.85   Kern, Marion L. Cemeteries in the Town of Austerlitz: Names Identified on
         Tombstones from 1754-1984. Rhinebeck, N.Y.: Wambach Communications
         Group, 1985.

35.86   King, Rufus. "Genealogical Items from the Long Island Star." New York
         Genealogical and Biographical Record 48 (1917): 411-13. Includes a few
         death notices, 1809-11.

35.87   *------. "Marriages and Deaths from the Suffolk Gazette." New York
         Genealogical and Biographical Record 24 (1893): 86-87. For the years
         1804-8.

35.88   *Kneale, Grace. "Early Death Items from Zenger's New York Journal."
         New York Genealogical and Biographical Record 47 (1916): 393-94. For
         the years 21 July 1726 to 13 Feb. 1744.

35.89   Lloyd, J. Tombstone Names in Suffolk County, New York. Long Beach,
         Calif.: M. S. Lloyd, 1986.

35.90   Lunt, Margaret. Tombstone Inscriptions from Riverside Cemetery, Riverside
         Near Broad Street, Plattsburgh, New York (Clinton County). [Toledo,
         Ohio], 1967.

35.91   McCabe, Clara J. "Vital Records from the Chenango County Newspapers."
         Tree Talks 18 (1978): 93.

35.92   ------. "Vital Records from the Chenango Republican, a Weekly Newspaper
         Published in Oxford, N.Y., from 7 Jan. 1829 to September 1830." Tree
         Talks 16 (1976): 165-66.

35.93   MacCormick, Elizabeth Janet. Death Notices, 1840-1843; 1870-1875,
         Saratoga Springs and Vicinity . . . Taken from Early Saratoga Papers, the

"Saratoga Whig," the "Sentinel," and the "Daily Saratogian." Jamaica, N. Y., 1944.

35.94   *"Madison County Newspaper Vital Records." Tree Talks 1 (1961): 4. For the years 1845-48.

35.95   Marriages and Deaths Compiled from "Buffalo Gazette"; Published 1811-1816 in the Village of Buffalo, Niagara County (Now Erie County) New York, on File at Buffalo Historical Society, Buffalo, N.Y. 5 vols. Buffalo, N.Y., 1934.

35.96   Marriages and Deaths from the "Evangelical Magazine and Gospel Advocate," 1839, Published in Utica, Oneida County, New York. Microfilm. Filmed at the New York Genealogical and Biographical Record Society, New York City, 1940. USIGS (American Periodicals: 1800-1850)

35.97   Meyer, Mary Keysor, and Joyce C. Scott. Cemetery Inscriptions of Madison Co., N.Y. N.p. 1960. For the towns of Fenner and Nelson.

35.98   Miscellaneous Bible, Cemetery, Newspaper and Family Records. . . . Copied by Agnes M. Grousset. William Dawes Chapter, 1978. (Daughters of the American Revolution. New York. Cemetery, Church and Town Records of New York State, v. 489) NN

35.99   Morrell, J. D. "Records from the Brooklyn Eagle." Ancestral Notes from Chedwato 11 (1964): 7-9. For the year 1841.

35.100   Mott, Hopper Striker. "Vital Statistics from the New York Weekly Museum, Published by J. Harrison, 3 Peck Slip, and the Telescope Published by William Burnet and Co., 201 Bowery." New York Genealogical and Biographical Record 49 (1918): 345-52. For the years 1801-24. Includes some death notices taken from stray copies of the newspapers.

35.101   Moyer, Robert V. "Vital Records from the Onondaga Standard." Tree Talks 16 (1976): 189-90.

35.102   Munsell, Joel. The Annals of Albany. 10 vols. Albany, N.Y.: J. Munsell, 1850-59. Contains a section entitled "Notes from the Newspapers," which includes deaths, beginning with a few for 1771.

35.103   ------. Collections on the History of Albany, from Its Discovery to the Present Time. 4 vols. Albany, N.Y.: J. Munsell, 1865-71. v. 1. pp. 432-96, includes death notices and many lengthy obituaries for 1859 and 1860; v. 2. pp. 68-218, for the years 1861 and part of 1862; v. 3. pp. 225-389, for the years 1865-67; v. 4. pp. 1-83, for 1868 and 1869.

35.104   Myers, Mrs. Lester F. "Deaths 1797-1820 from Combined File of Abstracts from Early Troy Newspapers in Troy Public Library." Tree Talks 6 (1966): 41.

35.105   ------. "Marriages and Deaths Copied from the Saratoga Daily Whig." Tree Talks 9 (1969): 50. For the year 1839.

35.106   *------. "Vital Records from the Onondaga Standard." Tree Talks 13
         (1973): 214-15. For the years 1836-42.

35.107   Naukam, Lawrence W. Monroe County, N.Y. Cemetery Record Index.
         Rochester, N.Y.: Rochester Genealogical Society, 1984.

35.108   New York Gazette; or, the Weekly Post-Boy. Marriages and Death Notices
         Copied from the "New York Gazette, or Weekly Post Boy," and Various
         Newspapers of Later Date, Published in New York 1744-1848. N.p., n.d.

35.109   Newspaper Marriages and Deaths of the Hudson River Valley. N.p., n.d.
         Microfilm. LN These transcripts are from newspapers of the Hudson
         River Valley north to Plattsburgh and of the Mohawk Valley to Utica,
         including some Pittsfield, Mass., Palmyra, Saratoga and other places,
         mostly 1784 to 1829, but a few through 1834. Microfilm of a
         handwritten card index which lists newspaper and date. reel 2. Deaths.

35.110   "Newspaper Obituaries from Northern Intelligencer of Plattsburgh, New
         York." Ancestral Notes from Chedwato 11 (1964): 5-6. For the year
         1825.

35.111   Nial, Loretta M. Tombstone Inscriptions in Cemeteries in Troy, Rensselaer
         County, N.Y., Indicating a Foreign Place of Origin. [Troy, N.Y.]: Nial,
         1976.

35.112   "Obituaries in the Brooklyn, (N.Y.) Eagle, April 28, 1907." Ancestral Notes
         from Chedwato 10 (1963): 103-4.

35.113   "Old New York and Trinity Church: A Collection of Extracts from News-
         papers, 1730-1790." Collections of the New York Historical Society,
         Publication Fund Series 3 (1870): 145-408. Extracts include obituaries
         from New York newspapers.

35.114   Onderdonk, Henry. Queens County in Olden Times: Being a Supplement to
         the Several Histories Thereof. Jamaica, N.Y.: C. Welling, 1865. Contains
         information taken from a variety of public documents and old news-
         papers. Entries are for the years 1639-1832, arranged chronologically.
         Death notices and obituaries are included, often giving the name of the
         newspaper from which they are taken.

35.115   "Oneonta Herald" Marriages and Deaths. Compiled by Helen O. Oliver.
         Oneonta, N.Y., 1975-76. (Daughters of the American Revolution. New
         York. Cemetery, Church and Town Records of New York State, v. 436).
         NN. For the years 1853, 1855-60.

35.116   Overbagh, Theodore S. Births, Marriages, and Deaths from the "Saugerties
         Post," Nov. 1878-Mar. 1895. Poughkeepsie, N.Y., 1970. Microfilm.

35.117   Perry, William Graves. The Old Dutch Burying Ground of Sleepy Hollow in
         North Tarrytown, New York; a Record of the Early Gravestones and
         Their Inscriptions. [Boston], 1953.

35.118   Poucher, J. Wilson, and Helen Wilkinson Reynolds. Old Gravestones of Dutchess County, New York: Nineteen Thousand Inscriptions. 1924. Reprint. Merrick, N.Y.: Richwood Publishing Co., [1976].

35.119   Poucher, John Wilson, M. M. Terwilliger, and Byron J. Terwilliger. Old Gravestones of Ulster County, New York; Twenty-two Thousand Inscriptions. Kingston, N.Y., 1931. Most of the inscriptions predate 1800.

35.120   Reynolds, Helen Wilkinson. Notices of Marriages and Deaths, about 4,000 in Number, Published in Newspapers Printed at Poughkeepsie, New York, 1778-1825. [Poughkeepsie, N.Y.: F. B. Howard, 1930]. (Collections of the Dutchess County Historical Society, v. 4)

35.121   Reynolds, Stanley I. Stanley I. Reynolds Collection. Waterloo, New York. Microfilm. Filmed at the Waterloo Library and Historical Society, 1970. USIGS. Included in this collection: Seneca County, New York newspapers, deaths and marriages, v. 1-6, 1817-1963. Ontario County, New York, deaths, marriage, cemetery records, v. 15-16, 1818-1836.

35.122   Rockefeller, Henry Oscar. Germantown, Columbia County, N.Y., Graveyard Inscriptions. . . . New York: [New York Genealogical and Biographical Society], 1920.

35.123   St. Lawrence University. Canton, N.Y. Necrology. Canton, N.Y., n.d.

35.124   Salmon, William. The Salmon Record of Marriages and Deaths of the Residents of Southold, Suffolk County, New York, from 1696 to 1811, Commenced by William Salmon and Continued by Members of the Salmon Family. With the Supplement from 1812 to 1880, by Nathaniel Hubbard Cleveland, 1879-82. NN. Photostat copies of clippings from the Long Island Traveler, Southold, L.I., Mar. 1879 to 27 Jan. 1882 and the Suffolk Times, Greenport, L.I., 4 Feb. 1882 to 8 July 1882, mounted and bound.

35.125   ------. The Salmon Records; a Private Register of Marriages and Deaths of the Residents of the Town of Southold, Suffolk County, N.Y., and of Persons More or Less Closely Associated with That Place, 1696-1811. . . . New York: New York Genealogical and Biographical Society, 1918. Reprinted from the New York Genealogical and Biographical Record. The 1918 edition does not contain the supplement.

35.126   Sampson, Clayburne B. Marriages and Deaths, 1857-1858, from the "Chautauqua Democrat," Jamestown, N.Y. Warren, Pa. Microfilm. Filmed by the Genealogical Society at the Warren County Historical Society, Warren, Pa., 1971. USIGS

35.127   Sawyer, Ray Cowen. Death Notices Published in the "Broome County Republican," a Weekly Newspaper of Binghamton, New York, from 1831-1870. New York, 1942.

35.128   Scott, Kenneth. "Genealogical Data from New York's First Newspaper." New York Genealogical and Biographical Record 95 (1964): 220-32. Abstracted from William Bradford's New York Gazette, 1726-44. Also includes deaths from Pennsylvania, New Jersey and the New England colonies.

35.129   *------. "Genealogical Data from the New York Mercury." New York Genealogical and Biographical Record 96 (1965): 77-90. For the years 1752-82. The New York Mercury ceased publication on Jan. 25 1768. Beginning with the issue of 1 Feb. 1768, the paper was known as the New York Gazette and Weekly Mercury and so continued until 10 Nov. 1783. Abstracts from the combined newspaper were begun in volume 99 (1968) and continued through volume 107 (1976).

35.130   ------. Genealogical Data from the "New York Post Boy," 1743-1773. Washington, D.C.: National Genealogical Society, 1970. (Special Publication of the National Genealogical Society, no. 35)

35.131   ------. "Genealogical Data from Zenger's New York Weekly Journal, 1733-1751." New York Genealogical and Biographic Record 96 (1965): 1-15.

35.132   ------. Marriages and Deaths from the "New Yorker" (Double Quarto Edition) 1836-1841. Washington, D.C.: National Genealogical Society, 1980. (Special Publication of the National Genealogical Society, no. 46) Consists of approximately 5,000 deaths and 3,000 marriages.

35.133   ------. Rivington's New York Newspaper: Excerpts from a Loyalist Press, 1773-1783. New York: New York Historical Society, 1973. (Collections of the New York Historical Society, John Watts DePeyster Publication Fund Series, v. 84)

35.134   Seth, Natalie M. Obituary Notices from the "Hudson River Chronicle," Sing Sing, New York, September 24, 1839 to April 16, 1850. Salt Lake City: Genealogical Society, 1977. Microfilm. USIGS

35.135   Shepard, Elmer Irwin. Orange County, New York Deaths, 1829-1857, from the "Independent Republican" and the "Goshen Democrat," Goshen, New York. Goshen, N.Y.: S. Weller and R. H. Siemers, 1967.

35.136   Sherburne, N.Y. Sherburne Genealogy Group. Deaths, Births and Marriages from Newspapers Published in Hamilton, Madison Co., 1818-1886, Inclusive. Sherburne, N.Y., 1956. Copied from newspaper filed in the archives of Colgate University, Hamilton, Madison County, New York. USIGS

35.137   Simpson, Robert L. An Index to the "Long Islander," 1865-1881: Marriages-Deaths. Huntington, N.Y.: Huntington American Revolution Bicentennial Committee, 1976.

35.138   *Smith, Mrs. L. P. "Deaths from the Western New Yorker." Tree Talks 8 (1968): 233. For 1842-43. The Western New Yorker was published in Warsaw.

35.139   Soanes, Mrs. Almeron B. "Deaths from Jamestown Journal, Chautauqua County, New York." Tree Talks 4 (1964): 74. For the years 1833-35.

35.140   Stark, Helen., "Deaths during the Year of 1872, Published in the Yates County Chronicle." Tree Talks 15 (1975): 86.

35.141   Staten Island Historical Society. Richmond, New York. Records of Marriages and Deaths from the "New York Magazine," 1790-1797, 1900-1905, 1924-1947; Bible Records. Richmond, N.Y. Microfilm. Filmed by the Genealogical Society, Richmond, 1967. USIGS New York Magazine is available for the years 1790-97 in American Periodicals: 18th Century.

35.142   Stevens, Marian F. An Index to the "Long Islander," 1839-1864: Marriages-Deaths. Huntington, N.Y.: Huntington Historical Society, 1974.

35.143   Sullivan Whig, Bloomingburgh, N.Y. Sullivan County, N.Y. Marriages, May 15, 1846-Nov. 15, 1850; Deaths, May 15, 1845-Aug. 4, 1848, Copied from the "Sullivan Whig," Published at Bloomingburgh, N.Y. N.p., n.d.

35.144   Sweetman and West Charlton Cemeteries; Saratoga County, New York. New York, 1938. Collected and compiled by the Federal Writers' Project.

35.145   Utica Sentinel and Gazette. Marriages and Deaths Taken from the "Utica Sentinel and Gazette" from June, 1825 to May, 1836. Utica, N.Y., 1939. Copied from papers at the Utica Public Library. NN

35.146   Van Voorhis, Elias William. Tombstone Inscriptions from the Churchyard of the First Reformed Dutch Church of Fishkill Village, Dutchess Co., N.Y. [New York: G. P. Putnam's Sons, 1882].

35.147   *"Vital Records from Old New York Newspapers." Journal of American Genealogy 1 (1921): 66. Includes death and marriage records from Hugh Gaine's Mercury 1755 to 1784 and from McClean's Independent Journal 1785 to 1787.

35.148   "Vital Records (Marriages and Deaths) from the Telescope." National Genealogical Society Quarterly 29 (1941): 15-17. For the year 1827. The Telescope was published in New York and Philadelphia. (American Periodicals: 1800-1850)

35.149   Voorhees, Lesley E. The Lesley E. Voorhees Records. Syracuse, N.Y.: History's People, 1965. Contains references to obituaries for Onondaga county.

35.150   Wiles, Harriett M. Deaths Copied from the "New World," Published by Park Benjamin, in New York City, Jan. 1, 1843-July 1, 1843. [New York?] 1951.

35.151   ------. Deaths Copied from the "Rural Repository," Published in Hudson N.Y. 3 vols. in 2. N.p. [1949-51]. v. 1. 12 June 1824-28 May 1825, 7 June 1828-3 June 1837; v. 2. 24 June 1837-6 June 1840, 19 June

1841-18 June 1842; v. 3. 16 Aug. 1845-20 Sept. 1851. (American Periodicals: 1800-1850)

35.152   ------. Deaths from the "Newark Gazette," "Newark Courier," and "Newark Union," Now the "Newark Courier-Gazette". . . . N.p., n.d.

35.153   ------. Marriages and Deaths Copied from Various Newspapers. N.p. 1949.

35.154   ------. Marriages and Deaths from the "Lyons Republican" and Inscriptions from the Lyons Rural Cemetery, Nelson, N.Y. and Aurora, N.Y. New York, 195-.

35.155   ------. Marriages and Deaths from the "Northern Whig" Published in Hudson, N.Y., 1823-1828. New York, 1952.

35.156   ------. Marriages and Deaths from the "Wayne Sentinel," a Newspaper Published in Palmyra, N.Y. New York: H. M. Wiles, 1933.

35.157   ------. Marriages and Deaths of Wayne County, New York, Copied from the "Newark Weekly Courier," Published at Newark, New York. New York, 1941.

35.158   Wilson, Robert J. New York State Cemetery Records. 2 vols. Tonawanda, N.Y.: Wilson, n.d.

35.159   Woodward, Mrs. Gordon H. Broome County Vital Dates from Church and Newspaper Records and Abstracts of Wills. Binghamton, N.Y., 1975-76. (Daughters of the American Revolution. New York. Cemetery, Church and Town Records of New York State, v. 442). NN

35.160   ------. "Marriages and Deaths from the Ithaca Journal and General Advertiser." Tree Talks 5 (1965): 43.

35.161   ------. "Marriages, Deaths and Miscellaneous Notices from Four Newspapers Published at Trumansburg, N.Y. Bound in a Single Book on File at the DeWitt Historical Society, Ithaca, N.Y." Tree Talks 9 (1969): 56. For the years 1828-46.

62   *Wright, Mrs. Richard N. "Vital Records from the Syracuse Daily Standard from January 1, 1851." Tree Talks 14 (1974): 9-10.

"Wyoming County Deaths Reported in Livingston County Newspapers Prior to 1850." Historical Wyoming 20 (1967): 85-87.

'mm, Louise Seymour. Death Notices of Revolutionary Veterans and Men and Women of the Revolutionary Period, from Kingston, New York Newspapers, 1826-1847. Woodstock, N.Y., 1937.

Marriage and Death Notices from Kingston, N.Y. Newspapers, -1830. . . . Woodstock, N.Y., 1940.

36. NORTH CAROLINA

36.1   Abandoned Cemeteries of Stanly County. [Albemarle? N.C.]: Stanly County Genealogical Society, 1981.

36.2   Absher, Levi. The Levi Absher Ledger. N.p., n.d. Diary of over 500 deaths in Wilkes County prior to 1911.

36.3   Aslund, Carolyn C., and Billie C. Ledbetter. Cemetery Inscriptions of Buncombe County, N.C. Asheville, N.C.: C. C. Aslund and B. C. Ledbetter, 1984-86.

36.4   Bahnsen, Jane Cutler. Index to Marriages and Obituaries in the "Western Carolinian," 1820-1823, 1831-1835, 1838-1842, and Scattered Issues. Chapel Hill, N.C.: n.p., 1935. NcU

36.5   Barfield, Anita W. They're Buried in Our Past. 2 vols. Whiteville, N.C.: A. W. Barfield and K. W. Duncan, 1983-84.

36.6   Britt, Morris F. Robeson County Cemetery Records. [North Carolina: M. F. Britt], 1982.

36.7   Brown, Betty Leach. Records from Trinity Cemetery in Randolph County, N.C. Archdale, N.C.: B. L. Brown, 1984.

36.8   Caldwell County, N.C., Cemeteries. Edited by Elizabeth P. Keller. Lenoir, N.C.: Caldwell County Genealogical Society, 1985.

36.9   Carpenter, Jake. "Catalogue of Death on Three-Mile Creek." North Carolina Folklore 1 (1948): 22. Excerpts from obituary notices, 1852-1914, for Penland.

36.10   Catawba County Cemeteries. 2 vols. Hickory, N.C.: Catawba County Genealogical Society, 1986-87.

36.11   Caudill, Edna Alford. Cemetery Records of Johnston County. 5 vols. [Smithfield, N.C.]: Johnston County Genealogical Society, [1980?].

36.12   Cemeteries of Bladen County, North Carolina. [Elizabethtown? N.C.: Bladen County Bicentennial Commission, 1985].

36.13   Cemetery Records of Carteret County, North Carolina. Carteret County, N.C.: Carteret Historical Research Association, 1982?

36.14   Cemetery Records of Davidson County, N.C. 3 vols. Lexington, N.C.: Genealogical Society of Davidson County, 1986. v. 1. Western section; v. 2. Southern section; v. 3. Central section.

36.15   Charlotte Democrat. Death Notices from the "Charlotte Democrat," 1871-1876. Charlotte, N.C.: Public Library of Charlotte and Mecklenburg County, 1963. NcC

36.16   Cotten, Elizabeth Henderson. <u>Index to Marriages and Obituaries in the</u>
         <u>"Minerva" (Raleigh), 1796-1821</u>. Chapel Hill, N.C.: University of North
         Carolina Library, 1956. NcU

36.17   ------. <u>Marriage and Death Notices from Raleigh, N.C. Newspapers,</u>
         <u>1796-1826</u>. Easley, S.C.: Southern Historical Press, 1977. Includes death
         notices from the <u>Minerva</u> and the <u>Star</u>.

36.18   Daughters of the American Revolution. North Carolina. <u>Genealogical</u>
         <u>Collection</u>. Washington, D.C.: Daughters of the American Revolution
         Library, n.d. Microfilm. Filmed for the Genealogical Society, 1971.
         USIGS. Includes marriage and death notices in newspapers published in
         Wilmington 1797-1842 and 1849-53.

36.19   ------. Genealogical Records Committee. <u>North Carolina Original Marriage</u>
         <u>Bonds of Mecklenburg and Johnston Counties, and Marriages and</u>
         <u>Obituaries from Early Newspapers of Wilmington, N.C</u>. N.p., 1958-59.
         Nc

36.20   ------. James Hunter Chapter, Madison. <u>Cemetery Records of Rockingham</u>
         <u>and Stokes Counties, North Carolina</u>. Madison, N.C.: The Chapter, 1978.

36.21   ------. John Penn Chapter. <u>Granville County, North Carolina Records</u>.
         1936. Microfilm. Includes inscriptions from the Banks Church cemetery,
         Clay cemetery, Elmwood cemetery, Shiloh graveyard, Fleming cemetery,
         Hicks cemetery, Lawrence cemetery, Minor cemetery, Mt. Energy
         cemetery, Tranquillity cemetery, Webb Cemetery, Gooch family cemetery.

36.22   ------. Stamp Defiance Chapter, Wilmington. <u>Records from Obituary and</u>
         <u>Marriage Notices As Published in the Following Newspapers in</u>
         <u>Wilmington, North Carolina: 1. The "Commercial," March 17, 1849 to</u>
         <u>March 15, 1851. 2. The "Wilmington Herald," May 14, 1851 to May 7,</u>
         <u>1853</u>. n.p., 1955.

36.23   Duke University, Durham, N.C. Library. <u>The "Durham Morning Herald"</u>
         <u>Index, 1930-1969</u>. Durham, N.C.: n.p., 1970. 9 vols.

36.24   Everton, Camille Bateman. <u>Cemeteries of Tyrrell County, Eastern Washington</u>
         <u>County, East Lake, Dare County</u>. [Charlotte, N.C.: H. Eaton Historical
         Publishers, 1985].

36.25   Fuller, Marian Camper. <u>Marriage and Death Notices in the "Hillsborough</u>
         <u>Recorder," 1820-1829, 1834-1858, 1860-1869, 1873, 1877, and a Few Odd</u>
         <u>Issues</u>. Chapel Hill, N.C.: n.p., 1946. NcU

36.26   ------. <u>Obituaries and Marriage Notices from the "Carolina Watchman"</u>
         <u>1832-1890: An Index</u>. Greenville, S.C.: A. Press, 1981.

36.27   Grantham, Rose L. <u>Death Notices from the "Mecklenburg Jeffersonian,"</u>
         <u>Charlotte, N.C., 1841-1849: An Index</u>. Charlotte, N.C.: Public Library of
         Charlotte and Mecklenburg County, 1966.

36.28   Greensboro, N.C. Public Library. Death Records from the Files of the "Greensboro (N.C.) Patriot," 1826-1899. Greensboro, N.C.: Greensboro Public Library, n.d. Gives name of person and date of paper in which the obituary was published.

36.29   Grice, Louise. Index to Biographies and Obituaries of North Carolina Physicians, Published in North Carolina Medical Journals and Transactions, 1849-1946. Chapel Hill, N.C.: n.p., 1949.

36.30   Haile, Margaret Wallis. Ivy Township Cemeteries, Buncombe County, North Carolina: Tombstone Inscriptions and Genealogical Identifications. Barnardsville, N.C.: Big Ivy Historical Society, 1985.

36.31   Hall, Lewis Philip. Marriage Notices, Obituaries, and Items of Genealogical Interest in the "Cape Fear Recorder," the "Peoples Press," and the "Wilmington Advertiser" from Aug. 26, 1829 to Dec. 24, 1833 (Abstracted). Wilmington, N.C.: n.p., 1958.

36.31a Harrison, Helen Dortch. Index to Marriages and Obituaries in the "Star" (Raleigh) 1810-1813, 1820, 1824-25. Chapel Hill, N.C.: n.p., 1952. NcU

36.32   Haywood, Carol, and Rose Grantham. Death Notices from the "Western Democrat," Charlotte, N.C., 1853-1870: An Index. Charlotte, N.C.: Public Library of Charlotte and Mecklenburg County, 1966. Microfiche. Sanford, N.C.: Microfilming Corporation of America, 1979.

36.33   Henry, Louis Carr. "Some North Carolina Vital Records. Part 1, Death Notices from the Raleigh Star, 1810." Daughters of the American Revolution Magazine 67 (1933): 119-22.

36.34   Hoots, Carl C. Cemeteries of Yadkin County, North Carolina. Spartanburg, S.C.: Reprint Co., 1985.

36.35   Hornaday, Mr. and Mrs. L. S. Piedmont North Carolina Cemeteries. Burlington, N.C.: L. S. Hornaday, [1981?].

36.36   Inscriptions on Stones in Thyatira Cemetery, 1755-1966. N.p. 1967.

36.37   Johnston, Hugh Buckner. Deaths and Marriages from Tarboro, North Carolina, Newspapers, 1824-1865. Easley, S.C.: Southern Historical Press, 1985.

36.38   ------. "Vital Statistics from the Tarboro Press, 1840-May, 1841 (Some Issues Missing)." National Genealogical Society Quarterly 34 (1946): 3-6.

36.39   Jones, Kathy Brooks. Buffalo Creek Chronicles. Sanford, N.C.: K. B. Jones, 1984. Contains tombstone inscriptions from Lee County, Chatham County, Harnett County, and adjacent areas in central North Carolina.

36.40   Kallam, Lemuel Wallace. Kallam Cemetery Survey Book of Surry County and Surrounding Areas: Active and Inactive Burying Grounds. [Mt. Airy, N.C.]: L. W. Kallam, 1982-84.

36.41 Kammerer, Roger E., and David E. Carpenter. Onslow Register: Records of Onslow and Jones County Citizens and Related Families. [Greenville, N.C.]: R. E. Kammerer, 1984.

36.42 Kellam, Ida Brooks. Marriage and Death Notices in Newspapers Published in Wilmington, North Carolina, 1797-1842; Marriage Contracts of New Hanover County Citizens, 1728-1855. Wilmington, N.C.: n.p., 1959.

36.43 Kellam, Ida Brooks, and Leslie H. Brown, Jr. Duplin County, North Carolina, Gravestone Records. 2 vols. Wilmington, N.C., 1960-61.

36.44 Kendall, Katherine K. "Marriage and Death Notices from Milton Newspapers, Caswell Co., 1818-54." North Carolina Genealogical Society Journal 4 (1978): 35-37.

36.45 Kirkpatrick, Ethel Meadows. Spring Creek Cemetery Survey. Hot Springs, N.C.: E. M. Kirkpatrick, 1985.

36.46 Lazenby, Mary Elinor. Lewis Grave Yard with Mention of Some Early Settlers along Fifth Creek, Iredell County, N.C. Statesville, N.C., 1944. Microfiche.

36.47 Lucas, Silas Emmett. Marriage and Death Notices from Raleigh, N.C. Newspapers, 1796-1826. Easley, S.C.: Southern Historical Press, 1977.

36.48 McClain, Mrs. William E., Jr. "Death Notices from the Charlotte Journal, Charlotte, North Carolina." Mississippi Genealogical Exchange 14 (1968): 65.

36.49 McEachern, Leora Hiatt. Duplin County Gravestone Records. Kenansville, N.C.: Duplin County Historical Society, 1978.

36.50 Miller, George Augustus. Cemeteries and Family Graveyards in Haywood County, N.C. Waynesville, N.C.: Miller, 1979.

36.51 Murphy, William L. Greene County, North Carolina Cemetery Records. Raleigh, N.C.: W. L. Murphy, 1983.

36.52 Navey, William R. Death Notices from the "Charlotte Journal," Charlotte, N.C., July 3, 1835-December 7, 1851. Charlotte, N.C.: Public Library of Charlotte and Mecklenburg County, 1964.

36.53 Neal, Lois Smathers. Abstracts of Vital Records from Raleigh, North Carolina Newspapers. Spartanburg, S.C.: Reprint Co., 1979-. v. 1. 1799-1819.

36.54 ------. "Excerpts from Early Raleigh Newspapers." North Carolina Genealogical Society Journal 3 (1977): 191.

36.55 News and Observer. Index. Greenville, N.C.: J. Y. Joyner Library, East Carolina University, 1967/69-. The News and Observer is published at Raleigh.

36.56   North Carolina. State Library, Raleigh. <u>Marriage and Death Notices from</u>
<u>"Raleigh Register and North Carolina State Gazette," 1799-1825</u>.
Compiled by Carrie L. Broughton, State Librarian, from the files in the
North Carolina State Library. 1944. Reprint. Baltimore: Genealogical
Publishing Co., 1962. Excerpted and reprinted from the <u>Biennial Report</u>
<u>of the State Library of North Carolina</u>, 1942-44.

36.57   ------. <u>Marriage and Death Notices in "Raleigh Register and North Carolina</u>
<u>State Gazette," 1846-1893</u>. Compiled by Carrie L. Broughton, State
Librarian. Raleigh, 1947. Reprint. Baltimore: Genealogical Publishing
Co., 1975. Originally published as <u>Bulletin of the North Carolina State</u>
<u>Library</u>. Also available in microfiche from Microfilming Corp. of
America, Sanford, N.C., 1979.

36.58   "North Carolina Deaths, Marriages, and Legal Notices, 1826-1830, Taken from
the Greensboro Newspaper." <u>Ridge Runners</u> 4 (1975): 99-121.

36.59   "Obituaries Prior to 1800." <u>North Carolina Historical Review</u> 9 (1932): 89-91.

36.60   "Obituary Notices from the <u>Biblical Recorder</u>, 1835-1877; 1877-1893; January
3, 1894-January 20, 1904." 3 vols. Unpublished typescripts in the Search
Room, North Carolina State Archive, Raleigh. The <u>Biblical Recorder</u> was
a Baptist journal published in Raleigh.

36.61   Pyatte, Martha A. <u>Lest We Forget: An Index to Avery County Cemeteries</u>.
2 vols. Rowland, N.C.: Pyatte, 1975.

36.62   Reeves, Henry, and Mrs. G. D. Koch. <u>Cemetery Inscriptions, Davidson (Old</u>
<u>Rowan) Co., North Carolina</u>. Lexington, N.C.: Reeves, 1970.

36.63   Satterfield, Virginia Lee. <u>Marriages and Deaths in the "Clayton Bud,"</u>
<u>Clayton, North Carolina, and the "Weekly Bud," Smithfield, North</u>
<u>Carolina, 1883-1887</u>. Clayton, N.C.: Satterfield, 1975.

36.64   Sebastian, Mr. and Mrs. Samuel. <u>Cemetery Records, Wilkes County Area,</u>
<u>North Carolina: Old Family and Church Cemetery Listings</u>. N.p.: Wilkes
Genealogical Society, [197-].

36.65   Sikes, Leon H. <u>Duplin County Cemetery Records</u>. Rose Hill, N.C.: Duplin
County Historical Society, 1983.

36.66   Spence, Wilma Cartwright. <u>Tombstones and Epitaphs of Northeastern North</u>
<u>Carolina; Consisting of Beaufort, Camden, Chowan, Currituck, Gates,</u>
<u>Hyde, Pasquotank, Perquimans and Washington Counties</u>. Baltimore:
Gateway Press, 1973.

36.67   Stanley, Donald W. <u>Forsyth County, N.C., Cemetery Records</u>. Edited by
Ann E. Sheek, and Hazell R. Hartman. 5 vols. Kernersville, N.C.:
Stanley, 1976-78. v. 1. Abbots Creek, Belews Creek, Bethania, Broadbay
Townships; v. 2. Clemmonsville, Kernersville, Lewisville, Middle Fork,
Old Richmond Townships; v. 3. Old Town, Salem Chapel Townships; v. 4.
South Fork, Vienna Townships and Salem Cemetery; v. 5. Winston-Salem.

36.68 Swindell, Martha Rebecca, and Romulus Sanderson Spencer, Jr. In Memory of . . . an Index to Hyde County Cemeteries. Fairfield, N.C.: Hyde History, 1973.

36.69 Taylor, Anne Hatcher. Inscriptions, Scrolls, and Vignettes of North Carolinians Born Before 1913, Gates and Hertford Counties. 2 vols. Winston, N. C.: Hatcher-Taylor Press, 1985-87.

36.70 Topkins, Robert M. Marriage and Death Notices from Extant Asheville, N.C. Newspapers, 1840-1870: An Index. Raleigh, N.C.: North Carolina Genealogical Society, 1977.

36.71 ------. "Marriage and Death Notices from Extant Lincolnton Newspapers 1836-1853." North Carolina Genealogical Society Journal 2 (1976): 62.

36.72 ------. "Marriage and Death Notices from the Iredell Express (Statesville), 1858-1865: An Index." North Carolina Genealogical Society Journal 3 (1977): 197-212.

36.73 ------. Marriage and Death Notices from the "Western Carolinian" (Salisbury, North Carolina) 1820-1842: An Index. 1975. Reprint. Spartanburg, S.C.: Reprint Co., 1983.

36.74 Townsend, Peggy Tyner. Vanishing Ancestors: Cemetery Records of Robeson County, North Carolina. 2 vols. [Red Springs, N.C.: Townsend], 1975-79.

36.75 Williams, Ruth Smith, Margarette Glen Griffin, and Hugh Buckner Johnston. Tombstone and Census Records of Early Edgecombe. Rocky Mount, N.C.: Dixie Letter Service, 1959.

36.76 Willis, Dixie T. Pamlico County, North Carolina Cemeteries; with Some Family Bible Records. Baltimore: Gateway Press, 1983.

36.77 Yadkin and Catawba Journal. Abstracts; Marriage Notices; Death Notices, 1824-1834. Salisbury, N.C.: n.p., 1968. NcC

36.78 Younts, Doris Ann. Dare County Cemeteries. Copied from the records of Leland Tillett. North Carolina: Albemarle Genealogical Society, 1983.

37. NORTH DAKOTA

37.1   Bismarck-Mandan Genealogical and Historical Society. McIntosh County Cemeteries. [Bismarck, N.Dak.]: The Society, [1978].

37.2   Cemeteries of North Dakota. 17 vols. Fargo, N.Dak.: Fargo Genealogy Society, 1972-. Vols. 1-14, 16 were issued by the Society under its earlier name, Fargo Genealogy Society; v. 15, 17 issued by Red River Valley Genealogy Society. v. 1-2. Cemeteries of Cass County; v. 3. Cemeteries of Griggs and Steele counties; v. 4. Cemeteries of Barnes county; v. 5. Cemeteries of Traill county; v. 6. Cemeteries of Grand Forks county; v. 7. Cemeteries of Ramsey county; v. 8. Cemeteries of Benson county; v. 9. Richland county; v. 10. Foster county cemeteries; v. 11. Cemeteries of Eddy county; v. 12. Cemeteries of Nelson county; v. 13. Cemeteries of La Moure county; v. 14. Cemeteries of Ransom county; v. 15. Towner county cemeteries; v. 16. Stutsman county cemeteries; v. 17. Burke county.

37.3   Ward County, North Dakota Cemetery Records. Minot, N.Dak.: Mouse River Loop Genealogical Society, 1983.

38. OHIO

38.1   Adams, Barbara, and Gene Mozley. <u>Memorial Records of Shelby County,</u>
        <u>Ohio, 1819-1975</u>. Baltimore: Gateway Press, 1977.

38.2   "Adams County, Ohio, Newspaper Accounts, Feb. 24, 1831-July 7, 1831; July
        30, 1831-March 3, 1832." <u>Gateway to the West</u> 1 (1968): 153-56.

38.3   Adamson, Lorena B. "Newspaper Items from <u>Zanesville Express and</u>
        <u>Republican Standard</u>." <u>Ohio Genealogical Quarterly</u> 7 (1943): 588.

38.4   <u>Akron Beacon Journal Index</u>. Prepared by the Newspaper Project, Work
        Projects Administration in Ohio. Akron, 1940-. Covers the years
        1929-38.

38.5   Amner, Mary Case. <u>Death Notices in the "Granville Times," 1880-1941</u>.
        Kent, Ohio: n.p., 1976.

38.6   Beach, Doris P. <u>Guernsey County, Ohio, Liberty Township Cemeteries</u>.
        Columbus, Ohio: D. P. Beach, 1986.

38.7   Beachy, Leroy. <u>Cemetery Directory of the Amish Community in Eastern</u>
        <u>Holmes and Adjoining Counties in Ohio</u>. 2d ed. Berlin, Ohio: L.
        Beachy, 1975.

38.8   Beam, Virginia Hamilton. <u>Obituary Clippings, from the Scrapbook of Etta</u>
        <u>and Emma Waln, Fayette County, Ohio 1888-1949</u>. N.p. 1977.

38.9   Bloomfield, Virginia Frances Jordan. <u>Obituaries Abstracted from the</u>
        <u>"Versailles Leader," Versailles Ohio, 1886-1912</u>. Fort Wayne, Ind.: Fort
        Wayne Public Library, 1971.

38.10   Bowen, Harriet Cole. <u>Gravestone Records of Lucas and Fulton Counties,</u>
        <u>Ohio</u>. . . . Adrian, Mich.: Bowen, 1944.

38.11   Bowman, Mary L. <u>Some Tombstone Inscriptions of Southwest Athens County,</u>
        <u>Ohio</u>. 5 vols. [Athens, Ohio]: Alexander Local Genealogical and Histor-
        ical Society, 1986. v. 1. Pleasanton, Woodyard, and others; v. 2. Bates,
        Creamer, and Hanning; v. 3. Gates, Haning, Jeffers, Martin, Quail, Trap,
        Minear, and Burson; v. 4. Town House, Bassett, Brooks, Cross Roads,
        Hewitt, and Ross; v. 5. Alexander-Union and Cumberland cemeteries.

38.12   Bricker, John W. <u>Cemetery Records of Delaware County, Ohio</u>. Galena,
        Ohio, 1970.

38.13   Broglin, Jana Sloan. <u>Defiance, Fulton, Henry, Paulding, Putnam, Williams</u>
        <u>and Wood Counties, Ohio, Newspaper Obituary Abstracts, 1838-1870</u>.
        N.p. 1987.

38.14   ------. <u>Obituaries Appearing in the "Swanton Enterprise," Swanton, Ohio,</u>
        <u>1922 thru 1978</u>. N.p. 198-?

38.15 Burgner, Jacob. Papers, 1859-1912. NUC MS 61-1264. Manuscript collection in the Rutherford B. Hayes Library, Fremont, Ohio. Burgner was an educator, author and local historian of Fremont, Ohio. His papers include a collection of obituaries. Also includes an index to a scrapbook (which has not been located) of 2000 obituaries of residents of Sandusky County.

38.16 Cemeteries of [named] Township, Gallia County, Ohio. 15 vols. Gallipolis, Ohio: Gallia County Historical Society, 1976-82. v. 1. Addison; v. 2. Cheshire; v. 3. Clay; v. 4. Gallipolis; v. 5. Green; v. 6. Greenfield; v. 7. Guyan; v. 8. Harrison; v. 9. Huntington; v. 10. Morgan; v. 11. Ohio; v. 12. Perry; v. 13. Raccoon; v. 14. Springfield; v. 15. Walnut.

38.17 Cemeteries of Berne Township. Lancaster, Ohio: Fairfield County Chapter of the Ohio Genealogical Society, 1983.

38.18 Cemeteries of Bristol and Meigsville Twps., Morgan Co., Ohio. [McConnelsville? Ohio]: Morgan County Genealogical Society and the Morgan County Historical Society, 1982.

38.19 Cemeteries of Center--Manchester Townships, Morgan County, Ohio. [McConnelsville, Ohio]: Morgan County Genealogical Society and the Morgan County Historical Society, 1983.

38.20 Cemeteries of Crawford County, Ohio. Galion, Ohio: Crawford County Chapter of the Ohio Genealogical Society, 1987.

38.21 Cemeteries of Penn-Windsor Townships, Morgan County, Ohio. [McConnelsville, Ohio]: Morgan County Genealogical Society and the Morgan County Historical Society, 1982.

38.22 Cemeteries of Richland Township. Lancaster, Ohio: Fairfield County Chapter of the Ohio Genealogical Society, 1984.

38.23 Cemetery Inscriptions, Ashtabula County, Ohio. Jefferson, Ohio: Ashtabula County Genealogical Society, 1977.

38.24 Cemetery Inscriptions of Brush Creek, Clay & Harrison Townships, Muskingum County, Ohio. Zanesville, Ohio: Muskingum County Genealogical Society, 1984.

38.25 Cemetery Inscriptions of Jefferson and Madison Townships, Muskingum County, Ohio. Zanesville, Ohio: Muskingum County Genealogical Society, 1984.

38.26 Cemetery Inscriptions of Newton and Springfield Townships, Muskingum County, Ohio. [Zanesville, Ohio?]: Muskingum County Genealogical Society, 1983.

38.27 Cemetery Inscriptions of Ottawa County, OH. [Port Clinton, Ohio?]: Ottawa County Chapter of the Ohio Genealogical Society, [197-].

38.28   Cemetery Inscriptions, Preble County, Ohio. Edited by Joan Bake Brubacker.
         [Eaton, Ohio, 1976?]

38.29   Cemetery Inscriptions, Stark County, Ohio. 7 vols. N.p.: Stark County
         Chapter, Ohio Genealogical Society, [1982-86].

38.30   Cincinnati Enquirer Index. Prepared by the Newspaper Index Project, Work
         Projects Administration in Ohio. Cincinnati, 1941-. Covers the years
         1934-38.

38.31   Cist, Charles. The Cincinnati Miscellany; or, Antiquities of the West and
         Pioneer History and General and Local Statistics. Compiled from the
         Western General Advertiser, from October 1st 1844, to April 1st 1846. 2
         vols. Cincinnati, Ohio: Clark Printer, 1845-46. Also available in
         Nineteenth Century American Literature on Microcards, Ser. A: The Ohio
         Valley, no. 363. Contains death notices (not included in index) and a
         few obituaries from the Western General Advertiser.

38.32   Clark, Marie Taylor. Tombstone Inscriptions of Grandview Cemetery,
         Chillicothe, Ohio, Ross County. [Chillicothe? Ohio]: Unigraphic, [1972].

38.33   Clegg, Michael Barren. Portage County, Ohio, Newspaper Obituary Abstracts,
         1825-1870. Fort Wayne, Ind.: M. B. Clegg, 1982.

38.34   ------. Trumbull County, Ohio, Newspaper Obituary Abstracts, 1812-1870.
         Indexed by Anne D. Budd. Fort Wayne, Ind.: M. B. Clegg, 1981.

38.35   "Cleveland Newspaper Digest January 1, 1822 to December 31, 1828."
         Certified Copy 6 (1977): 9.

38.36   Cleveland Plain Dealer Index. Prepared by the Newspaper Index Project,
         Work Projects Administration in Ohio. Cleveland, 1941-. For 1931,
         1933-38. 1933-38 are called v. 92-97 of the Annals of Cleveland, no.
         38.196

38.37   Clinton County Historical Society. Ohio. Genealogy Committee. Cemetery
         Records of Clinton County, Ohio, 1798-1978. Wilmington, Ohio: The
         Society, 1980.

38.38   "Clippings from Early Ohio Newspapers." Ohio Records and Pioneer Families
         10 (1969): 78-81. Includes obituaries for 1886-98, mostly from Mercer
         and Van Wert counties.

38.39   *"Clippings from Early Ohio Newspapers: Dayton Repertory, Ohio Watchman
         and Dayton Watchman." Ohio Records and Pioneer Families 3 (1962):
         33-34. Includes a few death notices for Montgomery county, 1818-33.

38.40   "Clippings from Early Ohio Newspapers: Scioto County Gazette." Ohio
         Records and Pioneer Families 9 (1968): 201-2. For 1819.

38.41   Cokonougher, Ralph W. Gravestone Inscriptions in Ross County, Ohio. New
         Holland, Ohio: Ralco Publishing Co., 1978.

38. OHIO

38.42   Colletta, Lillian Fiscus, and Leslie Puckett. Tombstone Inscriptions of Brown County, Ohio. Denville, N.J., 1963.

38.43   ------. Tombstone Inscriptions of Cherry Fork Cemetery, Adams County, Ohio, and Genealogical Gleanings. Denville, N.J., 1964.

38.44   Collins, Blanche. "Death Notices from the Western Intelligencer." Ohio Genealogical Quarterly 1 (1937): 22. For the years 1811-13.

38.45   *------. "Excerpts from the Eagle, Established 1817, by John Herman, Printer and Publisher, Lancaster, Fairfield County, Ohio." Ohio Genealogical Quarterly 1 (1937): 93. For the years 1817-31.

38.46   ------. "Gleanings from the Supporter, Printed by Nashee and Denny, Chillicothe, Ohio." Ohio Genealogical Quarterly 4 (1940): 305-9. Includes death notices for the years 1809-23.

38.47   ------. "Jefferson County Newspaper Notices." Ohio Genealogical Quarterly 2 (1938): 164-65. Includes death notices for 19 Dec. 1816-29 June 1820.

38.48   ------. "Notices from the Western Star, Lebanon, Warren County, Ohio." Ohio Genealogical Quarterly 5 (1941): 403-6. Includes death notices for 1810-24.

38.49   Conner, E. Margaret Masters. Pioneer Cemeteries of Guernsey County. Cambridge, Ohio: Conner and Goodpaster, 1963.

38.50   Coolman, Ford L., and Rachel W. Kreider. The Mennonite Cemeteries of Medina County, Ohio, with a Brief Historical Sketch of the Churches. [Wadsworth, Ohio]: F. L. Coolman, 1971

38.51   Coshocton Public Library. Index to Newspaper Obituaries, Coshocton County, Ohio, 1826-1908: In the Library's Microfilm Newspaper Files. Coshocton, Ohio: Coshocton Public Library, 1964.

38.52   Craig, Robert D. Brown County, Ohio Cemeteries. 2 vols. Cincinnati: Craig, 1963.

38.53   ------. Clermont County, Ohio, Records. 7 vols. N.p. 1964-. Includes cemetery inscriptions.

38.54   ------. Marriages, 1844-1847, and Deaths, 1844-1845 and 1847-1848 for the City of Cincinnati, Hamilton County, Ohio, That Were Extracted Out of Newspapers. Salt Lake City: Genealogical Society, 1965. Microfilm. USIGS

38.55   ------. Preble County, Ohio, Cemetery Inscriptions. Cincinnati: Craig, 1963.

38.56   *Dale, Raymond E. "Cincinnati (Ohio) Newspaper Notices (1847-1848)." Nebraska and Midwest Genealogical Record 12 (1934): 32-33. Only a small number of deaths listed here.

38. OHIO

38.57   <u>Darby and Jerome Townships, Union County, Ohio, Cemeteries</u>. Marysville, Ohio: Union County Chapter, Ohio Genealogical Society, 1982.

38.58   Daughters of the American Revolution. Ohio. <u>Genealogical Collection</u>. Washington, D.C.: Daughters of the American Revolution Library, n.d. Filmed for the Genealogical Society, 1970. Microfilm. USIGS Includes abstracts of genealogical interest from the <u>Clinton Republican</u>, Wilmington, 19 July 1866 through 31 Dec. 1868, and death records from old newspapers for Franklin county, 1811-32.

38.59   ------. Beech Forest Chapter, Williamsburg. <u>Monument Inscriptions Prior to 1900 from Cemeteries in Clermont County, Ohio</u>. 10 vols. in 1. [Evansville, Ind.: Unigraphic], 1952.

38.60   ------. Cincinnati Chapter. Genealogical Records Committee. <u>Death Records - the "Western Christian Advocate," Cincinnati, Ohio: A Collection of Death Records for April through August 7, 1846, January through March 14, 1855, January through February 20, 1861</u>. Cincinnati, Ohio: Cincinnati Chapter of the National Society Daughters of the American Revolution, 1979. (American Periodicals: 1800-1850)

38.61   ------. Columbus Chapter. <u>From Old Newspapers Franklin County, Ohio. Death Records from July 17, 1811 to October 18, 1832</u>. Columbus, Ohio: Daughters of the American Revolution, n.d. O

38.62   ------. Cuyhoga-Portage Chapter. Genealogical Records Committee. <u>Cemetery Inscriptions, Copley Township, Summit County, Ohio</u>. Akron, Ohio, 1959.

38.63   ------. George Clinton Chapter. <u>Abstracts from "Clinton Republican," 1870</u>. Wilmington, Ohio: Daughters of the American Revolution, n.d. O

38.64   ------. <u>Abstracts of Genealogical Interest from "Clinton Republican," Wilmington, Ohio, July 19, 1866 through December 31, 1868</u>. N.p., n.d. O

38.65   ------. Mahoning County. <u>Records of Administrators, Deaths, Marriages, etc., Collected from Mahoning Valley Newspapers 1839-1863</u>. Youngstown, Ohio: Daughters of the American Revolution, 1962. O

38.66   ------. Marietta Chapter. <u>Death Notices from Marietta Newspapers 1811-1830</u>. Microfilm. USIGS

38.67   ------. <u>Obituaries, Noble County, Ohio</u>. Marietta, Ohio: Daughters of the American Revolution, 1976.

38.68   ------. Wauseon Chapter. <u>Cemetery Inscriptions, Fulton County, Ohio</u>. 2 vols. Wauseon, Ohio: Daughters of the American Revolution, 1953-56. v. 1. Chesterfield, Dover, Franklin Pike, and Royalton townships; v. 2. Amboy, Fulton, Gorham, Swan Creek, and York townships.

38.69   ------. Western Reserve Chapter. <u>Obituaries of Ashtabula County, Ohio,</u>
         <u>1831-1869 at the Western Reserve Historical Society</u>. N.p.: Daughters of
         the American Revolution, 1972. O

38.70   Davidson, Edgar S. <u>Wellsville, 1852</u>. Wellsville, Ohio: Wellsville Historical
         Society, 1952. (Wellsville Echoes, v. 4, no. 4) Includes deaths and
         marriages from the <u>Wellsville Patriot</u>.

38.71   <u>Dayton Journal Index</u>. Prepared by the Newspaper Index Project, Work
         Projects Administration in Ohio. Dayton, 1940-. 5 vols. For the years
         1934-38.

38.72   <u>Death Notices from Marietta, Ohio Newspapers, 1811-1854</u>. Microfilm.
         Filmed by the Genealogical Society at Campus Martius Museum, Marietta,
         Ohio, 1973. USIGS

38.73   "Death Notices, Miamisburg, Montgomery County, Ohio, 1872-1873."
         <u>Gateway to the West</u> 2 (1969): 143.

38.74   <u>Deutsche Pionier. Erinnerungen aus dem Pionier-Leben der Deutschen in</u>
         <u>Amerika</u>, v. 1-18. Cincinnati, Ohio: Deutscher Pionier-Verein, 1869-87.
         This magazine published numerous lengthy and detailed obituaries.

38.75   Dickinson, Marguerite. <u>Obituaries Abstracted from Holmes County, Ohio</u>
         <u>Papers in "Farmer Hub" Office, Millersburg Library, Holmes County</u>
         <u>Historical Society and Western Reserve Historical Society</u>. N.p. 1973.
         Covers the years 1862-95.

38.76   Dickore, Marie Paula, and Robert D. Craig. <u>Hamilton County, Ohio,</u>
         <u>Cemetery Inscriptions</u>. 2 vols. Cincinnati: R. D. Craig, 1963.

38.77   Dillman, Alma G. <u>Obituary Index to Elyria, Ohio, Newspapers, 1830-1874</u>.
         Elyria, Ohio: Elyria Public Library, 1968.

38.78   Dove, Ivan, Joy Dove, and Ron Wintermute. <u>Licking County, Ohio</u>
         <u>Cemeteries, Perry Township</u>. Newark, Ohio: Licking County Genealogical
         Society, 1984.

38.79   Early Settlers' Association of the Western Reserve, Cleveland, Ohio. <u>Annals</u>, v.
         1-11, no. 6, 1880-1927; 1928-. Cleveland, Ohio: Early Settlers' Associa-
         tion of the Western Reserve, 1880-. 1880-1933 as Early Settlers' Associa-
         tion of Cuyahoga County.

38.80   Eynon, Nola R. <u>Noble County Cemeteries; Noble County, Ohio</u>. Cambridge,
         Ohio: Eynon and Eynon, 1965.

38.81   <u>Fairfield County Cemetery Inscriptions</u>. Compiled by Jean S. Collier.
         Columbus, Ohio: J. S. Collier, 1979.

38.82   "Fairfield County Early Newspaper Accounts." <u>Gateway to the West</u> 1 (1968):
         54-59. For the years 1826-44.

38.83   Fedorchak, Catharine Foreaker. "Items from Spirit of Democracy, Woodsfield, Monroe County, Ohio." Ohio Genealogical Society Report 14 (1974): 157-59. For the year 1874.

38.84   ------. Monroe County, Ohio Genealogical Records. 8 vols. Gary, Ind.: n.p., 1960-71. Contains obituaries and death notices for the years 1844-87, with a few later dates included.

38.85   Firelands Pioneer, v. 1-13, n.s., v. 1-. Norwalk, Ohio: Firelands Historical Society, 1858-.

         ------. Obituary Index, 1857-1909. Norwalk, Ohio: Firelands Historical Society, 1910. The Fire Lands consisted of Huron, Erie and part of Ottawa counties.

38.86   Fisher, Maxine Lynn, and Norma Lynn Ortman. Perry Co., Ohio. Junction City, Ohio: Perry County Chapter, Ohio Genealogical Society, 1985. Cemeteries, Thorn township, Perry county.

38.87   Franklin County, Ohio, Cemeteries. 8 vols. Columbus, Ohio: Franklin County Chapter of the Ohio Genealogical Society, 1980-84.

38.88   Franklin County, Ohio Death Records, 1811-1832, from Area Newspapers, July 17, 1811-Oct. 18, 1832, Alphabetically Arranged. Columbus, Ohio: Maxwell Publications, 1977.

38.89   From Old Newspapers, Franklin County, Ohio. Death Records from July 17, 1811 to October 18, 1832. Compiled by Rosalie R. Haddox, and Lorena B. Adamson. Columbus, Ohio: Columbus Chapter, Daughters of the American Revolution, 1972.

38.90   "From the Lancaster Gazette, Lancaster, Ohio, 1830-1833." Ohio Genealogical Quarterly 8 (1944): 664-66. Includes a few deaths.

38.91   Gilbert, Audrey. Obituary Abstracts 1850-1890 from "Eaton Register" and "Eaton Democrat" Newspapers in Eaton, Preble County, Ohio. 3 vols. Owensboro, Ky.: McDowell Publications, 1981-85.

38.92   Ginnery, Penny, Sue McCullough, and Doug McCullough. Cemeteries of Rushcreek Township, Fairfield County, Ohio. Lancaster, Ohio: P. D. Ginnery, 1986.

38.93   Gravestone Inscriptions of Scioto County, Ohio. 10 vols. [Minford, Ohio: C. R. Shoemaker], 1979-81.

38.94   Green, Karen Mauer. Pioneer Ohio Newspapers, 1793-1810: Genealogical and Historical Abstracts. Galveston, Tex.: Frontier Press, 1986.

38.95   Greene County, Ohio, Cemetery Inscriptions. Xenia, Ohio: Greene County Chapter, Ohio Genealogical Society, 1982-86. v. 1. Miami township; v. 2. Silvercreek township; v. 3. Jefferson, New Jasper, Caesarscreek, and Xenia townships; v. 4. Spring Valley and Sugarcreek townships; v. 5. Cedarville and Ross townships.

38.96 <u>Hamilton County, Ohio, Burial Records</u>. Edited by Mary H. Remler. [Cincinnati, Ohio]: Hamilton County Chapter of Ohio Genealogical Society, 1984.

38.97 Hayward, Elizabeth McCoy. <u>Vital Records from the "Baptist Weekly Journal," 1832 and 1833, and the "Cross and Baptist Journal," 1834</u>. Ridgewood, N.J.: n.p., 1947.

38.98 Helwagen, Martha W. "Clippings from Early Ohio Newspapers: <u>Democratic Herald and Workingman's Press</u>, Published Dayton, Ohio, Montgomery County." <u>Ohio Records and Pioneer Families</u> 4 (1963): 154-56. For the years 1836-39.

38.99 *------. "Clippings from Early Ohio Newspapers: <u>Liberty Hall and Cincinnati Mercury</u>." <u>Ohio Records and Pioneer Families</u> 7 (1966): 30-32. For the years 1805-11.

38.100 ------. "Clippings from Early Ohio Newspapers: <u>People's Press</u>, Xenia, Ohio." <u>Ohio Records and Pioneer Families</u> 9 (1968): 143-44. For the years 1826-27.

38.101 Hixon, Mary J., and Frances Welch Hixon. 2 vols. <u>Cemetery Inscriptions of Jackson County, Ohio</u>. Baltimore: Gateway Press, 1982.

38.102 ------. <u>Soldiers Buried in Jackson County, Ohio</u>. [Jackson, Ohio?]: M. J. Hixon, 1983.

38.103 Hodge, Robert Allen. <u>Marriage and Death Notices from the Xenia (Ohio) "Torch-Light," 1844-1870</u>. Fredericksburg, Va.: Hodge, 1978.

38.104 Howard, Scotty, and Loraine Davis Howard. <u>Obituaries of Athens Countians and Their Families</u>. Athens, Ohio: Howard, 1984.

38.105 <u>Index to Cleveland Newspapers: "Cleveland Press" and "Plain Dealer,"</u> v. 1-. Cleveland: Public Library, General Reference Department, 1976-. Monthly with annual cumulations.

38.106 <u>Information Copied from Death Notices and Obituaries As Published in the "News-Herald," (Vol. 98), 1933, Hillsboro, Ohio</u>. Compiled by Evelyn Easter. Hillsboro, Ohio: Southern Ohio Genealogical Society, [1986].

38.107 <u>Interment Records of Greenwood Cemetery</u>. [Zanesville, Ohio?]: Muskingum County Genealogical Society, 1984.

38.108 "Items from the <u>Olive Branch</u>, Circleville, Ohio." <u>Ohio Genealogical Quarterly</u> 4 (1940): 324-27. Includes a few deaths, 1821-22.

38.109 Johnstown Genealogy Society. <u>Cemetery Inscriptions</u>. [Johnstown, Ohio]: Johnstown Genealogy Society, 1971.

38. OHIO

38.110   ------. Newark Cedar Hill Cemetery, Newark, Ohio, Licking County. 2
          vols. Johnstown, Ohio: Johnstown Genealogy Society, 1972-73.

38.111   Jones, Isabel Sutton. Lawrence Township Cemetery Inscriptions: Lawrence
          County, Ohio. Indexed by John L. E. Jones. Ironton, Ohio: Lawrence
          County Genealogical Society, 1984.

38.112   Kilner, Arthur R. Cemetery Tombstone Inscriptions and Photographs of
          Selected Greene County, Ohio, Pioneers from the 1700s and 1800s.
          Xenia, Ohio: A. R. Kilner, 1983.

38.113   "Knox County, Ohio Death Notices, September 25, 1849-March 4, 1851."
          Gateway to the West 1 (1968): 178-80.

38.114   Lambert, Marguerite N. Death Notices from Ohio Newspapers at the Logan
          County Historical Society, Bellefontaine, Ohio. Ann Arbor, Mich.:
          Lambert, 1976.

38.115   Lee, Charles R. History of Walnut Grove Cemetery. Naples, Fla.: Neapolitan
          Publishers, [1970]. Includes inscriptions.

38.116   McBride, David Newton, and Jane N. McBride. Cemetery Inscriptions of
          Highland County, Ohio. 2d ed. Hillsboro, Ohio, 1972.

38.117   McClintock, Mary. "Auglaize County, Ohio, Obituaries, 1877-1879." Ohio
          Records and Pioneer Families 9 (1968): 180-82.

38.118   McKitrick, Arthur. Cemetery Inscriptions from Washington County, Ohio.
          [Coal Run, Ohio: McKitrick, 197-].

38.119   "Marriages and Deaths from the Toledo Blade, Lucas County, Ohio,
          1841-1842." Ohio Records and Pioneer Families 18 (1977): 164-68.

38.120   Mart, Larry D. Clinton County, Ohio Newspapers Death and Obituary
          Abstracts, 1838 to 1867. Lima, Ohio: Mart, 1973.

38.121   ------. Clinton County, Ohio Obituaries, 1867-1875 and Selected
          Genealogical Notes. Lima, Ohio: n.p., 1976.

38.122   "Meigs County, Ohio Newspaper Accounts 1851-52." Gateway to the West 2
          (1969): 111.

38.123   Mercer County, Ohio, Cemetery Inscriptions. 2 vols. Celina, Ohio: Mercer
          County Chapter, Ohio Genealogical Society, 1984-86.

38.124   Midlam, Paul J., and Barbara Midlam. Cemetery Inscriptions of Marion
          County, Ohio. Marion, Ohio: Marion Area Genealogy Society, 1985.

38.125   Minderman, Edith Johnson. Ottawa, Sandusky, and Seneca Counties, Ohio,
          Newspaper Obituary Abstracts, 1836-1870. Fort Wayne, Ind.: M. B.
          Clegg, 1985.

38.126   Montgomery County, Ohio Cemetery Inscriptions. . . . 3 vols. Dayton, Ohio: Montgomery County Chapter of the Ohio Genealogical Society, 1982-84.

38.127   Moore, Denise Kay Mahan. Champaign County Records. 3 vols. Gautier, Miss.: D. K. M. Moore, 1982-84. v. 1. Cemetery records of Adams and Johnson townships; v. 2. Cemetery and church records of Mad River township, Jackson township; v. 3. Cemetery records of Concord Township, Jackson township.

38.128   Morrow County, Ohio, Tombstone Inscriptions. Mount Gilead, Ohio: Morrow County Genealogical Society, 1986.

38.129   Muskingum County, Ohio, Blue Rock and Salt Creek Cemetery Inscriptions. Zanesville, Ohio: Muskingum County Genealogical Society, 1983.

38.130   Muskingum County, Ohio: Cemeteries of Wayne Township. [Zanesville? Ohio]: Muskingum County Chapter, Ohio Genealogical Society, 1982.

38.131   Myers, James C., and Mary L. Myers. Cemeteries of Aid Township, Lawrence County, Ohio. Gallipolis, Ohio: Gallia County Historical Society, 1983.

38.132   ------. Cemeteries of Mason Township, Lawrence County, Ohio. [Gallipolis? Ohio]: Gallia County Historical Society, 1982.

38.133   Myers, Ruby M. "Old Newspaper Clippings Found in the Bible of Charlotte Couch Myers." Ohio Genealogical Society Report 17 (1977): 114-19.

38.134   Noble County, Ohio Cemetery Inscriptions. 3 vols. Caldwell, Ohio: Noble County Chapter of the Ohio Genealogical Society, 1984-85.

38.135   Oberlin College. Obituary Record of the Officers and Alumni. Oberlin, n.d. (Its Bulletin).

38.136   Obituaries from Bowerston, Ohio and Neighboring Communities; in Harrison and Carroll Counties. Compiled by Alpha H. Shiltz, and edited by David Shiltz. 2 vols. Sugar Grove, Ohio: D. Shiltz, 1977.

38.137   Obituaries of Ashtabula County, Ohio, 1831-1869 [at the] Western Reserve Historical Society. Compiled by the Western Reserve Chapter, Daughters of the American Revolution. Cleveland, 1972.

38.138   Obituaries, Vol. 3, 1900-1905, "Hillsborough Gazette," Ohio. Compiled by Evelyn Easter. Hillsborough, Ohio: Southern Ohio Genealogical Society, [198-?].

38.139   "Obituary Abstracts from the Central Christian Advocate, 1853-60." Ohio Record and Pioneer Families 18 (1977): 119-29. Includes only obituaries which refer to Ohio. The Central Christian Advocate was published for the Southwestern Conference of the Methodist Episcopal Church with offices in St. Louis.

38.140   "Obituary Abstracts from the <u>Pittsburgh Christian Advocate</u>, January 1864." <u>Ohio Records and Pioneer Families</u> 18 (1977): 129. Includes only obituaries which refer to Ohio.

38.141   <u>Obituary Extracts from Highland County, Ohio Newspapers, Hillsboro, Ohio 1883-1899</u>. Compiled by Evelyn Easter. Hillsboro, Ohio: Southern Ohio Genealogical Society, 1986.

38.142   <u>Obituary Index to Elyria, Ohio Newspapers, 1875-1883</u>. Compiled by Alma G. Dillman. Elyria, Ohio: Elyria Public Library, 1982. Extends the compiler's earlier (1968) work, <u>Obituary Index to Elyria, Ohio Newspapers, 1830-1874</u>, no. <u>38</u>.77.

38.143   <u>Obituary, Marriage, and Miscellaneous Newspaper Clippings 1880-1944</u>. Compiled by Elvina Dunn Moulton, and Julia Moulton. 1964. Microfilm. Rochester, N.Y.: Eastman Kodak Co., [1971?].

38.144   <u>Obituary Newspaper Clippings 1893-1934</u>. Compiled by Elvina Dunn Moulton. 1964. Microfilm. Cleveland: Micro Photo Inc., 1971?

38.145   <u>Ohio Cemetery Records</u>. Extracted from the <u>Old Northwest Genealogical Quarterly</u>, with an index by Elizabeth P. Bentley. Baltimore, Md.: Genealogical Publishing Company, 1984. Consists principally of tombstone inscriptions from cemeteries in northeastern and central Ohio. Includes a number of inscriptions from cemeteries in Haddam, Connecticut, and Rutland, Massachusetts, which were important departure points for migrations into the "Old Northwest."

38.146   "Ohio Death Notices, 1875, Church of the Brethren." <u>Gateway to the West</u> 6 (1973): 87-88. Death notices taken from the <u>Christian Family Companion and Gospel Visitor</u>, a Church of the Brethren publication published in Tyrone, Dale City, Pennsylvania.

38.147   Ohio Genealogical Society. Columbiana County Chapter. <u>Columbiana County, Ohio Cemetery Inscriptions</u>. Salem, Ohio: The Chapter, 1976.

38.148   ------. Pike County Chapter. <u>Evergreen Union Cemetery, Pike County, Waverly, Ohio: Tombstone Inscriptions</u>. Compiled by Virginia Horner Hinds. Waverly, Ohio: The Chapter, 1977.

38.149   ------. Union County Chapter. <u>York Township Cemeteries, Union County, Ohio</u>. [Marysville, Ohio]: The Chapter, [1981].

38.150   ------. Wood County Chapter. <u>Wood County, Ohio Cemetery Inscriptions, Indexed</u>. Bowling Green, Ohio: The Chapter, 1983. There are volumes for Milton, Washington, Bloom, Liberty, Plain, and Portage townships.

38.151   "Ohio Obituaries Published in the <u>Evangelical Messenger</u>, 1848-50." <u>Gateway to the West</u> 5 (1972): 45. The <u>Evangelical Messenger</u> was published in New Berlin, Pennsylvania, a publication of the Evangelical Church.

38.152   Ohio Source Records from the "Ohio Genealogical Quarterly". Baltimore:
          Genealogical Publishing Co., 1986. Includes newspaper extracts and
          cemetery records.

38.153   Ohio State Journal Index. Prepared by the Newspaper Index Project, Work
          Projects Administration in Ohio. Columbus, 1941-. For the years
          1934-39.

38.154   Perry County Cemetery Inscriptions. Compiled by Jean S. Collier.
          Columbus, Ohio: J. S. Collier, 1975.

38.155   "Pickaway County Early Newspaper Accounts 1821-1823." Gateway to the
          West 2 (1969): 57-59.

38.156   Pioneer Cemeteries of Southeastern Ohio, 1801-1980: The Mound Cemetery,
          Marietta, Ohio. Edited by E. Margaret Masters Conner. Cambridge,
          Ohio: Guernsey County Genealogical Society, 1981.

38.157   Powell, Esther Weygandt. Stark County, Ohio: Early Church Records and
          Cemeteries. Akron, Ohio, 1973.

38.158   ------. Tombstone Inscriptions and Family Records of Belmont County,
          Ohio. Akron, Ohio, 1969.

38.159   ------. Tombstone Inscriptions and Family Records of Carroll County, Ohio.
          Akron, Ohio, 1973.

38.160   ------. Tombstone Inscriptions and Family Records of Jefferson County,
          Ohio. Akron, Ohio, 1968.

38.161   ------. Tombstone Inscriptions and Other Records of Delaware County,
          Ohio: Including Portions of Morrow and Marion Counties. Akron, Ohio,
          1972.

38.162   Price, Carolyn. North Jackson Township Cemetery, Mahoning County, North
          Jackson, Ohio . . . . Akron, Ohio: C. Price, [1983].

38.163   Putnam County Cemeteries. Compiled by the Putnam County Genealogical
          Society. Evansville, Ind.: Whipporwill Publications, 1986. v. 1. Monroe
          Township.

38.164   Raber, Nellie Marie. "Western Christian Advocate," Cincinnati, Ohio, Death
          Notices from Volume Ten, April 21, 1843-April 12, 1844. Lakewood,
          Ohio: n.p., 1943. (American Periodicals: 1800-1850)

38.165   "Revolutionary Records; Obituaries from the Painesville Telegraph of 1829."
          Daughters of the American Revolution Magazine 31 (1907): 547. Contains
          only four obituaries.

38.166   Richland County, Ohio, Cemetery Records. Compiled by the Richland
          County Chapter of the Ohio Genealogical Society. Evansville, Ind.:
          Whipporwill Publications, 1981.

38.167   Robbins, Iona E. <u>Olena & Hull Cemeteries: Peru-Olena Road, Bronson Township, Huron County, Ohio</u>. Norwalk, Ohio: I. E. Robbins, 1985.

38.168   Sandusky County Pioneer and Historical Association, Fremont, Ohio. <u>Year Book</u>, 1913-24/29. Freemont, Ohio: The Association, 1913-14/29.

38.169   Schirack, Edna Erb, and Larry Schirack, Jr. <u>Obituaries from the "Columbus Citizen Journal," Columbus (Franklin Co.) Ohio, January 1, 1985-March 30, 1985</u>. [Greenville, Ohio: E. E. Schirack], 1985.

38.170   ------. <u>Obituaries Taken from the "Daily Advocate," Greenville, Ohio</u>. Greenville, Ohio: L. and E. Schirack, 1984.

38.171   Schlegel, Donald M. <u>The Columbus Catholic Cemetery: History and Records, 1846-1874</u>. Columbus, Ohio: Columbus History Service, 1983.

38.172   ------. <u>The Columbus City Graveyards: Containing Histories of the Franklinton, North, East, South, and Colored Graveyards of Columbus, Ohio, with a Consolidated List of All Known Lot Owners, Burials, Inscriptions, and Removals</u>. Columbus, Ohio: Columbus History Service, 1985.

38.173   Seaman, Vashti K. <u>Burial Records with Some Family Records of Four Cemeteries, Henry Co. O., near Ridgeville Corners</u>. Wauseon, Ohio, 1968.

38.174   Seder, Mrs. A. R. <u>Index to the Subjects of Obituaries (Sterbfälle, Todesanzeigen) Abstracted from "Der Christlilche Botschafter" of the Evangelical Church, 1836-1866</u>. N.p. 1967.

38.175   Short, Mrs. Don, and Mrs. Dale Bowers. <u>Cemetery Inscriptions, Darke County, Ohio</u>. Greenville, Ohio, 1968.

38.176   ------. <u>Cemetery Inscriptions, Preble County, Ohio</u>. Arcanum? Ohio, 1969.

38.177   Simon, Margaret Miller. <u>Canfield Township Cemetery and Death Records, Mahoning County, Ohio</u>. Youngstown, Ohio: Mahoning County Chapter, Ohio Genealogical Society, 1983.

38.178   ------. <u>Mahoning County, Ohio, Newspaper Obituary Abstracts, 1843-1870</u>. Edited by Michael Barren Clegg. Fort Wayne, Ind.: M. B. Clegg, 1983.

38.179   Sims, James, and Janet Sims. <u>Sandusky Co., OH Cemeteries</u>. Arvada, Colo.: Ancestor Publishers, 1979.

38.180   Snodgrass, Anne Burgstaller. <u>Clark County, Ohio Newspaper Abstracts, 1829-1832: Obituaries-Marriages and Selected Genealogical Notes</u>. [Ohio]: Clark County Genealogical Society, 1984.

38.181   ------. <u>Clark County, Ohio Newspaper Abstracts, 1833-1835: Obituaries-Marriages and Selected Genealogical Notes</u>. [Ohio]: Clark County Genealogical Society, 1986.

38.182 Sottek, James J. <u>A Star Rose in the West: A Short Account of the Toledo Foundations of the Oblates of St. Francis de Sales from 1943 to 1972</u>. Toledo, Ohio: Magers Printing, 1972. Appendix B: Necrology of the Oblates of St. Francis de Sales who have served in the Toledo-Detroit Province.

38.183 Stroup, Hazel. <u>Butler County, Ohio, Cemetery Records</u>. Mangilao, Guam: R. D. Craig; Hamilton, Ohio: Stroup, n.d.

38.184 <u>Summit County, Ohio, Cemetery Inscriptions</u>. 3 vols. [Akron? Ohio]: Summit County Chapter, Ohio Genealogical Society, 1979.

38.185 Thompson, Carl N. <u>Historical Collections of Brown County, Ohio</u>. Piqua, Ohio: Hammer Graphics, 1969. Pp. 1095-1174 contain death and obituary notices from various county newspapers on file in the Ohio Historical Library.

38.186 Timman, Henry R. <u>Newspaper Abstracts, Huron County, Ohio, 1822-1835</u>. Norwalk, Ohio: n.p., 1974.

38.187 <u>Toledo Blade Index</u>. Prepared by the Newspaper Index Project, Work Projects Administration in Ohio. Toledo, 1941-. For the years 1936-38.

38.188 <u>Tombstone Inscriptions and Other Records of St. Adelbert's Cemetery, Bagley Road, Middleburg Heights, Cuyahoga County, Ohio</u>. [Ohio]: Cuyahoga/West Chapter, Ohio Genealogical Society, 1981.

38.189 <u>Tombstone Inscriptions from the Cemeteries in Medina County, Ohio, 1983: "Whispers from the Past."</u> Compiled by the Medina County Genealogical Society. Evansville, Ind.: Whipporwill Publications, 1984.

38.190 <u>Tombstone Inscriptions, Fulton County, Ohio</u>. 2 vols. Swanton, Ohio: Fulton County Chapter, Ohio Genealogical Society, 1986.

38.191 <u>Tombstone Inscriptions . . . Ross County, Ohio</u>. 3 vols. Chillicothe, Ohio: Ross County Genealogical Society, 1986-87. v. 1. Green Township; v. 2. Colerain Township; v. 3. Liberty Township.

38.192 Towne, Jeanette C. <u>Cemeteries, Leroy Township, Lake County, Ohio</u>. N.p. 1977.

38.193 <u>Trumbull County, Ohio, Cemetery Inscriptions, 1800-1930</u>. N.p.: Trumbull County Chapter, Ohio Genealogical Society, 1983.

38.194 "Trumbull County, Ohio Newspaper Accounts." <u>Gateway to the West</u> 2 (1969): 27-30. For the year 1833.

38.195 <u>Tuscarawas County, Ohio Cemeteries</u>. 3 vols. New Philadelphia, Ohio: Tuscarawas County Genealogical Society, 1981-84.

38.196   U.S. Work Projects Administration. Ohio. <u>Annals of Cleveland--1818-1935:</u>
          <u>A Digest and Index of the Newspaper Record of Events and Opinions in</u>
          <u>Two Hundred Volumes.</u> 59 vols. in 47. Cleveland, 1936-38.

38.197   <u>Van Wert County, Ohio, Cemetery Inscriptions.</u> 3 vols. [Van Wert, Ohio]:
          Van Wert County Chapter, Ohio Genealogical Society, 1982-86.

38.198   Wagner, Charles W. <u>Cemetery Inscriptions of Fairfield County, Ohio.</u> N.p.
          1948?

38.199   Warren, Violet, and Jeannette Grosvenor. <u>A Monumental Work: Inscriptions</u>
          <u>and Interments in Geauga County, Ohio, through 1983.</u> Evansville, Ind.:
          Whipporwill Publications, 1985.

38.200   <u>Warren County Cemetery Records.</u> 5 vols. Lebanon, Ohio: Warren County
          Genealogical Society, 1984-86. v. 1. Morrow Township; v. 2. Harlan
          Township; v. 3 Union Township; v. 4. Clearcreek Township; v. 5.
          Hamilton Township.

38.201   Wayne County Historical Society (Ohio). Genealogical Section. <u>Wayne</u>
          <u>County, Ohio Burial Records.</u> 2d ed. Evansville, Ind.: Unigraphic, 1980.

38.202   Western Christian Advocate. <u>Obituaries and Marriages. Abstracted.</u> 2 vols.
          N.p.: Daughters of the American Revolution, 1944/45-54. v. 1. 1834-47;
          v. 2. 1847-48. In

38.203   Whiteman, Jane. <u>Athens County, Ohio, Cemetery Records.</u> Tulsa, Okla.: J.
          Whiteman, 1983.

38.204   *Wight, Willard. "Newspaper Items, the <u>Ohio Gazette</u>, Delaware, Ohio." <u>Ohio</u>
          <u>Genealogical Quarterly</u> 5 (1941): 452-55. For the years 1830-40.

38.205   Wilke, Katherine. <u>Newspaper Death Records, Darke County, Ohio.</u> 4 vols.
          N.p. 1968-. v. 1. 1850-80; v. 2. 1880-85; v. 3. 1886-91; v. 4. 1892-98.

38.206   ------. <u>Newspaper Gleanings, Union City, Randolph County.</u> N.p. 1969.
          v. 1. 1873-83.

38.207   <u>Wilkesville Township, Vinton County, Ohio, Cemetery Inscriptions.</u> Compiled
          by Frances Welch Hixon, and Mary J. Hixon. [Jackson, Ohio]: F. W.
          Hixon, M. J. Hixon, 1982.

38.208   Wilson, Linda H. <u>Cemetery Inscriptions of Brown County, Ohio.</u>
          Georgetown, Ohio: Wilson, 1977.

38.209   <u>Youngstown Vindicator Index.</u> Prepared by the Newspaper Index Project,
          Work Project Administration in Ohio. Youngstown, 1941-. For the years
          1933-38.

39. OKLAHOMA

39.1 *"Births, Deaths and Marriages from the Ames Enterprise, 1901-1905." Oklahoma Genealogical Society Quarterly 7 (1962): 340.

39.2 Bogle, Dixie. Cherokee Nation Births and Deaths, 1884-1901, Abstracted from "Indian Chieftain" and "Daily Chieftain" Newspapers. Owensboro, Ky.: Cook and McDowell Publications, 1980.

39.3 Carrigan, Evelyn. "Births, Marriages and Deaths from Tulsa Daily Democrat, Tulsa, Oklahoma." Tulsa Annals 13 (1978): 24-30. For the years 1910-11.

39.4 Carselowey, James Manford. Pryor Cemetery. Adair, Okla., 1962.

39.5 Chronicles of Oklahoma, v. 1-, 1921-. Oklahoma City: Oklahoma Historical Society, 1921-. Beginning with volume 4, 1926, into the 1970s, this series contained a necrology section with obituaries, often lengthy, of prominent Oklahoma pioneers. There are only annual indexes.

39.6 Cranor, Ruby. Talking Tombstones: Pioneers of Washington County. Bartlesville, Okla.: R. A. Cranor, 1983.

39.7 Dollar, Claudine. Cemetery Records of Jackson County, Oklahoma. Blair, Okla.: Pioneer Publishing Co., 1980.

39.8 Erickson, Mahlon Gustav. Payne County Cemetery Index Update: 21 Payne County Cemeteries. [Payne County, Okla.]: M. G. Erickson, [1984].

39.9 Evett, Leila Ford. Kiowa Cemetery. Ozark, Mo.: Yates Publishing Co., 1983?

39.10 LeFlore County, Oklahoma, Cemeteries. Rev. ed. 9 vols. Poteau, Okla.: Poteau Valley Genealogical Society, 1983-84.

39.11 LeFlore County, Oklahoma, Genealogical Records. 8 vols. Poteau, Okla.: Poteau Valley Genealogical Society, 1979-80. v. 1. The Wister area; v. 2. The Shady Point area; v. 3. The Howe-Monroe area; v. 4. The Cameron area; v. 5. The Bokoshe area; v. 6. Oakland Cemetery; v. 7. The Heavener area; v. 8. Talihina cemetery.

39.12 McClain Co., Ok., Death Records, 1882-1984: A Project of the McClain County OK Historical Society. Edited by Joyce A. Rex. Purcell, Okla.: McClain County, Oklahoma Historical Society, 1984.

39.13 Murphy, Polly Lewis. So Lingers Memory: Inventories of Fort Sill, Ok, Cemeteries: Main Post, Apache Indian, Comanche Indian and Comanche Mission Cemeteries, 1869-1985. Lawton, Okla.: P. M. Murphy, 1985. Fort Still was founded in 1869, with first recorded burial in that year. In addition to men and women in military service, wives and children of military men are also buried in Fort Sill cemeteries, as well as civilians who worked on the post. In addition, many Indians are interred in Fort Sill cemeteries.

39. OKLAHOMA

39.14   "Newspaper Obituaries from the Tuttle, Grady County, I. T. Standard August 15, 1907 to January 15, 1909." Oklahoma Genealogical Society Quarterly 22 (1977): 70-71.

39.15   Obituaries of Cherokee Strip Settlers. 2 vols. Enid, Okla.: n.p., n.d.

39.16   Obituaries Printed in the "Miami Daily District News" and the "Miami Daily News Record," 1923-1933. [Miami, Okla.]: R. L. O. Geouge, 1984.

39.17   Okmulgee Genealogical Society. Okmulgee County, Oklahoma, Cemetery Records. Okmulgee, Okla.: The Society, 1974.

39.18   Pioneer Genealogical Society. Cemetery Inscriptions, Kay County, Oklahoma. Ponca City, Okla.: The Society, [1978].

39.19   Pontotoc County Historical and Genealogical Society. Pontotoc County, Oklahoma, Cemetery Inscriptions. 5 vols. [Ada? Okla., 1969-71].

39.20   ------. Rosedale Cemetery, City of Ada, Oklahoma. Ada, Okla.: The Society, 1975.

39.21   Rinehart, Merle, and Noby Kennedy. Gone But Not Forgotten: Cemeteries of Blaine County, Oklahoma. [Geary, Okla.: M. Rinehart, 1982].

39.22   Shadows of the Past: Tombstone Inscriptions in Tulsa County, Oklahoma. Tulsa, Okla.: Tulsa Genealogical Society, 1986.

39.23   Stanley, Mack, and Bess Stanley. Cemeteries in or near Spiro, Oklahoma. 4 vols. [Spiro, Okla.: M. Stanley, 1982]. v. 1. Spiro cemetery; v. 2. New Hope cemetery; v. 3. Fairview cemetery; v. 4. Skullyville Indian cemetery.

39.24   Tedford, Sandra Haney, and Allene Banks Haney. Cemetery Inscriptions of Carter County, Oklahoma. 2 vols. Farmersville, Tex.: Search-N-Print, 1982-83.

39.25   Tiffee, Ellen. Hughes County, Oklahoma, Records: Marriage Book 1, 1907-1909; Calvin Cemetery. Howe, Okla.: Tiffee, 1983.

39.26   Tyner, James W., and Alice Tyner Timmons. Our People and Where They Rest. 12 vols. N.p. 1969-85.

39.27   Wagner, Ivan. Cemetery Records, Garfield County, Oklahoma. Enid, Okla.: Garfield County Genealogists, 1974.

39.28   Woods County Oklahoma Rural Cemeteries. Compiled by the Cherokee Strip Volunteer League. Alva, Okla.: The League, 1982.

40. OREGON

40.1   Adams, Golden V, and Larue P. Leslie. <u>Harney County, Oregon, Cemetery Records: Including Some Entries from Lake and Malheur Counties.</u> Provo, Utah: Adams, 1975.

40.2   Branigar, Thomas R. "Excerpts from the <u>Pacific Christian Advocate</u> 1864-1890." <u>Bulletin of the Whatcom Genealogical Society</u> 7 (1977): 105-6. The <u>Pacific Christian Advocate</u> was published in Portland.

40.3   Brown, Wythle F., and Lloyd E. Brown. <u>Sexton Records of Lone Fir Cemetery, East Portland</u>. Portland, Oreg.: Genealogical Forum of Portland, Oregon, 1981.

40.4   Daughters of the American Revolution. Oregon. Champeeg Chapter. <u>Vital Records from the "Newberg Graphic," 1889-1901</u>. N.p., n.d. Microfilm. Filmed for the Genealogical Society at the DAR Library, Washington, D.C., 1972. USIGS

40.5   Genealogical Forum of Portland, Oregon. <u>Yesterday's Roll Call; Statistical Data and Genealogical Facts from Cemeteries in Baker, Sherman and Umatilla Counties, Oregon</u>. Portland, 1970.

40.6   ------. Cemetery Research Committee for Washington County. <u>Cemetery Records of Northwest Washington County</u>. Portland, Oreg.: Genealogical Forum of Portland, Oregon, 1977.

40.7   Gurley, Mrs. Wayne E. "The <u>Hood River Glacier</u>." <u>Bulletin of the Genealogical Forum of Portland, Oregon</u> 23 (1973): 49-50. Vital records abstracted from existing newspapers on file at the Hood River County Library, for the years 1889-95.

40.8   Kluchesky, Patti. <u>Oregon, Lane County Cemeteries: Headstone Inscriptions</u>. 4 vols. Veneta, Oreg.: P. Kluchesky, 1982-85.

40.9   McKeeman, Opal. <u>Obituaries Taken from the "Oregonian," Portland, Oregon</u>. Portland, Oreg.: McKeeman, 1974. IaHi

40.10   Oregon Historical Society, Portland. <u>Oregon Historical Quarterly</u>, v. 1-, 1900-. Salem, Oreg.: W. H. Leeds, 1900-. Indexes: v. 1-40, 1900-39; v. 41-61, 1940-60. Obituaries can be located in the earlier volumes by using the cumulative indexes.

40.11   <u>Oregon Spectator Index</u>, 1846-54. Prepared by the W.P.A. Newspaper Index Project. 2 vols. N.p. 1941. The <u>Oregon Spectator</u>, the first newspaper on the Pacific Coast, was published in Oregon City.

40.12   Parry, Evelyn. <u>At Rest in Lincoln County</u>. Newport, Oreg.: Lincoln County Historical Society, 1979. (Publication of the Lincoln County Historical Society, no. 17).

40.13   Punelli, Janis. <u>Obituaries Taken from the "Oregonian," Portland Oregon, Listings from August 1964-October 1966, February 1967-March 1968</u>. N.p., n.d.

40.14   Ramsay, Daphne Hon, and Lottie LeGett Gurley. Wasco County, Oregon Cemetery Records: Records from Cemeteries outside the Dalles Area. Portland: Genealogical Forum of Portland, Oregon, 1979.

40.15   Secord, Jeanne M. Duncan, Lura Glass, and LaVina Hutchinson. Grant County Cemeteries. John Day, Oreg.: Secord Press, 1970.

40.16   Smith, Fern. Genealogical Data Copied from the "Pacific Christian Advocate" (Published in Oregon) for the Years 1864-1890. N.p., n.d. Microfilm. USIGS

40.17   Some Cemetery Records of Coos and Curry Counties Oregon: The Alice Hoover Wooldridge Collection. [Portland, Oreg.]: Genealogical Forum of Portland, Oregon, 1982.

40.18   Stoller, Ruth. Cemetery Inscriptions, Yamhill County, Oregon. 2 vols. N.p.: Yamhill County Historical Society, 1980-81. v. 1. Yamhill-Carlton-Lafayyette, and vicinity; v. 2. Sheridan-Willamina, and vicinity.

40.19   Strom, Ora. Jackson Co., Or. Cemeteries. 2 vols. Medford, Oreg.: Rogue Valley Genealogical Society, 1984-85.

40.20   Wojcik, Donna M. The Brazen Overlanders of 1845. Portland, Oreg.: Wojcik, 1976. Contains a list of persons who died in 1845 during the journey to Oregon or shortly after arriving in the Willamette. Also included is a list of Oregon newspapers and obituaries. Although these persons died in Oregon, they were born in other parts of the country.

40.21   Wolf, Keith. "Genealogical Items from the Oregon Free Press of 1848." Beaver Briefs 9 (1977): 31-32. The Oregon Free Press was published in Oregon City.

41. PENNSYLVANIA

41.1   Abstracts (Mainly Deaths) from the "Pennsylvania Gazette," 1775-1783.
        Compiled by Kenneth Scott. Baltimore: Genealogical Publishing Co.,
        1976.

41.2   Alverton and Tarr Cemeteries, East Huntington Township, Westmoreland
        County, Pa. Compiled by Della Reagan Fischer. [McKeesport, Pa.]:
        Fischer, 1976.

41.3   American Daily and General Advertiser, Philadelphia. Marriage and Death
        Notices, 1791-1839. Microfilm. Filmed by the Genealogical Society at
        the Historical Society of Pennsylvania, Philadelphia, 1964. USIGS

41.4   Appleby, Aimee. Surname Index to 49 Dauphin County Cemeteries,
        Pennsylvania. Laughlintown, Pa.: Southwest Pennsylvania Genealogical
        Services, 1980.

41.5   Beaver County Cemeteries. 4 vols. [Apollo, Pa.]: Closson Press, [1982-86].

41.6   Bethel, Dorothy. "Genealogical Data Found in the United Presbyterian, vol.
        XLVII, No. 12, Printed in Pittsburgh, Pa., March 21, 1889." Midwest
        Genealogical Register 12 (1977): 69-71.

41.7   Blatt, Milton K., and Luella E. Blatt. Fairview Cemetery of Salem Bellman's
        Church, Centre Township, Berks County, Pennsylvania; Lots, Lot Owners
        and Burials, 1884-1977. N.p.: Blatt, [1977?].

41.8   Bowman, John Elliot. Some Pennsylvania Veterans of the American
        Revolution; Items Alphabetically Arranged from Newspaper Files,
        1709-1855; Deaths of Revolutionary Veterans in or from Pennsylvania.
        N.p. 1928.

41.9   Brass, Lucas S. Muncy Cemeterys [sic] Graves: Names, Dates and Burial
        No's, Muncy, PA. Williamsport, Pa.: Lycoming County Genealogical
        Society, 1987.

41.10   Bronson, William White, and Charles R. Hildeburn. The Inscriptions in St.
        Peter's Church Yard, Philadelphia. Camden, N.J.: S. Chew, Printer, 1879.

41.11   Brossman, Schuyler C. The Schuyler C. Brossman Collection of Cemetery
        Inscriptions from Various Berks County, Pennsylvania Cemeteries, with a
        Few from Neighboring Areas, Including a Few from Lebanon, Schuylkill,
        and Lancaster Co., Pa.: Approximately 7,000 Inscriptions Compiled from
        1957 to 1975, with Notes and Obituaries As Available. 7 vols.
        Rehrersburg, Pa.: Brossman, 1975.

41.12   Burial Record of Zion's (Stone) Church: Graveyard and Cemetery Near
        Kreidersville, Northampton County, Pa. N.p. 1905. Includes records
        from 1771, to 17 Aug. 1905.

41.13   Butler County Cemetery Inventory. Compiled by the Butler County Historical
        Society. 2 vols. Evansville, Ind.: Whipporwill Publication, 1983. v. 1.
        The northern townships; v. 2. The north-central townships.

41. PENNSYLVANIA

41.14   Cameron County, Pennsylvania. Newspaper Obituaries, 1890-1902.
        Microfilm. Filmed by the Genealogical Society, Emporium, Pa., 1972.
        Contains the newspaper obituaries of Cameron County collected by the
        Cameron County Historical Society. USIGS

41.15   "Canal and Portage Register: Newspaper Items Published at Hollidaysburg,
        Blair County." Your Family Tree 15 (1969): 20-23. For the years
        1836-38.

41.16   Carson Valley Cemetery, Carson Valley, Pennsylvania: From Tombstone
        Inscriptions, Mortuary Records and Obituaries. Compiled by the Family
        Tree Climbers Heritage Club, Hollidaysburg Area Junior High School.
        Altoona, Pa.: Blair County Genealogical Society, 1984.

41.17   The Cemeteries of Mifflin County, Pennsylvania. 2 vols. Lewistown, Pa.:
        Mifflin County Historical Society, 1977.

41.18   Cemetery Records, Hill Grove Cemetery, Connellsville, Fayette County,
        Pennsylvania. Connellsville, Pa.: Connellsville Area Historical Society,
        1984.

41.19   Chauncey, Charles. Obituary Notice Collection, ca. 1909-24. Philadelphia.
        Historical Society of Pennsylvania. NUC MS 61-1453. A collection of
        obituaries of prominent Philadelphians.

41.20   Clark, Edward L. A Record of the Inscriptions on the Tablets and
        Gravestones in the Burial-grounds of Christ Church, Philadelphia.
        Philadelphia: Collins, Printer, 1864.

41.21   Closson, Bob, and Mary Closson. Index to "Mifflin County" Cemetery
        Records. Lewistown, Pa.: Mifflin County Historical Society, 1978.

41.22   ------. Surname Index to 52 Westmoreland County Cemeteries. [Apollo,
        Pa.]: Closson, 1976.

41.23   ------. Westmoreland County, Pa., Cemetery Records. [Apollo, Pa.]:
        Closson, 1980.

41.24   Clyde, John Cunningham. Genealogies, Necrology and Reminiscences of the
        Irish Settlement. N.p. 1879. Pertains to the Scotch-Irish in Northampton
        County.

41.25   Collins, Patricia Wainwright. Marriages and Deaths from the "Cambria
        Tribune," Johnstown, Pennsylvania. 5 vols. [Apollo, Pa.]: Closson Press,
        1981-86. For the years 1853-85.

41.26   Crawford County, Pa. Cemetery Inscriptions. Meadville, Pa.: Crawford
        County Genealogical Society and the Crawford County Historical Society,
        1982. Includes cemeteries of Beaver, East Fairfield, Fairfield, and
        Steuben townships.

41.27   Daughters of the American Revolution. District of Columbia. Patriots'
         Memorial Chapter. Births, Marriages and Deaths 1848-1850, Copied from
         "McMakin's Model American Courier," Published Weekly, on Saturday, in
         Philadelphia, Pennsylvania. Washington, D.C., n.d. Microfilm. USIGS

41.28   ------. Pennsylvania. Genealogical Collection. Washington, D.C., Daughters
         of the American Revolution Library, n.d. Microfilm. USIGS. Contains
         Hanover deaths from newspapers, 1828-1900; genealogical notes for Adams
         County, 1803-57, from Adams Sentinel; marriages and death notices from
         Westmoreland County weekly newspapers 1818-65.

41.29   ------. Fort Antes Chapter. Cemetery Inscriptions--Deaths, Marriages:
         Lycoming, Clinton and North Central Pennsylvania Counties. Jersey
         Shore, Pa.: Genealogical Records Committee, 1961. Includes some
         obituaries and death notices, 1873-1897.

41.30   Deaths and Marriages from the "Weekly Advertiser," 1796-1816. Reading,
         Pa., n.d. In. The Weekly Advertiser was published in Philadelphia.

41.31   Deaths Copied from "Norristown Register," 1804-1845, Norristown, Pa.
         Microfilm. Filmed by the Genealogical Society at the Historical Society
         of Montgomery County, Norristown, 1948. USIGS

41.32   Deaths from the "Chronicle of Times," 1822-1834. Reading, Pa., n.d. In.
         The Chronicle of Times was published in Reading.

41.33   "Deaths from the Philadelphia Repertory, 1810-1811." Publications of the
         Genealogical Society of Pennsylvania 11 (1930-32): 160-62. (American
         Periodicals: 1800-1850). The Philadelphia Repertory was a weekly literary
         magazine which included listings of marriages and deaths.

41.34   DeSantis, Loretta Barker, and Sally Glaser Dufford. Mercer County,
         Pennsylvania, Cemetery Inscriptions. 15 vols. Sharon, Pa.: Mercer
         County Genealogical Society, 1980-87.

41.35   "Dutton Records of Deaths, Marriages, etc., 1770-1870." Publications of the
         Genealogical Society of Pennsylvania 4 (1909): 23-100. A record of
         deaths kept by Hannah Dutton of Sugartown, which lists name, date of
         death and occasionally age and family relationships.

41.36   Dyer, John. Marriage, Births and Deaths: Extracts from the Diary of John
         Dyer. Doylestown, Pa.: Bucks County Historical Society, 1940.
         Microform. Transcribed from the original manuscript. Includes
         tombstone inscriptions.

41.37   Everyname Index to Tombstone Records by Schuyler C. Brossman. Fort
         Wayne, Ind.: Fort Wayne Public Library, 1980.

41.38   Eyerman, John. The Old Grave-yards of Northampton and Adjacent
         Counties in the State of Pennsylvania. Easton, Pa.: Oakhurst House, 1899.
         "Some of the yards having as many as one thousand stones, it has been
         deemed advisable to record only those which stand for persons born prior

to 1870. . . . Genealogical notes have been added to many of the names."--Introduction.

41.39 Fairview Cemetery, Altoona, PA: From Cemetery Records and Tombstone Inscriptions. Altoona, Pa.: Blair County Genealogical Society, 1986.

41.40 *Fendrick, Virginia Shannon. "Notices from the Franklin Repository, Chambersburg, 1802-1805." Publications of the Genealogical Society of Pennsylvania 11 (1930-32): 276-84.

41.41 Fischer, Della Reagan. Cemeteries, Fayette County, Pa. 2 vols. McKeesport, Pa.: Fischer, 1979.

41.42 ------. Death Notices from Weekly Newspapers, Westmoreland County, Pennsylvania, 1866-1900. 1969. Reprint. Laughlintown, Pa.: Southwest Pennsylvania Genealogical Services, 1983.

41.43 ------. Evangelical Lutheran and Reformed Cemetery Inscriptions of Somerset County, Pennsylvania. McKeesport, Pa., 1968.

41.44 ------. 14 Cemeteries, Westmoreland Co., Pa. McKeesport, Pa., 1972. Includes the following cemeteries: Fells, Guffey, Harrold Lutheran, U.M. Methodist, Mars Hill Baptist, Middletown, U.M., Milliron, Old Brush Creek, Old German, Old Mars, Porch, St. Clair, Zion Ev. Lutheran, Zion Reformed.

41.45 ------. Hoffmans or (Hope) Lutheran Church Records, 1813-1924, of South Huntingdon Township, Westmoreland County, Pennsylvania. McKeesport, Pa., 1969.

41.46 ------. Inscriptions: Scottdale Cemetery, Westmoreland County, Scottdale, Pa. McKeesport, Pa.: Fischer, 1979.

41.47 ------. Jacobs Lutheran Church and Cemetery, Masontown, German Twp., Fayette County, Pa. (1793-1885). McKeesport, Pa., 1974.

41.48 ------. Marriage and Death Notices from Weekly Newspapers, 1818-1865, Westmoreland County, Pennsylvania. 2d rev. ed. Laughlintown, Pa.: Southwest Pennsylvania Genealogical Services, 1977.

41.49 ------. Mount Pleasant Cemetery, Mount Pleasant Township, Westmoreland County, Mount Pleasant, Pa. McKeesport, Pa.: Fischer, 1979.

41.50 ------. St. Luke's United Church of Christ: Church and Cemetery Records, Mount Pleasant Twp., Westmoreland County, Pleasant Unity, Pa. McKeesport, Pa., 1974.

41.51 ------. Tombstone Inscriptions of Cemeteries, Somerset County, Pa. 3 vols. McKeesport, Pa.: Fischer, 1977.

41.52 ------. 27 Cemeteries: Westmoreland Co., Pa. McKeesport, Pa.: Fischer, 1970.

41. PENNSYLVANIA

41.53   Fitler, Elizabeth Parker. "Genealogical Gleanings from the <u>Pennsylvania Evening Post</u>, 1776." <u>Pennsylvania Genealogical Magazine</u> 28 (1973): 68-80. Includes obituaries from this Philadelphia newspaper. Volume 27, pp. 230-37 cite obituaries for 1775.

41.54   Franklin and Marshall College. Lancaster, Pa. Alumni Association. <u>Obituary Record . . . . A Record of the Lives of the Deceased Alumni of Marshall College and of Franklin and Marshall College</u>. 2 vols. Lancaster, Pa., 1897-1909. Covers the years 1837-1909. Also on Microfilm from the Genealogical Society USIGS.

41.55   <u>Genealogy Clippings from the "Indiana Countian," Indiana, Pennsylvania, May 1940-January 1942</u>. n.p., n.d. Death Notices from old newspaper files. In

41.56   Germantown Historical Society, Germantown, Pa. <u>Newspaper Items Relating to Germantown, Historical and Genealogical, 1721-1807</u>. Germantown, Pa., 1934. Includes death notices from Philadelphia newspapers.

41.57   *Gilpin, Isaac Glover. "The Gilpin Register." <u>Chester County Collections</u> 10 (1938): 344-46. Chester County vital records kept by Isaac Glover Gilpin for the years 1804-18.

41.58   Hamilton, Rosalie. <u>Burials of Aleppo Township, Greene Co., Pa</u>. Wind Ridge, Pa.: R. Hamilton, 1985.

41.59   Harrington, Jeanne S. "Susquehanna County Deaths, 1816-1849; Copied from the Susquehanna County, Pennsylvania Newspapers." <u>Proceedings and Collections of the Wyoming Historical and Geological Society</u> 22 (1938): 210-70.

41.60   Hayden, Horace Edwin. "Marriages and Deaths in the Wyoming Section of Pennsylvania, 1797-1810." <u>Proceedings and Collections of the Wyoming Historical and Geological Society</u> 7 (1902): 201-28. Compiled from files of Wilkes-Barre papers.

41.61   ------. "Record of Marriages and Deaths Noticed in the <u>Susquehanna Democrat</u>, Published at Wilkes-Barre, Pa., from Volume I, Number 4, July 3, 1810 to Volume VIII, Number 36, March 6, 1818." <u>Proceedings and Collections of the Wyoming Historical and Geological Society</u> 10 (1909): 167-91.

41.62   Hennen, Dorothy T. <u>Cemetery Records of Greene County, Pennsylvania: A Project of the American Revolution Bicentennial Observance, 1776-1976</u>. 13 vols. Waynesburg, Pa.: D. T. Hennen, 1975-1980.

41.63   Herchenroether, Nell Young. <u>Bethel United Presbyterian Church Cemetery Record</u>. Pittsburgh, Pa.: Herchenroether, 1985.

41.64   Hildeburn, Charles R. "An Index to the Obituary Notices Published in the <u>Pennsylvania Gazette</u> from 1728-1791." <u>Pennsylvania Magazine of History and Biography</u> 10 (1886): 334-49. The <u>Pennsylvania Gazette</u> was published in Philadelphia. The deaths listed in this article can be located by using the magazine's cumulative index.

41.65   <u>Hollidaysburg Presbyterian Cemetery: from Tombstone Inscriptions, Cemetery Maps, and Various Records</u>. Altoona, Pa.: Blair County Genealogical Society, 1982.

41.66   Imler, Robetta E. <u>Bedford County, Pennsylvania, Cemeteries</u>. 8 vols. Denver, Co.: Ancestor Publishers, 1975-81.

41.67   <u>Index to Marriages and Deaths in the "Friend," 1827-1883</u>. Philadelphia, Pa., n.d. PHi (American Periodicals: 1800-1850) The <u>Friend</u>, published in Philadelphia, was a religious and literary journal fostered by the Society of Friends.

41.68   <u>Index to Obituaries from the "Sunday Dispatch" 1868-1883</u>. Philadelphia, n.d. PHi The <u>Sunday Dispatch</u> was published in Philadelphia.

41.69   <u>Index to the Obituaries Published in the "Apollo Sentinel," Apollo, Kiskiminetas Twp., Armstrong Co., Pa., 1924-1941</u>. N.p., n.d. PHi

41.70   <u>Inscriptions of the Unity Presbyterian Church Cemetery, Unity Township, Westmoreland County, Pa</u>. Compiled by Della Reagan Fischer. N.p. 1976.

41.71   Iscrupe, William L. <u>Ligonier Valley Cemeteries</u>. 2 vols. Laughlintown, Pa.: Southwest Pennsylvania Genealogical Services, 1976. v. 1. Ligonier Borough and Township; v. 2. Ligonier Valley Cemetery.

41.72   Knoll, Annie Potteiger. <u>Rehrersburg, Pa., and Vicinity, Berks County: A Collection of Newspaper Clippings of Obituaries, Weddings, Births, etc., Relating to the Community from the Beginning of 1900's to 1970 in 4 Volumes</u>. Philadelphia, n.d. Microfilm. Filmed by the Genealogical Society at the Genealogical Society of Pennsylvania, 1967. USIGS

41.73   Kraynek, Sharon Lee DeWitt. <u>Allegheny County, Pa. Cemetery Records</u>. 11 vols. Apollo, Pa.: Closson Press, 1981-86.

41.74   Ladd, Rhoda English. <u>Morris Township, Tioga County, Pa.: Early History, Census 1850, 1860, 1870, 1880, 1889, Newspaper Obituaries, Cemeteries</u>. Wellsboro, Pa.: Ladd, 1977.

41.75   Ladd, Rhoda English, et al. <u>Cemetery Inscriptions and Historical Data: Tioga County, Pa</u>. Wellsboro, Pa.: Daughters of the American Revolution, Wellsboro Chapter, 1970-.

41.76   ------. <u>Newspaper File: Births, Deaths, Marriages and Historical Data Abstracted from the Local Newspaper File</u>. 7 vols. Wellsboro, Pa.: Ladd, 1982. v. 1. 1829-73; v. 2. 1874-80; v. 3. 1881-1885; v. 4. various dates from 1807-1930; v. 5. 1873-87; v. 6. 1888 through 1895; v. 7. 1896-1900. The newspapers abstracted were from Tioga county.

41.77   ------. <u>A Study of Some Lycoming County Township Census Records and Families. Also Added Cemetery Inscriptions and Family Data to Assist in Research: Lycoming County, Pennsylvania</u>. Wellsboro, Pa., 1980.

41.78   Lancaster County Historical Society. Lancaster, Pennsylvania. <u>Deaths and Marriages Abstracted from Newspapers, 1800-1906</u>. Microfilm. Microfilm made in 1976 by the Genealogical Society from the original cards at the Society in Lancaster. USIGS Material is abstracted from the newspapers of Lancaster and from M. Heisey's scrapbook.

41.79   Lewis, George C. "Record of Marriages and Deaths, 1828 to 1836." <u>Proceedings and Collections of the Wyoming Historical and Geological Society</u> 4 (1899): 133-56. Contains death notices taken from Wilkes-Barre and Kingston newspapers.

41.80   Lingle, Harry A., and Vera A. Lingle. <u>Index to Obituaries in the "Democratic Watchman," 1855-1888</u>. N.p., n.d. Supplement to John H. Wion's <u>Deaths in Central Pennsylvania</u>, no. <u>41</u>.154

41.81   Lontz, Mary Belle. <u>Tombstone Inscriptions of Centre County, Pennsylvania</u>. [Milton, Pa.]: M. B. Lontz, 1984.

41.82   ------. <u>Tombstone Inscriptions of Union County, Pennsylvania</u>. [Milton, Pa., 1967].

41.83   <u>Lutheran Cemetery, Newry, PA: From Cemetery Records and Tombstone Inscriptions</u>. Altoona, Pa.: Blair County Genealogical Society, 1984.

41.84   McClenahen, Dan. <u>Obituaries of Mifflin County, 1822-1880</u>. Reedsville, Pa.: D. McClenahen, 1982.

41.85   McFarland, K. T. H. <u>Inscriptions from Union Dale Cemetery, Allegheny (Now Pittsburgh), Pa</u>. 8 vols. Apollo, Pa.: Closson Press, 1985-86.

41.86   McQuillis, Shirley G, and William L. Iscrupe. <u>Marriages and Deaths from the Ebensburg Sky, Cambria County, Pennsylvania, 1831-1837</u>. Laughlintown, Pa.: Southwest Pennsylvania Genealogical Services, 1983.

41.87   ------. <u>Marriages and Deaths from the "Pittsburgh Gazette," Allegheny County, Pennsylvania, 1829-1833</u>. Laughlintown, Pa.: Southwest Pennsylvania Genealogical Services, 1983.

41.88   ------. <u>Surname Index to 71 Fayette County Cemeteries, Pennsylvania</u>. Laughlintown, Pa.: Southwest Pennsylvania Genealogical Services, 1980.

41.89   McRae, Joan M. <u>Marriage and Death Notices Extracted from Warren County, Pa. Newspapers</u>. 2 vols. N.p.: J. M. McRae, 1982-83. v. 1. 1848-65; v. 2. 1866-75.

41.90   Mapes, Lester D. "Deaths from the <u>Ladies Literary Portfolio</u> 1823-1829." <u>Publications of the Genealogical Society of Pennsylvania</u> 13 (1938-39): 225-27. (American Periodicals: 1800-1850). <u>Ladies Literary Portfolio: A</u>

General Miscellany Devoted to the Fine Arts and Sciences was published in Philadelphia.

41.91 Marriage and Death Notices from Germantown Newspapers, 1867-1890. N.p., n.d. Microfilm. Filmed by the Genealogical Society at the Germantown Historical Society, Philadelphia, 1973. USIGS

41.92 *"Marriage and Death Notices from the Philadelphia Saturday Evening Post." Pennsylvania Genealogical Magazine 27 (1972): 176-79. Notices from the 2 Feb. 1842 issue, the 8 Feb. 1845 issue and the 11 Dec. 1847 issue.

41.93 Marriage and Death Records, 1796-1896, Copied from Various Newspapers. n.p., n.d. Microfilm. USIGS Filmed by the Genealogical Society at the Historical Society of Berks County, Reading Pa., 1949. These records pertain to Berks County.

41.94 Marriages and Deaths Copied from the "Lafayette Aurora," Pottstown, Pa., 1825-1827. N.p., n.d. Microfilm. Filmed by the Genealogical Society at the Historical Society of Montgomery County, Norristown, Pa., 1948. USIGS

41.95 Marriages and Deaths Copied from the "Norristown Free Press," 1829-1837. N.p., n.d. Microfilm. Filmed by the Genealogical Society at the Historical Society of Montgomery County, Norristown, Pa., 1948. USIGS

41.96 Marriages and Deaths Copied from the "Norristown Herald," 1816-1834 and Other Years Prior. N.p., n.d. Microfilm. Filmed by the Genealogical Society at the Historical Society of Montgomey County, Norristown, Pa., 1948. USIGS

41.97 "Marriages and Deaths from the Bedford Gazette." Publications of the Genealogical Society of Pennsylvania 11 (1930-32): 175-79. Deaths for the years 1832-34.

41.98 Marriages and Deaths from the "Hamburg Schnellpost," 1845. Hamburg, Pa., n.d. In

41.99 Marriages and Deaths from the "Kutztown Neutralist," 1833-1837. Kutztown, Pa., n.d. In

41.100 "Memoranda from the Diary of John Dyer of Bucks County, Pa., 1763-1805." Publications of the Genealogical Society of Pennsylvania 3 (1906): 38-72. Includes death records of the area.

41.101 Miner's Journal, Pottsville, Pennsylvania. Marriages, Deaths, Burials, Obituaries, 1829-1855. N.p., n.d. Microfilm. Filmed by the Genealogical Society, 1970. USIGS

41.102 *"Muncy Luminary Notices of Marriages and Deaths 1842-81." Now and Then 9 (1949): 92-93.

41. PENNSYLVANIA

41.103 <u>New St. Patrick's Cemetery and Old St. Patrick's Cemetery, Newry, PA: From Cemetery Records and Tombstone Inscriptions</u>. Altoona, Pa.: Blair County Genealogical Society, 1984.

41.104 <u>Notices of Marriages and Deaths in "Poulson's American Dailey Advertiser."</u> 7 vols. Philadelphia: Genealogical Society of Pennsylvania, 1980. For the years 1791-1839.

41.105 "Obituaries of Pennsylvania Revolutionary Veterans, from Newspaper Files 1790-1855." <u>Publications of the Genealogical Society of Pennsylvania</u> 11 (1930-32): 81-86.

41.106 Obituaries of Philadelphians. Philadelphia, ca. 1880-1913. Newspaper clippings. PHi

41.107 *"Obituaries of Revolutionary Veterans from the <u>Franklin Repository</u> and the <u>Franklin Telegraphy and Democratic Advertiser</u>, etc." <u>Publications of the Genealogical Society of Pennsylvania</u> 11 (1930-32): 196-97.

41.108 Obituary Notices: 1879-1887. PHi. Scrapbook of newspaper clippings collected by Adele Barnsley.

41.109 Obituary Notices of Philadelphia. PHi. Scrapbook of Philadelphia obituaries from newspapers and church bulletins, 1838-73.

41.110 Order of the Founders and Patriots of America. Pennsylvania Society. <u>Necrology of the Pennsylvania Society of the Order of the Founders and Patriots of America, from Its Organization December 28, 1896</u>. Philadelphia: Order of the Founders and Patriots of America, 1912.

41.111 Parkinson, Sarah Woods. <u>Memories of Carlisle's Old Graveyard . . . Containing a List of the Inscriptions on All Stones in the Enclosure in 1898</u>. Carlisle, Pa.: Sentinel, 1930. In most cases, the entire epitaph was recorded.

41.112 Pennsylvania. Historical Society. <u>Deaths from Berks, Dauphin and Philadelphia Counties Newspapers, 1791-1864</u>. Philadelphia, n.d. Microfilm. Filmed by the Genealogical Society at the Historical Society of Pennsylvania, Philadelphia, 1964. USIGS

41.113 ------. <u>Marriage and Deaths in Philadelphia, 1838-1916</u>. Philadelphia, n.d. Microfilm. Filmed by the Genealogical Society at the Historical Society of Pennsylvania, Philadelphia, 1964. USIGS

41.114 Pennsylvania Gazette. <u>An Index to the Obituary Notices Published in the "Pennsylvania Gazette" from 1728-1791</u>. N.p. 1979. PHi

41.115 <u>Pennsylvania Newspaper Excerpts of Genealogical Interest Abstracted from Pennsylvania Newspapers 1798-1874 in the Collection of the Historical Society of Pennsylvania</u>. Philadelphia, n.d. Microfilm. In

41. PENNSYLVANIA

41.116 Penrose, Maryly Barton. "Necrology of Philadelphia 1870-1873." Pennsylvania Traveler 2 (1966): 45-48. This alphabetical listing was transcribed from page 221 of the Public Ledger Almanac, 1873, which listed deaths of leading Philadelphia citizens for 1870-73.

41.117 ------. Philadelphia Marriages and Obituaries 1857-1860, "Philadelphia Saturday Bulletin." Franklin Park, N.J.: Liberty Bell Associates, 1974.

41.118 Philadelphia Magazine and Review; or, Monthly Repository of Information and Amusement, v. 1, Jan.-June 1799. Philadelphia: Benjamin Davies, 1799. (American Periodicals: 1800-1850). Contains records of deaths and marriages for Philadelphians.

41.119 Philadelphia Magazine and Weekly Repository, of Polite Literature, v. 1, Jan.-Nov. 1818. Philadelphia: J. R. Chandler and G. Goodman, 1818. Subtitle varies. (American Periodicals: 1800-1850). Contains obituaries of Philadelphians.

41.120 Pleasants, Henry. The History of Old St. Davids Church, Radnor, Delaware County, Pennsylvania: With a Complete Alphabetical List of Wardens and Vestrymen, and of the Interments in the Graveyard, 1700-1906. Philadelphia: John C. Winston, 1907. Also available in microform. Sanford, N.C.: Microfilming Corporation of America, 1980.

41.121 Poor Richard's Almanac for 1867. . . . Philadelphia: A. Winch, 1866. Contains obituaries of Philadelphians.

41.122 *"Register of Marriages and Deaths, 1800-1801." Pennsylvania Magazine of History and Biography 23 (1899): 98-103. These records were copied from the Philadelphia Repository and Weekly Register. (American Periodicals: 1800-1850). The deaths listed here can be located by using the magazine's cumulative index.

41.123 Rentmeister, Jean R. Marriage and Death Notices Extracted from the "Genius of Liberty and Fayette Advertiser" of Uniontown, Pennsylvania, 1805-1854. Apollo, Pa.: Closson Press, 1981.

41.124 *Roach, Hannah Benner. "Deaths in the Skippack Region." Bulletin of the Historical Society of Montgomery County 8 (1951): 3-11. This is a translation of a German list of 641 deaths, 1793-1845 kept by Jacob Kemper, Philip Markley, and others of the Markley family.

41.125 Robinson, Mary Dummett Nauman. Gleanings from an Old Newspaper. . . . Lancaster, Pa.: Reprinted from the New Era, 1903. (Journal of the Lancaster County Historical Society, v. 7). Extracts from early Lancaster newspapers.

41.126 Saint John's Cemetery, Altoona, PA: From Cemetery Records and Tombstone Inscriptions. Altoona, Pa.: Blair County Genealogical Society, 1982.

41. PENNSYLVANIA

41.127 St. Vincent Archabbey, Latrobe, Pa. Necrologium monasterii Sti. Vincentii a Paulo ex Congregatione Americano-Cassinensi, Americae Septentrionalis. Typis Archiabbatiae Sti. Vincentii, 1907.

41.128 Samuel, Edith. "Index to the Deaths Mentioned in the American Weekly Mercury, 1724-1746." Pennsylvania Magazine of History and Biography 58 (1934): 37-60. The American Weekly Mercury was published in Philadelphia. The deaths listed here can be located by using the magazine's cumulative index.

41.129 Sather, Mrs. Clifford. "Vital Records from the Philadelphia Public Ledger 25 March 1836, Vol. I, no. 1." Bulletin of the Genealogical Forum of Portland, Oregon 23 (1974): 90.

41.130 Sawyer, Ray C. Pennsylvania Deaths and Marriages As Published in the "Christian Intelligencer" of the Reformed Dutch Church 1830-1870. Philadelphia, n.d. Microfilm. Filmed by the Genealogical Society at the Historical Society of Pennsylvania, Philadelphis, 1965. USIGS

41.131 Schneck, Cheryl Fidler. Abstracts of Death Notices Published in "The Press Herald" Newspaper of Pine Grove, Pennsylvania, Beginning January 3, 1879. Pine Grove, Pa.: C. F. Schneck, 198-?

41.132 Schooley, Janet R. The Digger's Index. Newell, Iowa: Bireline Publishing Co., 198-. This is a directory of cemeteries from many counties of Pennsylvania and includes tombstone inscriptions.

41.133 Schultze, Augustus. Guide to the Old Moravian Cemetery of Bethlehem, Pa., 1742-1910. Lancaster, Pa.: Pennsylvania-German Society, 1912. (Proceedings and Addresses of the Pennsylvania-German Society, v. 21.) Contains names of persons buried in the cemetery, with dates and other biographical notes.

41.134 Scott, Kenneth. Abstracts from "American Weekly Mercury," 1719-1746. Baltimore: Genealogical Publishing Co., 1974. The American Weekly Mercury was published in Philadelphia.

41.135 ------. Abstracts from the "Pennsylvania Gazette," 1748-1755. Baltimore: Genealogical Publishing Co., 1977.

41.136 ------. Genealogical Data from the "Pennsylvania Chronicle" 1767-1774. Washington, D.C.: National Genealogical Society, 1971. (National Genealogical Society, Washington, D.C. Special Publications, no. 37). The approximately 3600 persons listed are predominantly from Pennsylvania, New Jersey (which had no newspaper for this period), and Maryland.

41.137 7724 Tombstone Inscriptions of Richland Cemetery, Allegheny County, Dravosburg, Pa. Compiled by Della Reagan Fischer, and Frank Fischer. McKeesport, Pa.: Fischer, 1976.

41.138　Some Blair County, PA Cemeteries in Hollidaysburg Borough: Greenlawn, Holliday, Jackson, Old and New St. Mary's, Union. Altoona, Pa.: Blair County Genealogical Society, 1982.

41.139　Southwest Pennsylvania Genealogical Services. Revolutionary War Veteran's Grave Register, Somerset County, Pennsylvania. Laughlintown, Pa.: Southwest Pennsylvania Genealogical Services, 1979.

41.140　Steele, Patricia. Tombstone Hoppin': Cemetery Inscriptions of Jefferson County, Pa. 2 vols. [Brookville, Pa.]: P. Steele, 1980-81.

41.141　Steinmetz, Mary Owen. Deaths of Civil War Soldiers from the "Gazette and Democrat" for the year 1863 and 1864, Reading, Pennsylvania. Rehrersburg, Pa., 1971. Microfilm. Filmed by the Genealogical Society, 1974. Deaths for Berks County. USIGS

41.142　Stevenson, Helen. "Obituaries from the Philadelphia Record, Philadelphia, Pennsylvania, Tuesday Morning, July 25, 1882." Bulletin of the Seattle Genealogical Society 17 (1967): 601-2.

41.143　Stover, Robert. Abstracts from the "Republican Compiler," Adams County, Pennsylvania, 1831-1851. Baltimore: Gateway Press, 1976.

41.144　Stroh, Oscar H. Dauphin County Tombstone Inscriptions. Harrisburgh, Pa., 1985.

41.145　------. Pennsylvania German Tombstone Inscriptions. 2 vols. Harrisburg, Pa.: O. H. Stroh, 1980-84.

41.146　Summers, William. "Obituary Notices of Pennsylvania Soldiers of the Revolution." Pennsylvania Magazine of History and Biography 38 (1914): 433-60. These obituary notices were collected from the newspapers of Montgomery county.

41.147　Sunday Dispatch, Philadelphia, Pa. Death Notices, 1868-1884, and Small Pox Deaths, 1879-1882. Philadelphia, n.d. Microfilm. Filmed by the Genealogical Society at the Historical Society of Pennsylvania, Philadelphia, 1964. USIGS

41.148　Taylor, Vivian F. Memorials in Stone: Tombstone Inscriptions, Montgomery County, Pennsylvania, West Norriton Township. Norristown, Pa.: Historical Society of Montgomery County, Pa., [1985].

41.149　30 Perry County, Pennsylvania Cemetery Records: Complete Tombstone Inscriptions. N.p.: Closson Press, 1982.

41.150　Throop, Eugene F. Forest County, Pennsylvania Cemetery Inscriptions. Bowie, Md.: Heritage Books, 1987.

41.151　Wagenseller, George Washington. Tombstone Inscriptions of Snyder County, Penna. All the Epitaphs Taken from the Markers in Every Burying Ground of Snyder County. A Complete Record from the Time of the

41. PENNSYLVANIA

Settlement of This Territory by the Pioneers Before the Revolutionary
War Down to the Year 1904. Middleburgh, Pa.: Wagenseller Publishing
Co., 1904.

41.152   Waite, Frances Wise. Bucks County Tombstone Inscriptions. Doylestown, Pa.:
Bucks County Genealogical Society, 1984.

41.153   Washington Observer, Jan.-Dec. 1894. Washington, Pa.: Citizens Library,
1973. InFw. Newspaper clippings and index.

41.154   Wion, John H. Deaths in Central Pennsylvania: An Index to the Obituaries
Appearing in the "Democratic Watchman," Bellefonte, Pennsylvania.
2 vols. N.p. 1969. v. 1. 12 July 1889 to 22 Dec. 1905; v. 2. 5 Jan.
1906 to 24 Dec. 1920.

41.155   Wyoming Historical and Geological Society, Wilkes-Barre, Pa. Proceedings
and Collections, v. 1-22, 1858-1938. Wilkes-Barre, Pa.: Wyoming
Historical and Geological Society, 1858-1938.

41.156   Zeamer, Jacob K. Record of Burials in the Millersville Mennonite Cemetery
from July 1, 1908, to January 16, 1943. Millersville, Pa.: Millersville
Mennonite Church, 1943.

42. RHODE ISLAND

42.1   Arnold, James Newell. <u>Inscriptions on the Grave-stones in the Old Churchyard of St. Paul's Narragansett: North Kingstown, Rhode Island: With a Record of the Inscriptions in the Graveyard of the Old Church at Wickford</u>. Boston: Merrymount Press, 1909.

42.2   ------. <u>Vital Record of Rhode Island. 1636-1850. First Series. Births, Marriages and Deaths. A Family Register for the People</u>. 21 vols. Providence, R.I.: Narragansett Historical Publishing Co., 1891-.

42.3   Bowman, John Elliot. <u>Rhode Island Index: To the "Gold Star Record" of Massachusetts in the World War</u>. N.p. 1930. The <u>Gold Star Record</u> gives full military and naval records, decorations, and some family records.

42.4   ------. <u>Some Rhode Island Veterans of the American Revolution. Items Alphabetically Arranged from Newspaper Files, 1790-1855</u>. N.p. 1928.

42.5   Carter, Marion Williams Pearce. <u>The Old Rehoboth Cemetery, "the Ring of the Town": At East Providence, Rhode Island, Near Newman's Church</u>. Attleboro, Mass.: Carter, 1932.

42.6   <u>Cemeteries in South Kingstown, Rhode Island</u>. Kingston, R.I.: Pettaquamscutt Historical Society, 1979.

42.7   <u>Death Notices: Rhode Island</u>. N.p., n.d. RHi Contains miscellaneous obituaries.

42.8   <u>Dorr's Obituaries</u>. 12 vols. N.p. 1826-1883. RHi Scrapbook collection of newspaper obituaries, from New York, Providence, and other papers. The obituaries are for individuals from Rhode Island and other New England states.

42.9   Durfee, Grace Stafford. <u>Newport County, Rhode Island, Death, Birth, Marriage Notices 1897-1960's</u>. Boston, Mass., n.d. Filmed for the Genealogical Society, 1969. USIGS

42.10   Harris, Edward Doubleday. <u>A Copy of the Old Epitaphs in the Burying Ground of Block Island, R. I.</u> Cambridge, Mass.: Press of J. Wilson and Son, 1883.

42.11   Hart, Constant. "From the Records of Constant Hart, of Tiverton, R.I." <u>New England Historical and Genealogical Register</u> 105 (1951): 213-17. List of deaths in Tiverton 1792-1824, with some earlier ones. In a few instances, additional information is given about the deceased.

42.12   Mansfield, Helen Winslow. <u>Block Island Cemetery Records</u>. Providence, R.I.: Block Island Historical Society, 1956.

42.13   <u>Marriages and Deaths Reprinted from Odd Numbers of the "Newport Mercury" Previous to 1800. Also, Marriages and Deaths from Old "Newport Heralds," 1787 to 1790; Mounted Clippings from the "Newport Mercury," July 8, 1899-March 10, 1900</u>. Newport, R.I., 1899-1900. NN

42.14   "Notes from the Diary of Elisha Fish, 1785-1804." <u>New England Historical and Genealogical Register</u> 56 (1902): 121-32. Contains considerable death information for the town of Foster.

42.15   Quintin, Robert J. <u>Franco-American Burials of Rhode Island</u>. 2 vols. N.p.: R. J. Quintin, [1980?].

42.16   Rhode Island Historical Society. "Necrological Notices in <u>Proceedings</u> and <u>Quarterly</u>, 1872-1897." <u>Publications of the Rhode Island Historical Society</u> 5 (1897): 70-75.

------. <u>Necrology, 1913-14</u>. Providence, R.I.: Rhode Island Historical Society, 1916.

------. <u>Necrology, 1915</u>. Providence, R.I.: Rhode Island Historical Society, 1916.

------. <u>Proceedings</u>, 1872-1891/92; 1900/01-13/14. 34 vols. Providence, R.I.: Rhode Island Historical Society, 1872-92; 1902-14.

------. <u>Publications</u>, n.s., v. 1-8, April 1893-Jan. 1901. From 1893-1900 the <u>Publications</u> of the Society include its <u>Proceedings</u>. These early proceedings contain necrology sections.

43.1 Abrams, George Carter. <u>Newberry County, South Carolina, Cemeteries</u>. 2 vols. Newberry, S.C.: Newberry County Historical Society, 1982-85.

43.2 Bolt, James Leland, and Margaret Eltinge Bolt. <u>Epitaphs from Old Cemeteries of Laurens County, S.C</u>. 2 vols. Greenville, S.C.: A Press, 1983. v. 1. Church cemeteries; v. 2. Family cemeteries.

43.3 Bratcher, R. Wayne. <u>Anderson County Cemeteries</u>. 2 vols. Greenville, S.C.: A Press, 1985-86.

43.4 ------. <u>Cemetery Records of Abbeville County, South Carolina</u>. 2 vols. [Greenville, S.C.]: R. W. Bratcher, 1982.

43.5 Bryan, Evelyn McDaniel Frazier, and Gibson Howard Bryan. <u>Cemeteries of Upper Colleton County, South Carolina</u>. Jacksonville, Fla.: Florentine Press, 1974.

43.6 *Bulloch, Joseph Gaston Baillie. "Extracts from the <u>South Carolina Gazette</u>, 1732-1781." <u>National Genealogical Society Quarterly</u> 2 (1914): 47.

43.7 <u>Cemeteries in Dillon County and Upper Marion County</u>. N.p. 1976? A bicentennial project of the United Daughters of the Confederacy, the Colonial Dames of the XVII Century, and the Daughters of the American Revolution.

43.8 Crockett, Nancy, and Mamie Getts Davis. <u>Old Waxhaw Graveyard</u>. [Lancaster? S.C.], 1965.

43.9 Crowder, Louise Kelly. <u>Tombstone Records of Chester County, South Carolina and Vicinity</u>. [Chester, S.C., 1970-].

43.10 Curry, Emma. "Death Notices from the <u>South Carolina Gazette</u> 1781-1785." <u>National Genealogical Society Quarterly</u> 11 (1923): 53-57.

43.11 ------. "Early South Carolina Marriages and Death Notices from the <u>South Carolina Weekly Museum</u>, Charleston, S.C. 1797." <u>National Genealogical Society Quarterly</u> 11 (1922): 47-48.

43.12 Elzas, Barnett Abraham. <u>The Old Jewish Cemeteries at Charleston, S.C.: A Transcript of the Inscriptions on Their Tombstones, 1762-1903</u>. Charleston, S.C.: Daggett Printing Co., 1903.

43.13 ------. Papers. New York Historical Society. NUC MS. 60-1868. This is a collection of notes compiled by Rabbi Elzas about the Jews of Charleston. It includes copies of death, funeral and obituary notices of Jews from the newspapers of Charleston 1783-1897.

43.14 English, Elizabeth D. "Marriage and Death Notices from the <u>Edgefield Hive</u>." <u>South Carolina Historical Magazine</u> 42 (1941): 25-27. For the year 1830.

43.15 <u>The Epitaphs in St. Paul's Cemetery, Summerville, South Carolina, August, 1855-October, 1977</u> . . . . Summerville, S.C.: St. Paul's Church, 1977.

43. SOUTH CAROLINA

43.16   [No entry].

43.17   ------. Obituaries and Marriage Notices from the "Carolina Watchman,"
         1832-1890: An Index. Greenville, S.C.: A Press, 1981.

43.18   Gainey, Joseph R. Some Spartanburg County Cemeteries. Spartanburg, S.C.:
         Piedmont Historical Society, 1983.

43.19   Gilman, Caroline Howard. Record of Inscriptions in the Cemetery and
         Building of the Unitarian, Formerly Denominated the Independent
         Church, Archdale Street, Charleston, S. C., from 1777-1860. Charleston,
         S.C.: Walker, Evans and Co., Printers, 1860.

43.20   Glover, Beulah. In Memory of: Inscriptions from Early Cemeteries.
         Walterboro, S.C.: The Press and Standard, 1972. These epitaphs are from
         Colleton county.

43.21   Greenville County, SC Cemetery Survey. Compiled by Greenville Chapter of
         South Carolina Genealogical Society. 5 vols. Greenville, S.C.: A Press,
         1977-83.

43.22   Harley, Lillian H., and Pattie W. Heaton. Cemetery Inscriptions of
         Dorchester County, South Carolina. 3 vols. St. George, S.C.: Dorchester
         Eagle-Record Publishing Co., 1978-1980. Vol. 3 has the title Cemetery
         Inscriptions of Colleton and Orangeburg Counties, South Carolina.

43.23   Herd, Elmer Don. Marriage and Death Notices from the "Abbeville Banner,"
         1846-1860. N.p. 1980.

43.24   Holcomb, Brent H. Marriage and Death Notices from Camden, South
         Carolina Newspapers, 1816-1865. Easley, S.C.: Southern Historical Press,
         1978.

43.25   ------. Marriage and Death Notices from Columbia, South Carolina,
         Newspapers, 1792-1839. Easley, S.C.: Southern Historical Press, 1982.

43.26   ------. Marriage and Death Notices from "Pendleton (S.C.) Messenger,"
         1807-1851. Easley, S.C.: Southern Historical Press, 1977.

43.27   ------. Marriage and Death Notices from the "Charleston Observer,"
         1827-1845. Greenville, S.C.: A Press, 1980.

43.28   ------. Marriages and Death Notices from the "Charleston Times,"
         1800-1821. Baltimore: Genealogical Publishing Co., 1979.

43.29   ------. Marriage and Death Notices from the Up-country of South Carolina
         As Taken from Greenville Newspapers, 1826-1863. Columbia, S.C.:
         SCMAR, 1983

43.30   ------. Marriage and Death Notices from Upper S.C. Newspapers,
         1843-1865: Abstracts from Newspapers of Laurens, Spartanburg, Newberry
         and Lexington Districts. Easley, S.C.: Southern Historical Press, 1977.

43.31   ------. "Marriage and Obituary Notices from the <u>Unionville Journal</u> and <u>Unionville Times</u>." <u>South Carolina Magazine of Ancestral Research</u> 3 (1975): 214   For the years 1852-68.

43.32   ------. <u>Marriage, Death, and Estate Notices from Georgetown, S.C., Newspapers, 1791-1861</u>. Easley, S.C.: Southern Historical Press, 1979.

43.33   ------. <u>Record of Deaths in Columbia, South Carolina, and Elsewhere, As Recorded by John Glass, 1859-1877</u>. Columbia, S.C.: SCMAR, 1986. John Glass was a newspaperman as well as a lawyer, educator, and businessman.

43.34   ------. <u>York, South Carolina, Newspapers: Marriage, and Death Notices, 1823-1865</u>. Spartanburg, S.C.: Reprint Co., 1981.

43.35   Hood, Mildred K., and Margit S. Benton. <u>Berkeley County Cemetery Inscriptions</u>. [Charleston, S.C.]: Charleston Chapter, South Carolina Genealogical Society, [1985].

43.36   <u>Inscriptions from Old Cemeteries in Lancaster, South Carolina</u>. [Lancaster, S.C.]: Lancaster County Historical Commission, 1974.

43.37   Jervey, Clare. <u>Inscriptions on the Tablets and Gravestones in St. Michael's Church and Churchyard, Charleston, S.C., to Which Is Added from the Church Records a List of Interments of Persons to Whom There are No Stones</u>. Columbia, S.C.: State Company, 1906.

43.38   Jervey, Elizabeth H. "Death Notices from the <u>Gazette of the State of South Carolina</u>." <u>South Carolina Historical Magazine</u> 50 (1949): 127-30. For the period 12 May 1777-28 Mar. 1785.

43.39   ------. "Marriage and Death Notices from the <u>Charleston Courier</u> for 1806." <u>South Carolina Historical Magazine</u> 29 (1928): 258-63.

43.40   <u>Keowee Courier, 1849-1851; 1857-1861 and 1865-1868</u>. Easley, S.C.: Southern Historical Press, 1979. The <u>Keowee Courier</u> was first published in Pickens and moved to Walhalla February 1868. This compilation includes death notices and obituaries for Oconee county.

43.41   *Lesesne, J. M. "Marriage and Death Notices from the <u>Greenville Mountaineer</u> of Greenville, S.C." <u>South Carolina Historical Magazine</u> 49 (1948): 57-60. For the period 26 July 1826-4 June 1836.

43.42   *-----. "Marriage and Death Notices from the <u>Pendleton Messenger</u> of Pendleton, S.C." <u>South Carolina Historical Magazine</u> 47 (1946): 29-31. For the period 1807-23.

43.43   McClendon, Carlee T. <u>Edgefield Death Notices and Cemetery Records</u>. Columbia, S.C.: Hive Press, 1977. Includes death notices that appeared in the <u>Edgefield Hive</u> in 1830, the <u>Carolinian</u> 1829-33, and the <u>Edgefield Advertiser</u> 1836-62.

43.44　Marriage and Death Notices from Baptist Newspapers of South Carolina, 1835-1865. Spartanburg, S.C.: Reprint Co., 1981.

43.45　"Marriage and Death Notices from Early Columbia Newspapers." South Carolina Magazine of Ancestral Research 5 (1977): 94-100. For the years 1819-29.

43.46　"Marriage and Death Notices from the Southern Christian Herald." South Carolina Magazine of Ancestral Research 5 (1977): 152-56. The Southern Christian Herald was a periodical published in Columbia, 1834-38.

43.47　*"Marriage and Death Notices from the Southern Enterprise." South Carolina Magazine of Ancestral Research 9 (1981): 84-90. This newspaper was published in Greenville; these notices are for the years 1854-57.

43.48　"Marriage and Death Notices from the Sumter Gazette." South Carolina Magazine of Ancestral Research 9 (1981): 91-94. For the years 17 Sept. 1831-10 Aug. 1833.

43.49　*"Marriage and Death Records from the Chester Standard." South Carolina Magazine of Ancestral Research 1 (1973): 100-4. For the years 1855-62.

43.50　*"Marriage and Death Records from the Columbia Telescope and South Carolina State Journal." South Carolina Magazine of Ancestral Research 1 (1973): 119-22. For the years 1826-33.

43.51　*"Marriage and Obituary Notices from the Cheraw Intelligencer and Southern Register." South Carolina Magazine of Ancestral Research 1 (1973): 115-18. For the years 1825-26.

43.52　"Marriage and Obituary Notices from the Darlington Flag." South Carolina Magazine of Ancestral Research 1 (1973): 41-47. For the years 1851-52.

43.53　"Marriage and Obituary Notices from the Edgefield Advertiser." South Carolina Magazine of Ancestral Research 4 (1976): 203-7. For the years 1836-39.

43.54　*"Marriage and Obituary Notices from the Greenville Mountaineer." South Carolina Magazine of Ancestral Research 2 (1974): 66-70. For the years 1852-56.

43.55　"Marriage and Obituary Notices from the Unionville Journal." South Carolina Magazine of Ancestral Research 1 (1973): 37-41. For the years 1851-52.

43.56　Moss, Bobby Gilmer, and Dennis R. Amos. Tombstones and Cemeteries of Cherokee County, South Carolina and Surrounding Areas. 2 vols. Greenville, S.C.: A Press, 1984-85.

43.57　One Hundred and One Cemeteries in Marion County, South Carolina. Marion, S.C.: Marion County Historical Society, 1983.

43.58   Pickens County, South Carolina, Cemetery Survey. N.p.: South Carolina
         Genealogical Society, 198-.

43.59   *"Records Kept by Colonel Isaac Hayne." South Carolina Historical Magazine
         10 (1909): 145-70. Records of births, marriages and deaths kept by
         Colonel Isaac Hayne who was executed by the British in 1781. Much of
         the information apparently taken from the newspapers starting in the
         1740s and ending December 1779. Most of the records are for Colleton
         and Charleston counties.

43.60   Revill, Janie. Abstract of Marriages and Death Notices Published in Various
         Newspapers of Camden, South Carolina: Now on File in the Library of
         the University of South Carolina, at Columbia, South Carolina, 1822-1838.
         Columbia, S.C.: Revill, 1936.

43.61   ------. Marriage and Death Notices Abstracted from Newspapers Published
         in Camden, South Carolina, 1822-1842, on File in the South Carolina
         Room, University of South Carolina Library. Columbia, S.C.: n.p., 1936.

43.62   ------. Marriage and Death Notices Abstracted from Various Old
         Newspapers on File in the Library of the University of South Carolina,
         with Cross References, 1804-1865. N.p. 1936.

43.63   ------. Marriage and Death Notices from Newspapers on File in the Library
         of the University of South Carolina. Columbia, S.C.: n.p., 1935. For the
         years 1822-71.

43.64   ------. The "Pendleton Messenger:" Abstract Data from the Marriage and
         Death Notices, 1826 to 1851, More Than 2,240 Names Listed Alphabeti-
         cally. Sumter, S.C.: J. Revill, 1956.

43.65   Roach, B. W., and Sarah Roach. Oconee County, South Carolina Cemetery
         Survey. 2 vols. [Greenville? S.C.]: A Press, 1983-84.

43.66   Salley, Alexander Samuel. Death Notices in the "South Carolina Gazette,"
         1732-1775. 1917. Reprint. Columbia, S.C.: South Carolina Archives
         Department, 1965.

43.67   Schorn, Catherine S. "Marriage and Deaths from Pendleton Messenger."
         Tulsa Annals 9 (1974): 48-56. For c1833.

43.68   Seay, June Anderson. Saluda County, South Carolina Epitaphs (Formerly Old
         Edgefield District): Still Villages. Lexington, S.C.: J. A Seay, 1986.

43.69   ------. Silent Cities: A Tombstone Registry of Old Lexington District, South
         Carolina. Lexington, S.C.: J. A Seay, 1984.

43.70   Simpson, Robert F. Some South Carolina Marriages and Obituaries and
         Miscellaneous Information, 1826-1854. Memphis: C. R. Barham, 1978.
         Abstracted from the Greenville Republican, the Greenville Mountaineer,
         and the Laurensville Herald.

43.71   Smith, R. M. <u>Book of the Dead: An Alphabetical Arrangement of the Dead Buried in the Cemeteries of Anderson County Indexed by Numbers to the Cemeteries in Which Each Individual Is Buried</u>. 2d ed. Anderson, S.C.: Smith, 1967.

43.72   <u>Some Cemetery Records of Abbeville County, South Carolina</u>. Baltimore: Genealogical Publishing Co., 1982.

43.73   <u>Spartanburg County, S.C. Cemetery Survey</u>. [Mayo, S.C.]: South Carolina Genealogical Society, 1983?

43.74   Watson, Margaret J., and Louise M. Watson. <u>Tombstone Inscriptions from Family Graveyards in Greenwood County, S.C.</u> [Greenwood, S.C.: Drinkard Printing Co., 1972].

43.75   *Webber, Mabel L. "Death Notices from the <u>South Carolina and American Gazette</u> and Its Continuation the <u>Royal Gazette</u>, May 1766-June 1782." <u>South Carolina Historical Magazine</u> 16 (1915): 34-38. This was a Charleston newspaper.

43.76   ------. "Death Notices from the <u>South Carolina Gazette</u> from September 29, 1766 to December 19, 1774." <u>South Carolina Historical Magazine</u> 34 (1933): 55-61. The <u>South Carolina Gazette</u> was published in Charleston.

43.77   *-----. "Marriage and Death Notices from the <u>South Carolina Weekly Gazette</u>." <u>South Carolina Historical Magazine</u> 18 (1917): 37-41. For the years 1783-1827.

43.78   Whaley, Mrs. E. D. <u>Union County Cemeteries: Epitaphs of 18th and 19th Century Settlers in Union County, South Carolina and Their Descendants</u>. Greenville, S.C.: A Press, 1976.

43.79   Whitmire, Beverly T., and H. C. Schroder. <u>The Presence of the Past: Epitaphs of 18th and 19th Century Pioneers in Greenville County, South Carolina, and Their Descendants, Natives of Virginia, Pennsylvania, and Other Original Thirteen States, Together with Those Who Came from Ireland, Scotland, England, Germany, and Other Foreign Countries</u>. Baltimore: Gateway Press, 1976.

43.80   Wilkinson, Tom C. <u>Early Anderson County, S.C. Newspapers, Marriages and Obituaries, 1841-1882</u>. Easley, S.C.: Southern Historical Press, 1978.

43.81   "William Hort's Journal." <u>South Carolina Historical Magazine</u> 24 (1923): 40-47. A record of births, baptisms, marriages and deaths in Charleston and vicinity in the late eighteenth and early nineteenth centuries.

43.82   Wilson, Teresa E. <u>Marriage and Death Notices from the "Southern Patriot."</u> 2 vols. Easley, S.C.: Southern Historical Press, 1982-86. v. 1. 1815-30; v. 2. 1831-48.

43. SOUTH CAROLINA

43.83   Young, Willie Pauline. <u>A Brief History with Tombstone Inscriptions of Old Little River Church, Founded 1791, Abbeville County, South Carolina</u>. [Easley, S.C.: Southern Historical Press, 1981?].

43.84   ------. <u>Cemetery Inscriptions of "Old Greenville Presbyterian Church": Erected 1773</u>. N.p. [1947?].

44. SOUTH DAKOTA

44.1   Grave Records of Minnehaha County Cemeteries. Sioux Falls, S.Dak.: Sioux
        Valley Genealogical Society, [1982].

44.2   *Patton, Mrs. Gareth R. "A Continued Series of Vital Records Excerpted
        from the Black Hills Journal, a Local Paper, for the Year 1883." Black
        Hills Nuggets 1 (1968): 10. The Black Hills Journal was published in
        Rapid City.

44.3   Serr, Esther. The Belvidere Cemetery, 1910-1985, Belvidere, South Dakota,
        Including the Flat Top Zion Lutheran and the St. Peter's Lutheran
        Cemeteries. Rapid City, S.Dak.: Hillsview Press, 1985.

44.4   Some Black Hills Area Cemeteries, South Dakota. 3 vols. Rapid City,
        S.Dak.: Rapid City Society for Genealogical Research, 1973-81. Includes
        some Wyoming cemeteries.

44.5   South Dakota Historical Collections, v. 1-, 1902-. Pierre, S.Dak.: State
        Department of History, 1902-. Index: v. 1-16, 1902-32. Early volumes
        list deceased members while volumes 5-13 contain a necrology section
        which lists notable deaths of the year and occasionally includes some data
        about the deceased.

45. TENNESSEE

45.1   Alexander, Irene McBane. <u>Cemetery Records of Lawrence County, Tennessee:</u> <u>At Rest, with Supplement</u>. 1968. Reprint. Collinwood, Tenn.: Byler Press, 1984.

45.2   Allison, Linda S. "Tennessee Miscellany." <u>Genealogical Reference Builders</u> <u>Newsletter</u> 9 (1975): 4-5. For Clarksville, 1819.

45.3   Anderson, Gladys P., and Jill K. Garrett. <u>Humphreys County, Tennessee</u> <u>Cemetery Records</u>. 1966. Reprint. N.p. 1978. Part 1 has special title: <u>Remember, As You Pass By; Humphreys County, Tennessee, Cemetery</u> <u>Inscriptions</u>.

45.4   <u>Annotated Cemetery Records of West Wilson County Area of Tennessee</u>. [Mt. Juliet, Tenn.]: Mt. Juliet-West Wilson County Historical Society, [197-?].

45.5   Bates, Lucy Womack. <u>Roster of Soldiers and Patriots of the American</u> <u>Revolution Buried in Tennessee</u>. Rev. ed. Brentwood, Tenn.: Tennessee Society, National Society of the Daughters of the American Revolution, [1979].

45.6   Beam, Judith Ann. <u>Cemetery Records of Land Between the Lakes: (Betwixt</u> <u>the Rivers) 1814-1973</u>. N.p.: Winchester Printing Co., 1974.

45.7   Bennett, Charles M. <u>Washington County, Tennessee Tombstone Inscriptions,</u> <u>Plus Genealogical Notes</u>. N.p.: Rae, 1977.

45.8   Boyer, Reba Bayless. <u>Monroe County, Tennessee: Records, 1820-1870</u>. 2 vols. Athens, Tenn., 1969-70.

45.9   Burns, William A. <u>Death and Obituary Notices Garnered from "Herald-</u> <u>Tribune," Published in Jonesboro, Washington County, Tennessee</u>. Phoenix, Ariz.: Burns, 1967-73. v. 1. 1869-75; v. 2. 1875-96; v. 3. 1896-1902; v. 4. 1902-7.

45.10   Carrier, Jeffrey L. <u>Upon a Lonely Hill: The Cemeteries of Johnson County,</u> <u>Tennessee</u>. Mountain City, Tenn.: Carrier, 1985. Includes tombstone records from 282 cemeteries in Johnson county.

45.11   Carter, Edwin, and Clella Mae Carter. <u>Carroll Cemetery Records</u>. 3 vols. N.p.: Carter, 1981.

45.12   <u>Cemeteries of Hawkins County, Tennessee</u>. 2 vols. Rogersville, Tenn.: Hawkins County Genealogical Society, 1985-86. v. 1. Civil districts 1, 2 and 8; v. 2. Civil districts 3 and 4, and also selected cemeteries in Hamblen and Hancock counties.

45.13   <u>Cemetery Records of Franklin County, Tennessee</u>. Compiled by the Franklin County Historical Society, Winchester, Tennessee. Rev. ed. Baltimore: Gateway Press; Winchester, Tenn.: The Society, 1986.

45.14   <u>Cemetery Records of Giles County, Tennessee</u>. Pulaski, Tenn.: Giles County Historical Society, 1986.

45. TENNESSEE

45.15 Cemetery Records of Lincoln--Moore Counties, Tennessee. Compiled by
Helen C. Marsh, and Timothy R. Marsh. Rev. ed. Shelbyville, Tenn.:
Marsh Historical Publications, 1983. A revised and combined edition of
Lincoln and Moore County cemetery records originally published in
separate volumes in 1972 and 1975.

45.16 Creekmore, Pollyanna. "Death Notices, 1791-1813, from Knoxville
Newspapers and Sevier's Diary." Publications of the East Tennessee
Historical Society 19 (1947): 110-19.

45.17 Cross, Lee M., and Larry R. Spurling. Morgan County Tennessee Cemetery
Inscriptions. Bowie, Md.: Heritage Books, 1986.

45.18 Cumberland County, Tennessee Cemetery Records. Crossville, Tenn.: B. A.
N. Castillo, 1984. Includes some adjoining cemeteries.

45.19 Dalton, Lynette Hamilton, Cleo G. Hogan, and Robert E. Dalton. Cemetery
Records of Cheatham County, Tennessee. Memphis: Dalton and Dalton,
1986.

45.20 Darnell, Anita Whitefield, and Mary Lewis Roe Jones. Cemetery Records of
Fort Campbell, Kentucky. Clarksville, Tenn., [1970].

45.21 Darnell, Anita Whitefield, Mary Lewis Roe Jones, and Ann Evans Alley.
Cemetery Records of Montgomery County, Tennessee. N.p. 1968.

45.22 Daughters of the American Revolution. James Buckley Chapter. Weakley
County, Tennessee Cemetery Listings. 2 vols. Sharon, Tenn.: The
Chapter, 1980.

45.23 *"Deaths Taken from the Fayetteville Observer." Lincoln County Tennessee
Pioneers 1 (1970): 3-4. For the years 21 Jan. 1851-26 Mar. 1868.

45.24 Durrett, Jean McClanahan. Cemetery Records of Robertson County,
Tennessee. 3 vols. Ashland City, Tenn.: Ideal Printing Co., 1973-75.

45.25 East Tennessee Historical Society. Knoxville's First Graveyard, Tombstone
Inscriptions in the First Presbyterian Church Cemetery, 1800-1879.
Knoxville, Tenn., 1965.

45.26 Elam, Charlotte Adee Edmondson, Margaret Inabinet Ericksen, and Ruth
Wyckoff Hunt. Gravestone Inscriptions from Shelby County, Tennessee
Cemeteries. 2 vols. Memphis: Milestone Press, 1971-74.

45.27 Fields, Orville T. Cemeteries of Carter County Tennessee. N.p.: Fields,
1976.

45.28 Finch, Maggie. Book of Poetry, Obituaries, Newspaper Clippings, etc.,
1800's. Nashville, Tenn.: State Library and Archives, 1974. Microfilm.
USIGS

45.29   Fulcher, Richard Carlton. Clipped Obituaries, "Shelbyville Times-Gazette."
         Brentwood, Tenn.: R. Fulcher, 1979. Reproduces obituaries from the
         1950s and 1960s.

45.30   ------. Davidson County, Tennessee Death Records and Tombstone
         Inscriptions. Brentwood, Tenn.: R. Fulcher, 1979. Includes abstracts of
         death records in early newspapers to the year 1820.

45.31   ------. Tombstone Inscriptions of Davidson County, Tennessee. 4 vols.
         Rev. ed. Brentwood, Tenn.: R. Fulcher, 1986-. v. 1. Nashville East and
         part of Nashville West quadrants; v. 2. Kingston Springs, Bellevue, Oak
         Hill Scottsboro quadrants; v. 3. Forest Grove and Goodlettsville quadrants;
         v. 4. Nolensville, Antioch, and part of La Vergne quadrants.

45.32   Garrett, Jill Knight. Maury County, Tennessee Newspapers (Abstracts).
         2 vols. [Columbia, Tenn., 1965].

45.33   ------. Obituaries from Tennessee Newspapers. Easley, S.C.: Southern
         Historical Press, 1980. Obituaries of the nineteenth century.

45.34   ------. "Some Tennessee Obituaries from Tennessee Newspapers."
         Genealogical Reference Builders Newsletter 8 (1974): 11-13. For the
         years 1888-89, from the Maury Democrat, Columbia, Tennessee.

45.35   Garrett, Jill Knight, and Iris H. McClain. Old City Cemetery, Nashville,
         Tennessee, Tombstone Inscriptions. Columbia, Tenn.: Garrett, 1971.

45.36   ------. Sacred to the Memory: Hickman County, Tennessee, Cemetery
         Records. Columbia, Tenn., 1966.

45.37   ------. Some Rutherford County, Tennessee, Cemetery Records. Columbia,
         Tenn., 1971.

45.38   Gibbs, G. F. Scrapbooks and Collections, 1800s-1900s. Nashville, Tenn.:
         State Library and Archives, 1974. Microfilm. USIGS Contains
         newspaper clippings, obituaries, miscellaneous certificates and documents
         of Tennessee, many of Lawrence county.

45.39   Glass, Mrs. Quintard. Cemetery Inscriptions of Dyer County, Tennessee.
         Easley, S.C.: Southern Historical Press, 1977.

45.40   Grady, Jamie Ault. Tombstone Inscriptions and Death Records, Calvary
         Cemetery, Knoxville, Tennessee, 1869-1967: Macedonia Cemetery,
         Knoxville, Tennessee, 1851-1967. . . . Knoxville, Tenn.: Grady, 1969.

45.41   Graves, Marjorie B. Lewis County, Tennessee Cemetery Records. Columbia,
         Tenn.: P-Vine Press, 1979?

45.42   Grohse, William P. Excerpts from Old Newspapers, Hancock and Hawkins
         Counties, 1815-1921. Microfilm. USIGS

45.43   ------. Newspaper Clippings from Hancock County Tennessee Newspapers, 1970-1971. Microfilm. USIGS

45.44   ------. Obituaries of Hancock County, Tennessee, 1963-1974. Microfilm. USIGS Includes some obituaries from surrounding counties.

45.45   Hansen, Mary Ruth. "Hawkins County, Tennessee Newspaper Abstracts." Ridge Runners 2 (1974): 169-71. Includes a few death notices from a Rogersville newspaper for the period 1851-85.

45.46   Hickman County, Tennessee Cemetery Records. Compiled by Jill Knight Garrett, and Irish H. McClain. Columbia, Tenn.: P-Vine Press, 1982.

45.47   Hickman County, Tennessee Cemetery Records, Part II. Edited by Catherine Gaffin Lynn. Centerville, Tenn.: Lynn, 1976. A continuation of Sacred to the Memory, by J. K. Garrett, published in 1966.

45.48   Hill, Eldon Randolph, and Edith Wilson Hutton. Cemeteries and Tombstone Inscriptions Central Peninsula, Norris Reservoir, Union, and Campbell Counties TN. Oak Ridge, Tenn.: Clark Printing Service, 1985.

45.49   In the Shadow of the Smokies: Sevier County, Tennessee Cemeteries. Sevierville, Tenn.: Smoky Mountain Historical Society, 1984.

45.50   Johnson, Paul. Cemeteries of Claiborne County, Tennessee. Tazewell, Tenn.: P. Johnson, [1982].

45.51   Jones, Lewis P. Cemeteries in Chester County. N.p.: [L. P. Jones, 1982].

45.52   Key, F. C., Sue Woodward Maggart, and Jane Coward Turner. Smith County, Tennessee, Cemeteries South of the Cumberland River. Carthage, Tenn.: McDowell Publications, 1984.

45.53   Lightfoot, Marise Parrish. They Passed This Way. 2 vols. Mt. Pleasant, Tenn., 1964-70. v. 2. Maury County, Tennessee death records, from nineteenth century newspapers. T

45.54   Little, Edith B. Blount County, Tennessee, Cemetery Records: Including Bount sector of Loudon and Monroe Counties, Tennessee. Evansville, Ind.: Unigraphic, 1980.

45.55   Lucas, Silas Emmett. Obituaries from Early Tennessee Newspapers 1794-1851. Easley, S.C.: Southern Historical Press, 1978.

45.56   Lynch, Louise Gillespie. Cemetery Records of Smith County, Tennessee. Franklin, Tenn.: L. G. Lynch, 1978.

45.57   ------. Early Obituaries of Williamson County, Tennessee. N.p. 1977. Abstracted from Franklin Review, Maury Democrat, Nashville Gazette, and others.

45.58   Lynch, Louise Gillespie, and Volenia Wheatley Hays. <u>Cemetery Records of Williamson County, Tennessee</u>. Franklin, Tenn., [1969].

45.59   McBee, Joe David. <u>"Winchester Herald-Chronicle" Obituaries Name Index, 1975-1979</u>. St. Andrews, Tenn.: Future Publishing Co., 1980.

45.60   McCown, Mary Hardin, and Inez E. Burns. <u>Soldiers of the War of 1812 Buried in Tennessee: Names Abstracted from Colonel David Henley's "Wastebook", Regular and Militia Personnel for Period 1793-1798, in Southwest Territory (Tennessee)</u>. . . . Rev. ed. [Johnson City, Tenn.]: McCown, 1977.

45.61   McKibben, Joyce A. <u>Index to Obituaries in "The Appeal" (1843-1894)</u>. Memphis: John W. Brister Library, Memphis State University, n.d.

45.62   Marsh, Helen Crawford, and Timothy R. Marsh. <u>Cemetery Records of Bedford County, Tennessee</u>. Rev. ed. Shelbyville, Tenn.: Southern Historical Press, 1986.

45.63   Marsh, Timothy R., Helen C. Marsh, and Ralph D. Whitesell. <u>Cemetery Records of Marshall County, Tennessee</u>. Shelbyville, Tenn.: Marsh Historical Publications, 1981.

45.64   Mellen, George Frederick, 1859-1927. Papers, 1878-1926. Tennessee State Library and Archives. NUC MS. 61-1333. Mellen was an author, educator and member of the Tennessee State Legislature. His papers include 15 scrapbooks containing articles and obituaries clipped from the <u>Knoxville Sentinel</u>. There are indexes for seven volumes of the scrapbooks.

45.65   Morton, Dorothy Rich. <u>Cemetery Records from Fayette County, Tennessee</u>. N.p. 1974.

45.66   <u>The 1980 Cemetery Census of Hardin County, Tennessee: A Research Project of the Hardin County Historical Society, Inc</u>. Savannah, Tenn.: The Society, 1984.

45.67   Noblitt, Anne G. "Lincoln County, Tennessee Obituaries from the <u>Fayetteville Observer</u>, 1851-1852." <u>Ansearchin News</u> 21 (1974): 20. Contains only a few obituaries.

45.68   <u>Obituaries from the West Union Association United Baptists' Minutes, 1893-1946</u>. Huntsville, Tenn.: Scott County Historical Society, [1985].

45.69   Owens, Fae Jacobs, Margureitte Holcomb Boyd, and Faye Tennyson Davidson. <u>The Cemetery Records of Hardeman County, Tennessee</u>. 5 vols. Huntsville, Ark.: Century Enterprises, Genealogical Services, [1970-].

45.70   Ownby, Carl Mayfield. <u>Cemetery Inscriptions in the Smoky Mountain Area, Sevier County, Tennessee, Blount County, Tennessee, and Cohutta Georgia Area, Whitfield County, Georgia</u>. Cleveland, Tenn.: Ownby, [1975].

45.71   Reagan, Donald B. Cemetery Inscriptions in the Smoky Mountain Area, Sevier County, Tennessee. Knoxville, Tenn., [1974].

45.72   Reynolds, Buford. Greene County Cemeteries, from Earliest Dates to 1970-1971. N.p. [1971].

45.73   Rhinehart, Margret. Our People: The Tombstone Inscriptions of Van Buren County, Tennessee, with Genealogical Notes: Tombstones Copied 1973 to 1976. Spencer, Tenn.: M. Rhinehart, 1983.

45.74   Riverside Cemetery Inscriptions, 1830-1975: Jackson, Tennessee. Jackson, Tenn.: Mid-West Genealogical Society, 1975.

45.75   Ross, Ernest L. Historical Cemetery Records of Bradley County, Tennessee. 2 vols. [Cleveland, Tenn., 1973].

45.76   [Scott County Cemeteries]. 3 vols. Huntsville, Tenn.: Scott County Historical Society, [1983-84?].

45.77   Sherrill, Charles A. Tombstone Inscriptions of Grundy County Tennessee. Decorah, Iowa: Anundsen Publishing Co., 1977.

45.78   Smith, Jonathan Kennon. Genealogical Gleanings in Benton County, Tennessee. Memphis, 1974. Contains death notices in Camden newspapers 1882-90.

45.79   ------. Selective Gleanings from Camden, Tennessee Newspapers, 1882-1932. Memphis: Smith, 1977.

45.80   Smith County, Tennessee, Cemeteries: North of the Cumberland River. Compiled by Smith County Historical and Genealogical Society and Caney Fork Chapter, DAR. Rev. ed. Utica, KY: McDowell Publications, 1983.

45.81   Snell, William R., and Virginia Faye Taylor. Death Notices in the "Cleveland Banner" (Tennessee), 1865-1883. N.p.: Bradley County Historical Society; Cleveland, Tenn.: Book Shelf, 1981.

45.82   Snider, Margaret Cummings, and Joan Hollis Yorgason. Sumner County, Tennessee, Cemetery Records. Owensboro, Ky.: McDowell Publications, 1981.

45.83   Templin, David H., and Cherel Bolin Henderson. Stories in Stone: Jefferson County Cemeteries. Knoxville, Tenn.: D. H. Templin, 1986. v. 1. South of the French Broad River and Dumplin Valley sections.

45.84   Walker, Emily B. Cemetery Records of Northern Gibson County, Tennessee. 2 vols. South Fulton, Tenn.: E. B. Walker, 1985.

45.85   Williams, Charlotte A. Index to the "Tennessee Gazette" and the "Tennessee Gazette and Mero District Advertiser." Nashville, Tenn.: Williams, 1979. Published in Nashville. For the years 25 Feb. 1800-30 May 1807.

45. TENNESSEE

45.86   Wooten, John Morgan. <u>Scrapbook History of McMinn County, Tennessee</u>. Cleveland, Tenn., 1937. Microfilm. Filmed by the State Library and Archives, Nashville, n.d. USIGS Includes some obituaries.

46. TEXAS

46.1   *"Abstracts from <u>Texas Wesleyan Banner</u> 1850-1860." <u>Footprints</u> 22 (1979): 1-7. <u>Texas Wesleyan Banner</u> title changed to <u>Texas Christian Advocate</u>. Published in Houston and Galveston respectively.

46.2   Alexander, N. W. <u>Orange County, Texas, Cemeteries</u>. Beaumont, Tex.: Southeast Texas Genealogical and Historical Society, 1980.

46.3   Applen, June. <u>Cemetery Inscriptions, Rains County, Texas</u>. N.p.: J. Applen, 1981.

46.4   Atchison, Mrs. Joe. <u>Peoria Cemetery, Hill County, Texas, 1826-1978</u>. [Hillsboro, Tex.]: Atchison, 1979.

46.5   "<u>Austin City Gazette</u> 1839 Abstracts and Notes." <u>Austin Genealogical Society Quarterly</u> 18 (1977): 65-77.

46.6   *"Austin <u>Texas Sentinel</u> Newspaper Abstracts 1840." <u>Austin Genealogical Society Quarterly</u> 8 (1967): 104-5.

46.7   Banks, H. L., and Ellie Fortner Funk. <u>Bazette, Prairie Point and Baptist Cemeteries</u>. N.p. 197-.

46.8   Barber, Gwen Stewart, and Opal Wheeler Jackson. <u>Polk County, Texas Cemetery Inscriptions</u>. Lufkin, Tex.: Barber and Jackson, 1976.

46.9   Beard, Betty, and Dwayne Beard. <u>Van Zandt County, Texas Cemeteries</u>. 2 vols. Van, Tex.: Beard, 1976-77.

46.10   Biggerstaff, Inez. <u>Four Thousand Tombstone Inscriptions from Texas, along the Old San Antonio Road and the Trail of Austin's Colonists</u>. [Oklahoma City? 1952]. Published under the auspices of the Oklahoma Historical Society.

46.11   <u>Births, Deaths and Marriages from El Paso Newspapers through 1885 for Arizona, Texas, New Mexico, Oklahoma, and Indian Territory</u>. Compiled by the El Paso Genealogical Society. Easley, S.C.: Southern Historical Press, 1982.

46.12   *Blount, Lois Fitzhugh Foster. "Vital Statistics from the <u>Telegraph and Texas Register</u>." <u>Stirpes</u> 2 (1962): 42-45. These statistics are for the years 1837-44. The <u>Telegraph and Texas Register</u> was published in Houston.

46.13   <u>Bosque County Cemetery Records</u>. [Meridian?]: Bosque County Historical Commission, [1985?].

46.14   Brinley, Lorine. <u>Fort Bend County Cemetery Inscriptions</u>. 2 vols. [Houston, Tex.]: Brinley, [1985-].

46.15   ------. <u>Harris County, Texas, Cemetery Inscriptions</u>. 2 vols. Houston, Tex.: L. Brinley, 1985.

46.16   ------. <u>Orange County, Texas, Cemetery Inscriptions</u>. Houston: L. Brinley, 1985.

46.17   Bryant, Stella Vinson. <u>Pioneers of Yesteryear: Pleasant Mound "Public" Cemetery and Memorial Park, 1848-1973</u>. [Dallas: Pleasant Mount "Public" Cemetery Association, 1974].

46.18   Cass County Genealogical Society. <u>Cass County Cemeteries: Texas Records</u>. Atlanta, Tex.: Cass County Genealogical Society, 1976.

46.19   Castro County Genealogical Society. <u>Castro County Cemetery Records</u>. Dimmitt, Tex.: Printed by Dimmitt High School Duplication Practices Class and Neighborhood Youth Corps Students, [1969].

46.20   Cawthon, Juanita Davis. <u>Marriage and Death Notices, Cass County, Texas, 1883-1932</u>. Shreveport, La.: J. D. Cawthon, 1983.

46.21   ------. <u>Marriage and Death Notices: Marion County, Texas and Environs, 1853-1927</u>. Shreveport, La.: J. D. Cawthon, 1980.

46.22   ------. <u>Marriage and Death Notices: The "Texas Republican," Marshall, Texas, 1849-1869</u>. Shreveport, La.: Cawthon, 1978.

46.23   Cawyer, Shirley Brittain, and Weldon I. Hudson. <u>Eastland County, Texas, Cemetery Inscriptions</u>. 3 vols. [Stephenville, Tex.]: Cawyer, [1976?].

46.24   ------. <u>Erath County, Texas, Cemetery Inscriptions</u>. [Stephenville? Tex., 1973].

46.25   <u>Cemeteries of Baytown</u>. [Baytown, Tex.]: Baytown Genealogy Society, [1980].

46.26   <u>Cemetery Records of Cooke County, Texas</u>. Gainesville, Tex.: Cross Timbers Genealogy Society, 1980.

46.27   <u>Cemetery Records of Smith County, Texas</u>. 5 vols. Tyler, Tex.: East Texas Genealogical Society, 1981-87. v. 1. Oakwood and Rose Hill cemeteries; v. 2. Northwest quarter; v. 3. Southwest quarter; v. 4. Southeast quarter; v. 5. Northeast quarter.

46.28   Central Texas Genealogical Society. <u>McLennan County, Texas, Cemetery Records</u>. 8 vols. Waco, Tex., [1965-85].

46.29   Clay, Jon H. <u>The Kaufman Cemetery, Kaufman, Texas</u>. Dallas: Clay, [1980?]

46.30   <u>Clippings of the Deaths and Funerals from the "Dallas Morning News," Dallas, Texas, June 1955-Dec. 1957</u>. Microfilm. USIGS

46.31   <u>Clippings of the Obituaries and Anniversaries from the "Dallas Morning News," 1955-58</u>. Microfilm. USIGS

46.32   Cook, Janette Tigert. Concord Cemetery Association. [Tyler, Tex.: J. T. Cook, 1980]. Inscriptions for Morris and Titus counties.

46.33   Crawford, Helen Wooddell. Cemeteries. . . . 5 vols. [Jacksonville, Tex.]: Crawford, 1971-74. v. 1. Northwest Cherokee county; v. 2. Jacksonville; v. 3. Northeast Cherokee county; v. 4. Mid Cherokee county; v. 5. Southern Cherokee county.

46.34   ------. Newspaper Obituaries, Cherokee County, Texas, 1836-1908. Jacksonville, Tex.: H. W. Crawford, 1983.

46.35   Cushman, Evelyn D'Arcy. Cemeteries of Northeast Tarrant County, Texas. N.p.: E. D. Cushman, 1981.

46.36   Daigle, Annette Lemmon, Jordan Henry Murray, and Travis Edgert Smith. 140 Years Interment Data, Marion County, Texas. Shreveport, La.: Mid-South Press, 1987.

46.37   Darnell, Rubyann Thompson, Adrienne Bird Jamieson, and Helen Mason Lu. Dallas County, Texas, Genealogical Data from Early Cemeteries. Dallas, Tex.: Dallas Genealogical Society, 1982.

46.38   Daughters of the American Revolution. Texas. La Paisana Chapter. Collingsworth County, Texas Cemeteries, 1876-1976. N.p. 1976.

46.39   ------. Martha McGraw Chapter, Jefferson. Cemetery Records of Marion County, Texas, 1846 to June 1, 1960. [Jefferson, Tex.], 1960.

46.40   Daughters of the Republic of Texas. Cradle of Texas Chapter, Freeport. A List of Old Brazoria County, Texas, Cemeteries During or Before 1900. [West Columbia, Tex.: Modern Manifold Method, 1965]. Includes epitaphs.

46.41   *"Deaths from the Fort Worth Gazette." Texas Heritage 1 (1976): 176-77. For the years 1883-84.

46.42   Denson, Mrs. Howard, Mrs. Billy Burnes, and Mrs. Howard Graves. Bandera County Cemetery Records. N.p. 197-.

46.43   Dunn, Mary Franklin Deason. 71 Cemeteries, Rusk County, Texas. 2 vols. [Henderson, Tex.]: M. F. D. Dunn, 1982.

46.44   Elliott, Colleen Morse. "Articles about Texans from the Anderson Intelligencer, Anderson Court House, S.C." Footprints 20 (1977): 211-17. Includes obituaries, 1868-1882.

46.45   Ellis County, Texas Cemetery Records. 10 vols. Waxahachie, Tex.: Ellis County Genealogical Society, 1981-86.

46.46   Ericson, Carolyn Reeves, and Joel Barham Burk. Nacogdoches County Cemetery Records. 5 vols. Nacogdoches, Tex.: Ericson, [1974-78].

46. TEXAS

46.47   Fairview Cemetery, Gainesville, Cooke County, Texas. Edited by Sue Wood and Ronnie Howser. N.p.: Cross Timbers Genealogical Society, 1985.

46.48   Floyd, Verna Corn, and Vernelle Corn. Cemeteries in Robertson County, Texas. Houston: D. Armstrong Co., 1980.

46.49   Frazier, John Purnell. Northeast Texas Cemeteries. 2 vols. Shreveport, La.: J & W Enterprises, 1984-86. v. 1. Cemeteries from Cass, Camp, Titus, Marion counties; v. 2. Titus, Cass, Morris, Camp, Upshur, Hopkins counties.

46.50   Freestone County Cemetery Records and Short Histories. Edited by Betty Moss Morrow. 10 vols. Teague, Tex.: B. M. Morrow, 1986.

46.51   Gable, Bertha L. Red River Co. Texas Cemeteries. 4 vols. Clarksville, Tex.: B. L. Gable, 1984-86.

46.52   Gentry, Mrs. Herbert R. "Extracts from the Tri-Weekly State Gazette." Austin Genealogical Society Quarterly 4 (1963): 53. For the year 1868. The Tri-Weekly State Gazette was published in Austin.

46.53   *"Gleanings from the Fort Worth Gazette." Texas Heritage 2 (1976): 121-25. For the years 1883-84.

46.54   Goebel, Patsy, and Karen McWhorter. Cemetery Records of DeWitt County, Texas. Cuero, Tex.: P. Goebel, 1986.

46.55   Gone, But Not Forgotten: A Cemetery Survey of Crosby County, Texas. Crosbyton, Tex.: Crosby County Pioneer Memorial and Crosby County Historical Commission, 1983.

46.56   Gone, But Not Forgotten: A Survey of Cemeteries in Boerne and Surrounding Areas. Boerne, Tex.: Boerne Area Historical Preservation Society, 1983.

46.57   Gregg County, Texas, Cemeteries. 3 vols. Longview, Tex.: Library Development Association, 1984-86.

46.58   Groves, Truman Algie, and Rita Arline Nichols Groves. Interments in Motley County, Texas to March 1977 and Appendix to July 1978. N.p. 1978.

46.59   Hampton, O. V. Archer County, Texas Cemeteries. Wichita Falls, Tex.: North Texas Genealogical and Historical Association, 1970.

46.60   Hendrix, Don. Polk County Folks. [St. Louis, Mo.]: Ingmire Publications; Nacogdoches, Tex.: Ericson Books, 1984. This is a collection of newspaper obituaries and death notices, late nineteenth and early twentieth centuries.

46.61   Henry, Mrs. T. E., and Mrs. Sears Anderson. Grayson County, Texas, Cemetery Inscriptions and Related Family Data. 3 vols. Fort Worth, Tex.: Hudson Heritage Books, 1984.

46.62   Higley, Caroline. <u>Obituaries of People Who Lived in Amarillo, Texas and Vicinity, 1958</u>. Amarillo, Tex., n.d. InFw

46.63   Holder, Charlotte, and Georgiana Hurlbert. <u>Grayson County, Texas Cemetery Records</u>. N.p.: H & H Genealogical Services, 1983.

46.64   Houston County Historical Commission. <u>Houston County (Texas) Cemeteries</u>. 2d ed. Crockett, Tex.: Houston County Historical Commission, 1978. Indexes 192 cemeteries in Houston county.

46.65   Houston Post. <u>Newspaper Index</u>. Wooster, Ohio: Bell and Howell Co., 1976-. Monthly with annual cumulations.

46.66   Hudson, Weldon I., and Shirley Brittain Cawyer. <u>Comanche County, Texas: Country Cemeteries</u>. Fort Worth, Tex.: W. I. Hudson, 1983.

46.67   <u>In Remembrance: Cemetery Inscriptions in Runnels County</u>. San Angelo, Tex.: Anchor Publishing Co., 1985.

46.68   Janak, Robert. <u>Old Bohemian Tombstones</u>. Beaumont, Tex.: R. Janak, 1983.

46.69   Jenkins, Frank Duane. <u>Cemetery Inscriptions, Runnels County, Texas</u>. San Angelo, Tex.: San Angelo Genealogical and Historical Society, [1976?].

46.70   Johnson, Gladys Hanks. <u>Cemetery Records of Llano County Texas and Some Adjacent Areas</u>. N.p. 1971?

46.71   <u>Leon County Cemetery Records</u>. 2 vols. Centerville, Tex.: Leon County Genealogical Society, 1982.

46.72   Loftus, Carrie. <u>Bexar County, Texas, Selected Cemeteries (Early Burials)</u>. St. Louis, Mo.: F. T. Ingmire, 1985.

46.73   McCown, Leonard Joe. <u>Cemeteries of Indianola, Texas: Indianola Cemetery, Cemetery on the Ridge, Zimmerman Cemetery</u>. Irving, Tex.: McCown, 1979.

46.74   ------. <u>Cemeteries of Seadrift, Texas: Bindewald Cemetery, Stiernberg Cemetery, Seadrift Cemetery</u>. Irving, Tex.: McCown, 1980.

46.75   McLin, G. <u>Medina County, Texas, Cemeteries</u>. 2 vols. N.p.: G. McLin, 1985.

46.76   McMinus, J. <u>Frio County, Texas Selected Cemeteries</u>. St. Louis, Mo.: F. T. Ingmire, 1985.

46.77   Miltenberger, Rev. and Mrs. Gordon. <u>Johnson County, Texas Cemetery Inscriptions</u>. 3 vols. Cleburne, Tex., 1971-72.

46.78   <u>Montgomery County, Texas, Cemeteries</u>. 6 vols. [Cut and Shoot, Tex.: Clan MacBean Register, 1979-1982].

46.79   Moore, Billie Beth, Olive Moore Russell, and Velma Waters. <u>East Mound Cemetery, Matador, Motley County, Texas</u>. [Fort Worth, Tex., 1973].

46.80   Morris, Ann. <u>Obituaries Recorded in Panola County, Texas</u>. 2 vols. Tyler, Tex.: East Texas Genealogical Society, 1986-87. v. 1. 1873-1920; v. 2. 1921-35.

46.81   Muckleroy, David V. <u>Nacogdoches County, Texas, Funeral Home--Cemetery Records</u>. San Antonio, Tex.: Muckleroy, 1981. v. 1. 1 Jan. 1970-30 Sept. 1980.

46.82   <u>Navarro County Cemetery Records</u>. 5 vols. Corsicana, Tex.: Navarro County Genealogical Society, 1981-85.

46.83   Newhouse, Dean, and Patricia Newhouse. <u>Fannin County, Texas, Cemetery Inscriptions</u>. 2 vols. Honey Grove, Tex.: Newhouse Publications, 1983. v. 1. Town and community cemeteries . . . located in the northeast corner of Fannin county; v. 2. North central area of county.

46.84   <u>Obituaries from the "Daily Sentinel," Nacogdoches County, Texas</u>. 2 vols. San Antonio, Tex.: Family Adventures, [1984-].

46.85   <u>Obituaries of Travis County Texas, 1900-1940: As Found in Travis County Scrapbook in Barker Library, Austin, Texas</u>. [Austin]: Balcones Chapter, National Society of the Daughters of American Revolution, 1985.

46.86   Peavy, Ruth Riley. <u>Cemetery Records of Henderson and Surrounding Texas Co.'s</u>. Compiled for the Daniel McMahon Chapter, National Society of the Daughters of the American Revolution and the Henderson County Historical Survey Committee. [LaRue, Tex.: Peavy, 1974].

46.87   Pinkston, Mildred Cariker. <u>Obituaries of Early Pioneers, Shelby County, Texas</u>. [Center, Tex.]: M. C. Pinkston, 1983.

46.88   Pitts, Alice, Wanda O'Roark, and Doris Posey. <u>Collin County (Texas) Cemetery Inscriptions</u>. 2 vols. McKinney, Tex.: POP Publications, 1975-78.

46.89   Russ, Herbert. "Genealogical Abstracts from the <u>Fairfield Recorder</u>." <u>Quarterly of the Central Texas Genealogical Society</u> 12, no. 4 (1969): 10-12. For the period 25 Sept. 1885-9 Oct. 1885.

46.90   Russell, Meta G. <u>Travis County Cemetery Records</u>. Austin, Tex.: Travis County Historical Survey Committee, 1964-66.

46.91   San Jacinto County, Texas Historical Commission. <u>San Jacinto County, Texas Cemeteries</u>. Winston-Salem, N.C.: Hunter Publishing Co., 1977.

46.92   Sanders, John Barnette. <u>Index to the Cemeteries of Panola County, Texas, 1836-1964</u>. Center, Tex., [1966].

46.93 ------. Index to the Cemeteries of Sabine County, Texas, 1836-1964. N.p. 1964.

46.94 ------. Index to the Cemeteries of San Augustine County, Texas, 1836-1964. Center, Tex., 1964.

46.95 ------. Our Dead. Index to the Cemeteries of Shelby County, Texas, 1838-1964. Center, Tex., 1963-64.

46.96 Smith, Joyce Christerson, and Floy Mixon. Moore County Cemeteries and Death Records. Dumas, Tex.: J. Smith and F. Mixon, 1966.

46.97 *Smith, Mrs. Stanley. "Obituaries and Death Notices, 1855-1882 from the Texas Baptist." Footprints 12 (1969): 108-11.

46.98 Smith, W. Broadus. Brazos County, Texas, Cemetery Inscriptions. [Houston, Tex., 1967].

46.99 Southwestern Historical Quarterly, v. 1-, 1897-. Austin, Tex.: Texas State Historical Association, 1897-. Indexes: v. 1-40, 1897-1937; v. 41-60, 1937-56. The indexes can be used to locate information on the deaths of prominent Texans.

46.100 Speakman, Mary N., and Walter F. Speakman. Cemeteries of Clay County, Texas. Wichita Falls, Tex., 1973.

46.101 Stanley, Audie Ray, Lurline Stanley, and Douglas Ray Stanley. Upshur County Cemetery Records of Texas. Diana, Tex., 1974.

46.102 Tally-Frost, Stephenie Hillegeist, and Billie Douthitt. Cemetery Records of Leon County, Texas. Corpus Christi, Tex.: Tally-Frost, 1967.

46.103 Tedford, Sandra Haney, and Walterine Hollingsworth Sharp. Cemetery Inscriptions of Rockwall County, Texas. Farmersville, Tex.: Search N Print, 1979.

46.104 ------. Epitaphs of Southwest Fannin County, Texas. Farmersville, Tex.: Search N Print, 1984.

46.105 Texas Obituaries. Death Notices Taken from Early Texas Newspapers, 1835-1890. N.p., n.d. Microfilm. Filmed by the Genealogical Society at Salt Lake City, 1971. USIGS

46.106 Thompson, Robert Lee., and Kathy Lynn Penson. Cemetery Inscriptions of Hunt County, Texas. [Greenville? Tex.]: Thompson, 1977.

46.107 Titus County, Texas Cemetery Records. 2 vols. Mt. Pleasant, Tex.: Cypress Basin Genealogical and Historical Society, 1982-85.

46.108 Trinity County Cemeteries. Compiled and edited by the Trinity County Historical Commission. Burnet, Tex.: Nortex Press, 1980.

46.109 Tuck, June England, and Deborah Tuck Young. Hopkins County, Texas Cemetery Inscriptions. Sulphur Springs, 1985.

46.110 Turk, T. R. Obituaries from Papers Printed in Scurry County, Texas 1891 till 1925. N.p. 197-.

46.111 Turner, Ida Marie, and Adele W. Vickery. Cemeteries of Wood County, Texas. 4 vols. Mineola, Tex.: Turner and Vickery, 1970-72.

46.112 Usry, John M. Early Waco Obituaries and Various Related Items, 1874-1908. Waco, Tex.: Central Texas Genealogical Society, 1980.

46.113 ------. Index to Early McLennan County Deaths. Waco, Tex.: Central Texas Genealogical Society, 1987. Indexes cemetery records, newspaper obituaries, and other types of death records.

46.114 Vaughter, Betty. Cemetery Records of Armstrong County, Texas 1890-1963. Amarillo, Tex.: B. Vaughter, 1963.

46.115 Vickery, Adele W. Cemeteries of East Texas. Mineola, Tex.: Vickery, 1976.

46.116 Waring, Margaret, and Samuel J. C. Waring. Comanche County Gravestone Inscriptions. 2d ed. Comanche, Tex.: M. Waring, 1984.

46.117 West Texas Genealogical Society. Cemetery Records: Abilene, Taylor County, Texas, 1882-1960: Book 1: City Cemetery, Masonic Cemetery, Odd Fellows Cemetery. Abilene, Tex., 1961.

46.118 Wetzel, Hazel Ellis. Rural Cemetery Inscriptions, Brown County, Texas. Brownwood, Tex.: H. E. Wetzel, [1980].

46.119 Wimberly, Vera. Montgomery County, Texas: Unmarked Graves, Cemetery Locations: Differences Between Cemetery Readings and Funeral Home Records. Conroe, Tex.: Montgomery County Genealogical Society and Historical Society, 1985.

46.120 Winfield, Judy, and Nath Winfield, Jr. Cemetery Records of Washington County, Texas, 1826-1960. N.p.: Winfield, 1974.

46.121 Withers, Mary. "Items Abstracted from the Microfilmed Records of the Galveston News." Yellowed Pages 5 (1975): 92. For the year 1848.

46.122 Witty, Mrs. Brent. Hamilton County, Texas, Cemetery Records. N.p.: B. Witty, n.d.

46.123 Wright, Betty Davis. Cemetery Inscriptions, Garland, Dallas County, Texas. N.p.: B. D. Wright, 1983.

46.124 Wright, Mildred S. Hardin County, Texas Cemeteries. Beaumont, Tex.: Southeast Texas Genealogical and Historical Society, 1976.

46. TEXAS

46.125   ------. <u>Jasper County, Texas, Cemeteries</u>. Decorah, Iowa: Anundsen
Publishing Co., 1976.

46.126   ------. <u>Jefferson County, Texas Cemeteries</u>. 2 vols. Beaumont, Tex.:
Wright, 1979-81. v. 1. Oak Bluff Memorial Park, Port Neches; pt. 2.
Calvary Catholic Cemetery, Port Arthur Memory Gardens Cemetery,
Midcounty Live Oak Memorial Cemetery.

46.127   ------. <u>Liberty County, Texas Cemeteries</u>. Decorah, Iowa: Anundsen
Publishing Co., 1977.

46.128   ------. <u>Newton County, Texas Cemeteries</u>. Decorah, Iowa: Anundsen
Publishing Co., 1975.

46.129   Wright, Zelma H., and Mildred S. Wright. <u>Chambers County, Texas,
Cemeteries</u>. Decorah, Iowa: Anundsen Publishing Co., 1975.

47. UTAH

47.1 Church of Jesus Christ of Latter-Day-Saints. Church Historian's Office.
Obituary Index File to the "Tribune" and "Deseret News" Salt Lake City,
Utah, As of 31 December 1970. Salt Lake City: Church Historian's
Office, 1971. Microfilm. USIGS For the years 1850-1970. Over
1,000,000 entries in this index.

47.2 Martin, Phyllis J. Bluff Dale, Utah, Cemetery. Evanston, Wyo.: P. J.
Martin, 1983.

47.3 ------. Cemeteries in Morgan County, Utah. Evanston, Wyo.: P. J. Martin,
[1984].

47.4 ------. Cemeteries in Summit County, Utah. [Evanston, Wyo.]: P. J.
Martin, [1984].

47.5 ------. Randolph and Woodruff Cemeteries, Rich Co., Utah. [Evanston,
Wyo.]: P. J. Martin, [1983].

47.6 ------. Vinebluff and Old City Cemeteries, Nephi, Utah. [Evanston, Wyo.]:
P. J. Martin, 1983.

47.7 ------. West Jordan Cemetery, West Jordan, Utah. [Evanston, Wyo.]: P. J.
Martin, [1983].

47.8 Rogers, Sadie. East Millard Pioneers, Death Notices, As Published in the
"Progress," 1912-1937. N.p., 1938. Microfilm. Filmed by the
Genealogical Society at Salt Lake City, 1972. USIGS This newspaper
was published in Fillmore.

48. VERMONT

48.1   Burlington Free Press. <u>Index to the "Burlington Free Press" in the Billings Library, University of Vermont</u>. 10 vols. Montpelier, Vt.: Historical Records Survey, 1940-42. For the years 1848-70.

48.2   Churchill, Mary. <u>Cemeteries of Cavendish, Vermont</u>. Springfield, Vt.: Hurd's Offset Printing, 1976.

48.3   Coates, Walter John. <u>Cemetery Inscriptions from Pardon Jones, Shortt and Mitchell Cemeteries, Calais, Vt., South Woodbury, Vt., Rich-Hollister and Dwinell Cemeteries, Marshfield, Vt., Delano Cemetery, Hartford, Vt. Also Marriages and Deaths Listed in the "Rural Repository," Hudson N.Y. 1839-1840 and early settlers (about 1800-1822) from Vermont to Jefferson County, N.Y</u>. N.p. 1939-40. Microfilm. (American Periodials: 1800-1850). Filmed by the Genealogical Society at Montpelier, Vt., 1952. USIGS

48.4   Daughters of the American Revolution. Vermont. <u>Genealogical Collection</u>. Washington, D.C.: Daughters of the American Revolution Library, 1971. Microfilm. Filmed for the Genealogical Society, 1971. USIGS Includes early Vermont death notices from old newspapers containing notices of many deaths of Revolutionary soldiers.

48.5   ------. <u>Some Veterans of the American Revolution, Items Alphabetically Arranged from Newspaper Files, 1792-1857</u>. Microfilm. USIGS

48.6   Dodge, Nancy L. <u>Settlement and Cemeteries in Vermont's Northeast Kingdom: Including Indexed Transcriptions from Gravesites in Canaan, Lemington, Bloomfield, Brunswick, and Maidstone, Vermont, and in Hereford, Quebec</u>. Salem, Mass.: Higginson Books, 1986.

48.7   Driscoll, Marion Lang. "New England Records, Copied from <u>Universalist Watchman</u>, Published Montpelier, Vt., Issue of February 11, 1837." <u>National Genealogical Society Quarterly</u> 24 (1936): 105. Includes a few deaths from Vermont and New Hampshire.

48.8   Elwell, Levi Henry. <u>The Gravestone Inscriptions of Rupert, Bennington County, Vermont</u>. Amherst, Mass.: Composition and Presswork, 1913.

48.9   ------. <u>The Gravestone Records of Shaftsbury, Bennington County, Vermont</u>. Amherst, Mass.: Composition and Presswork, 1911.

48.10   Folson, Clara Abbott. "Death Records from <u>Vermont Journal</u>, Windsor, Vt." <u>Daughters of the American Revolution Magazine</u> 67 (1933): 394-97. For the period 12 Aug. 1826-5 Jan. 1827.

48.11   Hill, Ellen C., Bob Webster, and Lois Webster. <u>The Cemeteries of East Montpelier, Vermont, 1794-1973: An Inventory of Gravestones and Their Poetry</u>. 2d ed. N.p. 1974.

48.12   Jenks, Margaret R. <u>Middletown Springs and Ira Cemetery Inscriptions, Rutland County, Vermont</u>. Kirkland, Wash.: M. R. Jenks, 1983.

48. VERMONT

48.13   ------. Pawlet Cemetery Inscriptions, Rutland County, Vermont. Kirkland,
         Wash.: M. R. Jenks, 1985.

48.14   ------. Poultney Cemetery Inscriptions, Rutland County, Vermont.
         Kirkland, Wash.: M. R. Jenks, 1983.

48.15   ------. Tinmouth Cemetery Inscriptions, Rutland County, Vermont.
         Kirkland, Wash.: M. R. Jenks, 1985.

48.16   ------. Wells Cemetery Inscriptions, Rutland County, Vermont. Kirkland,
         Wash.: M. R. Jenks, 1981.

48.17   Middlebury College. Middlebury, Vt. Associated Alumni. Necrological
         Report of the Associated Alumni, 1867/68-.   Middlebury, Vt., 1868-.

48.18   Nichols, Joann H. Index to Known Cemetery Listings in Vermont. 2d ed.
         Brattleboro, Vt.: J. H. Nichols, 1982.

48.19   "Record of Deaths Kept by Mrs. Salley Dewey of Middlebury, Vt." New
         England Historical and Genealogical Register 71 (1917): 44-57. This
         private record is arranged chronologically, giving name, date of death,
         frequently family relationships, and age at death. For the years 1804-74.

48.20   Spies, Francis F. Early Vermont Marriages and Deaths, Mostly from Addison
         County, Vermont. Mount Vernon, N.Y., 1926. Microfilm. NN Most of
         the records are for the first half of the nineteenth century, although
         there are some as early as 1791 and as late as 1880.

49.   VIRGIN ISLANDS

49.1   Margolinsky, Jul.   299 Epitaphs from the Jewish Cemetery in St. Thomas, W.I., 1837-1916.   With an Index Compiled from Records in the Archives of the Jewish Community in Copenhagen.   Copenhagen, 1957.

50. VIRGINIA

50.1   Adams, James Taylor. <u>Family Burying Grounds in Wise County, Virginia</u>. Norton, Va.: Southwest Virginia, [1983?].

50.2   Association for the Preservation of Virginia Antiquities. Joseph Bryan Branch, Gloucester. <u>Epitaphs of Gloucester and Mathews Counties in Tidewater, Virginia, through 1865</u>. Richmond: Virginia State Library, 1959.

50.3   Baber, Lucy Harrison Miller. <u>Marriages and Deaths from the Lynchburg, Virginia Newspapers, 1794-1836</u>. Baltimore: Genealogical Publishing Co., 1980.

50.4   Barger, Virginia. <u>Tombstones in St. Luke's Church Cemetery, Isle of Wight County, Virginia</u>. Newport News, Va., 1970.

50.5   Bentley, John B. <u>Gravestone Inscriptions from the Cemetery of St. John's Episcopal Church, Hampton, Virginia</u>. Hampton, Va.: Hugh S. Watson Jr. Genealogical Society of Tidewater Virginia, 1975.

50.6   Borden, Duane Lyle. <u>Tombstone Inscriptions</u>. 9 vols. [Ozark, Mo.]: Yates Publishing Co., 1981-86.

50.7   Brown, Mary C. "Death Notices in the <u>Norfolk Gazette and Public Ledger</u>, 1804-1816." <u>Virginia Magazine of History and Biography</u> 63 (1955): 332-48.

50.8   <u>Burials in Augusta County, Virginia Cemeteries</u>. N.p.: Augusta County Historical Society, 1985.

50.9   Catron, Ada Grace. <u>Tombstone Inscriptions of Lee County, Virginia</u>. Pennington Gap, Va., 1966.

50.10   <u>Cemetery Records of Franklin County, Virginia</u>. Compiled by the Franklin County Historical Society. Baltimore: Gateway Press, 1986.

50.11   Chilton, Harriett A., and Mitzi Chilton Wilkerson. <u>Register of Old Concord Presbyterian Church, Appomattox County, Virginia - 1826-1878; Baptism 1826-1876, Membership 1826-1878, Obituary 1829-1854</u>. [Falls Church? Va.], 1973.

50.12   Chitwood, W. R. <u>Tombstone Inscriptions, East End Cemetery and St. Mary's Catholic Church Cemetery, Wytheville, Va</u>. Wytheville, Va.: Chitwood, 1977.

50.13   Clark, Patricia P. "Obituaries from the <u>Family Visitor</u>, April 6, 1822-April 3, 1824." <u>Virginia Magazine of History and Biography</u> 68 (1960): 58-91.

50.14   *Cocke, William Ronald. "Some Revolutionary Soldiers, Selected from the Obituary Notices Published in Early Virginia Newspapers." <u>Virginia Magazine of History and Biography</u> 35 (1927): 444-50. For the years 1814-38. Most of the notices are from the <u>Whig</u> and <u>Enquirer</u>, for persons who were born or who lived in Virginia.

50. VIRGINIA

50.15   Conner, E. R. <u>One Hundred Old Cemeteries of Prince William County, Virginia</u>. [Manassas? Va.]: E. R. Conner, 1981.

50.16   Cox, Elza B., and Phyllis G. Phillips. <u>Cemeteries, Floyd (Montgomery) County, Va., Indian Valley District</u>. Chicago, Ill.: Adams Press, 1979.

50.17   Dalton, Winston. "Winston Dalton's Register." <u>William and Mary Quarterly</u>, 2d ser. 14 (1934): 36-45. A nineteenth century register of births, deaths, and marriages for the northern part of Pittsylvania and the southern part of Bedford counties.

50.18   Douglas, William. <u>The Douglas Register, Being a Detailed Record of Births, Marriages, and Deaths, Together with Other Interesting Notes, As Kept by the Rev. William Douglas from 1750 to 1797</u>. . . . 1928. Reprint. Baltimore: Genealogical Publishing Co., 1966.

50.19   Ellsberry, Elizabeth Prather. <u>Cemetery Records of Page County, Virginia</u>. Chillicothe, Mo.: Ellsberry, [197-?].

50.20   ------. <u>Cemetery Records of Shenandoah County, Virginia</u>. Chillicothe, Mo.: Ellsberry, [197?].

50.21   Fleming, John Anderson. <u>Fauquier County, Virginia Tombstone Inscriptions</u>. Delaplane, Va.: N. C. Baird, 1984.

50.22   <u>"Follow the Periwinkle": Cemetery Records of Henry County, Virginia</u>. Compiled by the Henry County Historical Society. Danville, Va.: VA-NC Piedmont Genealogical Society, 1982.

50.23   <u>Graveyards of Arlington County, Virginia</u>. Arlington, Va.: National Genealogical Society, 1985. (Special Publication of the National Genealogical Society, no. 54)

50.24   Green, Laurie Boush, and Virginia Bonney West. <u>Old Churches, Their Cemeteries, and Family Graveyards of Princess Anne County, Virginia</u>. [Virginia Beach, Va.]: L. B. Green and V. B. West, 1985.

50.25   Griffin, Frances C. <u>Tombstone Inscriptions, Cedar Grove Cemetery, 1825, Norfolk, Virginia</u>. Chesapeake, Va.: Griffin, [1980?].

50.26   ------. <u>Tombstone Inscriptions, Elmwood Cemetery, 1853, Norfolk, Virginia</u>. Chesapeake, Va.: Griffin, [1980?].

50.27   Historical Records Survey. Virginia. <u>Inventory of Church Archives of Virginia. Guide to the Manuscript Collections of the Virginia Baptist Historical Society. Supplement</u>. Richmond, 1940-41. 2 vols. v. 1, Index to obituary notices in the <u>Religious Herald</u>, Richmond, Virginia, 1828-1938.

50.28   Hodge, Robert Allen. <u>Death Notices," Virginia Herald" (Fredericksburg, Virginia) 1788-1836</u>. Fredericksburg, Va.: R. A. Hodge, 1981.

50.29   ------. Fredericksburg, Virginia Death Records, 1853-1895. Locust Grove,
Va.: Germanna Community College, 1980.

50.30   ------. An Index for . . . the "Exponent," Culpeper, Virginia. 3 vols.
[Fredericksburg, Va.]: Hodge, [1972-?]. v. 1. 1881-82; v. 2. 1897-1901; v.
3. Miscellaneous issues, 1885-1906.

50.31   ------. An Index for the "Fredericksburg Ledger," 1865-1874.
Fredericksburg, Va., 1974.

50.32   ------. An Index for the "Fredericksburg News," 1853-1861.
Fredericksburg, Va., 1976.

50.33   ------. An Index for the "Virginia Herald" and "Fredericksburg Advertiser,"
1788-1791. Fredericksburg, Va.: R. A. Hodge, 1969.

50.34   ------. An Index for the "Virginia Herald" of Fredericksburg, Virginia.
Fredericksburg, Va.: R. A. Hodge, 1975. For the years 1802-1805.

50.35   ------. An Index to 172 Miscellaneous Issues of Orange County, Virginia
Newspapers Dating from 1872 through 1936: With Titles of the
"Gordonsville Gazette," the "Native Virginian," the "Piedmont Virginian,"
the "Orange Observer." Locust Grove, Va.: R. A. Hodge, 1983.

50.36   ------. An Index to the "Culpeper Exponent," Culpeper Virginia: Volumes
30 through 39, April 15, 1910 through April 8, 1920. Fredericksburg,
Va.: R. A. Hodge, 1982.

50.37   ------. An Index to the Death Notices in the "Virginia Star," Culpeper,
Virginia. Fredericksburg, Va.: R. A. Hodge, 1982. For the years
1919-1953.

50.38   ------. An Index to the "Democratic Recorder," 1842-1848 and "Weekly
Recorder," 1844-1847. Fredericksburg, Va.: R. A. Hodge, n.d.

50.39   ------. An Index to the "Fredericksburg Times" (Fredericksburg, Virginia):
Volumes 1 through 10, September, 1974 through August, 1984. Fredericksburg, Virginia: R. A. Hodge, [1985?].

50.40   ------. An Index to the "Free Lance," Fredericksburg, Virginia. 3 vols.
Fredericksburg, Va.: R. A. Hodge, 1985. v. 1. 10 Dec. 1896-29 Jan.
1898; v. 2. 31 Jan. 1898-23 Mar. 1899; v. 3. 25 Mar. 1899-10 May 1900.

50.41   ------. An Index to the "Northern Neck News" (Warsaw, Richmond County,
Virginia). 2 vols. Fredericksburg, Va.: R. A. Hodge, 1984. For the
years 16 May 1879-9 Apr. 1886.

50.42   ------. An Index to the Rappahannock Page of the "Virginia Star"
(Culpeper, Virginia). 3 vols. Fredericksburg, Va.: R. A. Hodge, 1985.
For the years 1936-38.

50.43   ------. Indexes for the "Virginia Herald," Fredericksburg, Virginia:
          1788-1791, 1792-1795, 1799-1800, 1802-1805, 1806-1809. 5 vols.
          Fredericksburg, Va.: R. A. Hodge, 1969-1976.

50.44   ------. Indexes to Miscellaneous Newspapers of Culpeper, Virginia,
          1859-1899, 1881-1882, 1882-1889, 1885-1906, 1897-1898. Fredericksburg,
          Va.: R. A. Hodge, n.d.

50.45   ------. Indexes to the "Virginia Herald" (Fredericksburg, VA.), 1867-1876.
          Fredericksburg, Va.: R. A. Hodge, 1984.

50.46   ------. Indexes to Volumes 1, 2, 5, 6, 7 and 8 of the "Weekly Advertiser,"
          Fredericksburg, Virginia, 1853-1860. Fredericksburg, Va.: R. A. Hodge,
          1983.

50.47   ------. Indices to Newspapers of Culpeper, Virginia: Arranged in the
          Following Order, Miscellaneous Titles and Dates, 1859-1899, 1882-1889,
          the (Culpeper) "Exponent," 1881-1882, 1885-1906, 1897-1898, 1898-1899,
          1899-1900, 1900-1901. Fredericksburg, Va.: R. A. Hodge, [198?].

50.48   ------. A Roster of the Citizen Burials in the Fredericksburg Confederate
          Cemetery, Fredericksburg, Virginia. Fredericksburg, Va.: R. A. Hodge,
          1981.

50.49   Hodge, Robert Allen, and Lois L. R. Hodge. Index, 1982 Death Notices,
          "Free Lance-Star," Fredericksburg, Virginia. Fredericksburg, Va., 1983.
          volumes also published for 1981, 1983, 1984.

50.50   ------. An Index to the Newspaper Death Notices, Fredericksburg, Virginia.
          9 vols. Fredericksburg, Va.: R. A. Hodge, 1983. This index includes
          names and dates of publication of death notices in six Fredericksburg
          newspapers, 1788-1981.

50.51   Howe, Henry. Historical Collections of Virginia. Charleston, S.C.: Babcock
          and Co., 1845. Contains some obituary notices from the American
          Almanac for 1832-44, of public figures and residents of Virginia and the
          District of Columbia. These notices were reprinted in Tyler's Quarterly
          10 (1928): 146-56.

50.52   Jett, Dora Chinn. Minor Sketches of Major Folk and Where They Sleep; the
          Old Masonic Burying Ground, Fredericksburg, Virginia. Richmond, Va.:
          Old Dominion Press, 1928.

50.53   King, George Harrison Sanford. Marriage Bonds and Ministers' Returns of
          Fredericksburg, Virginia, 1782-1850; Also, Tombstone Inscriptions from St.
          George Cemetery, 1752-1920. [Pine Bluff, Ark.], 1954.

50.54   Klein, Margaret C. Tombstone Inscriptions of King George County, Virginia.
          Baltimore: Genealogical Publishing Co., 1979.

50.55   ------. Tombstone Inscriptions of Orange County, Virginia. Baltimore:
          Genealogical Publishing Co., 1979.

50.56   ------. Tombstone Inscriptions of Spotsylvania County, Virginia. Palm Coast, Fla.: M. C. Klein, 1983.

50.57   Leach, Frank W. Extracts of Some of the Marriages and Deaths Printed in the "National Intelligencer," Washington, D.C. between the years 1806-1858. N.p., n.d. Microfilm. USIGS Most of these records are for prominent men and women of Virginia and Maryland.

50.58   "List of Deaths, Southampton County from Virginia Herald, Fredericksburg, 2nd November 1831." Quarterly of the Virginia Genealogical Society 15 (1977): 16.

50.59   "List of Obituaries from Richmond, Virginia Newspapers." Virginia Magazine of History 20 (1912): 282-91. For the years 1786-1825.

50.60   McConnell, Catherine S. High on a Windy Hill. Bristol, Tenn.: King Printing Co., 1968. This is a collection of epitaphs in Washington county.

50.61   Marriages and Deaths from Richmond, Virginia Newspapers, 1780-1820. Richmond, Va.: Virginia Genealogical Society, 1983. (Special Publication of the Virginia Genealogical Society, no. 8)

50.62   "Marriages and Obituaries from Bowen's Virginia Centinel and Gazette, Winchester, Virginia, 1792-1794." Virginia Genealogist 1 (1957): 38-43.

50.63   Matheny, John Clifton, and Emma Robertson Matheny. Vital Records of Highland County, Virginia. Richmond, Va.: J. C. Matheny, 1986.

50.64   Mihalyka, Jean Merritt, and Faye Downing Wilson. Graven Stone: Inscriptions from Lower Accomack County, Virginia, Including Liberty and Parksley Cemeteries. 2d ed. Bowie, Md.: Heritage Books, 1987. This is a revised and corrected edition of Graven Stones of Lower Accomack County, Virginia, 1986.

50.65   ------. Gravestone Inscriptions in Northampton County, Virginia. Rev. ed. Richmond, Va.: Virginia State Library, 1984.

50.66   Moore, Evelyn Lee. Behind the Old Brick Wall; a Cemetery Story. Compiled by Lucy Harrison Miller Baber. Lynchburg, Va.: Lynchburg Committee of the National Society of the Colonial Dames of America in the Commonwealth of Virginia, 1968.

50.67   Moore, Munsey Adams. Cemetery and Tombstone Records of Mecklenburg County, Virginia. Chase City, Va.: Munsey Moore Publishers, 1982.

50.68   Murphy, Malita Warden, and James L. Douthat. Gates to Glory: Cemeteries of Pulaski County, Virginia. Signal Mountain, Tenn.: J. L. Douthat, 1983.

50.69   Murphy, Mary Catharine. "Abstracts of Obituaries in Charlottesville Newspapers, 1860-1869." Magazine of Albemarle County History 23 (1964-65): 45-70.

50.70   ------. "Abstracts of Obituaries in Charlottesville Newspapers, 1827-1859."
         Magazine of Albemarle County History 19 (1960-61): 41-57.

50.71   Musselman, Cynthia L. Stafford County, Virginia, Cemeteries. Stafford, Va.:
         C. L. Musselman, 1983.

50.72   Norfolk, Va. St. Paul's Church (Protestant Episcopal) Altar Guild. St. Paul's
         Church, 1832. Norfolk, Va.: St. Paul's Church, 1934. Includes records of
         inscriptions on the tombstones in St. Paul's church yard, pp. 63-115.

50.73   "Obituaries, American Almanac 1832-44." Genealogist's Post 5 (1968): 20-28.

50.74   Obituaries of Norfolk, Virginia and Vicinities. Compiled by Frances C.
         Griffin. Chesapeake, Va.: F. C. Griffin, 198-.

50.75   Obituary Notices from the "Alexandria Gazette" 1784-1915. Compiled by the
         Staff of Lloyd House, Alexandria Library. Bowie, Md.: Heritage Books,
         1987.

50.76   Peterson, Phyllis Louise Willits. Scott County, Va., Cemetery Records.
         3 vols. [Vancouver, Wash.]: Willits, 1979-1984.

50.77   Pilson, O. E. Tombstone Inscriptions of the Cemeteries of Patrick County,
         Virginia. Baltimore: Gateway Press, 1984.

50.78   Primitive Baptists. North Carolina. Little River Primitive Baptist
         Association. Minutes of the Sessions, 1896-1951. N.p., n.d. Contains
         obituaries for Grayson County, Virginia. InFw

50.79   Rachal, William Munford Ellis. "Obituaries from the Central Gazette
         Charlottesville, Va., 1820-1827." Papers of the Albemarle County
         Historical Society 10 (1949-50): 31-38.

50.80   Ritchey, Andrew. "Obituaries from a Scrapbook." Virginia Appalachian
         Notes 4 (1980): 12-13. Obituaries for Franklin county.

50.81   Roanoke County Graveyards through 1920. Roanoke, Va.: Roanoke Valley
         Historical Society, [1986].

50.82   Rudd, Alice Bohmer. Shockoe Hill Cemetery, Richmond, Virginia; Register
         of Interments, April 10, 1822 -December 31, 1950. 2 vols. N.p., n.d.

50.83   Ryland, Elizabeth Hawes. King William County, Virginia, from Old
         Newspapers and Files. Richmond, Va.: Dietz Press, 1955. Deaths are
         listed on pages 118-29. Seldom gives the name of the newspaper from
         which the death notice is taken.

50.84   Sellman, Maude E. Mercer. Civil War Burials, Fredericksburg, Virginia.
         N.p.: Sellman, 1979.

50.85   Sheridan, Christine L., and Elsie W. Ernst. <u>Tombstones of Mathews County,</u> <u>Virginia, 1711-1986</u>. Mathews County, Va.: Mathews County Historical Society, 1988.

50.86   Stuntz, S. C. "Extracts from Old Newspapers." <u>Daughters of the American</u> <u>Revolution Magazine</u> 48 (1916): 434. Includes a few deaths, 1799-1801, from Alexandria newspapers.

50.87   ------. "Gleanings from <u>Alexandria, (Va.) Herald</u>, March 15-Sept. 10, 1816." <u>Daughters of the American Revolution Magazine</u> 49 (1916): 277-78. Contains records of marriages and deaths

50.88   Sweeny, Lenora Higginbotham. <u>Obituaries of Bedford County, Virginia</u> <u>Revolutionary War Soldiers</u>. N.p., 1939. Excerpt from the <u>Bedford</u> <u>Bulletin</u>, 5 January 1939.

50.89   <u>Tombstone Inscriptions of Norfolk County, Virginia</u>. Chesapeake, Va.: Norfolk County Historical Society of Chesapeake in cooperation with Great Bridge Chapter, Daughters of the American Revolution, 1979.

50.90   Triplett, Ralph L. <u>Frederick County, Virginia Obituaries</u>. 3 vols. Gore, Va., 1974. Covers early 1800s to 1974.

50.91   <u>Virginia Gazette Index, 1736-1780</u>. 2 vols. Williamsburg, Va.: Institute of Early American History and Culture, 1950. The <u>Virginia Gazette</u> of Williamsburg was the second oldest newspaper in the southern colonies. Death notices and obituaries were infrequently published, but the ones that do appear can be located through this index.

50.92   Virginia Gazette, Williamsburg. "Extracts from the <u>Virginia Gazette</u> for 1755-1756." <u>Virginia Genealogist</u> 1 (1957): 23-28. Abstracts of genealogical information from 20 issues of the <u>Virginia Gazette</u>, 6 June 1755-30 June 1756, discovered after the publication of the index in 1950, no. <u>50</u>.91.

50.93   Virginia State Library. Richmond. <u>Index to Obituary Notices in the</u> <u>"Richmond Enquirer" from May 9, 1804, through 1828, and the</u> <u>"Richmond Whig" from January, 1824, through 1838</u>. 1923. Reprint. Baltimore: Genealogical Publishing Co., 1974. Originally published as <u>Bulletin of the Virginia State Library</u> vol. 14, no. 4, October 1921.

50.94   Waldrep, George Calvin. <u>Halifax County Cemeteries</u>. Greenville, S.C.: A Press, 1985.

50.95   Wayland, John W. <u>Virginia Valley Records</u>. Strasburg, Va.: Shenandoah Publishing House, 1930. Indexes some obituaries from the <u>Harrisonburg</u> <u>Daily News</u>, 1866-1911. There are several reprint editions.

50.96   Winchester-Frederick County Historical Society. <u>2200 Gravestone Inscriptions</u> <u>from Winchester and Frederick County, Virginia: Death Dates Range from</u> <u>1700's to Early 1900's; Indexed</u>. Compiled and edited by Pearl W. Ritenour. Boyce, Va.: Carr Publishing Company, 1960.

50. VIRGINIA

50.97   Woodward, Eula Keblinger.   "Alexandria, Va. Records from the <u>Alexandria Herald</u>, 1818-1819."   <u>National Genealogical Society Quarterly</u> 5 (1916): 17-20.

50.98   ------.   "<u>Genius of Liberty</u> Clippings, 1820-21, Leesburg, Virginia." <u>National Genealogical Society Quarterly</u> 7 (1918): 31-32.

51. WASHINGTON

51.1   *Branigar, Thomas R. "Genealogical Abstracts, Northwest Enterprise
        1882-1886, Anacortes, Washington." Bulletin of the Whatcom Genealogical
        Society 7 (1977): 151-60.

51.2   Calvary Cemetery (Catholics). Compiled by the Tacoma-Pierce County
        Genealogical Society. Tacoma, Wash.: The Society, [1985?].

51.3   Cemeteries of Eastern Jefferson County, State of Washington. Port
        Townsend, Wash.: Jefferson County Genealogical Society, 1985.

51.4   Clark County Washington Cemetery Records. 2 vols. Vancouver, Wash.:
        Clark County Genealogical Society, 1981-82. v. 1. Old City Cemetery of
        Vancouver; v. 2. St. James Acres, Salmon Creek Methodist, St. James
        Lutheran, Pioneer, and Fisher.

51.5   Daughters of the American Revolution. Washington. Rainier Chapter. Vital
        Statistics of Washington Territory, November 27, 1852 to November 1,
        1862. Seattle: Daughters of the American Revolution, 1923. Includes
        obituaries and death notices from the first papers published in the
        Washington Territory at Olympia.

51.6   "Deaths from the Benton County Republican and the Prosser Bulletin."
        Bulletin of the Yakima Valley Genealogical Society 7 (1975): 67-68. For
        the years 1906-7.

51.7   Frey, Joyce Padol, Carole Bierman Sayers, and Donna Burkert Grothaus.
        Memorial Records of South King County, Washington. 2 vols. Seattle,
        Wash.: South King County Branch of the Seattle Genealogical Society,
        1981-83.

51.8   Gig Harbor Peninsula Area Cemeteries: Pierce County, State of Washington.
        [Tacoma, Wash.]: Tacoma-Pierce County Genealogical Society, 1982.

51.9   "Gleanings from the Bellingham Herald." Bulletin of the Whatcom
        Genealogical Society 6 (1975): 47-48. For the years 1918-51.

51.10   Irvine, Jessie Young. Scrapbook of Obituaries of Grays Harbor Pioneers
        Published in the "Aberdeen Daily World," 1895-1961. Olympia:
        Washington State Library, 1961. Microfilm. Wa

51.11   Kolb, Alexis Ann Alexander. Black Diamond Cemetery, Black Diamond,
        Washington. [Black Diamond? Wash.]: Kolb, 1980.

51.12   Lartigue, Weston, and Carrie Lartigue. Tombstone Inscriptions, Lincoln
        County, Washington. Spokane, Wash.: Eastern Washington Genealogical
        Society, 1974.

51.13   McNeill, Ruby Simonson. Columbia County Washington Newspaper Abstracts.
        Spokane, Wash.: R. S. McNeill, 1980-. v. 1. Apr. 1882-Dec. 1883.

51. WASHINGTON

51.14 ------. Lewis County, Washington, Newspaper Abstracts. 5 vols. Spokane, Wash.: R. S. McNeill, 1978. v. 1. 1884-86; v. 2. 1887-89; v. 3. 1890-93; v. 4. 1894-96; v. 5. 1897-99.

51.15 Naselle to Grays River and Knappton to Nemah, Washington: Cemetery Records and Genealogical Notes. Compiled by Roberta Evans Krause Yancy. [Naselle? Wash.]: Yancy, 1978.

51.16 "Obituaries from the Yakima Herald 1889." Bulletin of the Yakima Valley Genealogical Society 8 (1976): 97-101.

51.17 Pacific Northwest Quarterly, v. 1-, 1906-. Seattle: Washington University State Historical Society, 1906-. Indexes: v. 1-10, 1906-19, in v. 10; v. 11-20, 1920-29, in v. 20; v. 1-29, 1906-38, in v. 29; v. 45-47, 1954-56, with v. 44-47; v. 1-53, 1906-62, 1 vol. Beginning in volume 4 and continuing through volume 8 there is a special section of obituaries for pioneer citizens. To locate these, it is necessary to use the index to volumes 1-10 in volume 10. Additional obituaries can be located by using the other indexes. The index to volumes 1-53 is selective in its indexing of obituaries.

51.18 Pierce Co. Cemetery Records. 3 vols. Tacoma, Wash.: Tacoma-Pierce County Genealogical Society, 1982. v. 2. Oakwood Cemetery; v. 3. Calvary Cemetery (Catholic).

51.19 Prichard, Carolyn. "Genealogical Data Abstracted from the Chehalis Valley Vidette, Published Weekly at Montesano, Chehalis County, Washington Territory (Now Grays Harbor County)." Bulletin of the Seattle Genealogical Society 18 (1969): 105-8. For the year 1883.

51.20 Todd, Frances. "News from Friday Harbor Journal, San Juan County, Washington." Bulletin of the Whatcom Genealogical Society 7 (1976): 39. For the year 1931.

51.21 Tombstone Inscriptions: Adams County and Pend Oreille County, Washington. Spokane, Wash.: Eastern Washington Genealogical Society, [1976].

51.22 Tombstone Inscriptions, Stevens County, Washington. Compiled by Carrie Lartigue and Belva Pedersen. [Spokane, Wash.]: Eastern Washington Genealogical Society, 1976.

51.23 Tombstone Inscriptions, Whitman County. Compiled by Weston Lartigue, and Carrie Lartigue. 3 vols. N.p.: Eastern Washington Genealogical Society, 1972-73.

51.24 Townsend, Homer, and Alice Townsend. Obituaries from the Skamania County Pioneer Newspaper, Skamania County, Washington, 1900-1929. Goldendale, Wash.: H. Townsend, 1985.

51.25 Weatherly, Bob. Asotin County, Washington, Cemeteries, Some Garfield and Columbia County, Washington, and Wallowa County, Oregon, Cemeteries:

Their History and Headstone Inscriptions. Orting, Wash.: Heritage Quest, 1986.

51.26   Whatcom Genealogical Society. *Cemetery Records of Whatcom County*. 5 vols. Bellingham, Wash.: Whatcom Genealogical Society, 1973-76.

51.27   Winter, Jean. *Tombstone Inscriptions of Adams County, Washington*. [Pasco, Wash.]: Winters, 1972.

51.28   ------. *Tombstone Inscriptions of Columbia County, Washington*. [Pasco, Wash.]: Winters, 1972.

51.29   ------. *Tombstone Inscriptions of Franklin County, Washington*. [Pasco, Wash.]: Winters, 1971.

51.30   ------. *Tombstone Inscriptions of Klickitat County, Washington*. Pasco, Wash.: Winters, 1972.

51.31   ------. *Tombstone Inscriptions of Walla Walla County, Washington*. [Pasco, Wash.]: Winters, 1971-.

52. WEST VIRGINIA

52.1   Anderson, Stanley J. <u>Cemeteries of Northern Webster County</u>. [Cleveland, W.Va.], 1978.

52.2   Atkinson, Mary Davis. <u>Cemetery Records of Tyler and Pleasants Counties, West Virginia</u>. 2 vols. College Park, Md.: Atkinson, 1980.

52.3   Bailey, Ronzel L. <u>Cemeteries in Calhoun County, West Virginia</u>. Grantsville, W.Va.: Calhoun Historical and Genealogical Society, 1985.

52.4   Baisden, Louise, and Brenda J. Hensley. <u>Cemeteries of Logan County</u>. 2 vols. Logan, W.Va: Logan County Genealogical Society, 1983-84.

52.5   <u>Banks District Cemetery Readings, Upshur County, West Virginia</u>. Buckhannon, W.Va.: Upshur County Genealogical Society, 1984.

52.6   Carter, Eleanor Yost, and Kathleen Mahaffey Bogdan. <u>Cemetery Records of Marion County, West Virginia</u>. Fairmont, W.Va.: Marion County Genealogical Club, Marion County Library, 1983. For the Winfield district.

52.7   <u>Cemetery Readings; Preston County, West Virginia</u>. . . . Tomball, Tex.: Genealogical Publishing Co., 1977. Originally published in 1933 by Jeanna Robey Felldin.

52.8   Chapman, Odee. <u>"They Rest Quietley": Cemetery Records of Tucker County, West Virginia</u>. Marceline, Mo.: Walsworth Press, 1985.

52.9   Craig, Fred E. Papers, 1910-45. West Virginia University Library. NUC MS. 60-969. Clippings of obituaries from the <u>Reedy News</u>, a Roane County, West Virginia newspaper.

52.10   Cutright Family. Genealogical Materials, 1887-1950. West Virginia University Library. NUC MS. 60-1359. Includes obituaries clipped from newspapers of Buckhannon, Clarksburg, and Parkersburg, West Virginia.

52.11   Duffield, Ella May. <u>Charleston, Kanawha, West Virginia Deaths from the "Charleston Daily Mail" and "Gazette," 1945-1952</u>. Salt Lake City: Genealogical Society, 1966. Microfilm. USIGS

52.12   ------. <u>Parkersburg, Wood County, West Virginia, Deaths from the "Parkersburg News" Parkersburg, West Virginia and "Greenbrier Valley's Gateway" Ronceverte, West Virginia</u>. Salt Lake City: Genealogical Society, 1966. Microfilm. USIGS For the period Dec. 1945-May 1946.

52.13   <u>Graveyard History of Morgan County W. Va</u>. Berkeley Springs, W.Va.: Morgan County Historical and Genealogical Society, 1980.

52.14   Hassig, Carol. <u>Wetzel County, WV, Obituary Book, 1870-1940</u>. New Martinsville, W.Va.: Wetzel County Genealogical Society, 1981.

52.15   Historical Records Survey. West Virginia. <u>Cemetery Readings in West Virginia</u>. Charleston, W.Va.: Historical Records Survey, 1939.

52. WEST VIRGINIA

52.16   Hite, Mrs. H. Paul. Index to Wood County Cemetery Inscriptions. N.p.: West Augusta Historical and Genealogical Society, 1977.

52.17   Hodge, Robert Allen. An Index for the "Martinsburg Gazette," Martinsburg, West Virginia, v. 35-39, 1834-1839. Fredericksburg, Va., 1974.

52.18   ------. An Index for the "Martinsburg Gazette,"]Martinsburg, West Virginia, 1810-1815, 1823-1827, 1829-1831. 2 vols. Fredericksburg, Va., 1973.

52.19   Jacob, John G. Brooke County, Being a Record of Prominent Events, Occurring in Brooke County, W. Va., from the Settlement of the County, Until January 1, 1882. Wellsburg, W. Va.: Printed at the Herald Office, 1882. Contains a list of deaths in Brooke County from 1 January 1870 to 1882 on pages 188-93. Some of the deaths were copied from the Wellsburg Herald. Only the name, date, and age at death is given.

52.20   Lambert, Frederick B. Papers, ca. 1809-1959. West Virginia University Library. Microfilm. NUC Ms. 66-692. Includes obituaries from Guyandotte Valley area.

52.21   Machir, Violette Irene. Mason County, W. Va., Cemetery Inscriptions. 4 vols. Middleport, Ohio: Quality Print Shop, 1972-.

52.22   Moore, Fannie I., Gregg D. Moore, and Lena Frame Ball. Clay County Cemeterys. Belle, W.Va.: G. D. Moore, [1985].

52.23   [No entry].

52.24   Pendleton County Historical Society. Grave Register, Pendleton County, West Virginia. 2 vols. [Franklin? W.Va.: Pendleton County Historical Society], 1977-80.

52.25   Prince-Tharp, Barbara. Where They Lie: Cemeteries of Southern Harrison County. Lost Creek, W.Va.: B. Prince-Tharp, 1984.

52.26   Ramage, Donald Edward. Doddridge County and West Virginia Deaths. [Granada Hills, Calif.]: D. E. Ramage, 1983. Includes deaths recorded in the West Union Record from January 1901 through December 1904. The West Union Record was a county weekly newspaper.

52.27   ------. Doddridge County Cemeteries. [Granada Hills, Calif.]: D. E. Ramage, 1984.

52.28   Sponangle, Maycel M. Obituaries Cut from Pendleton Co., West Virginia Newspapers. Salt Lake City: Genealogical Society, 1970. Microfilm. USIGS

52.29   Stinson, Helen S. Nicholas County, West Virginia Cemeteries: Copied from the Original Tombstones, Includes Research Data on Smith-Jones-Williams-Foster Families of Southern West Virginia. Sommersville, W.Va.: Nicholas County Historical and Genealogical Society, 1983.

52. WEST VIRGINIA

52.30   Tetrick, Willis Guy. Obituaries from Newspapers of Northern West Virginia,
         Principally from the Counties of Barbour, Braxton, Calhoun, Doddridge,
         Gilmer, Harrison, Lewis, Nicholas, Pocahontas, Preston, Randolph,
         Ritchie, Taylor, Tucker, Tyler, Upshur, Webster and Parts of Marion,
         Wetzel and Wirt. 2d ser., vol. 1-. Clarksburg, W.Va., 1933. v. 1. 17
         Dec. 1931-28 May 1932; v. 2. 25 May 1932-8 Nov. 1932. Reprints the
         entire obituary.

52.31   Thayer, George, and Mary Thayer. Hancock County, West Virginia
         Cemeteries. Apollo, Pa.: Closson Press, 1983.

52.32   Tombstone Inscriptions and Burial Lots. Compiled by Bee Line Chapter,
         National Society of the Daughters of the American Revolution.
         Marceline, Mo.: Walsworth Publishing Co., 1981.

52.33   Triplett, Ralph L. Cemeteries of Hampshire County, W.Va., and Vicinity.
         [Kimberly, Idaho]: J. M. Secord, 1974.

52.34   Washington District Cemetery Readings. Buckhannon, W.Va.: Upshur County
         Genealogical Society, 1984.

52.35   Wood County Cemetery Inscriptions. 3 vols. Parkersburg, W.Va.: West
         Augusta Historical and Genealogical Society, [1978-83].

53. WISCONSIN

53.1   Cemetery Inscriptions of Monroe County, Wisconsin. N.p.: Monroe, Juneau, Jackson County Genealogy Workshop, [1985?].

53.2   Cemetery Inscriptions, Town of Mishicot, Manitowoc County, Wisconsin. [Mishicot, Wis.?]: Manitowoc County Genealogical Society, 1981.

53.3   Cemetery Inscriptions, Township of Cooperstown, Manitowoc County, Wisconsin. [Manitowoc, Wis.]: Manitowoc County Genealogical Society, 1981.

53.4   Cemetery Inscriptions, Township of Gibson, Manitowoc County, Wisconsin. [Manitowoc, Wis.]: Manitowoc County Genealogical Society, 1981.

53.5   Cushing, Myrtle, et al. Cemetery Inscriptions of Sauk County, Wisconsin. 6 vols. Sauk City, Wis: M. E. Cushing, 1980.

53.6   "Death Notices from the Advocate." Newsletter of the Wisconsin State Genealogical Society 21 (1974): 20. For the year 1851. The Advocate was published in Green Bay.

53.7   "Deaths and Marriages from the Watertown Democrat." Wisconsin Helper 2 (1968): 4. For the years 1864-65.

53.8   "Deaths from Buffalo County Journal." Newsletter of the Wisconsin State Genealogical Society 23 (1976): 19-20. For the years 1861-64. The Buffalo County Journal was published in Alma.

53.9   "Deaths from Oconto County Reporter." Newsletter of the Wisconsin State Genealogical Society 23 (1976): 94. For the year 1872.

53.10   "Deaths from the Appleton Post." Newsletter of the Wisconsin State Genealogical Society 24 (1978): 194. For the years 1866-69.

53.11   "Deaths from the Columbus Democrat." Newsletter of the Wisconsin State Genealogical Society 21 (1974): 22.

53.12   "Deaths from the Monroe Sentinenl." Newsletter of the Wisconsin State Genealogical Society 24 (1977): 78. For the years 1851-56.

53.13   "Deaths from the Prescott Journal." Newsletter of the Wisconsin State Genealogical Soceity 24 (1977): 88. For the year 1861.

53.14   "Deaths from the Wood County Reporter." Newsletter of the Wisconsin State Genealogical Society 25 (1978): 54. For the years 1858-61. The Wood County Reporter was published in Wisconsin Rapids.

53.15   "Deaths from Waukesha County Democrat." Newsletter of the Wisconsin State Genealogical Society 25 (1978): 104. For the year 1882.

53.16   Dieter, Herbert A. Here They Sleep: Compiled As a Memorium to Those Who Rest in 91 Cemeteries in Richland County, Wisconsin. rev. ed. N.p. 1979.

53.17　Foley, Wilma Whitehead. <u>Marriage and Deaths Abstracted and Indexed from the "Depere News," 1871-1883</u>. Dearborn, Mich.: Foley, 1976.

53.18　Gee, Patricia Foley. <u>Deaths in the "Green Bay Advocate," 1870-1880</u>. N.p. 1976.

53.19　"Genealogical Data from the <u>Grant County Herald</u>, the <u>Wisconsin Herald</u> and <u>Grant County Advertiser</u>, Published at Lancaster." <u>Newsletter of the Wisconsin State Genealogical Society</u> 22 (1975): 28. For the years 1843-45.

53.20　Gnacinski, Janneyne Langley. <u>Abstracts from Obituaries Published in Waukesha Wisconsin Newspapers, 1863-1881</u>. West Allis, Wis.: Gnacinski, 1971.

53.21　"<u>Grant County Herald</u> Marriages and Deaths." <u>Newsletter of the Wisconsin State Genealogical Society</u> 24 (1977): 27-28. For the years 1853-60. The <u>Grant County Herald</u> was published in Lancaster.

53.22　Habelman, E. Carolyn Wildes. <u>Genealogical Branches from Monroe County, Wisconsin</u>. 3 vols. La Crosse, Wis.: Midwest Graphics, 1973-75. Contains births, marriages, and deaths extracted from Monroe county newspapers, 1858-1920.

53.23　Historical Records Survey. Wisconsin. <u>Abstracts from Obituaries Published in Waukesha, Wisconsin Newspapers, 1863-1881</u>. West Allis, Wis., 1971. Microfilm. USIGS

53.24　Irvin, John M. <u>Tombstone Inscriptions of Cemeteries in Green County, Wisconsin</u>. 2 vols. Monroe, Wis.: Wisconsin Helper, 1969-71.

53.25　Kahlert, John. <u>Pioneer Cemeteries, Door County Wisconsin</u>. Baileys Harbor, Wis.: Meadow Lane Publishers, 1981.

53.26　Keibel, Albert. <u>The Obituary Book of St John's Evangelical Lutheran Church, Maribel, Wisconsin, 1875-1892</u>. Transcribed and translated by Robert A. Bjerke. Manitowoc, Wis.: University of Wisconsin Center-Manitowoc County, Manitowoc County Genealogical Society, 1986.

53.27　"Local News from the <u>Brandon Times</u> of Brandon, Wisconsin in Fond du Lac County." <u>Newsletter of the Wisconsin State Genealogical Society</u> 14 (1967): 5. For January 1889.

53.28　<u>Marathon County, Wisconsin, Cemetery Inscriptions: An Every-Name Index</u>. Edited by Jerome S. Lund, and Edith E. Carpenter. Wausau, Wis.: Marathon County Genealogical Society, 1986.

53.29　"Marriage and Death Records from <u>Green Lake Spectator</u>." <u>Newsletter of the Wisconsin State Genealogical Society</u> 21 (1975): 133-34. For the years 1864-66.

53.30   "Marriages and Deaths from the <u>Superior Chronicle</u>." <u>Newslettter of the</u> <u>Wisconsin State Genealogical Society</u> 25 (1978): 91-81. For the years 1855-57.

53.31   Marx, Joseph A. <u>God's Acre: A Necrology of the Diocesan Clergy of the</u> <u>Diocese of Green Bay</u>. Green Bay, Wis., 1939. Gives year of ordination, age, date of death and occasionally additional facts.

53.32   Matl, Glenn J., and Fran H. Matl. <u>City of Shullsburg: Indexed Cemetery</u> <u>Records, Evergreen Cemetery, Old St. Matthew's Cemetery, New St.</u> <u>Matthew's Cemetery, Sullivan Death Records, Lafayette County, State of</u> <u>Wisconsin</u>. N.p.: G. J. Matl, 1985.

53.33   Miller, Willis Harry. <u>Hudson Area Biography: A Group of Biographical</u> <u>Sketches As Contained in Obituaries Originally Published in the "Hudson</u> <u>(Wis.) Star-Observer</u>." 2 vols. Hudson, Wis.: Star-Observer Print, 1967-68.

53.34   ------. <u>Willow River Cemetery (Old Yard) Tombstone Inscriptions, Hudson,</u> <u>St. Croix Co., Wisconsin, and Deaths for St. Croix Co., Wisconsin,</u> <u>1870-1879, As Found in Volume 1 of Deaths in the Office of Register of</u> <u>Deeds, St. Croix Co., Court House, Hudson, Wis</u>. Hudson, Wis.: Star-Observer Publishing Co., 1974.

53.35   Milwaukee Journal. <u>Newspaper Index</u>. Wooster, Ohio: Bell and Howell Co., 1976-. Monthly with annual cumulations.

53.36   Noonan, Barry Christopher. <u>Index to Green Bay Newspapers, 1833-1840</u>. Madison, Wis.: Wisconsin State Genealogical Society, 1987.

53.37   <u>Obituary Index, 1939-1971, the "New North," "Rhinelander Daily News</u>." N.p. 1983. Microfilm.

53.38   <u>Obituary Index, Vol. 1: Stevens Point Journal, 1881-1952</u>. Produced by the Stevens Point Area Genealogical Society in cooperation with the University of Wisconsin-Stevens Point Area Research Center and Archives. Stevens Point, Wis.: The Society, 1987. Microform.

53.39   Park, Margaret Jane. <u>Honey Creek Cemetery, 1849-1974</u>. West Allis, Wis.: Park, 1974.

53.40   "Pierce County Marriage and Death Notices from Newspapers 1859-1861." <u>Newsletter of the Wisconsin State Genealogical Society</u> 16 (1969): 27-28.

53.41   Pruett, Dorothy Diehl. <u>Abstracts of Births, Marriage and Death</u> <u>Announcements Published in the "Lake Geneva, Wisconsin Regional</u> <u>News," May through December 1967</u>. Milwaukee, Wis.., 1968. Microfilm. Filmed by the Genealogical Society at Salt Lake City, 1970. USIGS

53.42   "Records from the <u>Columbus Democrat</u>, Published at Columbus, Wisconsin." <u>Wisconsin Helper</u> 1 (1967): 25. For 1875.

53. WISCONSIN

53.43   "Records from the Fox Lake Gazette in Dodge County." Wisconsin Helper 2 (1968): 40. For the years 1864-65.

53.44   Rentmeister, Jean R., Sally P. Albertz, and Andrew M. Chiello. Cemetery Inscriptions of Empire Township, Fond du Lac County, Wisconsin. Fond du Lac, Wis.: J. R. Rentmeister, 1985.

53.45   "Trempealeau County Messenger Marriage and Death Notices." Wisconsin Helper 1 (1967): 34. For the years 1875-76.

53.46   "Vital Records from the Republican and Press, 5 January 1899." Newsletter of the Wisconsin State Genealogical Society 13 (1966): 54. The Republican and Press was published at Neillsville.

53.47   Wisconsin Families, v. 1, June 1940-March 1941. Milwaukee, Wis.: Wisconsin Genealogical Society, 1940. Genealogical gleanings from Prairieville newspapers for 1845-46 which includes a few death notices.

53.48   Wisconsin Magazine of History, v. 1-, 1917-. Madison: State Historical Society, 1917-. Contains a necrology section through volume 33.

53.49   Wisconsin Necrology, 1846-1968. Madison: State Historical Society, n.d. Microfilm. USIGS

53.50   Wisconsin State Historical Society. Proceedings, v. 1-, 1854-. Madison: State Historical Society, 1854-. Many volumes of the Proceedings have obituaries for the Society's members.

54. WYOMING

54.1   Cheyenne Genealogy Society, Cheyenne, Wyoming. <u>Obituary Clippings, 1964-1965</u>. N.p. 1965. InFw

54.2   Field, Sharon Lass. <u>Fort Fetterman's Cemetery</u>. Cheyenne, Wyo., [1970].

54.3   Martin, Phyllis J. <u>Greenriver and Bryon Cemeteries in Sweetwater County, Wyoming</u>. [Evanston, Wyo.]: P. J. Martin, [1983].

54.4   ------. <u>Obituaries from Newspapers in Uinta County, Wyoming 1984 and 1985</u>. Evanston, Wyo.: P. J. Martin, [1986?].

54.5   ------. <u>South Lincoln Special Cemetery District, Lincoln County, Wyo</u>. [Evanston, Wyo.]: P. J. Martin, [1983].

54.6   ------. <u>Uinta County, Wyoming Cemetery Records</u>. [Evanston, Wyo.]: P. J. Martin, n.d.

54.7   <u>Natrona County, Wyoming, Cemetery Records</u>. Casper, Wyo.: Natrona County Genealogical Society, 1986.

54.8   <u>Obituaries from Newspapers in Uinta County, Wyoming 1982 and 1983</u>. [Evanston, Wyo.: P. J. Martin, 1984].

54.9   Reese, Viola. <u>Rock Springs, Sweetwater County, Wyoming Mountain View Cemetery Records and Obituary Records Copied from Newspapers</u>. Salt Lake City: Genealogical Society, 1959. Microfilm. USIGS

54.10   "Wyoming Statistics from the <u>Cheyenne Daily Sun-Leader</u>." <u>Genealogical Post</u> 4 (1967): 3-4. For the years 1899-1900. Includes death and marriage notices.

55. UNITED KINGDOM AND THE REPUBLIC OF IRELAND

55.1 Almanack, v. 1-, 1869-. London: Whitaker, 1869-. Generally known as
      Whitaker's Almanac. Although its scope is international, the necrology
      section is strongly British. AC85

55.2 Annual Biography and Obituary. . . . v. 1-21, 1817-37. London: Longman,
      Hurst, Rees, Orme, and Brown, 1817-37.

55.3 Annual Monitor. Quaker Records: Being an Index to the "Annual Monitor",
      1813-1892, Containing Over 20,000 Obituary Notices of Members of the
      Society of Friends, Alphabetically and Chronologically Arranged. Edited
      by Joseph Green. London: E. Hicks, 1894. BB372

55.4 Assam. List of Inscriptions on Tombs or Monuments in Assam. [Shillong: C.
      Francis, Press Superintendent at the Secretariat Printing Office, 1902].

55.5 Baptist Annual Register . . . Including Sketches of the State of Religion
      among Different Denominations of Good Men at Home and Abroad. . . .
      1790/93-1801/02. 4 vols. London, 1793-1802.

55.6 Baptist Handbook, 1860-. London, 1860-.

55.7 Beazley, Frank Charles. Calendar of Persons Commemorated in Monumental
      Inscriptions and Abstracts of Wills. . . . [St. Annes]: Printed for the
      Record Society, 1922. (Publications of The Record Society for the Publi-
      cation of Original Documents Relating to Lancashire and Cheshire, v. 76)
      This volume is an index to some 21,000 references to persons commemor-
      ated in monumental inscriptions or named in wills. Also available in
      microform. Teaneck, N.J.: Chadwyck-Healey, 1976.

55.8 Bellasis, Edward. Westmorland Church Notes, Being the Heraldry, Epitaphs,
      and Other Inscriptions in the Thirty-two Ancient Parish Churches and
      Churchyards of That County. Kendal: T. Wilson, 1888-89.

55.9 The Bengal Obituary, or, a Record to Perpetuate the Memory of Departed
      Worth: Being a Compilation of Tablets and Monumental Inscriptions from
      Various Parts of the Bengal and Agra Presidencies: To Which is Added
      Biographical Sketches and Memoirs of Such As Have Preeminently
      Distinguished Themselves in History of British India Since the Formation
      of the European Settlement to the Present Time. 1851. Reprint.
      London: British Association for Cemeteries in South Asia, 1983.

55.10 Berning, J. M. Index to Obituary Notices of Methodist Ministers, 1815-1920.
      [Johannesburg]: Public Library, 1969. This is an index and summary of
      the obituary notices in the minutes of the British and South African
      Methodist Conferences, 1815-1920.

55.11 Bigland, Ralph. Historical, Monumental and Genealogical Collections,
      Relative to the County of Gloucester. 2 vols. London: J. Nichols,
      1791-92.

55.12 Blundell, William. Crosby Records; a Chapter of Lancashire Recusancy.
      Containing a Relation of Troubles and Persecutions Sustained by William

Blundell, of Crosby Hall, Lancashire, Esq. (1560-1638), and an Account of an Ancient Burial Ground for Recusants, called the Harkirke. . . . Manchester: Chetham Society, 1887. (Remains, Historical and Literary, Connected with the Palatine Counties of Lancaster and Chester, n.s., v. 12) For the years 1611-1753.

55.13   Braga, José Maria. Tombstones in the English Cemeteries at Macao. Macao: Tipografia mercantil de N. T. Fernandes e filhos, 1940.

55.14   British Almanac, 1828-1914. 87 vols. London: Cassell, 1828-1914. Issues for 1828-88 bound with Companion to the Almanac; or, Yearbook of General Information. The earliest volumes have a section called "Chronicle of Events" which lists some deaths of prominent persons. Beginning with 1844 there is a necrology section.

55.15   Brydges, Samuel Egerton. Select Funeral Memorials. Kent: Printed at the Private Press of Lee Priory, by John Warwick, 1818. Contains epitaphs from English cemeteries.

55.16   Burke, John Bernard. Heraldic Register, 1849-1850, with an Introductory Essay on Heraldry, and an Annotated Obituary. . . . London: E. Churton, 1850.

55.17   Cansick, Frederick Teague. A Collection of Curious and Interesting Epitaphs, Copied from the Monuments of Distinguished and Noted Characters in the Ancient Church and Burial Grounds of Saint Pancras, Middlesex. 2 vols. London: J. R. Smith, 1869-72.

55.18   Catholic Directory, v. 1-. London: Burns and Oates, 1838-1970. Annual. BB458

55.19   Catholic Record Society, London. Obituaries. London, 1918. (Its Publications, v. 12) Contains obituaries of secular priests, 1722-1783 and from Laity's Directory, 1733-1839. Laity's Directory, after 1782, in addition to obituaries of secular priests, included those of nuns and lay brothers.

55.20   Catholic Who's Who, 1st-28th. 1908-52. London: Burns and Oates, 1908-52. Annual. Ceased. AJ225

55.21   Charterhouse. The Registers and Monumental Inscriptions of Charterhouse Chapel. Edited by Francis Collins. London: [Mitchell and Hughes], 1892.

55.22   Chester Public Library. Chester Newspaper Index, 1960-64. Chester: Chester Civic Amenities Committee, 1970.

55.23   Clarke, R. S. J. Gravestone Inscriptions: Belfast. 3 vols. Belfast: Ulster Historical Foundation, 1982-86. v. 1. Shankill graveyard and tablets in Christ Church and St. George's Church; v. 2. Friar's Bush and Milltown graveyards; v. 3. Balmoral cemetery, friends' burial ground and Malone Presbyterian Church.

55.24   ------. Gravestone Inscriptions: County Down. 19 vols. Belfast: Ulster-Scot Historical Society, 1966-79.

55.25   Collectanea franciscana. . . . Aberdeen: Typis Academicis, 1914-22. (British Society of Franciscan Studies, v. 5) Records of the Franciscan province of England with an early 14th century obituary, Cotton charter XXX, 40.

55.26   Collection of Epitaphs and Monumental Inscriptions, Chiefly in Scotland. Glasgow: D. Macvean, 1834. pt. 1. An theater of mortality; collected and Englished by R. Monteith. [Reprint of the Edinburgh edition of 1704]; pt. 2. A theater of mortality; or, A further collection of funeral inscriptions over Scotland; by Robert Monteith. [Reprint of the Edinburgh edition of 1713]; pt. 3. Additional inscriptions [chiefly collected by William Dobie and John Dunn].

55.27   A Collection of Epitaphs and Monumental Inscriptions, Historical, Biographical, Literary, and Miscellaneous. To Which is Prefixed, An Essay of Epitaphs. By Dr. Johnson . . . . 2 vols. London: Lackington, Allen and Co., 1806.

55.28   Conceptionists. The Diary of the "Blue Nuns" or Order of the Immaculate Conception of Our Lady, at Paris, 1658-1810. London: Catholic Record Society, 1910. (Its Publications, v. 8) An English community of nuns, founded about 1660, and dispersed during the French Revolution. Contains an obituary, 1661-1810, partly in French.

55.29   Cornish Epitaphs. Edited by John Keast, and Renée Keast. Redruth, [Cornwall]: D. Truran, 1981.

55.30   Court Register, a Monthly Record of Births, Marriages and Deaths Associated with the Aristocracy, etc., no. 1-21, 1861-65. BM

55.31   Cowper, J. Meadows. The Memorial Inscriptions of the Cathedral Church of Canterbury. [Canterbury: Cross and Jackman, 1897].

55.32   Crisp, Frederick Arthur. Monumental Inscriptions in the Church and Churchyard of Ellough, Suffolk. [London]: F. A. Crisp, 1889.

55.33   Crossley, Ely Wilkinson. The Monumental and Other Inscriptions in Halifax Parish Church. Leeds, Eng.: John Whitehead, 1909.

55.34   Dalrymple, Robert. Register of Marriages and Deaths of Acquaintances and Persons of Rank, 1805-20. British Museum. Additional MS. 22,151.

55.35   Dand, Middleton Henry, and J. C. Hodgson. Epitaphs and Monumental Inscriptions of Warkworth Church and Churchyard. Alnwick: H. H. Blair, 1890.

55.36   Derozario. The Complete Monumental Register: Containing All the Epitaphs, Inscriptions . . . in the Different Churches and Burial-Grounds, in and about Calcutta. . . . Calcutta: P. Ferris, 1815.

55.37   Dew, Walton N. The Monumental Inscriptions in the Hundred of Holt in the County of Norfolk. Edited by Walter Rye. Norwich: A. H. Goose, 1885.

55.38   "Documents Illustrating the History of S. Paul's Cathedral. Article XII. Kalendar and List of Obits Observed in S. Paul's Cathedral, Taken from the Statuta Majora, a Manuscript of the Time of Richard II." Publications of the Royal Historical Society, London: Camden Publications, n.s. 26 (1880): 61-106.

55.39   Dod's Parliamentary Companion, 1832-. London: Whitaker, 1832-. Annual. CJ329

55.40   Dominicana. Cardinal Howard's Letters, English Dominican Friars, Nuns, Students, Papers and Mission Registers. London: Catholic Record Society, 1925. (Its Publications, v. 25) Contains an obituary of English Dominicans, 1661-1827, pp. 126-36.

55.41   Dublin. Cathedral Church of the Holy Trinity. The Book of Obits and Martyrology of the Cathedral Church of the Holy Trinity, Commonly Called Christ Church, Dublin. Edited from the original manuscript in the Library of Trinity College, Dublin, by John Clarke Crosthwaite. Dublin: Irish Archeological Society, 1844. (Its Publications, no. 4)

55.42   ------. St. Mary's Abbey. Chartularies of St. Mary's Abbey, Dublin: With the Register of Its House at Dunbrody, and Annals of Ireland. Edited by John T. Gilbert. 2 vols. London: Longman, 1884. (Great Britain. Public Record Office. Rerum britannicarum medii aevi scriptores; or, Chronicles and Memorials of Great Britain and Ireland during the Middle Ages, no. 80) Contains obits of the Lacys, Burkes, Butlers, and Fitzgeralds, 1370-1536.

55.43   Dugdale, William. Durham Monuments: Or, the Shields of Arms, Effigies and Inscriptions in the Churches, Castles, and Halls of the County of Durham. Newcastle upon Tyne: Printed for the Newcastle upon Tyne Records Committee by Northumberland Press, 1925. (Publications of the Society of Antiquaries of Newcastle-upon-Tyne. Newcastle-upon-Tyne Records Committee, v. 5)

55.44   Duncan, Andrew. Elogiorun sepulchralium Edinensium delectus. Monumental Inscriptions Selected from Burial Grounds at Edinburgh. Edinburgh: Neill and Co., 1815.

55.45   Duncan, Leland L. Kentish Monumental Inscriptions; Inscriptions at Tenterden. Blackheath, Eng.: C. North, [1919].

55.46   ------. Monumental Inscriptions in the Churchyard and Church of All Saints, Lydd, Kent. Edited by Arthur Finn. Ashford, Kent: Headley Brothers, Invicta Press, [1927]. (Kent Archaeological Society. Records Branch. Kentish Monumental Inscriptions series, no. 2)

55.47   Dunkin, Edwin. Obituary Notices of Astronomers, Fellows and Associates of the Royal Astronomical Society. . . . London: Williams and Norgate, 1879. (New York: Readex Microprint, 1974)

55.48   Durham Cathedral. Liber vitae Ecclesiae dunelmensis; nec non obituaria duo ejusdem ecclesiae. Edited by Joseph Stevenson. London: J. B. Nichols, 1841. (Publications of the Surtees Society, v. 13)

55.49   ------. The Obituary Roll of William Ebchester and John Burnby, Priors of Durham, with Notices of Similar Records Preserved at Durham, from the Year 1233 Downwards. . . . Durham: G. Andrews, [1856]. (Publications of the Surtees Society, v. 31)

55.50   Dwelly, Edward. Devon Monumental Inscriptions. Fleet, Hants: E. Dwelly, 1918.

55.51   ------. Kent M.I., Being All the Monumental Inscriptions in the Parishes of Reculver-cum Hoath, Herne and Herne Bay. Herne Bay: Dwelly, 1914.

55.52   Edinburgh. Greyfriars' Churchyard. Register of Interments in the Greyfriars Buryingground, Edinburgh, 1658-1700. Edited by Henry Paton. Edinburgh: J. Skinner, 1902. (Publications of the Scottish Record Society, 26)

55.53   "English Benedictine Nuns of Our Blessed Lady of Good Hope in Paris, Now at St. Benedict's Priory, Colwich, Staffordshire. Notes and Obituaries, 1652-1861." Publications of the Catholic Record Society 7 (1911): 334-431.

55.54   "English Franciscan Nuns, 1619-1821, and the Friars Minor of the Same Province, 1618-1761." Publications of the Catholic Record Society 24 (1922): 259-314. This is a necrology of Franciscan friars.

55.55   Farrar, Robert Henry. Irish Marriages, Being an Index to the Marriages in "Walker's Hibernian Magazine," 1771 to 1812, with an Appendix from the Notes of Sir Arthur Vicars . . . Ulster King of Arms, of the Births, Marriages, and Deaths in the "Anthologia Hibernica," 1793 and 1794. 1897. Reprint. Baltimore: Genealogical Publishing Co., 1972.

55.56   Feltham, John, and Edward Wright. Memorials of "God's Acre," Being Monumental Inscriptions in the Isle of Man, Taken in the Summer of 1797. Edited by William Harrison. Douglas, Isle of Man: Manx Society, 1868. Microfiche. Bishops Stortford, Eng.: Chadwyck-Healey, 1974.

55.57   Finlayson, John. Inscriptions on the Monuments, Mural Tablets, at Present Existing in Christ Church Cathedral, Dublin: The Names (So Far As They Have Been Ascertained) of Persons Buried within That Church, But of Whom No Monumental Records Exist. . . . Dublin: Hodges, Foster, and Figgis, 1878.

55.58   Fisher, Payne. The Tombs, Monuments, &c., Visible in S. Paul's Cathedral (and S. Faith's beneath It) Previous to Its Destruction by Fire A.D. 1666. 1684. Reprint. 1885.

55.59   Foreign Office List and Diplomatic and Consular Year Book, 1806-1965. London: Harrison, 1806-1965. Annual. Ceased.

55.60   Garrett, Herbert Leonard Offley. Supplementary List of Inscriptions on Tombs or Monuments in the Punjab, North-West Frontier Province, Kashmir, Sind, Afghanistan, and Baluchistan. . . . Lahore: Superintendent of Government Printing, 1934. This is a supplement to no. 55.102.

55.61   Gibson, James. Inscriptions on the Tombstones and Monuments Erected in Memory of the Covenanters, with Historical Introduction and Notes. Glasgow: Dunn and Wright, [1879].

55.62   Gibson, Jeremy Sumner Wycherley. Monumental Inscriptions in Sixty Hampshire Churches. Hannington, Hampshire: J. S. W. Gibson, 1958.

55.63   Gilchrist, George, and Alexander McCracken. Memorials of Ayr Old Churchyard. Annan: G. Gilchrist, 1974.

55.64   ------. Memorials of Stapleton. Annan: G. Gilchrist, 1974.

55.65   Gilchrist, George, and Robert A. Shannon. Memorials of Applegarth and Sibbaldbie Parish. Annan: G. Gilchrist, 1971.

55.66   ------. Memorials of Caerlaverock Parish. Annan: G. Gilchrist, 1968.

55.67   ------. Memorials of Canonbie Parish. Annan: G. Gilchrist, 1969.

55.68   ------. Memorials of Ewes Parish. Annan: G. Gilchrist, 1968.

55.69   ------. Memorials of Kirkconnell, Parish of Kirkpatrick-Fleming. Annan: G. Gilchrist, 1966.

55.70   ------. Memorials of Kirkmichael Parish. Annan: G. Gilchrist, 1968.

55.71   ------. Memorials of Kirkpatrick-Juxta Parish. Annan: G. Gilchrist, 1972.

55.72   ------. Memorials of Langholm Parish. Annan: [. Gilchrist, 1968?].

55.73   ------. Memorials of Lochrutton. Annan: G. Gilchrist, 1974.

55.74   ------. Memorials of Ruthwell Parish. [Annan: G. Gilchrist, 1966].

55.75   ------. Memorials of St. Mungo Parish. [Annan: G. Gilchrist, 1966].

55.76   ------. Memorials of Torthorwald Parish. Annan: G. Gilchrist, 1968.

55.77   ------. Memorials of Trailflatt Parish (Now Included in Tinwald Parish). Annan: G. Gilchrist, 1971.

55.78   Gilchrist, George, R. A. Shannon, and M. Cowan. Memorials in Dornock Churchyard: With Index of Names with Ages and Dates of Death. [Annan?]: G. Gilchrist, [196-].

55.79   Giraldus, Cambrensis. Giraldi Cambrensis opera. Edited by J. S. Brewer. 8 vols. London: Longman, 1861-91. Vol. 7 contains obituary, 12th century, Lincoln cathedral, 153-64.

55.80   Grant, Francis James. Index to the Register of Burials in the Churchyard of Restalrig, 1728-1854. Edinburgh: J. Skinner, 1908. (Publications of the Scottish Record Society, 32)

55.81   Gravestone Inscriptions, County Antrim. Edited by R. S. J. Clarke. 2 vols. Belfast: Ulster Historical Foundation, 1977-81.

55.82   Guild of Corpus Christi, York, England. The Register of the Guild of Corpus Christi in the City of York. . . . Durham: Surtees Society, 1872. (Its Publications, v. 57) Contains obituary of deceased brothers and sisters, 1408-37.

55.83   Gumbley, Walter. Obituary Notices of the English Dominicans from 1555 to 1952. London: Blackfriars Publications, 1955.

55.84   Hall, Joseph. Memorials of Wesleyan Methodist Ministers, or, the Yearly Death Roll, from 1777 to 1840. London: Haughton, 1876.

55.85   Harris, James. Copies of the Epitaphs in Salisbury Cathedral, Cloisters, and Cemetery: Accompanied by Translations, and Notes Historical and Biographical . . . . Salisbury: Browdie and Dowding, 1825.

55.86   Haslewood, Francis. The Monumental Inscriptions, in the Parish of Saint Matthew, Ipswich, Suffolk. [Ipswich: Pawsey and Hayes], 1884.

55.87   ------. The Parish of Benenden, Kent: Its Monuments, Vicars, and Persons of Note. . . . Ipswich: Haslewood, 1889. Includes epitaphs.

55.88   ------. The Parish of Chislet, Kent: Its Monuments, Vicars, and Parish Officers. . . . Ipswich: Haslewood, 1887. Includes epitaphs.

55.89   Havergal, Francis Tebbs. Monumental Inscriptions in the Cathedral Church of Hereford. London: Simpkin, Marshall, 1881.

55.90   Henderson, John Alexander. Aberdeenshire Epitaphs and Inscriptions: With Historical, Biographical, Genealogical, and Antiquarian Notes. Aberdeen: Aberdeen Daily Journal Office, 1907.

55.91   Historical Register: Containing an Impartial Relation of All Transactions, Foreign and Domestick, with a Chronological Diary of All the

Remarkable Occurrences, viz. Births, Marriages, Deaths. . . . 23 vols. London: H. Meere, 1717-39.

55.92 Holt, Alexander. "A Chapter Necrology, Oct. 1670-Feb. 1678. From the Original MS. in the Bodleian Library, Oxford." Miscellanea of the Catholic Record Society 3 (1906): 98-104.

55.93 Holyrood Abbey. Register of Burials in the Chapel Royal or Abbey of Holyroodhouse, 1706-1900. Edinburgh: Lorimer and Gillies, 1900. (Publications of the Scottish Record Society, 25)

55.94 Hope, Sir William Henry St. John. The Obituary Roll of John Islip, Abbot of Westminster, 1500-1532, with Notes on Other English Obituary Rolls Westminster: Nichols, 1906. (Vetusta Monumenta of the Society of Antiquaries of London, v. 7, pt. 4)

55.95 Horringer, England (Parish). Horringer Parish Registers. Baptisms, Marriages, and Burials . . . 1558-1850. Woodbridge: G. Booth, 1900. Includes inscriptions from church and churchyard.

55.96 [Hovenden, Robert]. The Monumental Inscriptions in the Old Churchyard of St. Mary, Newington, Surrey. Part I. London, 1880.

55.97 Hughes Clarke, Arthur William. Monumental Inscriptions in the Church and Churchyard of St. Mary's, Wimbledon. London: Mitchell, Hughes and Clarke, 1934.

55.98 Index Society, London. Index of Obituary Notices . . . 1880-82. 3 vols. London: Index Society, 1882-84. (Publications of the British Record Society. . . . Index Society, v. 9, 12, 14) Microfiche. Cambridge, Mass.: Harvard University Library Microreproduction Service, 1987. Indexes for 1878 and 1879 were issued in the appendixes of the Reports of the 1st-2d annual meetings of the Index Society (Publications 4, 7). Obituaries from English and American periodicals.

55.99 ------. Index of Obituary Notices in the "Times," "Athenaeum Academy," "Builder," etc., from 1878 to 1882. London: Index Society, 1879-1884.

55.100 ------. Index to the Biographical and Obituary Notices in the "Gentleman's Magazine," 1731-1780. London: British Record Society, 1886-91. (Publications of the British Record Society. . . . Index Society, v. 15) AJ242 See no. 55.126

55.101 Index to Births, Marriages and Deaths, 1795-1820. Stafford: Staffordshire Record Society, 1968. Index to births, marriages and deaths that appeared in the Staffordshire Advertiser, 1795-1820.

55.102 Irving, Miles. A List of Inscriptions on Christian Tombs or Monuments in the Punjab, North-West Frontier Province, Kashmir, and Afghanistan; Possessing Historical or Archaeological Interest. 2 vols. Lahore: Printed at the Punjab Government Press, 1910-12. See no. 55.60.

55.103   Jervise, Andrew. Epitaphs and Inscriptions from Burial Grounds and Old Buildings in the North-east of Scotland. . . . 2 vols. Edinburgh: Edmonston and Douglas, 1875-79.

55.104   Kelly's Handbook to the Titled, Landed, and Official Classes, v. 1-101, 1880-1977. London: Kelly Directories, 1880-1977. Annual. AJ235

55.105   Lawrence-Archer, James Henry. Monumental Inscriptions of the British West Indies from the Earliest Date. . . . London: Chatto and Windus, 1875.

55.106   Layer, John. Monumental Inscriptions and Coats of Arms from Cambridgeshire, Chiefly As Recorded by John Layer About 1632 and William Cole Between 1742 and 1782. Edited for a committee of the Cambridge Antiquarian Society by W. M. Palmer. Cambridge: Bowes and Bowes, 1932.

55.107   Le Neve, John. Monumenta Anglicana: Being Inscriptions on the Monuments of Several Eminent Persons Deceased in or since the Year 1600 to the End of the Year 1718. 5 vols. in 4. London: W. Bowyer, 1717-19.

55.108   Le Neve, Peter. "Memoranda on Heraldry (1695-1729)." Topographer and Genealogist 3 (1858): 25. Includes death and funeral notices.

55.109   Light, Alfred W. Bunhill Fields; Written in Honour and to the Memory of the Many Saints of God Whose Bodies Rest in This Old London Cemetery. 2d ed. London: C. J. Farncombe and Sons, 1915. Bunhill Fields was a burying ground for dissenters.

55.110   McCann, Justin, and Hugh Connolly. Memorials of Father Augustine Baker and Other Documents Relating to the English Benedictines. London: Catholic Record Society, 1933. (Its Publications, v. 33)

55.111   M'Dowall, William. Memorials of St. Michael's: The Old Parish Churchyard of Dumfries. Edinburgh: Adam and Charles Black, 1876.

55.112   "Martilogium" (Martyrologium) of the Monastery of Syon, County Middlesex, Together with a Calendar Containing Notes Relating to the Monastery, Lists of Abbesses, Confessors, and Benefactors, an Obituary of Members Down to the Year 1639, After the Removal of the Congregation to Lisbon, etc. British Museum. Additional MS., 22,285.

55.113   *Mawson, Richard. "Obits (1720-29)." Genealogist, n.s. 2 (1885): 143.

55.114   May, Leonard Morgan. Charlton: Near Woolwich, Kent. Full and Complete Copies of All the Inscriptions in the Old Parish Church and Churchyard, Together with Notes on the History of the Manor and of the Families Connected with the Place. London: C. North, 1908.

55.115   Memorials of Castleton Parish. Compiled by George Gilchrist. . . . Annan: G. Gilchrist, 1971.

55.116   Military Obituary, 1853-54. London: Parker, Furnivall, and Parker, 1854. Continued as The Annual Military Obituary for 1855, 1856. London, 1856, 1857. BM

55.117   Mitchell, John Fowler, and Sheila Mitchell. Monumental Inscriptions (pre-1855) in Dunbartonshire. Edinburgh: Scottish Genealogy Society, 1969.

55.118   ------. Monumental Inscriptions (pre-1855) in North Perthshire. [Edinburgh]: Scottish Genealogy Society, 1975.

55.119   ------. Monumental Inscriptions (pre-1855) in Renfrewshire. Edinburgh: Scottish Genealogy Society, 1969.

55.120   ------. Monumental Inscriptions (pre-1855) in West Fife. Edinburgh: Scottish Genealogy Society, 1972.

55.121   ------. Monumental Inscriptions (pre-1855) in West Lothian. Edinburgh: Scottish Genealogy Society, 1969.

55.122   Monumenta Franciscana. . . . 2 vols. London: Longman, 1882. Vol. 2 includes obituary of the Franciscan convent at Aberdeen, 1469-1516.

55.123   Mordaunt, Edward A. B. Index to Obituary and Biographical Notices in "Jackson's Oxford Journal" (Newspaper) 1753-1853. London, 1904. v. 1. 1753-55. No more published.

55.124   Munby, Arthur Joseph. Faithful Servants: Being Epitaphs and Obituaries Recording Their Names and Services. London: Reeves and Turner, 1891. Contains 692 epitaphs, and 111 obituaries of servants who had served all grades of masters, from sovereigns to small tradesmen.

55.125   Musgrave, Sir William. Obituary Prior to 1800 (As Far As Relates to England, Scotland, and Ireland). . . . 1899. Reprint. [West Jordan, Utah: Stemmons Publishing, 1986]. AJ244 Originally published as v. 44 of the Publications of the Harleian Society.

55.126   Nangle, Benjamin Christie. "The Gentleman's Magazine" Biographical and Obituary Notices, 1781-1819: An Index. New York: Garland, 1980. Continues the indexes to biographical and obituary notices by R. H. Farrar and H. B. Wheatley, published by the Index Society of London and the British Record Society in 1886 and 1891, which cover the period 1731-80. AJ243. See no. 55.100

55.127   Obituaries in BCM, 1881-1945. N.p. 1985. This is an index to obituaries in the British Chess Magazine.

55.128   "Obituaries of Relatives of Abbess Newsham of St. Clare's Abbey, Darlington, 1759-1858." Publications of the Catholic Record Society. Miscellanea 6 (1909): 246-54.

55.129 "Obituary Notices of the English Benedictine Nuns of Ghent in Flanders, and at Preston, Lancashire (Now at Oulton, Staffordshire), 1627-1811." Publications of the Catholic Record Society. Miscellanea 11 (1917): 1-92.

55.130 "Obituary of Dom John Huddleston, O.S.B. . . ." Publications of the Catholic Record Society. Miscellanea 1 (1905): 123-32.

55.131 Oxford. University. Queen's College. The Obituary Book of Queen's College, Oxford, an Ancient Sarum Kalendar with the Obits of the Founders and Benefactors of the College. . . . Oxford: Clarendon Press, 1910. (Publications of the Oxford Historical Society, v. 56)

55.132 [Page-Turner, Frederick Augustus]. Genealogia Bedfordiensis; Being a Collection of Evidences Relating Chiefly to the Landed Gentry of Bedfordshire, A. D. 1538-1700. . . . London: Chiswick Press, 1890. Includes monumental inscriptions.

55.133 Paget, Alfred Henry. Epitaphs in the Graveyard and Chapel of the Great Meeting, Leicester. . . . Leicester: Clark and Satchell, 1912.

55.134 Partridge, Charles. Suffolk Churchyard Inscriptions. . . . 3 vols. [Bury St. Edmunds]: Suffolk Institute of Archaeology and Natural History, 1913-23.

55.135 Pettigrew, Thomas Joseph. Chronicles of the Tombs; a Select Collection of Epitaphs, Preceded by an Essay on Epitaphs and Other Monumental Inscriptions. . . . 1857. Reprint. New York: AMS Press, [1968].

55.136 Plarr, Victor Gustave. Plarr's Lives of the Fellows of the Royal College of Surgeons of England. . . . 2 vols. London: Simpkin, Marshall, 1930. EK174   Cites obituaries.

55.137 Ravenshaw, Thomas FitzArthur. Antiente Epitaphes (from A.D. 1250 to A.D. 1800). . . . London: J. Masters, 1878.

55.138 Reeves, John Anthony. An Abstract of Monumental Inscriptions in Salisbury Churches (Mainly up to 1852). Salisbury: Salisbury Museum, 1975.

55.139 Register and Magazine of Biography: A Record of Births, Marriages, Deaths, and Other Genealogical and Personal Occurrences, v. 1-2, Jan.-Dec. 1869. London: Nichols, 1869.

55.140 Rogers, Charles. Monuments and Monumental Inscriptions in Scotland. 2 vols. London: C. Griffin for the Grampian Club, 1871-72.

55.141 Roper, Ida M. The Monumental Effigies of Gloucestershire and Bristol. Gloucester: H. Osborne, 1931.

55.142 Royal Commonwealth Society. Library. Biography Catalogue. . . . London: Royal Commonwealth Society, 1961. AJ240   An index to biographical material, including obituaries held by the Society's library. Includes persons connected with British imperial affairs who were born in or actively connected with countries of the Commonwealth.

55.143   Rushen, Percy Charles. <u>The Churchyard Inscriptions of the City of London</u>. London: Phillimore, 1910.

55.144   Rye, Walter. <u>The Monumental Inscriptions in the Hundred of Tunstead, in the County of Norfolk</u>. Norwich: A. Goose, 1891.

55.145   ------. <u>Some Early English Inscriptions in Norfolk Before 1600, Mostly from (1) Churches, Monuments, Windows, Pulpits, Doors, and Seates; But Also from (2) Houses, Fire-places, etc</u>. London: Jarrolds, n.d.

55.146   <u>Sailor's Home Journal and Chronicle of the Royal Navy and Mercantile Marine</u>, v. 1- ?, 1853-63. BM G. K. S. Hamilton-Edwards, in <u>Tracing Your British Ancestors</u> (1967), states that this title contains many obituary notices of naval officers.

55.147   St. Werburgh's Abbey, Chester, England. <u>Some Obits of Abbots and Founders of St. Werburgh's Abbey, Chester</u>. London, 1912. (Publications of the Record Society for the Publication of Original Documents Relating to Lancashire and Cheshire, v. 64, pt. 2) Extracts from a Bodleian manuscripts written about 1195.

55.148   Sayers, Edward. <u>Transcripts of, and Extracts from, Records of the Past . . . from Inscriptions on Brasses, Tablets, Tombs, Tombstones, and Windows, in the Churches and Church-yards of West Tarring, Broadwater, and Christ Church, Worthing</u>. Worthing: W. J. C. Long, Caxton Printery, 1903.

55.149   <u>Scots Magazine</u>, v. 1-97, Jan. 1739-June 1826. 97 vols. Edinburgh: Sands, Brymer, Murray and Cochran, 1739-1825. G. K. S. Hamilton-Edwards, in <u>Tracing your British Ancestors</u> (1967), indicates this title contains many notices of birth, marriage and deaths. There is a manuscript index to it in the Lyon Office, Edinburgh.

55.150   Scott, Sheila A. <u>Monumental Inscriptions (pre-1855) in Peeblesshire</u>. Edinburgh: Scottish Genealogy Society, [1971].

55.151   Scottish Genealogy Society. <u>Pre-1855 Tombstone Inscriptions in Berwickshire</u>. 2 vols. Edinburgh: Scottish Genealogy Society, 1971.

55.152   Selkirkshire Antiquarian Society. <u>Gravestone Inscriptions Prior to 1855</u>. 2 vols. Selkirk: Selkirkshire Antiquarian Society, [1968]. v. 1. Selkirk, Ashkirk, and Lindean Old Churchyards; v. 2. Galashiels Old Cemetery, Ladhope, and Bevolie cemeteries.

55.153   Shotley, England (Suffolk). Parish. <u>Shotley Parish Registers, 1571 to 1850. With All Tombstone Inscriptions in Church and Churchyard</u>. Bury St. Edmund's: Paul and Mathew, 1911.

55.154   Simpson, Justin. <u>Obituary and Records for the Counties of Lincoln, Rutland and Northampton, from the Commencement of the Present Century to the End of 1859</u>. Stamford: W. R. Newcomb, 1861.

55.155 Simpson, William Sparrow. Documents Illustrating the History of S. Paul's Cathedral. 1880. Reprint. New York: Johnson Reprint Corporation, [1965]. (Publications of the Camden Society, n.s., 26) Contains obits, indulgences, etc., 1140–1712.

55.156 Smith, John. Monumental Inscriptions in St. Cuthbert's Churchyard, Edinburgh (Newer Portion). Edited by Sir James Balfour Paul. Edinburgh: J. Skinner for the Scottish Record Society, 1919. (Its Publications, 51)

------. Monumental Inscriptions in St. Cuthbert's Churchyard, Edinburgh (Older Portion). Edited by Sir James Balfour Paul. Edinburgh: J. Skinner for the Scottish Record Society, 1915. (Its Publications, 47)

55.157 Smith, Richard. Obituary of Richard Smyth, Secondary of the Poultry Compter, London: Being a Catalogue of All Such Persons As He Knew in Their Life, Extending from A.D. 1627 to A.D. 1674. Edited by Sir Henry Ellis. [London]: Camden Society, 1849. (Its Publications, v. 44) The records here are for persons residing in London, and were printed from a transcript of the Sloane manuscript in the British Museum, no. 886.

55.158 Snow, Terence Benedict. Obit Book of the English Benedictines from 1600 to 1912, Being the Necrology of the English Congregation of the Order of St. Benedict from 1600 to 1883. 1913. Reprint. Farnborough: Gregg International, 1970. This is a revision, enlargement and continuation, by H. N. Birt, of T. B. Snow's Necrology of the English Congregation of the Order of St. Benedict from 1600 to 1883.

55.159 Suffling, Ernest R. Epitaphia: A Collection of 1300 British Epitaphs, Grave and Gay, Historical and Curious, Annotated with Biographical Notes, Anecdotes, etc. London: L. Upcott Gill, 1909.

55.160 Surtees, Herbert Conyers, and James Wall. Memorial Inscriptions in Durham Cathedral. Cambridge, [Eng.]: Cambridge University Press, 1932.

55.161 Theatre World Annual (London): A Pictorial Review of West End Productions with a Record of Plays and Players, no. 1–16, 1949/50–1964/65. London: Rockliff, 1950–65. Annual. Ceased publication. BG54

55.162 Wainwright, Thomas. "Index to the Names of Persons Found in the Monumental Inscriptions in Devonshire Churches, Copied in the Years 1769–93." Report and Transactions of the Devonshire Association for the Advancement of Science, Literature, and Art 36 (1904): 522–41.

55.163 Ward, Wilfrid. "Death Bills; the Equivalent 300 Years Ago of the Modern Obituary; Illustrated by Death Bills of Benedictine Nuns of the English Convent at Ghent, Now at Oulton Abbey, Near Stone, Staffordshire." Nineteenth Century and After 78 (Dec. 1915): 1430–48.

55.164 Wells Cathedral. Dean Cosyn and Wells Cathedral Miscellanea by Dom Aelred Watkin. London: Butler and Tanner, 1941. (Publications of the

Somerset Record Society, v. 56) Contains a fragment of a Wells obit-book. Dean William Cosyn died in 1525.

55.165 Wesley Historical Society. An Index to the Memoirs, Obituary Notices, and Recent Deaths, Together with the References to the Local Histories of Methodism, As Contained in the "Armenian Magazine," 1778-1797; the "Methodist Magazine," 1798-1821; and the "Wesleyan Methodist Magazine," 1822-1839. Burnley: Wesley Historical Society, 1909-10. (Issued with its Proceedings, v. 7)

55.166 Who's Who: An Annual Biographical Dictionary, with Which Is Incorporated "Men and Women of the Time," v. 1-, 1849-. London: A. and C. Black, 1849-. Annual. AJ236

55.167 Wilson, James. The Monumental Inscriptions of the Parish Church and Churchyard, and Congregational Burial Ground, Wigton, Cumberland. Wigton, Cumberland: T. McMechan, 1892.

55.168 Wright, Philip. Monumental Inscriptions of Jamaica. London: Society of Genealogists, 1966.

55.169 Writings on British History, 1901-1933. 5 vols. London: Jonathan Cape, 1968-70. DC246-DC247. Obituaries are cited in vol. 1, pp. 161-87.

------. 1934-, v. 1-. London: Jonathan Cape, 1937-. Annual (irregular).

56.1   Abbaye de Sixt. <u>L'Obituaire de l'Abbaye de Sixt</u>. Annecy: Imprimerie commerciale, 1913.

56.2   Académie des inscriptions et belles-lettres, Paris. <u>Recueil des historiens de la France. Obituaires</u>. 7 vols. Paris: Impr. Nationale, 1902-80. v. 1-4. Obituaires de la province de Sens; v. 5-6. Obituaires de la province de Lyon; v. 7. Répertoire des documents nécrologiques francais.

56.3   <u>Almanach Hachette; petite encyclopédie populaire</u>. . . . 1894-1972. Paris: Hachette, 1894-1972. Annual.

56.4   Apt, France. St. Anne (Church). <u>Obituaire de l'église cathédrale d'Apt</u>. Publié par Fernand Sauve. Monaco: Impr. de Monaco, 1926. (Collection de textes pour servir à l'histoire de Provence, no. 5.)

56.5   Berger, Roger. <u>Le nécrologe de la Confrerie des jongleurs et des bourgeois d'Arras, 1194-1361</u>. 2 vols. Arras, 1963-70. (Commission départementale des monuments historiques du Pas-de-Calais. Mémoires, t. 11, 2, t. 13,2)

56.6   Beuchot, A. J. Q. <u>Nouveau nécrologe français: ou, Liste alphabétique des auteurs nés en France, ou qui ont écrit en francais, morte depuis le premier janvier 1800</u>. Paris: Chez Guitel, 1812.

56.7   <u>Bibliographie annuelle de l'histoire de France du cinquième siècle à 1939</u>, année 1955-. Paris: Centre National de la Recherche Scientifique, 1956-. Annual. DC155

56.8   Bonshommes de Craon (Grandmontensian priory). <u>Cartulaire et obituaire du prieuré des Bonshommes de Craon</u>. Laval: A. Goupil, 1905-6.

56.9   Chevalier, Cyr Ulysse Joseph. <u>Nécrologe et cartulaire des Dominicains de Grenoble</u>. . . . Romans: Impr. de H. Rosier, 1870. (Documents historiques inédits sur le Dauphine, pt. 5.)

56.10   Delisle, Léopold Victor. <u>Rouleaux des morts du IXe au XVe siècle</u>. Recueillis et publiés pour la Societe de l'histoire de France. . . Paris: J. Renouard, 1866. (Its Publications, 135.)

56.11   Devaux, Jean. <u>Index funereus chirurgorum Parisiensium</u>. . . . Trivoltii et Paris: Stephanum Ganeau, 1714.

56.12   Franciscans. Angers. <u>L'obituaire et le nécrologe des cordeliers d'Angers, 1216-1790</u>. Angers: Germain et G. Grassin, 1902.

56.13   Gazette de France. <u>Table ou abrégé des cent trente-cinq volumes de la "Gazette de France," depuis son commencement en 1631 jusquà la fin de l'année 1765</u>. 3 vols. in 1. Paris: Impr. de la Gazette de France, 1766-67.

56.14   Hunt, Noreen. <u>Cluniac Monasticism in the Central Middle Ages</u>. [London]: Macmillan, [1971]. Includes a Cluniac necrology from the time of Abbot Hugh, by J. Wollasch.

56.15   Kunstler, Charles. <u>Discours . . . Institut de France, Académie des beaux-arts, seance publique annuelle du 11 décembre 1974</u>. Paris: Institut de France, 1974.

56.16   LeMans. Saint-Julien (Cathedral). <u>Nécrologe-obituaire de la cathédrale du Mans</u>. . . . Au Mans: la Société, 1906. (Archives historiques du Maine, 7.)

56.17   Le Monde, Paris. <u>Index Analytique</u>, 1965-. Paris: Le Monde, 1967-. Annual. Retrospective indexing, 1944/45-, in progress.   AF88-AF89

56.18   Lyons. Saint-Jean-Baptiste (Cathedral). <u>Obituarium Lugdunensis ecclesiae. Nécrologe des personnages illustres et des bienfaiteurs de l'Église métropolitaine de Lyon du IXe au XVe siecle</u>. . . . Lyon: N. Scheuring, 1867.

56.19   Molinier, Auguste Emile Louis Marie. <u>Les obituaires français au moyen âge</u>. Paris: Impr. Nationale, 1890.

56.20   <u>Nécrologe des hommes célèbres de France, par une société de gens de lettres</u>. 17 vols. Paris: Impr. de Moreau, 1767-82.

56.21   <u>Obituaire de l'Abbaye de Beaupré, ordre de Cîteaux, diocèse de Toul</u>. Publié par l'abbe Jacques Choux. Nancy: Société d'archéologie lorraine, 1968. (Recueil de documents sur l'histoire de Lorraine, no. 25.)

56.22   <u>Obituaire israélite: le Mamorbuch de Metz, vers 1575-1724 traduit de l'hébreu, avec une introduction et des notes par Simon Schwarzfuchs</u>. Metz: [Société d'histoire et d'archéologie de la Lorraine], 1971.

56.23   Paris. Université. Institut francais de presse. Section d'histoire. <u>Tables du journal "Le temps"</u>, v. 1-, 1966-. In progress. Contents: v. 1. 1861-65; v. 2. 1866-70; v. 3. 1871-75; v. 4. 1876-80; v. 5. 1881-85; v. 6. 1886-88; v. 7. 1889-91; v. 8. 1892-94; v. 9. 1895-97; v. 10. 1898-1900.   AF90

56.23a   Parisse, Michel. <u>Le necrologe de Gorze; contribution a l'histoire monastique</u>. Nancy: Universite de Nancy II, 1971. (Annales de l'Est. Memoire, no. 40)

56.24   Port-Royal des Champs (Abbey of Cistercian nuns). <u>Nécrologe de l'abbaie de Nôtre-Dame de Port-Roial des Champs, Ordre de Cîteaux, Institut du saint sacrement</u>. . . . Amsterdam: Chez N. Potgieter, 1723.

56.25   Poulet, Robert. <u>Billets de sortie</u>. Paris: Nouvelles Éditions Latines, 1975. A collection of 76 literary obituaries published in the Belgian satirical journal <u>Pan</u>. Most of the obituaries are for French writers and critics.

56.26   Prémontré, France. Abbaye. <u>L'obituaire de l'abbaye de Prémontré (XIIe S - ms. 9 de Soissons)</u>. Louvaine: P. Smeesters, 1913.

------. 2me partie. Tongerloo: Impr. de l'abbaye, 1925.

56.27   Raunié, Émile. <u>Épitaphier du vieux Paris: recueil général des inscriptions</u> <u>funéraires des églises, couvents, collèges, hospices, cimetières et charniers,</u> <u>depuis le moyen âge jusquà la fin du XVIIIe siecle</u>. 5 vols. Paris: Impr. nationale, 1890-.

56.28   Ritz, Louis. <u>Le nécrologe de l'Abbaye de Talloires</u>. Chambéry: Impr. Générale savoisienne, 1913. (Extrait des Mèmoires de l'Académie de Savoye. Documents, vol. 8.)

56.29   Rouen. Nôtre-Dame (Cathedral). <u>Obituaire de l'église cathédrale de Rouen</u> <u>pour l'année capitulaire 1791</u>. Rouen: Impr. L. Gy, 1908. (Société rouennaise de bibliophiles. Publications, 63.)

56.30   <u>Rouleau mortuaire du b. Vital, abbé de Savigni, contenant 207 titres écrits en</u> <u>1122-1123</u>. . . . Paris: H. Champion, 1909.

56.31   Saint-Nicolas de Beauvais, France (Church). <u>Obituaires des églises</u> <u>Saint-Nicolas et Saint-Michel de Beauvais</u>. Paris: E. Champion, 1923. (Société académique d'archéologie, sciences et arts du département de l'Oise, Beauvais. Documents, v. 8.)

56.32   Solignac, France. Benedictine abbey. <u>Le rouleau des morts de l'abbaye de</u> <u>Solignac</u>. Limoges: Impr. Chapoulard frères, 1879.

56.33   Vanel, Jean Baptiste. <u>Les Bénédictins de Saint-Maur à Saint Germain-</u> <u>des-Prés, 1630-1792. Nécrologe des religieux de la Congrégation de</u> <u>Saint-Maur</u>. . . . Paris: H. Champion, 1896.

56.34   <u>Who's Who in France: dictionnaire biographique</u>, Ed. 1-, 1953/54-. Paris: Lafitte, 1953-. Biennial. AJ201

57. GERMANY

57.1   Arens, Fritz Viktor. <u>Die Inschriften der Stadt Mainz von früh-christlicher</u>
        <u>Zeit bis 1650</u>. Stuttgart: A. Druckenmüller, 1958.

57.2   ------. <u>Die Inschriften der Stadt Wimpfen am Neckar</u>. Stuttgart: A.
        Druckenmüller, 1958.

57.3   Augsburg. Zu den Barfüssern (Franciscan Monastery) Kirche. <u>Das</u>
        <u>Necrologium des Ordens der Mindern Brüder zu den Barfüssern in</u>
        <u>Augsburg 1270-1500</u>. Munich, 1955.

57.4   Benedictines. Bayerische Kongregation. <u>Necrologium Congregationis</u>
        <u>Benedictinae Bavaricae, 1836-1950</u>. Munich: F. S. Seitz, 1951.

57.5   <u>Bibliographie der deutschen Zeitschriftenliteratur, mit Einschluss von</u>
        <u>Sammelwerken</u>, v. 1-128, 1896-1964. Osnabrück: Felix Dietrich,
        1897-1964. Semiannual. (Internationale Bibliographie der
        Zeitschriftenliteratur, Abt. A.)   AE278

57.6   <u>Biographisches Jahrbuch und deutscher Nekrolog</u>, v. 1-18, 1896-1913. Berlin:
        G. Reimer, 1897-1917.   Annual.   AJ203

57.7   Colmar. Unterlinden (Convent of Dominican nuns). <u>L'Obituaire des</u>
        <u>dominicaines d'Unterlinden: édition critique du manuscrit 576 de la</u>
        <u>Bibliothèque de la ville de Colmar</u>. Compiled by Charles Wittmer.
        Strasbourg: P. H. Heitz, 1946.

57.8   <u>Deutsche Abschiede</u>. Edited by Gerhard Hay. Munich: Winkler, 1984.

57.9   <u>Deutsches biographisches Jahrbuch</u>. . . . v. 1-5, 10-11, 1914-23, 1928-29.
        Berlin: Deutsche Verlagsanstalt, 1925-32.   AJ204

57.10   Duckesz, Eduard. <u>Hakhme, AHW</u>. . . . Hamburg: A. Goldschmidt, 1908.

57.11   Floss, Heinrich Joseph. <u>Das Kloster Rolandswerth bei Bonn</u>. Cologne: J. M.
        Haberle, 1868.

57.12   Heinlein, Heinrich. <u>Der Friedhof zu Leipzig in seiner jetzigen Gestalt; oder</u>
        <u>Vollständige Sammlung aller Inschriften auf den ältesten und neuesten</u>
        <u>Denkmälern daselbst</u>. Leipzig, 1844.

57.13   <u>Jahresberichte für deutsche Geschichte</u>, v. 1-15/16, 1925-39/40. Leipzig:
        Koehler, 1927-42. Annual. DC183a

        ------. n.s. v. 1-, 1949-. Berlin: Akademie-Verlag, 1952-. v. 1-2,
        Annual; v. 3-, Beinnial.

57.14   Kürschners deutscher Literatur-Kalender. <u>Nekrolog zu Kürschners</u>
        <u>Literatur-Kalender, 1901-1935</u>. Berlin: de Gruyter, 1936. BD854

        ------. <u>Nekrolog 1936-1970</u>. Berlin: de Gruyter, 1973. For the years after
        1970, use the annual volumes.

57. GERMANY

57.15 <u>Kürschners deutscher Musiker-Kalender, 1954</u>. 2d ed. Berlin: de Gruyter, 1954. BH206. In the appendix there is a list of 1,500 musicians who had died since the first edition.

57.16 Kutzbach, Karl August. <u>Autorenlexikon der Gegenwart</u>. Bonn: Bouvier, 1950. BD855

57.17 Monumenta Germaniae historica. <u>Necrologia Germaniae</u>. 5 vols. Berlin: Weidmann, 1886-1920.

57.18 <u>Nekrolog der Teutschen für das neunzehnte Jahrhundert</u>. Edited by Friedrich Schlichtegroll. 5 vols. Gotha: J. Perthes, 1802-6.

57.19 Neumullers-Klauser, Renate. <u>Die Inschriften der Stadt und des Landkreises Heidelberg</u>. Stuttgart: A. Druckenmüller, 1970.

57.20 Pudor, Fritz. <u>Lebensbilder aus dem rheinisch-westfälischen Industriegebiet, Jahrgang 1960-1961. Neue Folge der Nekrologe aus dem Rheinisch-Westfälischen Industriegebiet</u>. Cologne: Westdeutscher Verlag, 1966.

------. <u>Nekrologe aus dem rheinisch-westfalischen Industriegebiet, Jahrgang 1939-1951</u>. Düsseldorf: A. Bagel, 1955.

57.21 Rath, Josef Theodor. <u>Mortuarium der deutschen Provinz der Kongregation vom Heiligen Geist, 1857-1975</u>. Knechtsteden: Missionsverlag, 1976.

57.22 Roth, Fritz. <u>Restlose Auswertungen von Leichenpredigten und Personalschriften für genealogische Zwecke</u>. 6 vols. Boppard, Rhine: Selbstverlag, 1959-67.

57.23 Stemplinger, Eduard. <u>Nachrufe für die 1915-1919 dahingegangen lieben Mitglieder des Bayer. Gymnasiallehrervereins</u>. Munich: F. P. Datterer, 1920.

57.24 Stepner, Salomon. <u>Inscriptiones Lipsienses: Locorum Publicorum, academicorum, pariter ac senatoriorum, memorabiles</u>. Leipzig: Elias Fiebig, Druckts Christoph Uhmann, 1675.

57.25 Struck, Wolf Heino. <u>Das Nekrologium II des St. Lubentius-Stiftes zu Dietkirchen a. d. Lahn</u>. Mainz: Selbstverlag der Gesellschaft fur Mittelrheinische Kirchengeschichte, 1969. (Quellen und Abhandlungen zur mittelrheinischen Kirchengeschichte, v. 11.)

57.26 Wattenbach, Wilhelm. <u>Deutschlands Geschichtsquellen im Mittelalter bis zur Mitte des dreizehnten Jahrhunderts</u>. 6th rev. ed. 2 vols. 1893-94. Reprint. Darmstadt: Wissenschaftliche Buchgesellschaft, 1976. DC189. On pages 437-460 there is a bibliography of necrologies for the Middle Ages.

57.27 <u>Wer ist wer? Das deutsche who's who</u>, v. 1-, 1905-. Berlin: Arani, 1905-. AJ211

57.28   Wulf-Mathies, Monika. Typologische Untersuchungen zum deutschen Gelehrten-Nekrolog des 19. und 20. Jahrhunderts dargestellt am Beispiel des Historiker-Nachrufs. Hamburg, 1969. Dissertation--Hamburg.

57.29   Zahn, Peter. Die Inschriften der Friedhöfe St. Johannis, St. Rochus und Wohrd zu Nürnberg. Munich: A. Druckenmüller, 1972.

57.30   Zeitungs-Index, v. 1-, no. 1-, Jan./Mar. 1974-. Munich: Verlag Dokumentation, 1974-. Quarterly. AF92

58. OTHER FOREIGN COUNTRIES

58.1 Abdul Majid. Vaffiyat-i Majidi: ya Nasri marsiye, murattib 'Abdulqavi Dariyabadi. Lakhnau: 'Abdulmajid Dariyabadi Akadmi: milne ka patah, Sidq'i Jadid Buk Ejansi, 1978.

58.2 Académie royale des sciences, des lettres et des beaux-arts de Belgique, Brussels. Annuaire (Indexes). Tables des notices biographiques publiées dans l'Annuaire (1835-1914). Brussels: Hayez, 1919.   AJ125

------. Commission royale d'histoire. Inventaire des obituaires belges (collégiales et maisons religieuses). Brussels: Kiessling, P. Imbreghts, 1899.

58.3 Admont, Austria (Benedictine Abbey). Admonter Totenroteln (1442-1496) von Fritz Bünger. Münster in Westf.: Aschendorff, 1935.

58.4 Argus, Melbourne. Index to the "Argus," 1846-1854. Melbourne: Library Council of Victoria, 1976.

58.5 Arkhivnyi zbirnyk v svitlu pam'iat' D-ra IUriia Lypy, 1900-1944: v 40-littia ioho herois'koi smerty. Chicago: Ukrainian Archives of the Ukrainian Medical Association of North America, 1984.

58.6 Aydarus, Abd al-Qadir ibn Shaykh. Tarikh al-nur al-safir An akhbar al-qarn al-Ashir. [Egypt, 198-].

58.7 Bibliographie der Schweizergeschichte, 1913-83. Zurich: Leemann, 1914-83. Annual. Ceased. AJ373

58.8 Bloch, Isaac. Inscriptions tumulaires des anciens cimetières israélites d'Alger: recueillies, traduites, commentées et accompagnées de notices biographiques. Paris: A. Durlacher, 1888.

58.9 Blunt, Edward Arthur Henry. List of Inscriptions on Christian Tombs and Tablets of Historical Interest in the United Provinces of Agra and Oudh. Allahabad: Government Press, United Provinces, 1911.

58.10 Borja Pavón, Francisco de. Necrologías de varios contemporáneos distinguidos, especialmente Cordobeses. . . . Cordoba: Est. tip. de La Union, 1892.

58.11 Brandstetter, Josef Leopold. Repertorium über die in Zeit- und Sammelschriften der Jahre 1812-1890, 1891-1900, enthaltenen Aufsätze und Mitteilungen schweizergeschichtlichen Inhaltes. 2 vols. Basel: A. Geering, 1892-1906. AJ374

58.12 British Museum. Egerton MS. 3059. Obit-book of the Collegiate Church of Augustinian Canons of St. Germain at Mons, in Belgium.

58.13 Bykov, P. V. Pavel Antipovich Potiekhin: pamiati byvshago predsiedatelia Gorodskoi komissii po narodnomu obrazovaniiu v Petrogradie 10 ianvaria 1916 goda. Saint Petersburg: [Gorodskaia tip.], 1916.

58.14 <u>Canadian Annual Review of Politics and Public Affairs</u>, v. 1-, 1960-. Toronto: University of Toronto Press, 1961-. Annual. CG165

58.15 <u>Canadian Medical Directory</u>, 1955-. Toronto: Seccombe House, 1954-. Annual. EK144

58.16 <u>Canadian News Facts</u>, v. 1, no. 1-, Jan. 16, 1967-. Toronto: Marpep, 1967-. Biweekly with monthly indexes cumulating quarterly and annually. DB206

58.17 <u>Canadian Periodical Index</u>, 1928-47. Toronto: Public Libraries Branch, Ontario Department of Education, 1928-47. Continued by <u>Canadian Index to Periodicals and Documentary Films: An Author and Subject Index</u>, Jan. 1948-Dec. 1959, with annual volumes 1960-63 (v. 13-16); title changed with v. 17 to <u>Canadian Periodical Index. Index de périodiques canadiens</u>, v. 17-. Ottawa: Canadian Library Association, 1964-. Monthly with annual cumulations. AE269-AE271

58.18 Capuchins. Provincia di Bologna. <u>Necrologium fratrum minorum Capuccinorum provinciae Bononiensis nec non illorum qui in eadem supremum diem obierunt a P. Augustino a Fusiniano anno 1786 inscriptum et a P. Humile a Camugnano recognitum</u>. Bologna: Typ. S. Joseph, 1949.

58.19 Carnochan, Janet. <u>Inscriptions and Graves in the Niagara Peninsula</u>. Niagara-on-the-Lake: Niagara Advance Print, [1928?].

58.20 <u>Cemetery Inscriptions for Lunenburg and Queens Counties</u>. [Bridgewater, N.S.]: South Shore Genealogical Society, 1981.

58.21 Champion, Benjamin William. <u>Family Entries, Births, Deaths, Marriages, with Some Personalities, Institutions and Oddments in the Hunter Valley District, 1843-1884: Register</u>. 6 vols. [Newcastle, N.S.W.]: B. W. Champion, 1973.

------. <u>1884-1890: Register 2</u>. 6 vols. [Newcastle, N.S.W.]: B. W. Champion, 1974.

58.22 Cipriano da Serracapriola. <u>Necrologia dei Frati minori cappuccini della provincia religiosa di Foggia 1530-1968</u>. Foggia: Curia provinciale dei Cappuccini, 1969.

58.23 Contarini, Giovanni Battista. <u>Menzioni onorifiche de'defunti scritte nel nostro secolo; ossia, Raccolta cronologica, alfabetica di necrologie, biografie, prose e poesie che furono pubblicate e che si pubblicheranno in memoria dei defunti del presente secolo XIX, di quelli che sono veneti, a noi noti</u>. Venice: Tip. all'Ancora, 1845.

------. <u>Menzioni onorifiche de'defunti scritte nel nostro secolo; ossia, Raccolta cronologica, alfabetica di lapidi, necrologie, biografie, prose e poesie dei defunti nell'anno 1846-1870</u>. Venice, 1846-70. Continues the previous title which included the years 1801 to 1845.

58. OTHER FOREIGN COUNTRIES

58.24   Crawford Cemetery, Dalhousie Township, Lanark County. . . . Ottawa: Ottawa Branch, Ontario Genealogical Society, 1977.

58.25   Current Digest of the Soviet Press, v. 1-, Feb. 1 1949-. New York: Joint Committee on Slavic Studies, 1949-. Weekly. AF100

58.26   Curtis, R. B., and Coral Lindsay. Elmview Cemetery, Kars, Ontario, North Gower Township. . . . [Ottawa]: Ontario Genealogical Society, 1974.

58.27   Dalkin, Robert Nixon. Colonial Era Cemetery of Norfolk Island. Sydney: Pacific Publications, 1974.

58.28   Derozario, M. The Complete Monumental Register: Containing All the Epitaphs, Inscriptions . . . in the Different Churches and Burial-grounds, in and about Calcutta. . . . Calcutta: P. Ferris, 1815.

58.29   Egidi, Pietro. Necrologi e libri affini della Provincia romana, a cura di Pietro Egidi Rome: Tip. del Senato, 1908-. v. 1. Necrologi della citta di Roma. (Fonti per la storia d'Italia. Antichità, secoli XI-XV, no. 44-)

58.30   Einsiedeln, Switzerland (Benedictine Abbey). Das Totenbuch des Klosters Einsiedeln 861-1973. Einsiedeln: [Kloster, Peter J. Salzgeber], 1973.

58.31   Fordyce, Alexander Dingwall. Gleanings from the Church-yard: A Selection of Old Inscriptions. [N.p. 1880]. Microfiche. Ottawa: Canadian Institute for Historical Microreproductions, 1980. Reproduction of original in the National Library of Canada.

58.32   ------. The Monumental Inscriptions in the Cemetery at Belleside, Fergus (Ontario). Fergus: A. Fordyce, 1883. Microfiche. Ottawa: Canadian Institute for Historical Microreproductions, 1980. Reproduction of original in the Library of the Public Archives of Canada.

58.33   Fraser, Alex W. Williamstown. Belleville, Ont.: Mika Publishing Co., 1976. Includes epitaphs.

58.34   Fraser, Alex W., and Rhoda P. Ross. Gravestones of Prescott County. Lancaster, Ontario: Highland Heritage, 1985. Includes inscriptions from Barb and McLaughlin cemeteries.

58.35   Gandhi, Mohandas Karamchand. Homage to the Departed. Compiled and edited by S. B. Kher. Ahmedabad: Navajivan, 1958. Contains tributes written by Gandhi in addition to tributes written at his death.

58.36   Gendai bukkosha jiten: 1980-1982. Tokyo: Nichigai Asoshietsu, 1983.

58.37   Genève. Saint Pierre (Cathedral). Obituaire de l'Eglise cathédrale de Saint-Pierre de Genève, avec une introduction, des notes et un index par Albert Sarasin. Geneva: J. Jullien, 1882. (Société d'histoire et d'archéologie de Genève. Mémoires et documents, v. 21)

58. OTHER FOREIGN COUNTRIES

58.38   Gianetto, Stella M. <u>Midland's Past Inhabitants: Tombstone Inscriptions of the Cemeteries of Midland, Simcoe County, Ontario</u>. Toronto: Ontario Genealogical Society, 1979.

58.39   Götebergs kungl. vetenskapa- och vitterhetssamhälle. <u>Minnestal hållna i Göteborgs k. vetenskaps- och vitterhets-samhälle å dess högtidsdagar 1893-1899</u>. Göteborg: D. F. Bonniers, 1899.

      ------. 1900-1903. Göteborg: W. Zachrissons, 1903.

      ------. 1909-1918, 1919-1923, 1924-1927. Göteborg: Elanders, 1918, 1927.

58.40   Gordon, Elizabeth M., et al. <u>Munster Union Cemetery</u>. . . . Ottawa: Ottawa Branch, Ontario Genealogical Society, 1977.

58.41   Goulet, J. Napoleon. <u>Nécrologe de St. Anselme, Dorchester, 1830-1976</u>. Montreal: Editions Bergeron, 1978.

58.42   Gravel, Albert. <u>Obituaire du clergé séculier de l'archidiocèse de Sherbrooke, de 1874 à 1968</u>. Sherbrooke, 1969.

58.43   <u>Guide to Indian Periodical Literature</u>, v. 1-, 1964-. Gurgaon: Prabhu Book Service, 1968-. Quarterly. AE283

58.44   Hale, R. Wallace. <u>Northwestern York County Cemeteries</u>. [Woodstock, N.B.: Poverty Press, 1982].

58.45   ------. <u>Southern Carleton County Cemeteries</u>. 4 vols. Woodstock, N.B.: Poverty Press, [1982-83].

58.46   Hanks, Carole. <u>Early Ontario Gravestones</u>. Toronto and New York: McGraw-Hill Ryerson, [1974].

58.47   Hauterive (Cistercian Abbey). <u>Le nécrologe de l'abbaye cistercienne d'Hauterive</u>. Berne, 1957.

58.48   <u>Hij is reeds aan de overzijde: Necrologieen van schrijvers</u>. . . . Amsterdam: Rap, 1986.

58.49   Horno Liria, Luis. <u>Convecinos de ayer</u>. . . . Saragossa, 1978. (Publicación de la Institución Fernando el Catolica, no. 678. Temas Aragoneses, 20)

58.50   Ibn Khallikan. <u>Ibn Khallikan's Biographical Dictionary</u>. Translated from the Arabic by Bn Mac Guckin de Slane. . . . 4 vols. Paris: Printed for the Oriental Translation Fund of Great Britain and Ireland, 1842-71.

58.51   <u>Index India</u>, v. 1, no. 1-, Jan./Mar. 1967-. Jaipur: Rajasthan University Library, 1967-. Quarterly. AE284

58.52   An Index of Marriage and Death Notices from Manitoba Newspapers. Compiled by Kathleen Rooke Stokes, et al. [Winnipeg]: Manitoba Genealogical Society, 1986. For the years 1859-81.

58.53   Index to New Zealand Periodicals, 1940-. Wellington: New Zealand Library Association, 1940-. Annual. AE297

58.54   Index to Obituaries in the "Pacific Islands Monthly," August 1945-December 1979, vols. 16-50. Canberra: Pacific Manuscripts Bureau, Research School of Pacific Studies, Australian National University, 1981.

58.55   Index to South African Periodicals, v. 1-, 1940-. Johannesburg: Public Library, 1941-. Annual. AE306

58.56   Indian News Index: A Quarterly Subject Guide to Selected English Newspapers of India, v. 1-7, 1965-71. Ludhiana: Panjab University Extension Library, 1965-71. AF97

58.57   Jakubíček, Milan. V letech 1963-1967 zemřeli. Brno: Univ. knihovna, rozmn, 1969. (Na pomoc knihovnikum a čtenářum, 41)

         ------. V roce 1969 zemřeli. Brno: Univ. knihovna, rozmn., 1970. (Na pomoc knihovnikum a čtenářum, 25)

58.58   Johnson, Keith A., and Malcolm R. Sainty. Sydney Burial Ground: Elizabeth and Devonshire Streets, the Sandhills (Monuments Relocated at Bunnerong). Sydney: Genealogical Publications of Australia, 1973.

58.59   Kennedy, James Y., and Rita Aubrey. The Merivale Cemeteries. Ottawa: Ottawa Branch, Ontario Genealogical Society, 1981.

58.60   Koronowo, Poland (Cistercian Abbey). Liber mortuorum Monasterii Coronoviensis o. Cist. Wydal ks. Alfons Mankowski. Torun, 1931. (Towarzystwo naukowe w Toruniu. Fontes, v. 25)

58.61   Le Blanc, Genevieve. Obituaire; Lac-aux-Chicots, Saints-Thecle, 1870 a 1975. Montreal: Editions du Bien Public, 1975.

58.62   Lewis, John Penry. List of Inscriptions on Tombstones and Monuments in Ceylon, of Historical or Local Interest, with an Obituary of Persons Uncommemorated. Colombo: H. C. Cottle, 1913.

58.63   Lund. Diocese. Libri memoriales Capituli Lundensis. Lunde domkapitels gaveboger ("Libri datici Lundenses") paa ny udg. ved C. Weeke af Selskabet for udgivelse af kilder til dansk historie. 1884-89. Reprint. Copenhagen: Selskabet for Udgivelse af Kilder til Dansk Historie, 1973.

         ------. Kapitel. Necrologium Lundense; codex mediaevalis VI[tus] Bibliothecae Universitatis Lundensis. Copenhagen: E. Munksgaard, 1960. (Corpus codicum Danicorum Medii Aevi, v. 1). Facsimile of a manuscript which came into existence about 1123 and received subsequent additions and entries throughout the Middle Ages. The manuscript was first transcribed and edited in 1923 by Lauritz Weibull.

58.64   Lutz, Markus. Nekrolog denkwurdiger Schweizer aus dem achtzehnten Jahrhundert, nach alphabetischer Ordnung bearbeitet für Freunde vaterländischer Kultur und Geschichte. . . . Aarau: H. R. Sauerländer, 1812.

58.65   McKenzie, Donald A. Death Notices from the "Christian Guardian," 1836-1850. Lambertville, N.J.: Hunterdon House, 1982.

------. Death Notices from the "Christian Guardian," 1851-1860. Lambertville, N.J.: Hunterdon House, 1984.

58.66   ------. More Notices from Methodist Papers: 1830-1857. Lambertville, N.J.: Hunterdon House, 1986.

58.67   Margolinsky, Jul. Gravpladserne pa Mosaisk nordre kirkegard i Møllegade 1693-1953. Copenhagen, 1956.

58.68   Meiller, Andreas von. Auszüge aus bisher ungedruckten Necrologien der Benedictiner-Klöster St. Peter in Salzburg und Admont in Steiermark, dann der Propstei St. Andrä an der Traisen in Oesterreich unter der Enns. Vienna: Aus der kaiserlichköniglichen Hof- und Staatsdruckerei, 1858.

58.69   Mengenangkan Zaini: kumpulan tulisan p2 s di media pers Jakarta berhubung dengan meninggalnya pelukis Zaini pada hari Minggu, tanggal 25 September, 1977. [Jakarta]: Sinar Harapan, [1977].

58.70   Meyer, Wilhelm Josef. Zuger Biographien und Nekrologe. Bio-bibliographie bis Ende 1912. Zug: W. Wyss, 1915.

58.71   Moodie, E. Marjorie, and Bruce S. Elliott. The Hazeldean Cemeteries. Ottawa: Ottawa Branch, Ontario Genealogical Society, 1980.

58.72   Moore, Robert M. "Vital Statistics from the Chatham Journal, 1841-1844." Detroit Society for Genealogical Research Magazine 13 (1949): 13-17.

58.73   Mummu Bhai. Jangal udas hai. Lahaur: Gul Rang Pablisharz, 1984.

58.74   Necrologi di soci defunti: nel decennio dicembre 1945-dicembre 1955. Rome: Accademia nazionale dei Lincei, 1956.

58.75   Necrologus virorum ecclesiasticorum utriusque cleri tum saecularis tum regularis qui in missione Batava defuncti sunt ab anno domini 1730 ab annum 1830, toto hoc centum annorum spatio. Addito ad calcem elencho Archipresbyterorum districtus Hollandiae ac Zeelandiae, ab anno domini 1727 ad annum 1831. Batavia: J. W. Van Leeuwen, 1833.

58.76   Neiske, Franz. Das Altere Necrolog des Klosters S. Savino in Piacenza. Munich: W. Fink, 1979.

58.77   New Brunswick Historical Society. <u>Loyalists' Centennial Souvenir</u>. . . . Saint John, N.B.: J. & A. McMillan, 1887. Includes inscriptions from the old burial-ground, Saint John, N.B.

58.78   North Cumberland Historical Society. <u>The Cemeteries of North Cumberland</u>. [Pugwash, Nova Scotia, 1969]. (Its Publication, no. 3.)

58.79   Notre-Dame à Huy (Collegiate Church). <u>L'obituaire de la Collégiale Notre-Dame à Huy, par Christine Renardy et Joseph Deckers</u>. Brussels: Palais des Academies, 1975.

58.80   <u>Obituario calahorrano del siglo XV</u>. . . . Logroño: Instituto de Estudios Riojanos, 1976. (Biblioteca de temas riojanos. Estudios 9).

58.81   Oliveira, Betty Antunes de. <u>North American Immigration to Brazil: Tombstone Records of the "Campo" Cemetery, Santa Barbara, Sao Paulo State, Brazil</u>. Rio de Janeiro: Oliveira, 1978.

58.82   Orlandi, Stefano. <u>Necrologio di S. Maria Novella; testo integrale dall'inizio MCCXXXV al MDIV corredato di note biografiche tratte da documenti coevi con presentazione del P. Innocenzo Taurisano</u>. 2 vols. Florence: L. S. Olschki, 1955.

58.83   <u>Pakistan Press Index: A Monthly Index to Newspapers of Pakistan</u>, v. 1-, Apr. 1966-. Karachi: Documentation and Information Bureau, 1966-. Monthly. AF99

58.84   [No entry].

58.85   Pauw, Napoléon de. <u>Obituarium Sancti Johannis. Nécrologe de l'église St. Jean (St. Bavon) à Gand, du XIIIe au XVIe siecle</u>. Brussels: F. Hayez, 1889. (Académie royale des sciences, des lettres et des beaux-arts de Belgique. Commission royale d'histoire. Publication, v. 13.)

58.86   Pavićević-Slapski, Ljubomir P. Oproštajne besede. Belgrade: Izdanje autora, Zablačka 8, 1968-.

58.87   <u>Pei chuan chi</u>. 60 vols. 1893. Reprint. [Yang-chou shih]: Yang-chou ku chi shu tien, 1984.

58.88   Poledna, Petr. <u>V roce 1978 zemřeli</u>. Brno: Státní vedecka knihovná, 1979.

58.89   Potter, Elizabeth Margaret. <u>Obituaries in "The Star" 1925-1927: A Bibliography</u>. Johannesburg: University of the Witwatersrand, Department of Bibliography, Librarianship and Typography, 1969.

58.90   Reid, William D. <u>Death Notices of Ontario</u>. Lambertville, N.J.: Hunterdon House, 1980.

58.91   <u>Repertorium der verhandelingen en bijdragen betreffende de geschiedenis des vaderlands, in tijdschriften en mengelwerken tot op 1900 verschenen</u>. Leiden: Brill, 1907. DC427

------. v. 2-5. Leiden: Brill, 1913-53. Includes material for 1901-39.

58.92 Repertorium van boeken en tijdschriftartikelen betreffende de geschiedenis van Nederland, v. 1-, 1940-. Leiden: Brill, 1943-. Triennial since 1942. Index, 1940-50. DC428

58.93 Richter, Vilhelm. Dødsfald i Danmark 1761-1890. 2 vols. 1901-7. Reprint. Copenhagen: Dansk historisk handbogsforlag, 1976.

58.94 Ross, Rhoda P., and Alex W. Fraser. Gravestones of Stormont County. Lancaster, Ontario: Highland Heritage and the Glengarry Genealogical Society, 1985. Includes inscriptions from the city of Cornwall: Old St. Columban's Catholic cemetery, 4th Street; St. John's Presbyterian cemetery, Sydney Street; and Maple Grove Anglican cemetery, Vincent Massey Drive.

58.95 Roy, Pierre Georges. Les cimetières de Québec. 1941. Reprint. [Pawtucket, R.I.: Quintin, 1982?].

58.96 St. Pierre, Rosaire. Mariages et nécrologe de Saint-Vallier, 1713 à 1795. Québec: Société de Généalogie de Québec, 1977.

58.97 Sainty, Malcolm R., and Keith A. Johnson. Index to Birth, Marriage, Death and Funeral Notices in the "Sydney Herald." 4 vols. Sydney: M. R. Sainty and K. A. Johnson, 1972. For the years 18 Apr. 1831 through 30 Sept. 1853.

58.98 Schofield, B. "Obit book from the Church of St. Germanus, Mons." British Museum Quarterly 7 (1932-33): 110-11.

58.99 Small, Darell, and Fern Small. The Clarence Cemetery: Ottawa River Front, Part of Lot 13, Township of Clarence, County of Russell, Ontario. . . . [Ottawa]: Ottawa Branch, Ontario Genealogical Society, [1979].

58.100 Small, Fern, and Ken Collins. Horne Cemetery & Point Alexandria United Church Cemetery, Wolfe Island, Ontario. Ottawa Branch, Ontario Genealogical Society, 1975. Includes epitaphs.

58.101 ------. Trinity Church Anglican Cemetery, Concession VI-Lot 3, Wolfe Island, Ontario. . . . Kingston, Ontario: Kingston Branch, Ontario Genealogical Society, 1980.

58.102 Société d'histoire de la Suisse romande. Mélanges. Lausanne: G. Bridel, 1863. (Société d'histoire de la Suisse romande. Mémoires et documents, v. 18). Contains "Nécrologes des églises cathédrales de Lausanne et de Sion et de l'église paroissiale de Granges."

58.103 Sommerfeldt, Wilhelm Preus. Nekrologer i dagsaviser, 1936-1939: Bergens Tidende, Dagsposten, Fredrelandsvennen, Hamar Stiftstidende, Morgenbladet, Stavanger Aftenblad, Tromso Stiftstidende. Oslo: Halvorsens Bokhandel, 1946. (Norsk bibliografisk bibliotek, v. 12.)

58. OTHER FOREIGN COUNTRIES

58.104   Sorgato, Gaetano. <u>Memorie funebri antiche e recenti</u>. 11 vols. Padua: Coi tipi del Seminario, 1856-62.

58.105   Sydney. Public Library of New South Wales. Mitchell Library. <u>Australian Periodical Index</u>, 1944/49-60/63. Sydney, 1950-64. AE262

58.106   Ubieto Arteta, Antonio. <u>Obituario de la catedral de Pamplona</u>. Pamplona: Diputacion foral de Navarra, Institucion "Principe de Viana," 1954.

58.107   Wachstein, Bernhard. <u>Die Grabschriften des alten Judenfriedhofes in Eisenstadt</u>. Vienna: A. Holzhausen, 1922.

58.108   ------. <u>Die Inschriften des alten Judenfriedhofes in Wien</u>. Auftrage der Historischen kommission der Israelitischen kultusgemeinde in Wien. Vienna: W. Braumuller, 1912.

58.109   Waefelghem, Raphael van. <u>Le nécrologe de l'abbaye du Parc</u>. Brussels: Misch et Thron, 1908.

58.110   Weber, Eldon D. <u>Monumental Transcriptions</u>. Toronto: Ontario Genealogical Society, 1977. Includes records of 60 burial grounds in Central North Simcoe county.

58.111   Wiesener, Anthon Mohr. <u>Dødsfald i Bergen 1765-1850</u>. [Bergen]: J. D. Beyer Boktr., 1925.

58.112   Wolff, Egon. <u>Sepulturas de israelitas, S. Francisco Xavier, Rio de Janeiro</u>. Sao Paulo: Universidade de São Paulo, Faculdade de Filosofia, Letras e Ciencias Humanas, Centro de Estudos Judaicos, 1976.

58.113   ------. <u>Sepulturas de israelitas-II: Uma Pesquisa em mais de trinta cemiterios nao israelitas</u>. Rio de Janeiro: Cemitério Comunal Israelita, 1983.

58.114   ------. <u>Sepulturas de israelitas-III: as Mishpakhot de Belém</u>. Rio de Janeiro, 1987.

58.115   Woodhouse, Anthony John. <u>Obituaries in "The Star" 1902-1903: A Bibliography</u>. Johannesburg: University of the Witwatersrand, Department of Bibliography, Librarianship and Typography, 1969.

58.116   Zawadzky, Alfonso. <u>Necrologio de San Francisco de Cali</u>. Cali: Talleres graficos Palazquez, 1933.

NOTES

1. National Union Catalog, Pre-956 Imprints: A Cumulative Author List Representing Library of Congress Printed Cards and Titles Reported by Other American Libraries. 685 vols. London: Mansell, 1968-80. AA125

   ------. 1956 through 1967, 1968-1972, 1973-1977, 1978-. 1970-. Publisher varies.

2. Union List of Serials in Libraries of the United States and Canada. 3d ed. 5 vols. N.Y.: Wilson, 1965. AE182

3. New Serial Titles: A Union List of Serials Commencing Publication After Dec. 31, 1949, 1950-70 Cumulative. 4 vols. N.Y.: Bowker, 1973. There are cumulations for 1971-75 in 2 vols.; 1976-80 in 2 vols; 1981-85 in 6 vols; 1986-87 in 4 vols. AE183

4. OCLC Data Base. Online Computer Library Center, Columbus, Ohio. An online file of more than 15 million records of books and other library material. Terminals are available in many libraries for locating books and serials in the United States.

5. Hoornstra, Jean, and Trudy Heath. American Periodicals: 1741-1900: An Index to the Microfilm Collections; American Periodicals, 18th Century; American Periodicals, 1800-1850; American Periodicals 1850-1900, Civil War and Reconstruction. Ann Arbor, Mich.: University Microfilms International, 1979. AE26

6. Library of Congress Catalog. Books: Subjects. A Cumulative List of Works Represented by Library of Congress Printed Cards, 1950-54. 20 vols. Ann Arbor, Mich.: J. W. Edwards, 1955. There are cumulations for 1955-59 in 22 vols.; 1960-64 in 25 vols.; 1965-69 in 42 vols.; 1970-74 in 100 vols. AA130 Title changed to U.S. Library of Congress. Subject Catalog, 1975-82. AA131

7. Milner, Anita Cheek. Newspaper Indexes: A Location and Subject Guide for Researchers. 3 vols. Metuchen, N.J.: Scarecrow Press, 1977-82. AF84

8. U.S. Library of Congress. Catalog Publication Division. Newspapers in Microform: United States 1948-83. 2 vols. Wash.: Library of Congress, 1984. AF26

9. Guide to Reference Books. Edited by Eugene P. Sheehy. 10th ed. Chicago: American Library Association, 1986.

10. USIGS. Bibliographic information for items so designated was taken from the microfilm of the card catalog of the library of the Genealogical Society of the Church of Jesus Christ of Latter-Day Saints in Salt Lake City, Utah. The library will lend the item if it is available in microform through its branch libraries.

APPENDIX

OBITUARY CARD FILES

ALABAMA

Alabama Department of Archives and History Library
624 Washington Avenue
Montgomery, Ala. 36130
Card file consists of 136 drawers of obituaries clipped from Alabama newspapers from the 1950s through 1979.

Birmingham Public Library
Tutwiler Collection of Southern History and Literature
2020 Park Place
Birmingham, Ala. 35203
Since 1978, a file of obituaries has been maintained, from the Birmingham News and the Birmingham Post Herald.

COLORADO

Colorado Historical Society Library
1300 Broadway
Denver, Colo. 80203
Files of births, marriages and death notices from newspapers from the 1860s to the 1940s.

Denver Public Library
Genealogy Division
1357 Broadway
Denver, Colo. 80203
Maintains an obituary file which indexes obituaries appearing in the Denver Post and the Rocky Mountain News from 1940 to date. (see 8.1)

CONNECTICUT

Hartford Public Library
500 Main Street
Hartford, Conn. 06103
Since 1945, has been indexing obituaries of prominent Hartford citizens from the Hartford Times.

DELAWARE

Historical Society of Delaware
505 Market Street Mall
Wilmington, Del. 19801
Maintains a surname file that includes obituaries indexed from newspapers.

HAWAII

Hawaii State Archives
Honolulu, Hawaii 96813
Card index to obituaries appearing in Honolulu newspapers from 1844 to 1950. It is not a complete index to all deaths for this period which appeared in newspapers.

APPENDIX: OBITUARY CARD FILES

INDIANA

Indiana State Library
Indiana Division
140 North Senate Avenue
Indianapolis, Ind. 46204
Maintains a subject/name index to Indianapolis newspapers, from 1898 to date which includes some obituaries of prominent citizens.

South Bend Public Library
122 West Wayne
South Bend, Ind. 46624
Card index to obituaries from the South Bend Tribune 1940 to date, and to obituaries from 1838-68 from South Bend newspapers.

Valparaiso Public Library
103 Jefferson Street
Valparaiso, Ind. 46383
The staff of the Genealogy Department have surname indexed the early papers of Porter County, Indiana, including obituaries. Complete through 1894.

IOWA

State Historical Society of Iowa Library
402 Iowa Avenue
Iowa City, Iowa 52240
Newspaper clippings file which contains many obituaries. These clippings are from newspapers from all parts of Iowa and are especially strong for the period from 1920 to the early 1950s.

LOUISIANA

New Orleans Public Library
219 Loyola Avenue
New Orleans, La. 70140
Card file of approximately 523,000 cards to which are added about 25,000 new cards per year. For the years 1804-11; 1814-15, 1849-72 (German newspapers only); 1860-March 1866; 1876-1972. The indexing is in progress and will eventually cover the entire period from 1804-1972.

MARYLAND

Maryland Historical Society Library
201 West Monument Street
Baltimore, Md. 21201
Card file of obituaries, marriages and biographical items from Maryland newspapers, from late eighteenth century to the present. Approximately 250,000 entries.

APPENDIX: OBITUARY CARD FILES

MAINE

> Maine State Library
> LMA Bldg., State House Station 64
> Augusta, Maine 04333
> Obituaries from the Waterville Sentinel, Kennebec Journal, and Bangor Daily News for 1 Sept. through 31 Dec. 1976. Newsclippings mounted on individual cards and arranged alphabetically by surname of deceased.

MONTANA

> Montana Historical Society Library
> 225 North Roberts St.
> Helena, Mont. 59601
> 15 drawers of obituaries in various Montana newspapers. More complete for the nineteenth century to 1920.

NEW HAMPSHIRE

> New Hampshire Historical Society Library
> 30 Park Street
> Concord, N.H. 03301
> Card file of approximately 30,000 cards which index biographical sketches and obituaries from New Hampshire newspapers for notable New Hampshire citizens.

NEW JERSEY

> Archives and Genealogy
> New Jersey State Library
> P. O. Box 1898
> Trenton, N.J. 08625
> Card files for deaths, 1937-39, 15 drawers. Part of the Historical Records Survey Works Projects Administration. Based on county records, church records, municipal records and newspapers.

NEW YORK

> Queens Borough Public Library
> Long Island Division
> 89-11 Merrick Blvd.
> Jamaica, N.Y. 11432
> Name index (60 drawers) of births, deaths and marriages from Long Island newspapers

OHIO

> Cleveland Public Library
> History, Biography and Travel Dept.
> 325 Superior Avenue
> Cleveland, Ohio 44114
> 800,000 entries to death notices from Cleveland newspapers, 1833 to date.

APPENDIX: OBITUARY CARD FILES

UTAH

Utah State Historical Society Library
300 Rio Grande
Salt Lake City, Utah 84101
Maintains file of obituaries clipped from major Utah newspapers since 1940.

VIRGINIA

Virginia Historical Society Library
P. O. Box 7311
Richmond, Va. 23221
Obituary file of approximately 30,000 cards covering notices to Virginia newspapers prior to 1820.

WISCONSIN

State Historical Society of Wisconsin Library
816 State Street
Madison, Wis. 53706
Index to selected Wisconsin obituaries 1846 to date.

APPENDIX: LIST OF ONLINE DATABASES

Obituaries can be located in the following BRS databases:

Agricola and Backfile (CAIN,CAIB)
Arts and Humanities Search (AHCI)
CAB Abstracts (CABA)
Computer and Mathematics Search (CMCI)
Current Contents Search (CCON)
Legal Resource Index (LAWS)
Magazine Index (MAGS,MSAP)
Mathfile (MATH)
Medical and Psychological Previews (PREV)
MEDLINE and Backfiles (MESH,MS82,MS76,MS71)
National Newspaper Index (NOOZ)
Newsearch (DALY)
Nursing and Allied Health (NAHL)
Psychological Abstracts (PSYC)
Religion Index (RELI)
Social SciSearch (SSCI)
Sociological Abstracts (SOCA)
Sport Database (SFDB)
Trade and Industry (TSAP)
Zoological Record (ZREC)

Many of the above databases, or equivalent databases, are also available through DIALOG Information Retrieval Service.

INDEX

Abbaye de Beaupre, Meurthe-et-Moselle, Fr. 56.21
Abbeville (co.), S.C. 43.4,72,83
Abbeville Banner, Abbeville, S.C. 43.23
Aberdeen Daily World, Aberdeen, Wash. 51.10
Aberdeenshire, Scot. 55.90
Abilene, Tex. 46.117
Absher, Levi, diary 36.2
Accomack (co.), Va. 50.64
Acquackanonk, N.J. 33.22
Actors and actresses 1.9,22,26,43,67,72,75,79,102,120,140,156,160,162,170,175;
    2.26,67-68,90-91,114; 55.161
Acworth, N.H. 32.17,27
Ada, Okla. 39.20
Adair (co.), Ky. 20.26
Adams (co.), Ill. 16.166
Adama (co.), Ohio 38.2,43
Adams (co.), Pa. 41.143
Adams (co.), Wash. 51.21,27
Adams Sentinel, Gettysburg, Pa. 41.28
Addison (co.), Vt. 48.20
Adel, Iowa 18.1
Admont, Aus. 58.3,68
Adrian, Mich. 25.31
Afro-Americans 1.95-96; 2.1,71,87,101,124
Agriculturists 1.39
Akron Beacon Journal, Akron, Ohio 38.4
Alabama 2.34,73,77,83
Alabama Christian Advocate, Birmingham, Ala. 3.2,22
Alaskan, Sitka, Alaska 4.3
Albany, N.Y. 35.102-3
Albion New Era, Albion, Ind. 17.40
Alcorn (co.), Miss. 27.16
Aleppo, Pa. 41.58
Alexandria, Va. 50.86
Alexandria Gazette, Alexandria, Va. 50.75
Alexandria Herald, Alexandria, Va. 50.87,97
Algiers, Alg. 58.8
Allegan (co.), Mich. 25.3,10,63
Allegan County Pioneer Society, Allegan, Mich. 25.3
Allegan Gazette, Allegan, Mich. 25.56
Allegheny (co.), Pa. 41.73,87,137
Allen (co.), Ind. 17.1,44,50,73,90,100-101,114-15,137,156
Allen (co.), Kans. 19.72
Allen (co.), Ky. 20.56,88
Alma, Wis. 53.8
Alta, Calif. 7.1-2
Alta California, San Francisco 7.14-15
Altoona, Kans. 19.9
Altoona, Pa. 41.39,126
Amador (co.), Calif. 7.3
Amarillo, Tex. 46.62
Amenia, N.Y. 9.37

INDEX

Arizona 46.11
Arizona Champion, Flagstaff, Ariz. 5.9
Arizona Daily Star, Tucson, Ariz. 5.1
Arizona Pioneers' Historical Society, Tucson, Ariz. 5.4
Arkansas 2.27,55,103
Arkansas (co.), Ark. 6.9
Arkansas Advocate, Little Rock, Ark. 6.43
Arkansas Gazette, Little Rock, Ark. 6.28,44
Arlington (co.), Va. 50.23
Arminian Magazine, London 55.165
Armstrong (co.), Pa. 41.69
Armstrong (co.), Tex. 46.114
Army 2.119; 55.116
Aroostook (co.), Maine 22.27
Arras, Fr. 56.5
Art critics 1.174
Art historians 1.21,51,56,104,127-29,174
Art teachers, 1.174
Artists 1.21-22,43,51,55,104,121,127-29,174,179; 2.11,123; 56.15; 58.69
Asheville, N.C. 36.70
Ashtabula (co.), Ohio 38.23,69,137
Asotin (co.), Wash. 51.25
Assam, India 55.4
Associate Presbyterian Church 2.50
Assumption (parish), La. 21.39
Astoria Argus, Astoria, Ill. 16.147,150
Astronomers 1.23-24,84,143,153; 55.47
Atchison (co.), Kans. 19.16
Atchison, Mo., 28.4
Atchison County Journal, Rockport, Mo. 28.3
Athenaeum Academy, London 55.99
Athenian, Athens, Ga. 13.97
Athens (co.), Ohio 38.11,104,203
Athens, Ga. 13.16,48,67,97
Athletes 2.90
Atlanta Argus, Atlanta, Ill. 16.144
Auburn, N.Y. 35.14,41
Auburn Gazette, Auburn, N.Y. 35.43
Augauga (co.), Ala. 3.28 (vol. 106)
Auglaize (co.), Ohio 38.117
Augsburg, Ger. 57.3
Augusta (co.), Va. 50.8
Augusta, Ga. 13.33,62,72
Augusta, Maine 22.1,17,24
Augusta Chronicle, Augusta, Ga. 13.97
Augusta Chronicle and Gazette, Augusta, Ga. 13.24
Aurora, N.Y. 35.154
Austerlitz, N.Y. 35.85
Austin, Tex. 46.6,52
Austin City Gazette, Austin, Tex. 46.5
Australia 58.4,21,97,105
Austria 58.3,108

Blackford (co.), Ind. 17.2,7
Blacks see Afro-Americans Bladen (co.), N.C. 36.12
Blaine (co.), Nebr. 30.25
Blaine (co.), Okla. 39.21
Blair (co.), Pa. 41.15-16,39,65,83,103,126,138
Block Island, R.I. 42.10,12
Bloomingburgh, N.Y. 35.13,143
Bloomington, Ill. 16.49,181
Bloomington, Ind. 17.45,99,102
Blount (co.), Tenn. 45.54,70
Bluffdale, Utah 47.2
Blytheville, Ark. 6.56
Boerne region, Tex. 46.56
Boise (co.), Idaho 15.5
Bologna, It. 58.18
Bond (co.), Ill. 16.12,15,127
Bonner (co.), Idaho 15.8
Bonner Springs, Kans. 19.47
Bonneville (co.), Idaho 15.4
Boone (co.), Ill. 16.182
Boone (co.), Mo. 28.47,75,150
Boonville Enquirer, Boonville, Ind. 17.107
Boonville Standard, Boonville, Ind. 17.107
Bosque (co.), Tex. 46.13
Boston, Mass. 2.33,45-46; 24.2,3,11,13-14,17,19-21,24,26,37,53,55,74,76,81,87,91
Boston Advertiser, Boston 2.8; 24.66
Boston Courier, Boston 24.93
Boston Evening Transcript, Boston 24.82
Boston Gazette, Boston 24.71
Boston Journal, Boston 24.93
Boston Post, Boston 24.93
Boston Recorder, Boston 24.54
Boston Recorder and Telegraph, Boston 2.58-59; 24.26,45
Botanists 1.4,25,39,70,101,153
Bourbon (co.), Ky. 20.1,6,109
Bowdoin College, Brunswick, Maine 22.2
Bowen, Nathan, personal record 24.9
Bowens' Virginia Centinel and Gazette, Winchester, Va. 50.62
Bowling Green, Ky. 20.47
Boyle (co.), Ky. 20.39
Bradley (co.), Ark. 6.10
Bradley (co.), Tenn. 45.75
Branch (co.), Mich. 25.11
Brandon Times, Brandon, Wis. 53.27
Braxton (co.), W.Va. 52.30
Brazil 58.81,112-14
Brazoria (co.), Tex. 46.40
Brazos (co.), Tex. 46.98
Breckinridge (co.), Ky. 20.8
Bremen, Maine 22.11
Bremer (co.), Iowa 18.18
Brevard (co.), Fla. 12.12

Brewster, Mass. 24.58
Bridgehampton, N.Y. 35.2
Bridgeport, Conn. 9.21
Bridgeton, Mo. 28.133
Bridgewater, Conn. 9.22
Bridgewater, Mass. 24.52
Bristol, Eng. 55.141
Bristol, Maine 22.11
Broadwater, Eng. 55.148
Brooke (co.), W.Va. 52.19
Brookfield, Conn. 9.40
Brooklyn Daily Union, Brooklyn, N.Y. 35.54
Brooklyn Eagle, Brooklyn, N.Y. 35.7,22,99,112
Brooklyn Eagle and King's County Democrat, Brooklyn, N.Y. 35.53
Broome (co.), N.Y. 35.159
Broome County Courier, Binghamton, N.Y. 35.31
Broome County Republican, Binghamton, N.Y. 35.127
Brown (co.), Ill. 16.168
Brown (co.), Ind. 17.62,134-35
Brown (co.), Kans. 19.18,65,69
Brown (co.), Ohio 38.42,52,185,208
Brown (co.), Tex. 46.118
Browning Leader Record, Browning, Mo. 28.125
Brownville, Nebr. 30.9
Brunswick, Maine 22.2,10,36
Buchanan (co.), Iowa 18.11
Buchanan (co.), Mo. 28.128-29,153,173
Buckhannon, W.Va. 52.10
Buckland, Mass. 24.16
Bucks (co.), Pa. 41.36,100,152
Buffalo (co.), Nebr. 30.2
Buffalo, N.Y. 35.49,95
Buffalo County Journal, Alma, Wis. 53.8
Buffalo Gazette, Buffalo, N.Y. 35.95
Builder, London 55.99
Bullitt (co.), Ky. 20.67
Bulloch (co.), Ga. 13.19
Buncombe (co.), N.C. 36.3,30
Bunhill Fields, London 55.109
Bunker Hill Gazette, Bunker Hill, Ill. 16.117
Bunker Hill Press, Bunker Hill, Ind. 17.118
Burgner, Jacob 38.15
Burke (co.), Ga. 13.38,79
Burlington, Ill. 16.21
Burlington, N.J. 33.10
Burlington Free Press, Burlington, Vt. 48.1
Burritt, Ill. 16.94
Bushnell, Ill. 16.22
Businessmen 2.32,111,121; 57.20
Butler (co.), Ala. 3.2,22
Butler (co.), Ky. 20.16,41
Butler (co.), Mo. 28.18

Charleston (co.), S.C. <u>43</u>.59
Charleston, S.C. <u>43</u>.6,10-13,19,27-28,37-39,66,75-77,81-82
<u>Charleston Courier</u>, Charleston, S.C. <u>43</u>.39
<u>Charleston Daily Mail</u>, Charleston, W.Va. <u>52</u>.11
<u>Charleston-Enterprise</u>, Charleston, Mo. <u>28</u>.76
<u>Charleston Gazette</u>, Charleston, W.Va. <u>52</u>.11
<u>Charleston Observer</u>, Charleston, S.C. <u>43</u>.27
Charlevoix (co.), Mich. <u>25</u>.64
Charlotte, N.C. <u>36</u>.27,32
<u>Charlotte Democrat</u>, Charlotte, N.C. <u>36</u>.15
<u>Charlotte Journal</u>, Charlotte, N.C. <u>36</u>.48,52
Charlotteville, Va. <u>50</u>.69-70,79
Charlton, Eng. <u>55</u>.114
Charlton, N.Y. <u>35</u>.81
Chatham (co.), N.C. <u>36</u>.39
<u>Chatham Journal</u>, Chatham, Ont., Can. <u>58</u>.72
Chautauqua (co.), N.Y. <u>25</u>.75; <u>35</u>.30,48,139
<u>Chautauqua Democrat</u>, Jamestown, N.Y. <u>35</u>.126
Cheatham (co.), Tenn. <u>45</u>.19
<u>Chehalis Valley Vidette</u>, Montesano, Wash. <u>51</u>.19
Chelmsford, Mass. <u>24</u>.86
Chemists <u>1</u>.18,49-50,143,154
Chenango (co.), N.Y. <u>35</u>.18,91
<u>Chenango Republican</u>, Oxford, N.Y. <u>35</u>.92
<u>Cheraw Intelligencer and Southern Register</u>, Cheraw, S.C. <u>43</u>.51
Cherokee (co.), Ala. <u>3</u>.55
Cherokee (co.), Ga. <u>13</u>.50
Cherokee (co.), Kans. <u>19</u>.56
Cherokee (co.), S.C. <u>43</u>.56
Cherokee (co.), Tex. <u>2</u>.55; <u>46</u>.33-34
Cherokee Indians <u>39</u>.2,26
<u>Cherokee Sentinel</u>, Cherokee, Kans. <u>19</u>.21
Cherokee Strip <u>39</u>.15
Cherry Fork, Ohio <u>38</u>.43
<u>Cherry Valley Gazette</u>, Cherry Valley, N.Y. <u>35</u>.27
Cheshire, Eng. <u>55</u>.7,147
Chess players <u>55</u>.127
Chester (co.), Pa. <u>41</u>.57
Chester (co.), S.C. <u>43</u>.9
Chester (co.), Tenn. <u>45</u>.51
Chester, Eng. <u>55</u>.22,147
Chester, N.Y. <u>35</u>.24
<u>Chester Standard</u>, Chester, S.C. <u>43</u>.49
Chesterfield, N.H. <u>32</u>.9
<u>Chesterton Tribune</u>, Chesterton, Ind. <u>17</u>.95-96
<u>Chestertown Telegraph</u>, Chestertown, Md. <u>23</u>.40
<u>Chestertown Telescope</u>, Chestertown, Md. <u>23</u>.40
Cheyenne, Wyo. <u>54</u>.1
<u>Cheyenne Daily Sun-Leader</u>, Cheyenne, Wyo. <u>54</u>.10
Chicago, Ill. <u>16</u>.36-40,53,73,100
Chicago Archdiocese <u>16</u>.71
<u>Chicago Sun-Times</u>, Chicago, Ill. <u>16</u>.41

Clay (co.), Ala. 3.6
Clay (co.), Fla. 12.17
Clay (co.), Ill. 16.173-74
Clay (co.), Iowa 18.15
Clay (co.), Minn. 26.3
Clay (co.), Mo. 28.23,70,88-89,136
Clay (co.), Tex. 2.55; 46.100
Clay (co.), W.Va. 52.22
Clayton (co.), Ga. 13.2
Clayton Bud, Clayton, N.C. 36.63
Clear Creek (co.), Colo. 8.11
Clergy 1.152; 2.51
    Baptist 2.12-13; 55.5-6
    Catholic 7.37; 16.71; 21.7; 24.17; 28.137; 53.31; 55.18-20,92;
    56.4-5,8-9,12,14,22,24; 57.3,11,17; 58.3,18,22,42;
    Episcopal 2.48-49
    Jewish 2.86
    Lutheran 2.18,80
    Methodist 13.18; 55.10,84,165
    Presbyterian 2.50,117; 3.45; 13.103
    Protestant Episcopal 2.36
    United Church of Christ 2.116
Clermont (co.), Ohio 38.53,59
Cleveland (co.), Ark. 6.13
Cleveland, Ohio 38.35,196
Cleveland Banner, Cleveland, Tenn. 45.81
Cleveland Plain Dealer, Cleveland, Ohio 38.36,105
Cleveland Press, Cleveland, Ohio 38.105
Clifton Park, N.Y. 35.17
Clinton (co.), Ind. 17.24,65
Clinton (co.), Ky. 20.17
Clinton (co.), Mich. 25.17
Clinton (co.), Mo. 28.173
Clinton (co.), N.Y. 35.90
Clinton (co.), Ohio 38.37,120-21
Clinton (co.), Pa. 41.29
Clinton, Ill. 16.134-35
Clinton, Maine 22.12
Clinton, N.Y. 35.72
Clinton Herald, Clinton, Iowa 18.53,55
Clinton Republican, Wilmington, Ohio 38.58,64
Cluniacs 56.14
Cluny, Fr. 56.14
Cobb (co.), Ga. 13.13,92
Coconino Sun, Flagstaff, Ariz. 5.9
Coeur d'Alene, Idaho 15.1
Coffee (co.), Ga. 13.14
Colbert (co.), Ala. 3.28 (vol. 56)
Colby College, Waterville, Maine 22.5
Colchester, Ill. 16.115
Cole (co.), Mo. 28.21,80
Colebrook, N.H. 32.5

Flushing Observer, Flushing, Mich. 25.4

Foggia, It. 58.22

Folklorists 1.22,43,107,171

Fond du Lac (co.), Wis. 53.44

Foreign Office, Gt. Brit. 55.59

Forest (co.), Pa. 41.150

Forrest (co.), Miss. 27.10

Forsyth (co.), Ga. 13.78

Forsyth (co.), N.C. 36.67

Fort Bend (co.), Tex. 46.14

Fort Campbell, Ky. and Tenn. 20.30; 45.20

Fort Fetterman, Wyo. 54.2

Fort Huachuca, Ariz. 5.6

Fort Knox, Ky. 20.67

Fort Sill, Okla. 39.13

Fort Wayne, Ind. 17.55,84,160

Fort Wayne Journal Gazette, Fort Wayne, Ind. 17.56-58,121-22,149

Fort Wayne News Sentinel, Fort Wayne, Ind. 17.58,121,149

Fort Worth Gazette, Fort Worth, Tex. 46.41,53

Foster, R.I. 42.14

Fountain (co.), Ind. 17.66

Fountain and Journal, Mount Vernon, Mo. 28.12-13

Fowlerville, Mich. 25.15

Fox Lake Gazette, Fox Lake, Wis. 53.43

Framingham, Mass. 24.6

Franciscans 55.25,54,122; 56.12; 57.3; 58.116

Frankfort, Ill. 16.74

Frankfort, Ky. 20.3,93

Franklin (co.), Ala. 3.28 (vol. 16)

Franklin (co.), Ill. 16.31-32,58,68,82

Franklin (co.), Ky. 20.22,93

Franklin (co.), Maine 22.26-27

Franklin (co.), Mass. 24.34

Franklin (co.), Miss. 27.24

Franklin (co.), Ohio 38.58,61,87-89,169,171

Franklin (co.), Tenn. 45.13

Franklin (co.), Tex. 46.115

Franklin (co.), Va. 50.10,80

Franklin (co.), Wash. 51.29

Franklin (parish), La. 21.1

Franklin, La. 21.24

Franklin and Marshall College, Lancaster, Pa. 41.54

Franklin Planters' Banner, Franklin, La. 21.21

Franklin Repository, Chambersburg, Pa. 41.40,107

Franklin Review, Franklin, Tenn. 45.57

Franklinville, N.Y. 35.11

Frederica, Ga. 13.72

Frederick (co.), Md. 23.18-19,29,43

Frederick (co.), Va. 50.6,90,96

Frederick, Md. 23.29,43

Fredericksburg, Va. 50.28-29,33-34,38,40,45-46,48-50,52-53,58,84

Fredericksburg Ledger, Fredericksburg, Va. 50.31

Geneva, Switz. 58.37
Genius of Liberty and Fayette Advertiser, Uniontown, Pa. 41.123
Gentleman's Magazine, London 1.86; 2.20; 55.98,100,126
Geochemists 1.33-34
Geographers 1.3,31,35,74,101,158
Geologists 1.3-4,33-34,101,143,153
George (co.), Miss. 27.38
Georgetown, D.C. 11.4,10
Georgetown, Maine 22.13
Georgetown, S.C. 43.32
Georgia 2.73,77,83,95
Georgia Enterprise, Covington, Ga. 13.44
Georgia Gazette, Savannah, Ga. 13.7,28
Georgia Journal, Milledgeville, Ga. 13.29,35,75,86
Georgia Messenger, Macon, Ga. 13.30,87
Georgia Republican and State Intelligencer, Savannah, Ga. 13.31
Georgia State Gazette and Chronicle, Augusta, Ga. 13.62
Georgia Telegraph, Macon, Ga. 13.48
Georgiana, Ala. 3.22
Gering, Nebr. 30.19
Gering Courier, Gering, Nebr. 30.21
German Americans 38.74,171,174
Germantown, N.Y. 35.122
Germantown, Pa. 41.56,91
Germantown Historical Society, Germantown, Pa. 41.56
Gettysburg, Pa. 41.28,143
Ghent, Belg. 58.85
Gibson (co.), Ind. 17.140
Gibson (co.), Tenn. 45.84
Gibson, Wis. 53.4
Gig Harbor region, Wash. 51.8
Giles (co.), Tenn. 45.14
Gilmer (co.), W. Va. 52.30
Gilpin, Isaac Glover, personal record 41.57
Gilyard, Thomas, personal record 9.15
Glascock (co.), Ga. 13.5
Glass, John 43.33
Glastenbury, Conn. 9.35
Gloucester (co.), Va. 50.2
Gloucestershire, Eng. 55.11,141
Gold Star Record of Massachusetts, Boston 42.3
Golden Era, San Francisco 7.14
Goochland (co.), Va. 50.18
Goodhue, Joseph, diary 24.84
Goodland, Kans. 19.13
Gordonsville Gazette, Gordonsville, Va. 50.35
Gorham, Maine 22.14
Gorze, Alsace-Lorraine 56.23a
Goshen, N.Y. 35.16
Goshen Democrat, Goshen, N.Y. 35.135
Grady (co.), Ga. 13.94
Grady (co.), Okla. 39.14

Grand Army of the Republic 16.20; 19.35
Grand Haven Tribune, Grand Haven, Mich. 25.58
Grand Lodge of Kansas 19.31
Grandin, Mo. 28.115
Granite Monthly, Manchester, N.H. 32.12
Grant (co.), Ark. 6.23
Grant (co.), Ind. 17.41,64
Grant (co.), Oreg. 40.15
Grant County Advertiser, Lancaster, Wis. 53.19
Grant County Herald, Lancaster, Wis. 53.19,21
Grantham, N.H. 32.15
Granville (co.), N.C. 36.21
Granville Times, Granville, Ohio 38.5
Gratiot (co.), Mich. 25.17
Gratiot County Herald, Ithaca, Mich. 25.54
Graves (co.), Ky. 20.43-44,99
Grays Harbor (co.), Wash. 51.10,19
Grayson (co.), Tex. 46.61,63
Grayson (co.), Va. 50.78
Grayville, Ill. 16.76
Green (co.), Ky. 20.54
Green (co.), Wis. 53.24
Green Bay, Wis. 53.31,36
Green Bay Advocate, Green Bay, Wis. 53.6,18
Green Lake Spectator, Green Lake, Wis. 53.29
Greenbrier Valley's Gateway, Ronceverte, W.Va. 52.12
Greene (co.), Ala. 3.28 (vols. 14,16,63,87,108),41-42
Greene (co.), Ill. 16.169-70
Greene (co.), Ind. 17.17,89
Greene (co.), Iowa 18.34
Greene (co.), Mo. 28.81-82
Greene (co.), N.C. 36.51
Greene (co.), Ohio 38.95,112
Greene (co.), Pa. 41.58,62
Greene (co.), Tenn. 45.72
Greenfield Gazette and Courier, Greenfield, Mass. 24.16,22,61,66
Greenport, N.Y. 35.10,124
Greensboro, N.C. 36.58
Greensboro Patriot, Greensboro, N.C. 36.28
Greensborough, Ala. 3.28 (vol. 34)
Greenup (co.), Ky. 20.92
Greenville (co.), S.C. 43.21,79
Greenville, Miss. 27.29
Greenville, Ohio 38.170
Greenville, S.C. 43.29,47,84
Greenville Advocate, Greenville, Ala. 3.2,22
Greenville Advocate, Greenville, Ill. 16.6
Greenville Mountaineer, Greenville, S.C. 43.41,54,70
Greenville Republican, Greenville, S.C. 43.70
Greenwich, N.J. 33.1
Greenwood (co.), S.C. 43.74
Gregg (co.), Tex. 46.57

Grenoble, Fr. 56.9
Grinnell Herald, Grinnell, Iowa 18.25
Groton, Conn. 9.5
Groton, Mass. 24.38-39
Groveland, Mass. 24.94
Grundy (co.), Mo. 28.55
Grundy (co.), Tenn. 45.77
Guernsey (co.), Ohio 38.6,49
Guild of Corpus Christi, York, Eng. 55.82
Guntersville Reservoir region, Ala. 3.14
Gurley Herald, Gurley, Ala. 3.48
Guthrian, Guthrie Center, Iowa 18.52
Guthrie (co.), Iowa 18.36-37,40,51-52
Guyandotte region, W.Va. 52.20
Haddam, Conn. 9.31-32; 38.145
Hagerstown, Md. 23.11,43
Haines, Ill. 16.16
Halifax (co.), Va. 50.94
Halifax, Eng. 55.33
Hall (co.), Ga. 13.63
Hall (co.), Nebr. 30.10
Hallowell Register, Hallowell, Maine 22.15
Halycon, Greensborough, Ala. 3.28 (vol. 34)
Hamblen (co.), Tenn. 45.12
Hamburg Schnellpost, Hamburg, Pa. 41.98
Hamilton (co.), Ill. 16.180
Hamilton (co.), Ind. 17.25,52,161
Hamilton (co.), Ohio 38.54,76,96
Hamilton (co.), Tex. 46.122
Hamilton, N.Y. 35.18,136
Hamilton College, Clinton, N.Y. 35.72
Hampden, Mass. 24.29
Hampden Federalist, Hampden, Mass. 24.26
Hampden region, Mass. 24.28
Hampshire (co.), W.Va. 52.33
Hampshire, Eng. 55.62
Hampshire Gazette, Northampton, Mass. 24.46
Hampton, Va. 50.5
Hamptonburgh, N.Y. 35.25
Hancock (co.), Ind. 17.104
Hancock (co.), Ky. 20.8,62
Hancock (co.), Maine 22.27,31,37
Hancock (co.), Tenn. 45.12,42-44
Hancock (co.), W.Va. 52.31
Hanford Sentinel, Hanford, Calif. 7.55
Hanover, Mass. 24.41
Hanover, N.H. 32.4
Hanover, N.J. 33.28
Hanover, Pa. 41.28
Hardeman (co.), Tenn. 45.69
Hardin (co.), Ill. 16.57,81
Hardin (co.), Ky. 20.57,67

Jefferson (co.), Wash. 51.3
Jefferson (co.), W.Va. 52.32
Jefferson City, Mo. 28.80,139
Jenks' Portland Gazette, Portland, Maine 22.46
Jennings (co.), Ind. 17.35,85,119
Jessamine (co.), Ky. 20.1
Jewell (co.), Kans. 19.27
Jews 1.69,86,92,112,138,183; 2.17,86; 13.57,60,72; 42.12-13; 43.12; 49.1;
    56.22; 57.10; 58.8,67,107-8,112-14
Jo Daviess (co.), Ill. 16.86-88
Johannesburg, S.Afr. 58.89,115
Johnson (co.), Iowa 18.13-14,33
Johnson (co.), Kans. 19.28
Johnson (co.), Mo. 28.162
Johnson (co.), Nebr. 30.11
Johnson (co.), Tenn. 45.10
Johnson (co.), Tex. 2.55; 46.77
Johnson's Island Confederate Cemetery, Ohio 2.97
Johnston (co.), N.C. 36.11
Johnstown, Pa. 41.25
Jones (co.), Ga. 13.1
Jones (co.), Miss. 27.6
Jones (co.), N.C. 36.41
Jonesboro, Ark. 6.41
Jonesboro, Tenn. 45.9
Kalamazoo (co.), Mich. 25.78
Kalkaskian and Leader, Kalkaska, Mich. 25.27
Kanawha (co.), W.Va. 52.11
Kandiyohi (co.), Minn. 26.9
Kane (co.), Ill. 16.21,93,121
Kanesville, Iowa 18.32
Kansas 18.46; 39.15
Kansas City Genealogist, Kansas City, Mo. 28.120
Kansas Medical Journal, Topeka, Kans. 19.36
Kansas State Historical Society, Topeka, Kans. 19.30
Katonah, N.Y. 35.4
Kaufman, Tex. 46.29
Kay (co.), Okla. 39.18
Keene, N.H. 32.10
Kemper, Jacob, personal record 41.124
Kenai Peninsula Borough, Alaska 4.1
Kennebec (co.), Maine 22.26-27
Kennebec Journal, Augusta, Maine 22.17
Kennebec Valley, Maine 22.24
Kent (co.), Md. 23.17
Kent (co.), Mich. 25.42,46,83
Kent, Eng. 55.51
Kent Inquirer, Chestertown, Md. 23.40
Kenton (co.), Ky. 20.58
Kentucky 2.74; 28.31; 38.97,202
Kentucky Reporter, Lexington, Ky. 20.110
Keokuk, Iowa 18.43

Lancaster (co.), S.C. 43.8,36
Lancaster, Mass. 24.51
Lancaster, Ohio 38.45,90
Lancaster, Pa. 41.54,78,125
Lancaster, Wis. 53.19,21
Lancaster County Historical Society, Lancaster, Pa. 41.78
Lancaster Gazette, Lancaster, Ohio 38.90
Land between the Lakes, Ky. and Tenn. 20.4; 45.6
Landscape architects 1.3,21
Lane (co.), Oreg. 40.8
Langholm, Scot. 55.72
Lansing State Republican, Lansing, Mich. 25.22,25,30
Lansingburgh, N.Y. 35.20-21
Lapeer (co.), Mich. 25.28
La Plata, Colo. 2.55
La Porte (co.), Ind. 17.21-22
Larue (co.), Ky. 20.5
La Salle (co.), Ill. 16.56
Lassen (co.), Calif. 7.43-44,46-47
Lassen Advocate, Susanville, Calif. 7.47
Latrobe, Pa. 41.127
Lauderdale (co.), Ala. 3.7,21,28 (vols. 43,123)
Lauderdale (co.), Miss. 27.14
Lauderdale Times, Florence, Ala. 3.34
Laurel (co.), Ky. 20.18,77
Laurens (co.), S.C. 43.2
Laurens, S.C. 43.30
Laurensville Herald, Laurens, S.C. 43.70
Law teachers 1.57,91,93-94
Lawrence (co.), Ala. 3.10
Lawrence (co.), Ark. 6.11
Lawrence (co.), Ill. 16.9
Lawrence (co.), Ind. 17.62
Lawrence (co.), Mo. 28.106,110
Lawrence (co.), Ohio 38.111,131-32
Lawrence (co.), Pa. 41.63
Lawrence (co.), Tenn. 45.1,38
Lawrence, Tenn. 45.28,38
Lawrence County Journal, Mount Vernon, Mo. 28.13
Lawrence Daily World, Lawrence, Kans. 19.25
Lawyers 1.57,91,93-94; 2.40; 13.76; 16.23
Lea (co.), N.Mex. 34.3
Leavenworth Conservative, Leavenworth, Kans. 19.43,45
Lebanon (co.), Pa. 41.11
Lebanon, Mo. 28.43
Lebanon, N.H. 32.15
Lebanon, Ohio 38.48
Lee (co.), N.C. 36.39
Lee (co.), Va. 50.9
Lee, Mass. 24.88-89
Leesburg Genius of Liberty, Leesburg, Va. 50.98
Le Flore (co.), Okla. 39.10-11

Leicester, Eng. 55.133
Leighton News, Leighton, Ala. 3.13
Leipzig, Ger. 57.12,24
Le Mans, Fr. 56.16
Lenawee (co.), Mich. 25.7
Leon (co.), Fla. 12.14,21
Leon (co.), Tex. 46.71,102
Leslie's Illustrated Newspaper, N.Y. 2.24
Lewis (co.), Idaho 15.6
Lewis (co.), Ky. 20.114
Lewis (co.), N.Y. 35.36
Lewis (co.), Tenn. 45.41
Lewis (co.), Wash. 51.14
Lewis (co.), W.Va. 52.30
Lewiston, Maine 22.22
Lewiston Weekly Journal, Lewiston, Maine 22.30
Lexington (co.), S.C. 43.69
Lexington, Ky. 20.2,28,64,93,110
Lexington, Mass. 24.15
Lexington, Nebr. 30.13
Lexington, S.C. 43.30
Leyden, Mass. 24.34
Liberty (co.), Ga. 13.102
Liberty (co.), Tex. 46.127
Liberty Hall and Cincinnati Mercury, Cincinnati, Ohio 38.99
Liberty Tribune, Liberty, Mo. 28.88-89,174 (vol. 2)
Librarians 1.45,106,115-16
Librettists 1.67,124
Licking (co.), Ohio 38.78,109-10
Licking Valley Register, Covington, Ky. 20.36
Limestone (co.), Ala. 3.28 (vols. 61,209),30,62
Lincoln (co.), Ark. 6.37
Lincoln (co.), Eng. 55.154
Lincoln (co.), Ky. 20.1,37
Lincoln (co.), Maine 22.11,27
Lincoln (co.), Mo. 28.114
Lincoln (co.), Oreg. 40.12
Lincoln (co.), Tenn. 45.15,67
Lincoln (co.), Wash. 51.12
Lincoln (Co.), Wyo. 54.5
Lincoln Cathedral, Lincoln, Eng. 55.79
Lincolnton, N.C. 36.71
Linguists 1.22,32,43,158
Linlithgowshire, Scot. 55.121
Linn (co.), Iowa 18.21-24,26
Linn (co.), Mo. 28.58,125
Litchfield (co.), Conn. 2.38
Litchfield, Conn. 9.23
Little Crosby, Eng. 55.12
Little River (co.), Ark. 6.38
Little Rock, Ark. 6.15,28,43-44
Littleton, Colo. 8.6

Macao 55.13
McClain (co.), Okla. 39.12
McDonald (co.), Mo. 28.101,105
McDonough (co.), Ill. 16.22,89,115,145,147,149,157
McDuffie (co.), Ga. 13.5
Mackinac Island, Mich. 25.80
McLean (co.), Ill. 16.52,78,120,144,181
McLean (co.), Ky. 20.68
McLennan (co.), Tex. 46.28,113
McMakin's Model American Courier, Philadelphia 41.27
McMinn (co.), Tenn. 45.86
Macomb, Ill. 16.90
Macomb Journal, Macomb, Ill. 16.145,151; 18.41; 19.53
Macon (co.), Ill. 16.64,175
Macon (co.), Mo. 28.60,118
Macon, Ga. 13.30,48,57,85,87
Macon Beacon, Macon, Miss. 27.32
Macon County Poor Farm, Decatur, Ill. 16.175
Macoupin (co.), Ill. 16.116-19,142,178
Madera (co.), Calif. 7.23
Madison (co.), Ala. 3.27-28 (vols. 54,59,80,161,165,173,203)
Madison (co.), Ark. 6.5,55
Madison (co.), Idaho 15.4
Madison (co.), Ill. 16.127,130
Madison (co.), Ind. 17.34,47,120
Madison (co.), Ky. 20.1
Madison (co.), Miss. 27.23
Madison (co.), N.Y. 35.18,94,97,136
Madison (co.), N.C. 36.45
Madison Courier, Madison, Ind. 17.42
Magee's Creek Baptist Association 21.40
Mahoning (co.), Ohio 38.65,162,177-78
Maine 2.125; 32.28
Maine Farmer, Augusta, Maine 22.24,42
Maine Gazette, Bath, Maine 22.6
Maine Historical Society, Portland, Maine 22.25,43
Mainz, Ger. 57.1
Man, Isle of 55.56
Manatee (co.), Fla. 12.20
Manhattan Mercury, Manhattan, Kans. 19.41
Manhattan Republic, Manhattan, Kans. 19.61,67
Manitoba, Can. 58.52
Manitowoc (co.), Wis. 53.2-4
Marathon (co.), Wis. 53.28
Marblehead, Mass. 24.9
Maribel, Wis. 53.26
Maries (co.), Mo. 28.96
Marietta, Ohio 38.66,72,156
Marion (co.), Ala. 3.4,54
Marion (co.), Fla. 12.13
Marion (co.), Ill. 16.16-18
Marion (co.), Iowa 18.16

Mennonites <u>16</u>.92; <u>18</u>.33; <u>38</u>.50; <u>41</u>.156
Mercer (co.), Ky. <u>20</u>.19,109
Mercer (co.), Ohio <u>38</u>.38,123
Mercer (co.), Pa. <u>41</u>.34
Meredith, N.H. <u>32</u>.24
Metcalfe (co.), Ky. <u>20</u>.75
Meteorologists <u>1</u>.101,153
Methodist Episcopal Church <u>28</u>.90-91; <u>38</u>.139
<u>Methodist Magazine</u>, London <u>55</u>.165
Methodists <u>2</u>.63,65,96,115; <u>13</u>.54; <u>38</u>.60,139-40,164,202; <u>40</u>.16; <u>46</u>.1;
    <u>55</u>.165; <u>58</u>.66
Methuen, Mass. <u>24</u>.59
Metz, Fr. <u>56</u>.22
Miami (co.), Ind. <u>17</u>.146
<u>Miami Daily News Record</u>, Miami, Okla. <u>39</u>.16
<u>Miami District News</u>, Miami, Okla. <u>39</u>.16
Miamisburg, Ohio <u>38</u>.73
Michigan <u>17</u>.122; <u>38</u>.10
Michigan. University <u>25</u>.81
<u>Michigan Christian Herald</u>, Kalamazoo; Detroit, Mich. <u>25</u>.48
Michigan Pioneer and Historical Society, Lansing, Mich. <u>25</u>.49
Middle East <u>58</u>.6
Middle West <u>2</u>.2,103
Middleboro, Mass. <u>24</u>.93
Middlebury, Vt. <u>48</u>.17,19
Middlebury College, Middlebury, Vt. <u>48</u>.17
Middlesex (co.), Conn. <u>9</u>.31
Middlesex (co.), Eng. <u>55</u>.17,112
Middletown, N.Y. <u>35</u>.66
Middletown Springs, Vt. <u>48</u>.12
Midland (co.), Mich. <u>25</u>.51
Mifflin (co.), Pa. <u>41</u>.17,21,84
Milford, Conn. <u>9</u>.1,14,25
<u>Milford Times</u>, Milford, Mich. <u>25</u>.53
Milledgeville, Ga. <u>13</u>.29,35,59,75,86
<u>Millennial Harbinger</u>, Bethany, Va. <u>20</u>.13; <u>28</u>.122
Miller (co.), Ga. <u>13</u>.12
Miller (co.), Mo. <u>28</u>.62,154
Millersburg, Ohio <u>38</u>.75
Millersville, Pa. <u>41</u>.156
Milton, Mass. <u>24</u>.60
Milton, N.Y. <u>35</u>.55
Milton, N.C. <u>36</u>.44
<u>Milwaukee Journal</u>, Milwaukee, Wis. <u>53</u>.35
Mineralogists <u>1</u>.4,101,143,153,159
<u>Miners' Journal</u>, Pottsville, Pa. <u>41</u>.101
<u>Minneapolis Star</u>, Minneapolis, Minn. <u>26</u>.11
<u>Minneapolis Tribune</u>, Minneapolis, Minn. <u>26</u>.11
Minnesota Historical Society, Saint Paul, Minn. <u>26</u>.13
<u>Mishawaka Enterprise</u>, Mishawaka, Ind. <u>17</u>.51
Mishicot, Wis. <u>53</u>.2
Missionaries <u>1</u>.177

Montgomery (co.), Va. 50.16
Montpelier, Vt. 48.7
Montrose, Iowa 18.50
Moore (co.), Tenn. 45.15
Moore (co.), Tex. 46.96
Morgan (co.), Ala. 3.28 (vol. 74),39
Morgan (co.), Ind. 17.26
Morgan (co.), Ky. 20.76
Morgan (co.), Ohio 38.18-19,21
Morgan (co.), Tenn. 45.17
Morgan (co.), Utah 47.3
Morgan (co.), W.Va. 52.13
Mormons 2.48; 47.1
Morning Star, Dover, N.H. 22.47
Morrill Journal, Morrill, Kans. 19.40
Morris (co.), N.J. 33.3-6,28
Morris (co.), Tex. 46.32,49
Morris, Conn. 9.23
Morris, Pa. 41.74
Morrison, Ill. 16.172
Morristown, N.J. 33.3,6
Morrow (co.), Ohio 38.128,161
Motley (co.), Tex. 46.58,79
Moulton, Ala. 3.10
Moultrie (co.), Ill. 16.65,92
Mount Holly Mirror, Mount Holly, N.J. 33.24
Mount Hope, Kans. 19.11
Mount Vernon, Ky. 20.9
Mount Vernon, Mo. 28.12-13
Moving picture producers and directors 1.9,22,26,67,72,75,102,120,140,156,160
  162
Mower (co.), Minn. 26.16
Muhlenberg (co.), Ky. 20.46
Muncy, Pa. 41.9
Muncy Luminary, Muncy, Pa. 41.102
Music teachers 1.124
Musicologists 1.124
Muskegon (co.), Mich. 25.14
Muskingum (co.), Ohio 38.24-26,107,129-30
Myers, Charlotte Couch 38.133
Nacogdoches (co.), Tex. 46.46,81,84
Namasket Gazette, Middleboro, Mass. 24.93
Nashville, Tenn. 3.35; 45.35,85
Nashville Democrat, Nashville, Ill. 16.85
Nashville Gazette, Nashville, Tenn. 45.57
Natchez, Miss. 27.9,11
Natchitoches, La. 21.26,33
Natchitoches Courier, Natchitoches, La. 21.28
Natchitoches Union, Natchitoches, La. 21.27
Natick, Mass. 24.6,18
National Banner, Nashville, Tenn. 3.35
National Intelligencer, Wash., D.C. 2.82; 11.3; 50.57

Selma Free Press, Selma, Ala. 3.23
Seneca (co.), N.Y. 35.59-60,121
Seneca (co.), Ohio 38.125
Seneca Falls, N.Y. 35.58
Sens, Fr. 56.2 (vols. 1-4)
Sentinel Echo, London, Ky. 20.77
Serbia, Yugos. 58.86
Servants 55.124
Seventh-day Adventists 2.92
Sevier, John, diary 45.16
Sevier (co.), Tenn. 45.49,70-71
Seward, Ill. 16.97
Shaftsbury, Vt. 48.9
Shakers 20.96
Shannon (co.), Mo. 28.44
Sharon, Conn. 9.37
Shawnee (co.), Kans. 19.42,64
Shelby (co.), Ala. 3.8,28 (vol. 244)
Shelby (co.), Ill. 16.14,67,80
Shelby (co.), Ky. 20.1,97
Shelby (co.), Mo. 28.69
Shelby (co.), Ohio 38.1
Shelby (co.), Tenn. 45.26,61
Shelby (co.), Tex. 46.87,95
Shelby Daily Union, Shelbyville, Ill. 16.132
Shelbyville Democrat, Shelbyville, Ill. 16.131
Shelbyville Times-Gazette, Shelbyville, Tenn. 45.29
Shelter Island, N.Y. 35.73
Shenandoah (co.), Va. 50.6,20
Sherbrooke (co.), Quebec, Can. 58.42
Sherburne (co.), Minn. 26.9a
Sherman (co.), Kans. 19.13
Sherman (co.), Oreg. 40.5
Shiawassee (co.), Mich. 25.9,17,34,36,55,73,84
Shotley, Eng. (Suffolk) 55.153
Shullsburg, Wis. 53.32
Sidell, Ill. 16.79
Signal of Liberty, Ann Arbor, Mich. 25.29
Simpson (co.), Ky. 20.102
Sing Sing, N.Y. 35.134
Singers 1.67,79; 2.98
Sinologists 1.119
Sitka, Alaska 4.3
Sixt, Fr. 56.1
Skamania (co.), Wash. 51.24
Skippack, Pa. 41.124
Smith (co.), Tenn. 45.52,56,80
Smith (co.), Tex. 46.27,115
Smithfield, N.C. 36.63
Snyder (co.), Pa. 41.151
Social scientists 1.157

Sociologists 1.100
Solano (co.), Calif. 7.56
Soldiers 2.70,76,78,119; 5.6; 9.17; 16.80; 17.120; 25.32,61; 38.102
   American Revolution 2.28-31,37-38,43-44,53,59,76,100,102; 3.1; 9.3; 13.75,84;
   16.52; 22.3,10,16,20; 23.8; 24.45; 32.1,27; 33.2; 35.19,164; 38.165;
   41.8,105,107,139,146; 42.3-4; 45.5; 48.4-5; 50.14,88
   Black Hawk War, 1832 16.44
   Civil War, Confederate 2.72,76,79,97; 11.5; 13.10,15; 28.176; 50.84
   Civil War, Union 2.76; 11.5; 16.20; 19.35; 27.11; 32.6; 41.141; 50.84
   French and Indian Wars 9.3
   Spanish War 19.66
   War of 1812 16.52; 20.24; 45.60
   World War I 2118; 24.48; 31.1; 42.3
Solignac, Fr. 56.32
Somerset (co.), Maine 22.26-27
Somerset (co.), Pa. 41.25,43,51,139
Somerset Bugle, Somerset, Ind. 17.165
Somonauk, Ill. 16.141
Sonoma (co.), Calif. 7.54,57
Sons of Colorado, Denver 8.14
South Africa 58.55,89,115
South Alabamian, Greenville, Ala. 3.2
South Carolina 2.34,77,83
South Carolina and American General Gazette, Charleston, S.C. 43.75
South Carolina Gazette, Charleston, S.C. 43.6,10,66,76
South Carolina State Journal, Columbia, S.C. 43.50
South Carolina Weekly Gazette, Charleston, S.C. 43.77
South Carolina Weekly Museum, Charleston, S.C. 43.11
South Dakota 2.109
South Hadley, Mass. 24.69
South Holland, Ill. 16.72
South Kingstown, R.I. 42.6
South Whitley, Ind. 17.88
South Woodbury, Vt. 48.3
Southampton (co.), Va. 50.58
Southern Advocate, Huntsville, Ala. 3.28 (vols. 86,101,148)
Southern Banner, Athens, Ga. 13.48,97
Southern Centinel and Universal Gazette, Augusta, Ga. 13.33
Southern Christian Advocate, Columbia, S.C. 13.54
Southern Christian Herald, Columbia, S.C. 43.46
Southern Enterprise, Greenville, S.C. 43.47
Southern Illinois Herald, Carbondale, Ill. 16.19
Southern Lutheran, Charleston; Columbia, S.C. 2.64
Southern Messenger, Greenville, Ala. 3.2
Southern Patriot, Charleston, S.C. 43.82
Southern Patriot, Savannah, Ga. 13.34
Southern Recorder, Milledgeville, Ga. 13.35,59
Southern states 2.23,34-35,73,77,83,95,97
Southern Telegram, Rodney, Miss. 27.37
Southern Watchman, Athens, Ga. 13.97
Southold, N.Y. 35.73,124-25
Southwestern Christian Advocate, Nashville, Tenn. 2.96

Soviet Union see Russia
Spain 58.10,49,80,106
Spalding (co.), Ga. 13.10
Sparta, N.J. 33.9
Spartanburg (co.), S.C. 43.18,73
Spartanburg, S.C. 43.30
Spencer (co.), Ind. 17.126,141,166
Spencer, N.Y. 35.71
Spirit of Democracy, Woodsfield, Ohio 38.83
Spirit of the Times, Greenville, Ala. 3.2,22
Spiro region, Okla. 39.23
Spotsylvania (co.), Va. 50.56
Spring River Fountain, Mount Vernon, Mo. 28.13
Springdale News, Springdale, Ark. 6.46
Springfield, Ill. 16.35,176
Springfield, Mo. 28.82
Springfield Republican, Springfield, Mass. 24.80
Stafford (co.), Va. 50.71
Stafford Courier, Stafford, Kans. 19.68
Staffordshire, Eng. 55.101,163
Staffordshire Advertiser, Stafford, Eng. 55.101
Stamford, Conn. 9.10
Stanislaus (co.), Calif. 7.7
Stanley (co.), N.C. 36.1
Stapleton, parish church, Eng. 55.64
Star, Johannesburg, S.Afr. 58.89,115
Star, Raleigh, N.C. 36.17,31a,33
Star-Journal, Hope, Ind. 17.72
Star of Pascagoula, Pascagoula, Miss. 27.17
Stark (co.), Ohio 38.29,157
Statesmen 1.65; 55.39
Statesville, N.C. 36.72
Statisticians 1.63
Staunton, Ill. 16.128
Staunton Star, Staunton, Ill. 16.119
Staunton Times, Staunton, Ill. 16.116,119
Stearns (co.), Minn. 26.9a
Stephenson (co.), Ill. 16.33
Sterling Gazette, Sterling, Ill. 16.172
Steuben (co.), Ind. 17.93
Steuben (co.), N.Y. 35.67
Stevens (co.), Wash. 51.22
Stevens Point Journal, Stevens Point, Wis. 53.38
Stewartstown, N.H. 32.5
Stewartsville region, Mo. 28.173
Stockton, Calif. 7.18,51
Stockton Times, Stockton, Calif. 7.29
Stockton Valley Association 20.17
Stokes (co.), N.C. 36.20
Stonington, Conn. 9.34
Stratford, Conn. 9.21
Stratford, N.H. 32.5

Taylor (co.), W.Va. 52.30
Tazewell (co.), Ill. 16.138,144
Teachers see Educators
Tecumseh Chieftan, Tecumseh, Nebr. 30.11
Tekonsha News, Tekonsha, Mich. 25.77
Telegraph and Texas Register, Houston, Tex. 46.12
Telescope, N.Y. 35.100,148
Television producers and directors 1.9,22
Teller (co.), Colo. 8.8
Temps, Le, Paris, Fr. 56.23
Tennessee 2.74,77; 3.25; 20.4,70
Tennessee Baptist, Nashville, Tenn. 2.23
Tennessee Gazette, Nashville, Tenn. 45.85
Tenterden, Eng. 55.45
Terrebonne (parish), La. 21.10-13
Texas 2.27,55
Texas (co.), Mo. 28.39,151
Texas Baptist, Anderson, Tex. 46.97
Texas Christian Advocate, Galveston, Tex. 46.1
Texas Republican, Marshall, Tex. 46.22
Texas Sentinel, Austin, Tex. 46.6
Texas Wesleyan Banner, Houston, Tex. 46.1
Theatre critics 1.67
Theatrical managers 1.67
Theatrical producers and directors 1.9,22,67,140,170,175; 2.26,91,114; 55.161
Theologians 1.150,152
Times, Charleston, S.C. 43.28
Times, London 1.137,164-65; 55.99
Times-Democrat, Davenport, Iowa 18.53
Times-Union, Warsaw, Ind. 17.103
Tinmouth, Vt. 48.15
Tioga (co.), Pa. 41.75-76
Tippah (co.), Miss. 27.18,20-21
Tippecanoe (co.), Ind. 17.117
Tippecanoe Banner, Maysville, Ky. 20.94
Tipton (co.), Ind. 17.74,143
Tishomingo (co.), Miss. 27.1
Titus (co.), Tex. 46.32,49,107
Tiverton, R.I. 42.11
Toledo, Ohio 37.182
Toledo Blade, Toledo, Ohio 38.119,187
Tompkins (co.), N.Y. 35.59
Topeka, Kans. 19.42
Topsham, Maine 22.39
Torchlight, Xenia, Ohio 38.103
Toronto, Ont., Can. 58.65
Torthorwald, Scot. 55.76
Towson, Md. 23.5
Trail, Denver, Colo. 8.14
Trailflatt, Scot. 55.77
Travis (co.), Tex. 46.85,90
Trempealeau County Messenger, Whitehall, Wis. 53.45

United Spanish War Veterans <u>19</u>.66
United States Military Academy <u>2</u>.119
<u>Universalist Watchman</u>, Montpelier, Vt. <u>48</u>.7
Universities see Colleges and universities
Upshur (co.), Tex. <u>46</u>.49,101,115
Upshur (co.), W.Va. <u>52</u>.5,30,34
Utica, N.Y. <u>35</u>.96,109
<u>Utica Sentinel and Gazette</u>, Utica, N.Y. <u>35</u>.145
Valencia (co.), N.Mex. <u>34</u>.1
Valparaiso, Ind. <u>17</u>.106,153-54
Van Buren (co.), Ark. <u>6</u>.8,48
Van Buren (co.), Iowa. <u>18</u>.9
Van Buren (co.), Tenn. <u>45</u>.73
<u>Vandalia Union</u>, Vandalia, Ill. <u>16</u>.133
Vanderburgh (co.), Ind. <u>17</u>.92
Van Wert (co.), Ohio <u>38</u>.38,197
Van Zandt (co.), Tex. <u>46</u>.9,115
<u>Variety</u>, N.Y. <u>1</u>.140
<u>Vedette</u>, Panora, Iowa <u>18</u>.52
Venice, It. <u>58</u>.23
Vermilion (co.), Ill. <u>16</u>.25,29
<u>Vermont Journal</u>, Windsor, Vt. <u>48</u>.10
Vernon (co.), Mo. <u>28</u>.9
Vernon (parish), La. <u>21</u>.22
Vernon, Mich. <u>25</u>.34
Vernonburg, Ga. <u>13</u>.72
<u>Versailles Leader</u>, Versailles, Mo. <u>28</u>.176
<u>Versailles Leader</u>, Versailles, Ohio <u>38</u>.9
Veterans see Soldiers
Vicksburg, Miss. <u>27</u>.11
Vienna, Aus. <u>58</u>.108
<u>Vienna Progress</u>, Vienna, Ga. <u>13</u>.80
Vigo (co.), Ind. <u>17</u>.62,91,157-58
Vincentown, N.J. <u>33</u>.11
Vinton (co.), Ohio <u>38</u>.207
Vinton, Calif. <u>7</u>.45
<u>Vinton Eagle</u>, Vinton, Iowa <u>18</u>.30
<u>Virden Recorder</u>, Virden, Ill. <u>16</u>.142
Virginia <u>2</u>.74,77; <u>11</u>.2; <u>55</u>.123
<u>Virginia Gazette</u>, Williamsburg, Va. <u>50</u>.91-92
<u>Virginia Herald</u>, Fredericksburg, Va. <u>50</u>.28,33-34,43,45,58
<u>Virginia Star</u>, Culpeper, Va. <u>50</u>.37,42
Volusia (co.), Fla. <u>12</u>.2,3
Voorhees, Lesley E., personal record <u>35</u>.149
Wabash (co.), Ind. <u>17</u>.8,10,18,59,88,98,165
<u>Wabash Courier</u>, Wabash, Ind. <u>17</u>.165
<u>Wabash Plain Dealer</u>, Wabash, Ind. <u>17</u>.165
<u>Wabash Star</u>, Wabash, Ind. <u>17</u>.165
<u>Wabash Times</u>, Wabash, Ind. <u>17</u>.165
<u>Wabash Weekly Gazette</u>, Wabash, Ind. <u>17</u>.164
Waco, Tex. <u>46</u>.112
Wahkiakum (co.), Wash. <u>51</u>.15